BOOK HISTORY

BOOK HISTORY

Volume 7

2004

Edited by

Ezra Greenspan
Southern Methodist University

Jonathan Rose
Drew University

The Pennsylvania State University Press
University Park, Pennsylvania

Graduate Student Essay Prize

Book History offers an annual prize to the outstanding graduate student essay submitted to our journal. The competition is open to anyone pursuing a course of graduate studies at the time of submission. The winning author will receive an award of $400, and the essay will be published in *Book History*. Articles should be submitted to either of the editors at the addresses below.

The Graduate Student Essay Prize for 2004 is awarded to Neil Safier for his article "'. . . To Collect and Abridge . . . Without Changing Anything Essential': Rewriting Incan History at the Parisian Jardin du Roi."

ISSN 1098-7371
ISBN 0-271-02245-0

Published by The Pennsylvania State University Press,
University Park, PA 16802-1003

The Pennsylvania State University Press is a member of the Association of American University Presses.

It is the policy of The Pennsylvania State University Press to use acid-free paper for the first printing of all clothbound books. Publications on uncoated stock satisfy the minimum requirements of American National Standard for Information Sciences—Permanence of Paper for Printed Library Materials, ANSI Z39.48–1992.

Book History is the annual journal of the Society for the History of Authorship, Reading and Publishing, Inc. (SHARP). Articles dealing with any part of the American hemisphere, Judaica, or the Middle East should be submitted to Professor Ezra Greenspan, Department of English, Southern Methodist University, P.O. Box 750435, Dallas, TX 75275-0435, USA, egreensp@smu.edu. All other articles should be submitted to Professor Jonathan Rose, Department of History, Drew University, Madison, NJ 07940, USA, jerose@drew.edu.

Book History is sent to members of SHARP and to institutions holding subscriptions. For information on membership in SHARP, contact Barbara A. Brannon, SHARP, P.O. Box 30, Wilmington, NC 28402-0030, USA, membership@sharpweb.org. For information on institutional subscriptions, contact the Journals Department, the Pennsylvania State University Press, Suite C, 820 North University Drive, University Park, PA 16802-1003.

CONTENTS

Book Dedications and the Death of a Patron: The Memorial
Engraving in Chapman's *Homer*   1
    John A. Buchtel

An Invitation to Buy and Read: Paratexts of Yiddish Books in
Amsterdam, 1650–1800   31
    Shlomo Berger

". . . To Collect and Abridge . . . Without Changing Anything
Essential": Rewriting Incan History at the Parisian Jardin
du Roi   63
    Neil Safier

Recovering *The French Convert:* Views of the French and the Uses
of Anti-Catholicism in Early America   97
    Thomas S. Kidd

"*Jane Eyre* Fever": Deciphering the Astonishing Popular Success of
Charlotte Brontë in Antebellum America   113
    Cree LeFavour

Uncle Tom's Cabin in the *National Era:* An Essay in Generic
Norms and the Contexts of Reading   143
    Barbara Hochman

Another Look at "The Life of 'Dead' Hebrew": Intentional
Ignorance of Hebrew in Nineteenth-Century Eastern European
Jewish Society   171
    Iris Parush
    Translated by Saadya Sternberg

Bringing Books to a "Book-Hungry Land": Print Culture on the
Dakota Prairie   215
    Lisa Lindell

Books Worthy of Our Era? Octave Uzanne, Technology, and
the Luxury Book in *Fin-de-Siècle* France 239
Willa Z. Silverman

The Writer, the Critic, and the Censor: J. M. Coetzee and the
Question of Literature 285
Peter D. McDonald

Reading: The State of the Discipline 303
Leah Price

Contributors 321

ADVISORY EDITORS

BOOK DEDICATIONS AND THE DEATH OF A PATRON

The Memorial Engraving in Chapman's *Homer*

John A. Buchtel

The death of a patron could be devastating. In early modern England, most writers depended upon the patronage of the nobility, as the numerous book dedications of the era bear witness. These dedications, whose pleadings for patronage, protection, and place we almost unthinkingly label "fulsome" and "sycophantic," can be difficult for us to take seriously today. Yet, considered as integral physical parts of the books in which they appeared, book dedications provide significant insights into the operations of the patronage system and the expectations early modern writers had of their readers.[1] Particularly rich opportunities for exploring how dedications frame their works arise in changes made following a patron's death, a situation that often forced former clients to confront anew the conventional language of their dedications.

I wish to thank Terry Belanger, David Vander Meulen, Gordon Braden, Katharine Maus, and the anonymous readers for their thoughtful comments and insightful suggestions. Thanks are also due the cheerfully helpful staffs of the Library of Congress and the Folger, Beinecke, and Houghton Libraries. This essay benefited greatly from the lively discussions initiated by Elizabeth Eisenstein and carried on by fellow participants in the 1999 Folger Institute Seminar, "Divine Art, Infernal Machine." A shortened version was presented at the 2003 annual meeting of the Bibliographical Society of the University of Virginia.

This essay explores the significance of the changes George Chapman made to his translation of Homer following the death of his patron, Henry, Prince of Wales (1594–1612), focusing in particular on the iconography of the Columns of Hercules in Chapman's memorial engraving commemorating the lost prince. Chapman's iconography creates a myth of Prince Henry as the Herculean hero who embodies the balance between the outward power of Achilles and the inward equanimity of Ulysses: Chapman's understanding of the relationship of Homer's two epics becomes clear only in a reading that takes the book's front matter into account. Chapman links the engraving's imagery to his laments for Prince Henry's unfulfilled patronage in the memorial sonnet that appears beneath the columns, attempting thereby to reinforce his contemporaneous appeals to the king and Privy Council. Forming a subtext to all of Chapman's appeals for patronage after Prince Henry's death, including the curious dedication of his *Epicede* to one Henry Jones, is a serious indebtedness revealed by a lengthy lawsuit between Chapman and his creditors, a lawsuit whose pressures add a note of desperation to Chapman's patron seeking. Chapman's Herculean ideal, and its loss, as expressed in the memorial dedication to Prince Henry, link inextricably with his own laureate ambitions and their failure.

By the time *The Whole Works of Homer, Prince of Poetts, in his Iliads, and Odysses* was published in 1616, Prince Henry was already some three or four years in the grave—yet *The Whole Works* retains the dedication of the *Iliad* to Henry unaltered from the two editions printed during his lifetime, in 1609 and 1611.[2] The retention of a dedication to a dead patron was a common enough practice in early modern England, but it occurred mostly in reprints of works by writers who were themselves deceased. For new editions of books by living authors in need of continued patronage, the normal pattern involved rededication, as Chapman had done following the death of the *Iliad*'s first dedicatee, the Earl of Essex.[3] The stakes involved in retaining the dedication to Prince Henry were high. As the future Henry IX, Prince Henry had stood at the center of potential opposition to the policies of his father, King James; by voicing too loud a lament for the lost prince, Chapman risked offending the king.[4] On the other hand, Prince Henry, already growing powerful as a young patron in 1608 or 1609, when he first commanded Chapman to finish his translation of Homer, had promised Chapman the handsome sum of £300 and "a good pension" upon completion of the translation, a promise that went unfulfilled at Henry's death.[5] Chapman had served without pay in the prince's household, and his hopes for substantial remuneration seem only to have compounded his genuine grief at the loss of the prince.[6]

The publication of *The Whole Works of Homer* as a substantial folio in 1616 introduced two notable additions to Chapman's book, in the form of two new plates in the preliminaries: a memorial engraving and a portrait of the author. Together the engravings illuminate Chapman's motives for retaining the original dedication to the prince and his approach to securing his unfulfilled reward; they also shed light on Chapman's understanding of the social function of his book. Chapman's translation of the *Odyssey*, the first twelve books of which were published in 1614, bore a dedication to the Earl of Somerset.[7] Two years later, nearly four years after Henry's death, the *Iliad* and the *Odyssey* first appeared together—a prime opportunity to alter the dedications, as Chapman had done in 1611. Yet *The Whole Works* gives no indication that Chapman sought new or additional patrons; instead he simply retained the original dedications. The book is a reissue of the unsold sheets of the 1611 *Iliad* and the 1614 *Odyssey*, so the retention of the dedications would have been the path of least resistance for the bookseller. But Chapman was clearly involved in the reissue's two added engraved plates, thereby confirming his willingness to let the original dedications stand. If anything, the new memorial engraving draws particular attention to the *Iliad*'s having been dedicated to Prince Henry, thus intensifying the thrust of the original dedication and extending it over the entire book, including the *Odyssey*.[8] The poet uses the engraving as part of a strategy to heighten the praise of his late patron.

The memorial engraving features Prince Henry's badge set between two Corinthian columns (see Figure 1). The badge consists of three ostrich feathers standing within a coronet, with the prince's motto *Ich Dien* ("I serve") underneath, surrounded by the angular rays of the sun shining out from behind. The two columns are labeled at their midpoints respectively "ILIAS" and "ODYSSÆA"—the titles of Homer's two epics. Between the columns extends a horizontal banner reading "MUSAR: HERCUL: COLUM:" identifying them as the muses' Columns of Hercules. Together the columns and banner form a massive capital "H," as Arthur Hind notes.[9] Underneath the banner, resting between the bases of the columns, is the motto "NE VSQUE" ("no further"), a paraphrase of the more common *Ne Plus Ultra*. Together motto and image allude to the famous device of the Hapsburg emperor Charles V.[10] The entire image stands above a sonnet, also engraved, "To the Imortall Memorie, of the Incomparable Heroe, Henrye Prince of Wales," followed by a pair of couplets "Ad Famam," one in Latin and one in English, brief meditations on the vagaries of Fame. In some copies, the blank space beneath the banner and above the motto reveals the watermark, which, extraordinarily, matches the engraving, with two columns joined by a banner so as to form an "H" (along with a bunch of grapes and various decorative flourishes between the columns).[11] The similarity of the images may be coincidental, but it is striking enough to raise the extremely unusual possibility that the paper was

Figure 1.   George Chapman's memorial engraving for Prince Henry (*Whole Works of Homer*, 1616). Illustrations provided by the Beinecke Rare Book and Manuscript Library, Yale University.

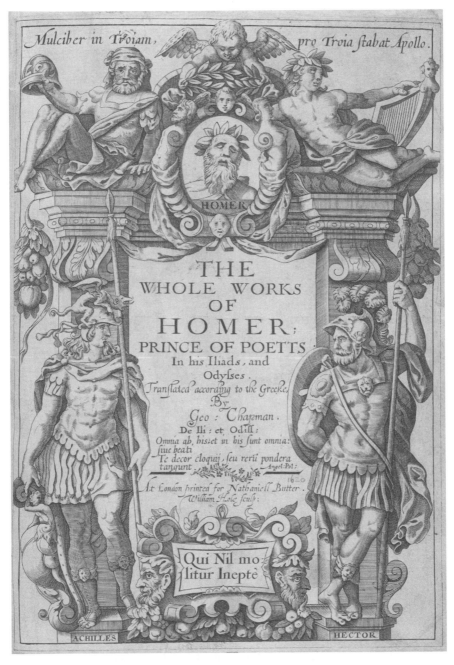

Figure 2. General title page to Chapman's *Whole Works of Homer* (1616).

specially selected for this reason, and perhaps even that the watermark inspired the engraving.[12]

The memorial engraving normally falls immediately after the engraved general title page and may be conjugate with it (see Figure 2). The general title for *The Whole Works,* signed by William Hole, is a reworking of the title page of the 1611 *Iliads* (itself an enlargement of the title page of the 1609 twelve-book *Iliads*). Hind deduces that Hole was also responsible for the other two engravings; Hole had collaborated closely with Chapman on other occasions.[13] As Margery Corbett and Ronald Lightbown show in their detailed description, the general title to *The Whole Works* makes the largest possible claims for Homer.[14] Chapman presents the title of his translation among citations from authorities describing Homer as the principal poet of antiquity. (One of the quotations reads in translation, "All things descend from these works: in them are all things, whether the beauty of the divine eloquence touch you or the weightiness of the matter.")[15] Chapman has Hole give Homer a laurel wreath and the title "Prince of Poets" lest anyone should miss the point. Readers need not wait for Chapman's citations, later in the preliminaries, of further authorities on behalf of Homer (and against the partisans of Virgil as the greater poet) to gain a distinct impression of the book's pretensions.

On the verso of the general title in some copies appears an engraved frontispiece portrait of Chapman (Figure 3). Billowing clouds surround the poet's head, and the clouds are in turn encircled by a band giving Chapman's name, age, and his title as "HOMERI METAPHRASTES." The set of Latin and English verses beneath Chapman's portrait, engraved respectively in italic and secretary hands, celebrates the achievement of a translator who touches both current senses of the word *metaphrast*. Chapman, they claim, has at once captured the true spirit of his original, yet has powerfully transformed Homer's Greek into muscular, living English verse. Noticeably absent from the crown of Chapman's head is the laurel wreath that Homer himself wears—yet the clouds surrounding his head hint at something one step beyond enwreathment, toward something like an apotheosis to the level of "divine" Homer.[16] Laurel wreath or no, the portrait engraving clearly indicates the laureate ambitions, frustrated though they might be, of great Homer's metaphrast.[17] In most copies, the leaf carrying Chapman's portrait faces the memorial engraving. As soon as one opens the book and turns over the title page, one is confronted with the visage of the laureate poet, introducing his *magnum opus,* looking across the page toward images symbolizing the lost hopes of a would-be king of England. The juxtaposition of portrait and memorial ties Chapman's laureate claims to the contemplation of the loss of the prince. Chapman does so *in memoriam:* he summons up not an actual princely authority but a counterfactual,

Figure 3. Frontispiece portrait of George Chapman (*Whole Works of Homer,* 1616).

a potential, an authority that might have been. Not until after his patron's death does Chapman place a self-portrait in his book; memorializing the prince thus serves as a self-authorizing move.

Contemplation of the potential of the departed prince is precisely what the genre features of Chapman's memorial engraving ask of the reader. The engraving has the formal characteristics of a typical three-part emblem: the symbolic picture (the emblem proper), the brief and cryptic motto, and the epigram, which meditates more or less directly on the juxtaposed picture and motto. Alastair Fowler notes, "Almost invariably the emblem was a collective genre. . . . Emblems typically came in series, or at least in book-length collections."[18] The memorial is anomalous, a stand-alone emblem, set loose as it were from the context of the dozens of other emblems one would find in an emblem book, and privileged, not unlike its cousins the frontispiece and the printer's device, by prominent placement in the front matter of the book. Yet the memorial engraving is not quite alone, following as it does the portrait and the engraved title page, both containing strongly emblematic features (the title with its motto, the portrait with both motto and epigram): Chapman's memorial engraving gathers a good deal of its force through the emblem's collective nature.[19] Fowler remarks that "the emblematic frontispiece was often described as the 'soul' or 'ratio' (meaning) of the book."[20] In *The Whole Works of Homer,* the book's *ratio* develops through the interplay of the three engravings in the preliminaries, linking the classical authority of the author, the laureate ambitions of the translator, and the glory of the patron. The collection of emblematic engravings ends abruptly, leading into the text of the book's primary dedication, a long poem that both presents the book to Prince Henry and outlines the manner in which Chapman expected Prince Henry to read it. As the last of the three engravings and as the engraving that mediates between title, frontispiece, and dedication, the emphasis falls upon the memorial engraving.

The reading of emblems and devices formed a standard part of educated entertainment in the Renaissance, and given Prince Henry's own interests, the members of his household must have been particularly well versed in the rules of the game. As in most Renaissance courts, Henry and his followers were heavily involved in the elaborate visual symbolism of pageantry and masques, as well as of tilting.[21] Moreover, Prince Henry encouraged the production of emblem books themselves. Henry Peacham presented Prince Henry with a manuscript emblem book in 1610, and in 1612 Peacham dedicated his printed *Minerva Britanna* to the prince.[22] Peacham made part dedications—that is, dedications of individual parts of the book, subservient to the primary or blanket dedication to Prince Henry—of several of *Minerva Britanna*'s individual emblems to various of the prince's officeholders.[23] Part dedications like Peacham's may have operated as a primitive form of subscription publication, as an intermediary stage between writers selling their copies of a book and the printed subscription lists acknowledging advance sales that would emerge within just a few years as a method of financing the publication of certain kinds of books.[24] In any case, Peacham's forty part dedicatees would have been very likely to own copies of the book. It could easily have passed through the hands of many of the prince's servants and could thus have established something of a common emblematic vocabulary within Prince Henry's court circle.[25] The juxtaposition of the emblem's typical elements in Chapman's memorial engraving would suggest to readers trained in interpreting emblem books that the various elements were meant to be read as parts of a whole, relating to and playing off each other. The parlor-game sensibility normally involved in reading emblem books would have been overshadowed by the gravity of the subject matter, the habits of amusement replaced by the habiliments of contemplative mourning. The disbanded members of the prince's household must have read Chapman's memorial engraving as a touchingly appropriate homage to their beloved prince.

By 1616 it must have been growing evident that Prince Henry, whose body had been laid to rest in the tomb of Henry VII, was never going to get a tomb or statue of his own. The "Toomb, Arms, Statue" of Chapman's memorial sonnet suggest that Chapman has figuratively taken upon himself the task of constructing Prince Henry's tomb. The architectural designs for the general title page and the *pictura* of the columns serve as a two-dimensional representation of the poet's desire to erect a permanent, quasi-architectural memorial on behalf of his dead patron, something along the lines of the structures found among the ruins of ancient Greece or Rome. The motto and the banner appear in large roman capital letters, in letterforms noticeably different from those of the general title page. The capitals of the memorial engraving evoke a sense of classical monumentality such as that preserved in the inscriptional capitals on Trajan's Column in Rome and as picked up during the Renaissance in the typography and the woodcuts depicting ruined ancient monuments in Francesco Colonna's *Hypnerotomachia Poliphili* (Venice: Aldus, 1499), a book Chapman is likely to have known.[26]

Chapman's portrayal of the twin columns evokes this spirit, visually affirming a generic connection between chiseled epitaph and engraved epigram, between the monument and the dedication. Dedications of whatever kind are a species of explicit performative utterance: the sentence beginning "I dedicate" has the power to cause its object, book or church or monument, to be specially designated with the dedicatee's name.[27] Like dedication, the presentation ceremony formula, "I present," is also performative.

The difference involves the direct and the desired effects of the action: "I present" accompanied by the act of kneeling with a book in one's outstretched hands is a straightforward act of gift, the client placing ownership of that copy in the hands of the patron. "I dedicate" involves a kind of super-ownership: the locution causes the work itself, at least figuratively, to become the patron's, and the work remains the patron's regardless of who owns copies. Just as a dedicated church is God's at the same time that it exists for its priests and parishioners, a book dedication declares the book to be the patron's at the same time that it belongs to the owners of individual copies.[28] Both the act of presentation and the act of dedication involve an often tacit negotiation in which the client expects or at least hopes for a reciprocal (and preferably lopsided) response to the performance from the patron.

The act of commemoration, as in Chapman's memorial engraving, is likewise a kind of performative utterance, but unlike dedication and presentation, the communication operates in only one direction. The sentence "I commemorate" devotes its object to the remembrance of the dead, with no expectation of reciprocal benefit from the deceased. Whereas a book dedication's praise normally includes or implies a direct request for or acknowledgment of benefits from the patron, a commemorative dedication becomes a variation on the theme of sheer devotion—a great deal more like the dedication of a church, in fact, than an ordinary book dedication. The loyalty of memory is more sacrosanct than the devotion of ordinary service.

But, as the analogy of the church dedication shows, the exchange may be more complex. The dedicators of a church lack the power to oblige Deity or patron saint to give a blessing in return for their devotion, yet their dedication always involves the expectation that God will look down with pleasure. Even though the deceased dedicatee of a book is absent from any possible readership of the book, such a dedication still carries hopes for patronage, as the emphasis on financial need in Chapman's plaintive memorial sonnet makes clear. Chapman's memorial engraving reminds us that the funeral elegy is itself a genre of patronage, though literary historians seldom explore the full implications of this.[29] The memorial dedication and the funeral elegy are related: like other occasional kinds, both may function as genres of patronage, but both tend to do so indirectly. The very phrase "to the memory of" signals the actual audience: not the dedicatee, but those who cherish the dedicatee's memory.

Chapman's engraving evokes the remembrance of Prince Henry by placing Henry's badge between the two pillars, thereby identifying them as the prince's possessions. In heraldry, as A. C. Fox-Davies explains, a badge was its owner's "sign-mark indicative of ownership; they were stamped upon his belongings . . . and they were worn by his retainers . . . badges had very extensive decorative use."[30] Prince Henry's badge frequently appears, for instance, stamped on the bindings of books belonging to his library.[31] A number of works dedicated to Prince Henry, like Chapman's *Homer,* include the prince's badge printed in their preliminaries.[32] Peacham's *Minerva Britanna,* the most elaborate example, turns the badge into an emblematic frontispiece opposite the book's main dedication. Other appearances of the prince's badge are even more striking, none more so than that in *Coryats Crudities* (1611), which displays the badge set within a blazing fireball of a sun, in a full-page woodcut printed opposite the book's main dedication to the prince.[33] Whereas the badge as a decoration on a bookbinding marks the individual *copy* as the prince's, the badge printed within the text of a book marks the *work* as his possession. Marking the text of one's book with the badge of one's prince, like dedicating the book with his printed name, is a way both of declaring fealty and of submitting the work to the "ownership" of the patron, according to the feudal notions of property inherent in the patronage system.

The placement of Prince Henry's badge as a prominent part of Chapman's memorial engraving thus advertises the prince's rights of ownership over the other elements of the emblem. By labeling the two pillars in the emblem "Ilias" and "Odysses," the artist indicates that the memorial Chapman has "built" for the prince comprehends the totality of the two works. The memorial engraving relies on the commonplace that literary works outlast architectural monuments and thus better serve to perpetuate the memory of a patron. In structuring his emblem around the image of the Columns of Hercules, Chapman constructs a two-dimensional representation of one of the fabulous lost architectural monuments of antiquity. The mythical Columns had taken on a remarkable emblematic afterlife as the *impresa* of Emperor Charles V, the Hapsburg ruler who oversaw much of the Spanish colonization of the New World.[34] Charles V began using the Columns of Hercules as his device in 1516, and it became a familiar and widely used iconographic topos in coins and emblem books. English royal pageantry took up the image of the columns as early as the reign of Henry VIII, and the Elizabethans used it to celebrate England's victories over the Spanish.[35]

The image of the Columns of Hercules came down to the Renaissance as a myth in which the heroic Hercules marks the boundaries of the known world at the Straits of Gibraltar—Boccaccio even describes the columns as the thirteenth of the Labors of Hercules.[36] Depending upon its context, the image takes one of two senses. It is either a warning—beware the wide expanse of sea beyond these markers—or it is a symbol of heroic ambition: to pass beyond the columns is to partake of the "Ulyssean aspirations" described in Dante to surpass the bounds set by Hercules, exploring the world "beyond the straits of Gibraltar."[37] As with other emblems and *imprese,* "epigram and picture might offer an *embarras de richesses* of meanings separately," so one relies upon the placement of components together to determine which of the rival meanings to take.[38] As the emblem of the columns appears in the *impresa* of Charles V, it typically accompanies the emperor's motto, *Plus Ultra* ("further beyond"). According to Rosenthal, the imperial motto "was to be read, in combination with the columns, as a prepositional phrase, 'further beyond the Columns of Hercules,' with the inference that the institution or dignity represented by the symbol usually placed between the columns would be carried beyond those old limitary markers."[39] The iconography of Charles V thus partakes of the heroic Ulyssean connotations of the image. As Gordon Braden elaborates, the imperial device was "the concomitant to an empire of unprecedented expanse, one that could lay claim to being the real and indeed hyperbolic successor to Rome."[40]

At first glance, for a reader knowing of Prince Henry's desire to wage war with the Roman Catholic powers of the Continent, and of his intense interest in the exploration of the New World by the Virginia Company, Chapman's emblem might appear to mean that "Prince Henry would have gone further beyond the Columns of Hercules" in his military and colonial achievements.[41] The redeployment of the emperor's iconography on behalf of a future ruler of Britain might be seen as a means of staking rival imperial claims. This sense of the columns, that of heroic ambition, appears in an earlier work of Chapman's. In *The Teares of Peace* (1609), a bizarre dream-vision dedicated to Prince Henry, Homer appears to Chapman, commanding him to translate his works for the prince.[42] Praising the achievements of King James, Chapman begins:

> Now that our Soveraign, the great King of Peace,
> Hath (in her grace) outlabour'd Hercules;
> And, past his Pillars, stretcht her victories.[43]

Chapman's use of the Columns of Hercules here is not unambiguous.[44] For Chapman, they could simultaneously be interpreted as an emblem of James's pacifistic policies and as an expression of Britain's imperial ambitions. In 1609 a discussion of England's king stretching the victories of peace past the Pillars of Hercules must have called to mind the recent settlement at Jamestown—a peaceful settlement, in terms of England's rivalry with Spain, but an imperialistic achievement all the same. Chapman takes the columns as one of the all-but-impossible labors of Hercules; surpassing them serves as an emblem of remarkable effort, an exceptional achievement, outlaboring the mightiest of the men of mythical antiquity. The appearance of the Columns of Hercules in *The Teares of Peace,* at the outset of the work that announces to the world Chapman's project to finish his translation of Homer under the patronage of Prince Henry, is an expression of Renaissance optimism. Chapman associates the image's heroic import both with his work of translation and with Henry's sponsorship of it.

The Columns of Hercules reappear in an elegy Chapman wrote almost immediately after Prince Henry's death, the *Epicede,* but with their other major connotation as a limitary or cautionary symbol.[45] Combined as it is with a report on the funeral itself, and entered in the stationers' register only a few days after Henry's death, Chapman's *Epicede* takes the stance of a quasi-official report on the prince's loss. Toward the end of this long poem, Chapman writes:

> But let the world be now a heape of death,
> Life's joy lyes dead in him, and challengeth
> No lesse a reason: If all motion stoode
> Benumb'd and stupified, with his frozen blood;
> And like a Tombe-stone, fixt, lay all the seas
> There were fit pillers for our Hercules
> To bound the world with: Men had better dye
> Then out-live free times; slaves to Policie. (595–602)

Much of the *Epicede* paraphrases a Latin elegy by the humanist Homeric commentator Chapman relied on so much, Angelus Politianus, but the Columns of Hercules do not appear in Chapman's source.[46] As so often with Chapman's poetry, the lines are cryptic; the twin pillars figure forth the rigidity resulting from the benumbing of "all motion" and the fixing of the seas. The image encompasses all inward and outward activity on the earth in terms of the two most vital of fluids, both of which normally signify flux and change: the motion of the blood in all living creatures, and the undulating waves of the seas that are necessary for the most significant forms of commerce and exploration.

Chapman applies the Columns of Hercules to Prince Henry in ways that combine their two senses. The cautionary sense of Henry's twin columns is a political one: freedom is preferable to the slavery of "Policie" (that is, statecraft based in "cunning, craftiness, dissimulation" — *OED*). Henry's death marks the end of this freedom. The connotation of ambition too is present: Henry has moved the columns far beyond the physical borders of the known world, where Hercules left them, into a metaphysical realm. "Our Hercules" is Prince Henry himself, constructing his own memorial, setting the boundaries not at Gibraltar but upon life itself. This convoluted imagery does not manifest itself directly in the depiction of the columns in Chapman's memorial engraving, but these previous uses of the columns were undoubtedly on Chapman's mind when he chose the image for the memorial engraving.

Chapman's substitution in his memorial engraving of *usque* for *ultra* appears to be unique, a humanist's verbal *sprezzatura* in an original and more grammatically correct adaptation of the usual motto.[47] By adding the negative and modifying the wording of the motto to *ne usque*—"no further," "no higher," "not completely"—Chapman emphasizes that Prince Henry is lost.[48] The cautionary connotation of the columns makes little sense in interpreting the memorial engraving, because it is not possible for a deceased Henry to heed an admonition not to go beyond the columns. Instead, the message of Chapman's emblem reads something like this: "Prince Henry reached the limits of the world of the Muses, the point beyond which one can go no further: the twin pillars of Homer's *Odyssey* and *Iliad*." As a patron, Henry inspired the translation of the greatest of the Greek poets, and no other patron remains to go beyond his accomplishment.[49] Yet the connotations of *usque* also introduce a sense in which Henry's achievement is incomplete: his pledge to Chapman never came to fruition, just as Chapman never had the opportunity to present a copy of the combined works of Homer to his prince. Chapman insists that there is no higher epic to dedicate to a patron, and he repeatedly points out that his work is uniquely worthy of attention and reward, as in his assurance to the Earl of Northampton: "Nor needes your Lordshippe doubt giving President to any, no one being able, of this Nature, to alledge ye like service; None but my self having done homer; wch will sufficiently distinguish it from any other."[50]

Chapman has no higher patron to seek, save only the king and his council. The sonnet in Chapman's memorial emblem confirms this sense of desperation. The opening lines are syntactically obscure, yet verbally striking. Chapman creates a sense of spareness by the ellipsis of the definite article, heavy enjambment, and frequent alliteration:

> Thy Toomb, Arms, Statue; All things fitt to fall
> At foote of Deathe; And worship Funerall
> Forme hath bestow'd: for Forme, is nought too deare:
> Thy solid Virtues yet; eternis'd here;
> My bloode, and wasted spirritts have onely founde
> Commanded Cost: And broke so riche a grounde,
> (Not to interr; But make thee ever springe)
> As Arms, Toombs, Statues; everye Earthy thinge,
> Shall fade and vanishe into fume before:

> What lasts; thrives lest: yet; welth of soule is poore;
> And so tis kept: Not thy thrice sacred will
> Sign'd with thy Deathe; moves any to fullfill
> Thy Just bequests to me: Thow, dead then; I
> Live deade, for giving thee Eternitie.[51]

The Petrarchan devotion of the sonnet form, as it appears during the height of the vogue under Queen Elizabeth, had been adapted in some measure as a figuration of patron/client relations. As various critics have pointed out, attempts to adapt Petrarchan language to similar purposes under James were not so successful. Here, in his memorial for Prince Henry, Chapman literalizes the code of the Petrarchan sonnet, removing all traces of the amorous subtext of Petrarchan language. The devotion of Chapman's memorial sonnet is purely patronal. Chapman's praise for Prince Henry is not the hyperbole of a lovestruck courtier pining for some pretty Laura. The structure of Chapman's sonnet echoes this: instead of the normally interlocking stanzas of the Petrarchan or English sonnet forms, the poet employs heroic couplets, distancing his sonnet from its Petrarchan fellows as he immortalizes his "incomparable heroe." The half-rhyme in the final couplet touchingly calls attention to one of the inherent problems in the patronage system: the authorial *I* who grants *eternitie* depends in a very real way upon the continued attention of the *Thow* whom the sonnet addresses.

As an earnest vehicle for patronage, the sonnet form has here lost much of its playfulness. Chapman's concerns with lack of patronage are vocal and plain, and in case his readers should miss the point, he appends an additional pair of couplets "Ad Famam":

> To all Tymes future, This Tymes Marck extend;
> Homer, no Patrone found: Nor Chapman freind.
> Ignotus nimis omnibus;
> Sat notus, moritur sibi.

Chapman reverses the famous quotation from Seneca's *Thyestes,* which had only recently found its now familiar context in Bacon's "Of Great Place":

> Certainly men in great fortunes are strangers to themselves, and while they are in the puzzle of business they have no time to tend their health, either of body or mind. *Illi mors gravis incubat, qui notus nimis omnibus, ignotus moritur sibi.* [Death lies heavily on the man who, too well known to others, dies a stranger to himself.] In place there is licence to do good and evil, whereof the latter is a

curse; for in evil the best condition is not to will, the second not to can. But power to do good is the true and lawful end of aspiring.[52]

Perhaps Chapman knew the manuscript of the revised *Essays,* or the 1612 edition based on it—which Bacon had intended to dedicate to Prince Henry—in which the quotation first appears. Regardless, Chapman might have added that men in great fortunes ought to tend to the health, body, and mind of their clients as well as their own, and that the power of the great to do good includes the judicious and generous dispensing of patronage.

Chapman probably writes hyperbolically in saying that he is "too much unknown to all." The earlier editions of the *Iliad* had included a total of twenty multiple dedicatory sonnets bound in at the back, and Chapman seems to have been banking on the new *Whole Works'* gaining a favorable reception from several of these earlier dedicatees, a number of whom were members of the Privy Council.[53] Chapman regarded his work and the prince's promise as a matter of state, as becomes clear in his having sent a letter to the king requesting that his situation be looked into by the Privy Council.[54] Chapman's petition to the Privy Council itself reveals both the weightiness with which he viewed the matter and the extent of his desperation:

> Vouchsafe (most honord Lordes) your free consideration of my enforc't suyte; That attending, fower yeares our late lost Prince; in a service commaunded by his highnes (being the translation of Homers Iliads out of the Greeke) And being promist, wth his often Princely protestation of likinge, (bothe out of his owne rare towardnes, and confirmation of the best in the Homericall language) three hundred poundes; And uppon his deathbed a good Pension during my life;—Commaunding me to go on wth the Odysses; All wch Sir Tho: Challenor can truly wittnesse; yet never receyvinge pennye; but incurringe seaven score poundes debt, by my tyme spent in that service, wch all know I could have employde to the profitt of as great a Summ; The want whereof, wthout your charitable Prevention must ende in my endles imprisonment; It may please your most equall Lordshippes, not to value such a worke, at a lesse Rate, then any Mechanicall service; Nor his extraordinarie Princely promisse, lighter than a customarie debt; But to this my first suyte and last Refuge, stand just & consionable Sanctuaries; For wch: the little Rest of my poore ould life, shall ever pray knowinglie and faithfullie for yow.[55]

For one who had aimed so high, and with so much at stake, rededication was not an option; indeed, Chapman may have deliberately planned for the publication of *The Whole Works of Homer,* with its reissue of the dedication to Prince Henry, its newly added memorial engraving, and the reappearance of the *Iliad*'s dedicatory sonnets, to coincide with his petition to the Privy Council.

A potent irony thus manifests itself in Chapman's laureate ambitions for *The Whole Works of Homer.* The very work that most fully stakes Chapman's laureate claims, through the vehicle of the author's portrait, is also the work that, in the memorial engraving and mourning sonnet for Prince Henry, most poignantly laments the failure of the poet's laureate pretensions to be recognized. Richard Helgerson groups Chapman among such other poets with failed laureate ambitions as Samuel Daniel and Michael Drayton. Helgerson finds that Chapman, toward the end of his career, "drifted . . . into querulousness," just as Daniel "drifted into prose" and Drayton "into isolation from his audience."[56] Even as he hints that a common malady afflicted these poets, Helgerson offers no convincing explanation for the failure of their ambitions. Notably missing from Helgerson's analysis is the three poets' common investment of their poetic stock in the praise of Prince Henry.[57] Henry's death was not the sole contributing factor to the failure of their ambitions, yet it is not insignificant that the transitions Helgerson describes in each of their careers took place after the prince's death. Wilks shows how, after Prince Henry's death, many of his courtiers were shut out not only from the offices they expected under the future king but from any role in government at all—Chapman, he maintains, was a victim of this policy.[58] The discontent this policy engendered not only played a major role in the events leading up to the Civil War but also helped to shape the poetic trends of the ensuing decades. The degree to which poetic self-presentation takes its shape from the choice of patron, and the degree to which choice of patron shapes both work and poetic career—not to mention the degree to which the vicissitudes of Fortune and Death might diminish or even demolish a patron's ability to do so—are far more important than Helgerson allows.

Chapman made consistently bad choices of patrons: Essex executed, Prince Henry dead at an early age, Somerset disgraced. Daniel and Drayton both had strong Spenserian leanings, leanings that manifested themselves in Chapman as well and that Prince Henry encouraged. None of the Spenserians enjoyed extensive prominent literary patronage after Prince Henry's death. Spenser's influence exhibits itself in many of the hundreds of elegies on Prince Henry.[59] Chapman's *Epicede* is prominent among these elegies, with its "verbal allusions" to Spenser and its reference to Archbishop Abbott, which "emphasizes Henry's inheritance of the leadership of the Leicester/Sidney group," according to Dennis Kay. Kay reads Chapman's *Epicede* as "a scarcely veiled claim to laureateship, and to poetic primacy."[60]

In view of the strength of Chapman's claims, and of the similar boldness in *The Whole Works of Homer*, Kay makes surprisingly little of the extremely odd disjunction between these claims and the lack of ambition in Chapman's two-page prose dedication of the *Epicede* to his "best friend," Henry Jones.

In the dedication to Jones, Chapman renounces future patron-seeking, and possibly even the vocation of a poet, in terms that sound like a vow of monastic retreat from public life. "This so farre unexpected publication of my gratitude" appears simply to be a public acknowledgment thanking a friend for his loyalty and affection:

> My truest Friend:
> The most unvaluable and dismaifull loss of my most deare and Heroicall Patrone, Prince HENRY, hath so stricken all my spirits to the earth, that I will never more dare, to looke up to any greatnesse; but resolving the little rest of my poore life to obscuritie, and the shadow of his death; prepare ever hereafter, for the light of heaven.

Chapman goes on to call the dedication an "unprofitable signe of my love," further cementing the idea that the dedication is merely familiar. Little is known about Jones apart from Chapman's dedication, although he seems to have been "on the periphery" of Prince Henry's court circle.[61] Chapman hints that Jones may have done him a favor; Jones may even have taken him in, if the repast Chapman mentions is literal: "A little, blest, makes a great feast (my best friend)." In its language of brotherly affection, the dedication contains strikingly leveling sentiment: "There may favours passe betwixt poore friends, which even the richest, and greatest may envy." The conclusion praises Jones for his "extraordinary and noble love and sorrow, borne to our most sweet PRINCE," which "entitles you worthily to this Dedication which . . . I conclude you as desertfull of, at my hands, as our Noblest Earles." Chapman's praise for the obscure Henry Jones forms a sharp contrast with the chivalric magnificence of the virtual court, full of the noblest earls, which Chapman had created in the multiple dedicatory sonnets at the end of the *Iliad*.

Given the dignity Chapman had sought as a poet laureate to the Prince of Wales, it is striking in this context to discover that Chapman gave a presentation copy of the 1611 *Iliad* to Henry Jones, in a sense placing Jones among the company of the various noble dedicatees to whom Chapman presumably also gave copies of his book.[62] That Chapman should turn in the dedication of his *Epicede* to a friend instead of a nobleman seems strange, given Chapman's ambitions. The language of Chapman's dedication to Jones gives every appearance of familiarity, conviviality, and mere gratitude. Few of Chapman's contemporaries would have suspected that the serious debts he complains about to the Privy Council were directly related to the dedication to Jones. For, far from being the dedication of a poet laureate, the dedication to Jones is the dedication of a man who has narrowly escaped debtors' prison, a dedication deeply implicated in a series of financial transactions that blur the lines between friendship, patronage, and commerce.

A fascinating story emerges from the archival researches of C. J. Sisson and Robert Butman into a chancery case involving Chapman and Henry Jones.[63] Jones, it turns out, kept careful track of his beneficences to Chapman, which he regarded as loans. In 1612, sometime before Prince Henry's illness, Chapman agreed to sign a bond for £100 plus interest, confident, Wilks argues, of his coming payment for the translation of Homer and for a masque in preparation under Henry's patronage to celebrate the coming wedding of the prince's sister, Elizabeth.[64] Henry's death and Chapman's dedication of the *Epicede* to Jones coincide with "satisfactory financial arrangements made by Jones on Chapman's behalf."[65] Later, Chapman's lawyers were able to persuade the judge that Jones had given the bond for £100 to Chapman in exchange for the dedication. The *Epicede* turns out to be a work of patronage—not noble patronage, but the patronage of a son of a sheriff of London, a member of the wealthy merchant class.[66] The end result of the suit is the formalization of a marketplace commodification of dedications, potentially even establishing legal precedent for the notion that dedications could be bought and sold as a kind of goods or chattels.

In the meantime, still owing money to Jones, Chapman reneged on his vow not to "looke up to any greatnesse" and sought patronage elsewhere. Amid a flurry of works published in this period, he had a funeral elegy, *Eugenia,* printed privately in 1614, on the death of William, Lord Russell, and dedicated to Russell's son Francis. Chapman resolved to produce "Anniversaries," à la Donne, "for as many yeares as God shall please to give me life and facultie." No further commemorations of Russell by Chapman are known, and his hopes for the family's patronage evidently went nowhere.[67] Chapman turned in the same year to the king's favorite, Robert Carr, Earl of Somerset. Butman suggests that Chapman, in celebrating Somerset's marriage to Frances Howard in *Andromeda Liberata,* hoped for Somerset's assistance as the bond came due to Henry Jones.[68] The poem contained certain infelicities of subject matter that led to the publication, later that year, of *A Free and Offenceless Justification, of a Lately Publisht and Most Maliciously Misinterpreted Poem,* in which Chapman vigorously denied that the first poem's monster, from whom Andromeda/Lady Frances is liberated, was meant as an allegory on her former husband, the Earl of Essex. Whether or not Chapman was able to win Somerset over with the

Justification and the New Year's gift of the dedication of the *Odyssey*, his patronage was apparently insufficient to allow Chapman to meet his obligations.[69] By 1615 Somerset had been disgraced, and Chapman probably fled to his elder brother's estate in the country to escape imprisonment for debt.[70]

All this while, none of Chapman's published works mentioned Prince Henry's promised reward. Finally came the memorial engraving in *The Whole Works of Homer* and its accompanying suit to the Privy Council. After a series of new works either eschewing patronage or seeking out new patrons, Chapman returned to the lament of the death of his beloved prince. In contrast to the dedication to Henry Jones, Chapman's memorial sonnet in *The Whole Works* speaks boldly and frankly about his deservedness of substantial, noble patronage. Addressing the departed prince, Chapman implies that the king himself is at fault for failing to honor his dying son's wish that Chapman be recompensed for his translation: "Not thy thrice sacred will / Sign'd with thy Death; moves any to fullfill / Thy Just bequests to me."

In seeking redress from the king, framing the prince's badge between the Columns of Hercules might have seemed natural to Chapman, if he reflected upon the some dozen references throughout the *Iliad* to Jove's lost son Hercules. Unlike Ulysses, Hercules is not actually a character in the *Iliad* or the *Odyssey*, yet Homer's frequent references to him create such an important subtext that he emerges as a sort of proto-character, a shade whose presence ineluctably inhabits the narrative's background. The *Iliad* and *Odyssey* construct Hercules as an already transported hero, a lost son of Jove. Over and over Homer's epic epithets for Hercules identify him as Jove's son, emphasizing both the hero's mortality and his father's love for him: "his affected Hercules"; "As though Jove's love to Ilion in all degrees were such / As twas to Hercules, his sonne"; "Jove ever since did grieve, / Since his deare issue Hercules did by his vow atchieve / Th'unjust toyles of Eurystheus."[71]

By presenting Prince Henry as a Hercules figure, Chapman paints him not only as a departed saint of Hercules-like import and character—as a lost son of the king—but also as a paragon of virtue. The richness of Homer's treatment of Hercules provides also, indirectly, that most basic function of the funeral elegy, consolation, a consolation based upon the comparison of Prince Henry with the two heroes of the *Iliad* and the *Odyssey*, and of Homer's comparison of them with Hercules. In Book 18 of the *Iliad*, Achilles meditates on the inevitability of death:

> Not Hercules himselfe shund death, though dearest in the grace
> Of Jupiter; even him Fate stoopt, and Juno's crueltie;
> And if such Fate expect my life, where death strikes I will lie.
>
> (18.111–13)

Chapman offers implicit consolation to the English people. If, as Achilles learns, the son of Zeus himself is susceptible to the grave, if even the greatest hero must yield to death, England cannot expect her king's son to avoid it.

The *Odyssey* offers similar comfort in its description of Hercules in relation to Homer's other great hero. Where Achilles merely meditates on the dead Hercules, Ulysses confronts face to face the greatest of the heroes of generations past, at the culmination of Ulysses' visit to Hades in the *Odyssey*. Recognizing Ulysses, Hercules identifies himself with him. At this moment, as Karl Galinsky points out, "nobody else is present; Odysseus alone is worthy to be Herakles' companion."[72] They are two of a kind, and Ulysses goes back to the upper world "strengthened" and prepared to face the task the entire narrative has been building up to, the slaughter of the suitors. But it is not actually Hercules whom Ulysses has seen, but the hero's shade. Ulysses receives assurance that Hercules himself "feasting lives amongst th'immortall States": Hercules is with the gods.[73] By implication, Chapman reassures his reader that the new Hercules, Prince Henry, is in heaven.

The Herculean hero emerges in Chapman's thought as the *ne plus ultra,* the pinnacle of Renaissance heroism. According to Graham Parry, the protagonists of Chapman's tragedies ultimately point to and are influenced by Prince Henry:

> The preoccupation with valorous heroic figures that is such a feature of Chapman's work, the various attempts at presenting the "complete man" of the Renaissance in such characters as Bussy and Clermont, great and integrated beings who are "young, learned, valiant, virtuous and full mann'd," acquire a comprehensible context if we see Chapman working in the court of a young prince who himself embodied these qualities and who actively strove to create a heroic atmosphere at that court. Chapman both responded to and contributed to that atmosphere by his plays.[74]

Chapman's expressions of the heroic ideal in the tragedies—Charlotte Spivack even calls Bussy and Byron "Herculean heroes"—are of a piece with his explorations in the epic translations.[75] As patron of the acting company for which Chapman wrote, as well as the patron of the Homeric translations, Prince Henry is both the inspiration and the goal for Chapman's heroic urgings.

The summation of Chapman's heroic ideal comes after Prince Henry's death in the much-quoted lines from the dedication of the *Odyssey* to Somerset:

> And that your Lordship may in his Face take view of his Mind, the
> first word of his *Iliads* is μῆνιν, wrath; the first word of his *Odysses,*
> ἄνδρα, Man—contracting in either word his each worke's Propo-
> sition. In one, Predominant Perturbation; in the other, over-ruling
> Wisedome; in one, the Bodie's fervour and fashion of outward For-
> titude to all possible height of Heroicall Action; in the other, the
> Mind's inward, constant and unconquerd Empire, unbroken, unal-
> terd with any most insolent and tyrannous infliction. (*Odyssey,* 4)

Some critics take this statement to imply that Ulysses and the inward
empire of the mind are Chapman's ideal, while Achilles and active heroism
fall short. But George Lord sees it as an expression of the complementar-
ity of Chapman's ideas in the *Iliad* and the *Odyssey:* "Where the passion
of Achilles overcomes restraints in the one, the wisdom of Odysseus tri-
umphs over 'perturbation' in the other. The distinction is carried out
through the antithesis of body and mind."[76]

In its reminder that Chapman planned originally to dedicate *both* epics
to Prince Henry, Chapman's memorial engraving for the prince suggests a
resolution of synthesis, not antithesis. Chapman does not reject so much as
moderate Achilles, tempering his wrath with Ulysses' maturity. The memorial engraving sets forth the third term: the banner joining the two columns
labeled "*Ilias*" and "*Odyssaea*" announces that these two works, the tales
respectively of Achilles' outward heroism and Ulysses' inward governance,
are the muses' Columns of Hercules. Resting between and above the columns, as the standard of Hercules himself, is the badge of Henry, Prince
of Wales. The massive capital "H" formed by the columns and banner represents the initial both of Henry and of Hercules, conflated out of images
representing Homer's two epics and their respective heroes. Chapman's
ideal hero is Hercules, as reconstituted in Prince Henry: a *ne usque,* an
ideal beyond which none can go. Chapman's primary dedication to Prince
Henry in the *Iliad* holds up just this balance between the active and contemplative in the picture it paints of the virtuous prince, who

> in his minde
> Holds such a scepter as can keepe confinde
> His whole life's actions in the royall bounds
> Of Vertue and Religion.
> (*Whole Works,* sig. *2)

Prince Henry as Hercules is the figure in whom the two ideals meet, the
hero in whom active and contemplative strike the proper symmetry.[77]

Chapman's *Homer* responds richly to a paratextual reading, through which we find that Chapman's allegorizing tendencies require the entire *Whole Works of Homer* to be read in light of its would-have-been patron. Chapman's myth of Prince Henry is a literary one, and Chapman's laureate failure is a failure of patronage. But that literary myth relies on a political myth. Those who see Chapman as a poet only of the empire of the mind forget that Chapman, for a brief time, "had threatened to become one of the foremost propagandists of Henry's movement."[78] The godly prince who rules the empire of the mind must also, in order to fulfill the full range of Renaissance magnificence, in order to be able to dispense patronage liberally, in order to fill his court with the intonations of a laureate poet, rule a real empire, one that stretches far beyond the Columns of Hercules.

Chapman's quest for the fulfillment of Henry's promise, alongside his association of Henry with the Columns of Hercules, resonates powerfully with Sir Philip Sidney's *Defense of Poesy,* a work with which Chapman, who quotes it in the dedications to the 1609 *Iliad,* was evidently intimately familiar.[79] At the conclusion of the *Defense,* Sidney makes it clear that he is addressing nobles who ought to be serving as patrons. As his final blow in defense of poetry, Sidney argues for the immortality that poets can give. "Lastly," he writes, patrons should believe poets "when they tell you they will make you immortal by their verses. Thus doing, your name shall flourish in the printers' shops; thus doing, you shall be of kin to many a poetical preface; thus doing, you shall be most fair, most rich, most wise, most all, you shall dwell upon superlatives; thus doing, though you be *libertino patre natus* [the son of a freed-man], you shall suddenly grow *Herculea proles* [a descendant of Hercules]."[80] Chapman's use of the Columns of Hercules paints Prince Henry as a son of Hercules who established as his greatest accomplishment the twin columns of the works of Homer, a translation which itself merits description as a labor of Hercules.[81] In the final line of his *Defense,* Sidney pronounces a curse on nobles who fail to patronize poetry, that "when you die, your memory die from the earth for want of an epitaph." Following Sidney, Chapman seems determined not only to ensure that Prince Henry's memory live, but also to call his own capacity for creating memorials to the attention of the highest remaining patrons in the land. Chapman's memorial engraving, and his retention of his original dedication to Prince Henry, form part of a calculated, desperate last attempt to persuade the king and his council of the virtue of making good on a brilliant prince's promise to a poet of laureate distinction.

Notes

1. No serious history of early modern English book dedications as such has yet appeared to complement Karl Schottenloher's study of German dedications or Wolfgang Leiner's of dedications in France. Gérard Genette identifies dedications as *paratexts,* that is, liminal texts whose juxtaposition with the main body of the works they accompany mediates between book and reader (*Paratexts: Thresholds of Interpretation,* trans. Jane E. Lewin [Cambridge: Cambridge University Press, 1997]). Several studies of individual patrons contain useful if limited observations on English book dedications; most notable is Louis Knafla, "The 'Country' Chancellor: The Patronage of Sir Thomas Egerton, Baron Ellesmere," in *Patronage in Late Renaissance England* (Los Angeles: William Andrews Clark Memorial Library, 1983). Jason Scott-Warren's *Sir John Harington and the Book as Gift* (Oxford: Oxford University Press, 2001) represents a promising recent trend in the serious examination of the role of dedications and presentation copies in their own right.

2. Chapman's dedication to Prince Henry first appears in the twelve-book *Iliad* (*Homer Prince of Poets,* 1609; Short-title Catalogue [hereafter STC] 13633); it is unaltered in the complete twenty-four-book translation (*The Iliads of Homer Prince of Poets,* 1611; STC 13634) and in *The Whole Works of Homer* (1616; STC 13624). These dates follow the conjecture of the STC.

3. The two portions of the *Iliad* dedicated to Essex appeared in 1598: *Seauen Bookes of the Iliades of Homere, Prince of Poets* (STC 13632) and *Achilles Shield* (STC 13635). Franklin B. Williams Jr. lists more than 125 rededications resulting from the death of a patron in an appendix to his *Index of Dedications and Commendatory Verses in English Books Before 1641* (London: Bibliographical Society, 1962), 240–54.

4. The most useful study of Prince Henry is Timothy V. Wilks, *The Court Culture of Prince Henry and His Circle, 1603–1613* (D.Phil. diss., University of Oxford, 1988). J. W. Williamson focuses on possible points of tension between Henry and James in *The Myth of the Conqueror: Prince Henry Stuart, a Study in 17th-Century Personation* (New York: AMS Press, 1978).

5. Chapman's petition to the Privy Council containing the details of Prince Henry's promise is printed in A. R. Braunmuller, *A Seventeenth-Century Letter Book: A Facsimile Edition of Folger MS. V.a. 321 with Transcript, Annotation, and Commentary* (Newark: University of Delaware Press, 1983), 396.

6. Wilks, *Court Culture of Prince Henry,* 74–75, 275.

7. STC 13636. The date follows the conjecture of the STC.

8. The *Odyssey*'s original dedicatee, Somerset, had fallen into disgrace by 1615. In *The Whole Works* Chapman lets the dedication stand but draws no attention to it; the memorial dedication to Prince Henry supersedes it. Chapman's dedication of *Pro Vere, Autumni Lachrymae* to Somerset in 1622, after his release from the Tower, suggests that Chapman remained loyal to his patron during the intervening years.

9. Arthur M. Hind, *Engraving in England in the Sixteenth and Seventeenth Centuries: A Descriptive Catalogue with Introductions, Part II: The Reign of James I* (Cambridge: Cambridge University Press, 1955), 332.

10. On the origins, dispersal, and adaptations of Charles V's device, see Earl Rosenthal, "*Plus Ultra, Non Plus Ultra,* and the Columnar Device of Emperor Charles V," *Journal of the Warburg and Courtauld Institutes* 34 (1971): 204–28; and "The Invention of the Columnar Device of Emperor Charles V at the Court of Burgundy in Flanders in 1516," *Journal of the Warburg and Courtauld Institutes* 36 (1973): 198–230.

11. I have not yet been able to decipher the papermaker's initials in the banner. The watermark is clearly visible in copies at the Library of Congress (PA 4018 .A3 1616 Fabyan) and

the Houghton (f STC 13624); it can also be detected in two of the Folger copies (13624—in the leaf containing the title page—and 13624.25). It closely matches two watermarks reproduced in the Gravell Watermarks Database (COL.040.1 and COL.020.1, in documents written respectively in 1613 and 1620; http://ada.cath.vt.edu:591/dbs/gravell/). Raymond Gaudriault, citing Edward Heawood, gives 1613 as the date of the earliest known example of the design (which he terms *piliers*) in *Filigranes et Autres Caractéristiques des Papiers Fabriqués en France aux XVIIe et XVIIIe Siecles* (Paris: CNRS, 1995), 146; no. 861. Heawood infers that the paper is probably French and calls the image "posts" ("Papers Used in England After 1600. I. The Seventeenth Century to c. 1680," *Library*, 4th ser., 11 [1931]: 287–88). Since Inigo Jones—Prince Henry's Surveyor—probably collaborated with William Hole on Chapman's title page, it is worth noting that a similar watermark appears in some of his drawing paper (Edward Heawood, *Watermarks, Mainly of the 17th and 18th Centuries* [Hilversum, Holland: Paper Publications Society, 1950], nos. 3508–9). Many thanks to John Bidwell, David Vander Meulen, David Whitesell, and Stephen C. Jones for their assistance on the watermarks.

12. The rest of the book is printed on a different paper, bearing a pot watermark. Even if the pillars watermark is not coincidental, the explanation for its use could be as insignificant as a worker in the print shop having a joke with paper he happened to have on hand, or William Hole choosing it on a whim. It is nonetheless plausible to propose that Chapman, collaborating with Hole and maybe Inigo Jones, might have requested the paper for the engraving.

13. Hind, *Engraving in England,* 332. On Chapman's collaboration with Hole, see Wilks, *Court Culture of Prince Henry,* 251–52. Sir Roy Strong argues that the design for the title page of the *Iliad* originated with Inigo Jones and details Hole's close relationship with Prince Henry's court generally; see his *Henry, Prince of Wales and England's Lost Renaissance* (London: Thames and Hudson, 1986), 130–31.

14. Margery Corbett and Ronald Lightbown, *The Comely Frontispiece: The Emblematic Title-page in England, 1550–1660* (London: Routledge & Kegan Paul, 1979), 112–18.

15. Ibid., 113. The quotation comes from the fifteenth-century humanist and translator of Homer, Angelus Politianus.

16. Compare the portrayals of Homer and Chapman in the engraved title page to *The Crowne of All Homers Workes* (1624; STC 13628).

17. Chapman's only modern scholarly editor describes the memorial engraving as "a rather mediocre engraved plate . . . with two mourning columns. . . . Much more important is the handsome engraved portrait of Chapman" (*Chapman's Homer: The Iliad*, ed. Allardyce Nicoll, 2d ed., corr. [Princeton: Princeton University Press, 1967], xix). Nicoll omits the text of the verses as well as the images they accompany.

18. Alastair Fowler, "The Emblem as a Literary Genre," in *Deviceful Settings: The English Renaissance Emblem and Its Contexts,* ed. Michael Bath and Daniel Russell (New York: AMS Press, 1999), 14.

19. Fowler observes that "the emblematic title-page . . . historically preceded the emblem collection itself. One might almost think of the frontispiece as an emblem *pictura*, with the title as the motto. . . . On the same analogy, an epigraph might supply the epigram, or the text itself be the *explicatio*. The relationship of frontispiece to text was consciously considered" (ibid., 18).

20. Ibid. Compare the title of Ben Jonson's epigram on the frontispiece to Sir Walter Raleigh's *History of the World* (originally intended for dedication to Prince Henry): "The Minde of *The Front*" (1614; STC 20637).

21. See Graham Parry, *The Golden Age Restor'd: The Culture of the Stuart Court, 1603–1642* (Manchester: Manchester University Press, 1981), chaps. 2 and 3.

22. STC 19511. Peacham's manuscript presentation copy to Prince Henry survives as British Library MS Royal 12A LXVI. Alan Young describes the manuscript in *Henry Peacham's Manuscript Emblem Books*, vol. 5 of *The English Emblem Tradition* (Toronto: University of Toronto Press, 1988), xviii.

23. Williams, *Index of Dedications,* xxi.

24. Minsheu's *Guide into the Tongues* (1617) is usually cited as the first example of subscription publishing, although Williams argues that it falls somewhere between patronage and subscription; see "Scholarly Publication in Shakespeare's Day: A Leading Case," *Joseph Quincy Adams Memorial Studies* (Washington, D.C.: Folger Shakespeare Library, 1948), 769–70.

25. Fowler posits "an emblematic mind-set" in Renaissance culture that even extended, by way of the memory arts, into the realm of associative thinking and dreams, producing a "shared analogical world-picture" ("Emblem," 8–9).

26. As Stanley Morison puts it, the Aldine roman types were "inspired not by writing but by engraving; not script but sculpture" (*A Tally of Types,* 3rd ed. [Boston: David R. Godine, 1999], 49–50). Chapman's interests included neo-Latin humanists of the sort that Aldus published, including Angelus Politianus; he could also have known the *Hypnerotomachia* in the partial translation of Sir Robert Dallington, who would become a key figure in Prince Henry's court (1592; STC 5577).

27. Cf. Scott-Warren, *John Harington,* 2.

28. On church dedications, see Nicholas Orme, *English Church Dedications, with a Survey of Cornwall and Devon* (Exeter: University of Exeter Press, 1996).

29. Alastair Fowler uses the term "poem of patronage" (with little explanation) to describe the subgenres of the country house poem and the epithalamium—but not funeral elegy—in *A History of English Literature* (Cambridge: Harvard University Press, 1987), 99–100. Dennis Kay, whose *Melodious Tears: The English Funeral Elegy from Spenser to Milton* (Oxford: Clarendon Press, 1990) provides the otherwise excellent service of placing the funeral elegies for Prince Henry in the context of the larger English tradition, scarcely touches on the elegies' relationships to literary patronage. He relegates to a footnote the fascinating observation that Prince Henry's sister Elizabeth paid Joshua Sylvester for his *Lachrimae Lachrimarum,* one of the most important of the collections of elegies memorializing the prince's death (195 n. 183).

30. A. C. Fox-Davies, *The Art of Heraldry: An Encyclopaedia of Armory* (1904; reprint New York: Arno, 1976), 329.

31. The British Library's online Database of Bookbindings contains several examples of bindings stamped with Henry's badge: http://prodigi.bl.uk/bindings/. Mirjam Foot states that at least eighteen bindings with Henry's feathers are still extant; see *The Henry Davis Gift: A Collection of Bookbindings,* vol. 1, *Studies in the History of Bindings* (London: British Library, 1978), 44 n. 5.

32. The printing of Henry's badge seems to have been limited to books with literary aspirations, and despite Fox-Davies's assertion that the badge is not specifically tied to the principality of Wales (330), it appears mostly in books printed after Prince Henry's investiture in 1610.

33. STC 5808; the woodcut reappears in the preliminaries to Henry Peacham's *Graphice* (1612; STC 19507), a work not otherwise dedicated to Prince Henry. The Folger Shakespeare Library has copies of *Coryats Crudities* and *Coryats Crambe* bound in vellum gold-stamped with Henry's badge (shelf marks STC 5808 Copy 1 and STC 5807, respectively). The Folger *Crudities* is not the dedication copy bound in red velvet that Coryate describes in the *Crambe,* which is still housed in the British Library. The Folger copies may have been bought for one of Henry's libraries in addition to (or in ignorance of) the presentation, or they may have belonged to a member of his household.

34. The fascination with rulers' iconography, and the need for explanations of the import of devices such as those of Charles V, must have contributed significantly to the trend of compiling collections of such images, as in Girolamo Ruscelli's *Le Imprese Illustri* (Venice, 1566), which in some editions includes Charles's *impresa*, as does Claude Paradin's *Devises Heroïques* (Lyon, 1551). Such sociopolitical pressures qualify somewhat Fowler's explanation of the origins of the tripartite emblem as "a modal transformation of epigram by *impresa*" ("Emblem," 5).

35. For Henry VIII, see Mary E. Hazard, "'Order Gave Each Thing View': 'Shows, Pageants and Sights of Honour' in *King Henry VIII*," *Word & Image* 3 (1987): 100. For Elizabeth I, see Frances A. Yates, "Queen Elizabeth as Astraea," *Journal of the Warburg and Courtauld Institutes* 10 (1947): 55–56, pl. 17; and *Astraea: The Imperial Theme in the Sixteenth Century* (London: Routledge & Kegan Paul, 1975), 57–58, 102–3, and 116–17.

36. Rosenthal, "*Plus Ultra*," 212.

37. Ibid., 227; *Inferno* XXVI.90–142 in *Dante Alighieri's Divine Comedy*, vol. 1, trans. Mark Musa (Bloomington: Indiana University Press, 1996). See Musa's notes, vol. 2, 349ff.

38. Fowler, "Emblem," 10.

39. Rosenthal, "Invention," 199.

40. Gordon Braden, *Petrarchan Love and the Continental Renaissance* (New Haven: Yale University Press, 1999), 135.

41. This sense appears in a variant of Charles V's device in the 1516 Brussels funeral procession of Ferdinand the Catholic of Aragon, with the motto "Ulterius nisi morte": "had he not died, he would have gone further" (Rosenthal, "*Plus Ultra*," 224 n. 87). On Prince Henry's interest in the Virginia Company, see Wilks, *Court Culture of Prince Henry*, 8 n. 4.

42. *Euthymiae Raptus; or The Teares of Peace* (1609); STC 4976.

43. Sig. A3, lines 1–3.

44. *Pace* Williamson, who reads Chapman's work as a straightforward part of the "alternate myth" that figured Prince Henry as an overseer of British fecundity rather than as a warrior-prince (*The Myth of the Conqueror*, 85–86).

45. *An Epicede or Funerall Song: on the Most Disastrous Death, of the High-borne Prince of Men, Henry Prince of Wales* (1612; STC 4974).

46. *The Poems of George Chapman*, ed. Phyllis Brooks Bartlett (New York: Modern Language Association of America, 1941), 451.

47. Rosenthal observes that *Plus Ultra* would more correctly read *Ulterius* ("*Plus Ultra*," 224). Henry Peacham gives the motto thus: "to say, as Hercules between his two pillars, *non ulterius*" (*The Complete Gentleman, The Truth of Our Times, and The Art of Living in London*, ed. Virgil B. Heltzel [Ithaca: Cornell University Press, 1962], 46).

48. Contrary to the common assumption that the negative form of the motto predated Charles V, it was not until the 1590s that the motto began to read either *ne* or *non plus ultra*, according to Earl Rosenthal ("*Plus Ultra*"). Many thanks to Dan Kinney and Gordon Braden for their assistance with the interpretation of the motto and device.

49. Chapman could conceivably have rededicated the entire *Whole Works* to Somerset, had Somerset not fallen into disgrace by the time of its publication. Such a rededication would have detracted from the book's former glory, and would have rendered it useless for the purpose of petitioning for Prince Henry's promised £300.

50. Braunmuller, *Seventeenth-Century Letter Book*, 293.

51. Reprinted in Bartlett's edition of Chapman's *Poems* (388), but not in Nicoll's edition of the *Iliad*.

52. The modernized text and translation are from John Pitcher's edition of the *Essays* (Harmondsworth: Penguin, 1985).

53. There is no evidence of Chapman's multiple dedications' resulting in substantial remuneration. I argue elsewhere that Chapman's purpose in attaching the multiple dedications

at the back of the *Iliad,* which imitates a similar move in Spenser's *Faerie Queene,* was less to gain supplementary financial reward than to redound to the glory of his book's primary dedicatee. See "'This Heroicall, and Princely Traine': Spenser, Prince Henry, and the Dedications to Chapman's *Homer,*" chapter 2 of my *Book Dedications in Early Modern England: Francis Bacon, George Chapman, and the Literary Patronage of Henry, Prince of Wales* (Ph.D. diss., University of Virginia, 2004).

54. Braunmuller, *Seventeenth-Century Letter Book,* 29.

55. Ibid., 396. Chapman's letter to the Earl of Northampton (as Lord Privy Seal) apparently accompanied the petition (293).

56. Richard Helgerson, *Self-crowned Laureates: Spenser, Jonson, Milton, and the Literary System* (Berkeley and Los Angeles: University of California Press, 1983), 53.

57. Drayton dedicated the first installment of his *magnum opus, Poly-Olbion* (1612; STC 7226), to Prince Henry, and records survive of pension payments to Drayton out of the prince's privy purse. Daniel, whose primary patronage came from the queen but who also looked to Henry, dedicated his closet drama *Philotas* (1605; STC 6239) to the prince.

58. Wilks, *Court Culture of Prince Henry,* 253 and chap. 10 generally. See also David Norbrook, *Poetry and Politics in the English Renaissance,* rev. ed. (Oxford: Oxford University Press, 2002), especially chaps. 8–9.

59. Kay, *Melodious Tears,* 125ff.

60. Ibid, 201–2.

61. Wilks, *Court Culture of Prince Henry,* 10–11. R. C. Bald identifies Jones as a servant of Lord Ellesmere (*John Donne: A Life* [Oxford: Clarendon, 1970], 97). Ellesmere had extensive contacts within Prince Henry's household; Ellesmere's son John Egerton attended the prince.

62. The presentation copy to Jones is listed in Peter Beal, ed., *Index of English Literary Manuscripts* (New York: R. R. Bowker, 1980–), vol. 1, part 1, 191. The inscription is reproduced in the Christie's sale catalogue, *Books and Manuscripts from the Library of Arthur A. Houghton, Jnr* (13 and 14 June 1979), part 1, item 110, pl. 16. Its authenticity is discussed in L. A. Cummings, *Geo: Chapman: His Crowne and Conclusion; A Study of His Handwriting* (Salzburg: Institut für Anglistik und Amerikanistik, 1989), 146–49.

63. C. J. Sisson and Robert Butman, "George Chapman, 1612–22: Some New Facts," *Modern Language Review* 46 (1951): 185–90. The discussion that follows relies heavily on their research.

64. Wilks, *Court Culture of Prince Henry,* 251.

65. Sisson and Butman, "George Chapman," 186. One of Chapman's letters without addressee may refer to this deal: "For Godes love let me trouble you no more with wordes nor pistles, My offer is faire & satisfactorie; A suretie, bothe for the Principall & interest. . . . Be but Secur'de: your scrivener askes no more; Just dealing men are free though nere so poore. Here's Poetrie for you. Let me be free then" (Braunmuller, *Seventeenth-Century Letter Book,* 290).

66. Sisson and Butman, "George Chapman," 189. Henry Jones is a member of the same class whose aspirations to patronage Beaumont and Fletcher parody in *The Knight of the Burning Pestle* (1613; STC 1674).

67. Chapman, *Poems,* 455–56.

68. Sisson and Butman, "George Chapman," 189.

69. Nicoll, *Odyssey,* xviii.

70. Ibid., 190.

71. *Iliad* 8.318, 14.221–22, 19.127–29 (Chapman's translation, as reprinted in Nicoll).

72. G. Karl Galinsky, *The Herakles Theme: The Adaptations of the Hero in Literature from Homer to the Twentieth Century* (Totowa, N.J.: Rowman and Littlefield, 1972), 13.

73. *Odyssey* 11.821.

74. Parry, *Golden Age Restor'd,* 68.

75. Charlotte Spivack, *George Chapman* (New York: Twayne, 1967), 109.

76. George DeF. Lord, *Homeric Renaissance: The* Odyssey *of George Chapman* (London: Chatto & Windus, 1956), 41.

77. In Chapman's thought, laboring Hercules represents the achievements of the mind as well as of the body. In his letter to Northampton, Chapman presents his own intellectual efforts as a labor worthy of Hercules: "For if what Virgile divinely affirmes be true, yt easier it is to gaine ye Club from *Hercules,* then a verse from *Homer* (intending so to gaine & mannadge it, yt we make it our owne) I hope fewe els can plead to ye Prince so difficult a service?" Braunmuller, *Seventeenth-Century Letter Book,* 293.

78. Wilks, *Court Culture of Prince Henry,* 253. Wilks remarks that the strongly colonial themes in Chapman's *Masque of Lincoln's Inn and the Middle Temple* (performed for the wedding of Princess Elizabeth in 1613) found their way there under Prince Henry's influence.

79. In one of the dedicatory sonnets at the end of the 1609 *Iliad,* Chapman addresses Edward Wotton as "the right Noble, and (by the great eternizer of Vertue, Sir P. Sydney) long since, eterniz'd, Right vertuous, the accomplisht Lord Wotton" (sig. 2E4v). Chapman quotes from the first line of Sidney's *Defense of Poesy:* "When the right virtuous Edward Wotton and I were at the Emperor's court together."

80. Text and translations from *Sir Philip Sidney,* ed. Katherine Duncan-Jones (Oxford: Oxford University Press, 1989), 249.

81. Chapman compares his translation of the first twelve books of the *Odyssey* to the "Twelve Labours of your Thespian Hercules" in his dedication to Somerset.

An Invitation to
Buy and Read

Paratexts of Yiddish Books in Amsterdam,
1650–1800

Shlomo Berger

A book without preface is like a body without soul.
—Rabbi Meir Crescas, *The Book of
the Tashbets* (Amsterdam, 1741)

I

Much can be gleaned from an introduction or preface about the book to which it is prelude, the author, his ideas, and their context.[1] These texts have a distinctive structure and a specific logic, however, and they enable students of book history to propose another angle of research that aims at showing the place and position of the printed matter within a cultural setting. This can be an especially fruitful terrain in the world of Yiddish: a vernacular of the Ashkenazi Diaspora of Europe, a language that Jews spoke throughout the continent regardless of frontiers, a language that formed and united a people and helped forge its unique cultural blend. This was not the Jewish Latin—a fate that befell the scholarly, highbrow Hebrew—Yiddish was a vibrant, living vernacular. Yiddish paratexts of the early modern era can therefore shed light on books, their status and role in Ashkenazi society, and their importance to Jewish culture in Europe.

The theory of paratexts, as outlined by Gerard Genette, focuses on works of fiction and describes them as a "threshold of interpretation."[2] Paratexts, whether written or devised by authors, publishers, or any other promoter, are designed to persuade people to buy and read the book and to encourage them to receive the volume in the way they consider appropriate. Paratexts entice the reader to delve into the book and provide clues about how it is constructed, how it was conceived, and its object. The study of paratexts therefore deals with the sociology of literature, the intellectual background of authors, texts and their environment, and their impact on literary criticism. Paratexts enable us to reach beyond a "naïve" approach to literature and reveal an interim stage in book production usually considered to be a merely technical phase but in fact of much greater importance. Paratexts are not external but internal, ulterior literary devices that represent a legitimate section of literary criticism and booklore.

Despite Genette's theory, however, paratexts do not operate in one direction only into the text; often the text dictates the structure and content of its paratexts, taking the reader beyond the confines of the text.[3] While an author may seek acclaim as an artist and while the publisher may hope for financial success, paratexts operate within a web of considerations. Their object is to support the book while placing it within a wider cultural setting—dominant literary circles of the day, the potential audience among religious and other sections of society, financial considerations, and matters relating to form and content and their interrelation. Authors may not always be interested in these questions, but publishers definitely are. Their concern is to support the author and his book, and their strategy includes paratexts that place the book within a context.

Although most of the paratexts discussed here relate to nonfiction, this is no reason not to employ Genette's theory. Their basic function is no different from paratexts in fiction: namely, to persuade people to buy and read the book and to try to influence the way it is received. Clearly, readers view the text of a novel or poem from a specific perspective and exercise a certain freedom in forming an interpretation, so these paratexts may focus on intellectual, ethical, and aesthetic areas not touched on in nonfiction. After all, there is a world of difference between buying an anthology of short stories and buying a grammar or mathematics textbook. Yet this is more a question of content than of form or structure. Nonfiction has its own concerns, and these are reflected in its paratexts, too. As will be seen, publishers of nonfiction were just as keen to control the process of book production, maybe even more so.

2

From its earliest days, the market for Yiddish books was a popular, international market. Almost all Jewish boys attended school in order to learn to read and write Hebrew, ensuring that they could at least follow the prayer book. As a result, literacy may be assumed to have been more general among Jews than it was among non-Jews.[4] This led to a steady demand for books within Jewish communities. But the knowledge of Hebrew remained restricted to the reading of the prayer book and certain key religious texts, as well as to basic writing skills. The vernacular was Yiddish. Yiddish publications were produced primarily in order to reach the masses and were aimed at keeping ordinary Ashkenazi Jews true to their religion, nurturing their faith.[5] Although local Yiddish dialects presumably developed in the course of time, printed Yiddish continued to appear in a standard, more or less unified style—Western literary Yiddish—until well into the eighteenth century.[6] The same Yiddish books were read throughout the European continent. Indeed, publishers were a leading force behind the maintenance of Western literary Yiddish, for it ensured the continuation of the international market for Yiddish books.

From the sixteenth century on, four clusters of Yiddish printing activity took shape. From around 1500 to 1650, Yiddish books were produced in Italy, Poland, and in the German territories of central Europe, in cities like Basel, Frankfurt am Main, Frankfurt an der Oder, Fürth, and Prague.[7] In the early seventeenth century Yiddish publishing began to decline in Italy and Poland. Italy's small Ashkenazi community, living in a relatively liberal environment, preferred its literature in Italian (and in Hebrew for religious texts). At the same time, printing presses in Poland suffered in the political turmoil of the period, which severely affected Jewish communities and led to economic decline.

The fourth center of Hebrew, and, *mutatis mutandis*, of Yiddish printing, emerged in Amsterdam, where New Christians—descendants of converted Spanish and Portuguese Jews—were settling and returning to Judaism. They needed religious literature in Hebrew (as well as in Spanish and Portuguese)[8] to guide them back to traditional rabbinic Judaism. Members of this Sephardi community therefore took up printing in order to supply the growing demand for books.[9] This was facilitated and encouraged in seventeenth-century Amsterdam, then the most liberal publishing center in Europe.[10] Sephardi printers and publishers gladly widened their market to include Yiddish, as it was written in Hebrew characters.[11] In subsequent decades Ashkenazi Jews started to arrive in Holland: in the 1630s from the German territories following the Thirty Years' War, and from Eastern Europe as a result of the pogroms of 1648–49 and the ensuing Polish-Lithuanian wars of the 1660s.[12] This provided a new impetus for the Yiddish book industry, which assumed an international character from the outset. Indeed, Amsterdam's liberal atmosphere and its burgeoning publishing houses offered a ready alternative following the demise of the Italian and

Polish presses. Thus Amsterdam became the principal center of Yiddish printing for the entire "Land of Ashkenaz" for a century and a half. To maintain this vast international market for Yiddish books, Amsterdam's publishers clung to the use of Western Yiddish, eliminating local Dutch Yiddish dialect from their texts.[13] But as Jewish communities entered the modern world in the second half of the eighteenth century, and as the economy of the Dutch Republic declined, the story of the Yiddish language and Yiddish books took another turn. Jews in Western Europe gradually abandoned Yiddish in favor of the local vernacular, while publishing resumed in Eastern Europe, but now in another style of Yiddish—Eastern ("Modern") Yiddish—a new literary style based on local spoken dialects.[14]

3

As the product of a truly international market, data drawn from Amsterdam's Yiddish publishing industry shed light on the whole of the Ashkenazi Diaspora until the end of the eighteenth century, when the schism between Western and Eastern Europe became apparent. What we can learn about publishing in Amsterdam, therefore, has implications for Yiddish across the continent.

The inventory of Yiddish books from Amsterdam includes some five hundred titles.[15] Not all of these were new. A substantial section comprised reprints and new editions of books first printed in Amsterdam or abroad. Indeed, a vital aspect of Jewish publishing was its lax attitude toward the printed word. During the Middle Ages copyists occasionally altered their texts, adding and removing words and introducing other changes. In Jewish booklore this practice is known as the "tradition of the open book."[16] The practice was apparently not abandoned with the invention of print. Producers of new editions of existing titles assumed a similar liberty, so that many such editions actually became independent, original ones.[17] Because of the demand for books, many editions were printed on poor-quality paper, so that some books presumably perished without a trace. The Yiddish books published during this period include Bibles, rabbinic literature, works on ethics and customs, prayer books (translations of liturgy for the synagogue and for private ceremonies in the home and for the family), lamentations and prayers for women, textbooks, works on the cabbala, and works of history, geography, popular medicine, and poetry.[18] The impressive inventory of Yiddish books also reveals a distinctive group of publications, the "nongeneric genre" of translations.[19] As a young language (Jews began speaking Yiddish around 1000 CE, and the earliest surviving Yiddish text dates from 1272),[20] Yiddish was continually being enriched with translations from Hebrew as well as from European languages. Publications took a whole range of forms, from pedestrian, word-by-word renditions of texts, to attempts to present foreign compositions in Yiddish and place them in a Jewish context, to free adaptations. Indeed, several publications present the translator as "the translator and author,"[21] suggesting that considerable license could be taken.

Certain features of Yiddish books should be noticed. For one thing, religious books in Yiddish were in fact bilingual books, containing both Hebrew and Yiddish.[22] Although Yiddish was the language of the Ashkenazi masses, they could not turn the tables and introduce Yiddish liturgy into the synagogue.[23] Yet, because many were barely able to understand Hebrew, these texts were often accompanied by glosses that explained difficult Hebrew words and clarified the order and rules of worship and other rituals, or by Yiddish translations of the text.[24] Wherever the text concerned an area outside public liturgy, Yiddish was much more common—to the extent that it was sometimes used exclusively. Nevertheless, even a book written completely in Yiddish might occasionally contain a title page, an introduction, a preface, or a postface in Hebrew as well as Hebrew headers and footers. Here the publishing agent was attempting to place the book within a Jewish framework and increase its prestige.

If Roland Barthes announced the death of the author,[25] Yiddish books in Amsterdam belong to a period before the author's birth. Of course, people who wrote Yiddish books were not indifferent to fame and financial success. Yet two factors prevented the recognition of the author as the central agent of the book. First, traditionally, the text was what mattered, and the name of the author could be omitted or played down, especially in subsequent editions, as we shall see. Second, in the world of Yiddish publishing it was the publisher who assumed a central role: the author was the publisher's employee, except when a writer approached a publisher with funds to finance the book, in which case the author took a share of the responsibility for the book's publication. Indeed, many Yiddish short stories and other tales do not bear the author's name at all. These often appeared in anthologies compiled by an editor, who did not mention the names of the writers (if he even knew them), or in small publications of between four and ten pages on extremely cheap paper and again uncredited.[26] It is almost as if writers considered their compositions mere bagatelles, hardly worth attaching their name to. This was characteristic of Yiddish popular literature well into the nineteenth century.

The central position of the publisher is a vital aspect of Yiddish booklore. Alongside the author's, translator's, editor's, or compositor's preface, the publisher occasionally also included a preface, and in some cases the publisher's is the only preface. In fact, the author's or translator's preface frequently voiced the publisher's concerns. Both financial considerations and Jewish tradition played a role in the origin of this practice. Although for different reasons, Alistair McCleery pleads in a recent article for a place for the publisher in bibliology. The publisher, he claims, is often neglected in modern structural analyses of books or given a negative role as an enemy of the author and the arts, interested only in financial gain.[27] In Yiddish books, however, it is impossible to ignore the publisher. Moreover, in this antenatal age of the author, publishers assumed an even greater role in book production than that assigned by McCleery to their twentieth-century counterparts. In fact, they were often responsible for the form and the subject matter as well as the distribution and sale of a book.

4

Genette's categorization of paratexts includes title pages and prefaces, book titles, dedications, please-inserts, notes, and epitexts (i.e., paratexts not attached to the volume itself). And, as Genette repeatedly insists, there are endless combinations in the construction of paratexts. While this structural variation is clearly evident in Yiddish books from Amsterdam, the title page and preface remain the principal instruments. Book titles might be arbitrarily chosen, often alluding to tradition, while different books might occasionally bear the same title.[28] Dedications were not uncommon; notes were few and far between.

As Genette remarks, before the nineteenth century books were sold without covers.[29] It was generally up to the buyer, not the bookseller, to arrange for the book to be bound. The title page was therefore an ideal and logical space for information. Unlike the modern, technical, businesslike title page, its classical predecessor included "a veritable description of the book, a summary of its action, a definition of its subject, a list of its appendixes and so forth,"[30] while in Yiddish books the title page also provided information about other aspects of the production. Since this was the entryway to the book, it was also decorated, usually with a frontispiece (i.e., an illustration in the form of a portico framing the text).

Yiddish title pages reveal great variety in form, language, style, and content. In many cases the form of the title page depended on available funds, which also dictated the format of the book as a whole. Some books had no title page at all. Many of these were editions of short prose pieces, the Yiddish *mayse,* or tale, which most publishers considered the least important literary genre. Indeed, some famous anthologies of tales were compiled,

among them the *Mayse Bukh* (*The Book of Tales,* first published in Basel
in 1602),[31] a popular and widely acclaimed collection that consequently
appeared in well-prepared editions. Many tales, however, were published
in small booklets, containing one or two stories printed on a few pages of
cheap paper with used typesets. These were clearly intended as purely commercial enterprises designed to meet popular demand. Neither author nor
publisher thought these booklets deserved any embellishment and no one
believed they would earn respect or prestige by adding basic information
in the form of a title page. Usually the first page bears a title in bold letters,
underneath which the tale begins:

> A True Story/ That Happened in Amsterdam/
> And Took Place/ In 1797/
> Which Nobody Has Ever Seen

The story that follows this title, of a woman who tried to divorce her husband after ten years of childless marriage, runs to six pages (three folios).
The date of publication, 1798, appears at the bottom of the final page in
the form of a chronogram alluding to the story: "in the year you fostered
peace between husband and his wife." No information is given about the
author, publisher, or any other person responsible for the publication of
the story.

Where a title page is included, the text may occasionally be written in
Hebrew or in a mixture, usually of Hebrew followed by Yiddish. Hebrew
texts tend to follow the pattern set by traditional rabbinic writings. This
complex scholarly style includes all kinds of quotations and customary
abbreviations. These books usually dealt with religious subjects, and those
involved in the publication—from author to publisher—hoped thereby to
enhance their reputation.

Whether a book's subject is religious or not, the use of Yiddish signals
a different kind of text. It became almost commonplace for Yiddish title
pages (and prefaces) to be composed partly or entirely in verse, and they
convey an entirely different atmosphere from their Rabbinic Hebrew
counterparts. This trend probably developed from a combination of deeper
causes and frivolity. According to the *communis opinio,* although its
boundaries were sometimes vague, a division of labor existed between
Hebrew and Yiddish.[32] Important—that is, intellectual—books were (or
were supposed to be) written in Hebrew, and only these could claim a place
in the canon of Jewish literature. Yiddish books were written for the masses
and at best they held practical value. Since these compositions were never
considered important, authors and publishers could treat them with a certain levity. Indeed, even Eliah Levita, the famous sixteenth-century Hebrew

grammarian and translator/author of Yiddish masterpieces such as the *Bovo Mayse,* is known in Yiddish as *Eliah Bokher,* suggesting that his endeavors were considered follies, the pastime of a young man, a bachelor (*bokher*).[33] This frivolity is reflected in Yiddish title pages, which attempt to gain approval with art and wit.

Rhyming texts might be long or short and could include information on a wide range of topics: the subject matter of the book, its author, translation technique, an appeal to readers, technical details of book production. Almost all these texts end with a blessing and the conviction that the Messiah will soon come and lead the people of Israel back to his land. Detailed title pages occasionally compensated for the lack of prefaces, but this was certainly not the rule. One brief title page is found in a prayer book published in 1650:[34]

> Arranged according to German and Polish customs. And it includes the *Amida* prayer and the three Pilgrimages Holidays and also prayers of the Days of Awe. And it also includes the Chapters and Evening prayers and *Shir Hayikhud* as well as the Passover *Hagada.* All was fully and correctly translated. [The following text rhymes in Yiddish.] When you will read inside, your heart will know delight, since you'll understand what you are praying at prayers of evening and morning. Therefore, all of you: men, women, and maidens, come and see the beautiful, new prayer book. And buy it, [for] your money will not be wasted.

This title page gives the location of the intended market in Germany and Poland (reflecting the international nature of Amsterdam's Yiddish publishing industry); it mentions the various texts included, according to when these were used. It promises that the book is useful and that its purchase price will be money well spent. It also includes a second general address to its readers: men, women, and maidens. This formula is important because it occurs (in many variations)[35] in numerous Yiddish books throughout the centuries. The address to women and maidens, and the fact that the title of Yiddish literature's all-time best-seller, *Tsene-Rene,* derived from a verse in the Song of Songs ("Go out and watch, daughters of Tsion"), explains why for centuries Yiddish books were considered women's literature. Yet men could also be included as potential readers—mainly, here, because this was a prayer book. Indeed, it is now generally accepted that, in addition to writing intentionally for women, addressing them was also a smokescreen authors and publishers used to justify writing in Yiddish.[36] Hebrew was considered the language in which men read, Yiddish the women's vernacular. This title page and many others show that the dividing line was actually different: Hebrew was for scholarly writing and Yiddish for popular works. Moreover, it was evidently a flexible, continually shifting division.

An edition of the *Books of Tales* (Basel, 1602) was printed in Amsterdam in 1701. Its title page is wholly in rhyme and testifies to the publisher's liberal attitude toward later editions of books, as well as his attempt to (re)define its readership.

> Come, dear men and women, and look into this beautiful Book of Tales. Three hundred and more stories have been assembled. Some were constructed out of the *Talmud* and others from *Rabati* and *Bekhaye*. And you'll not miss stories of rabbi Yehuda the Righteous and you are offered stories from *Sefer Hasidim*. And you'll find also beautiful items from ethical books and *Yalkut*. **And other tales have been added in order to increase children's desire to read.** In order not to miss any of the tales, the characters of the alphabet have been added, numbering each one. **So this Book of Tales has been carefully prepared. This I promise you: letters that your eyes can clearly read as well as good ink and paper and, on top of this, it is not expensive. Now, dear people, lovers of reading Yiddish: I know that when you read in this book your hearts will be full of happiness. Books cannot be wrong when they include material from the Talmud and other holy books. Not all of us are scholars but all the same it is not smart to be ignorant. And so look into these books. If such Yiddish books are available, it is shameful if nobody reads them. So now we can follow the Torah in Hebrew or Yiddish and soon we shall experience the moment of returning to Erets Israel. Amen.**

The text reproduced in bold is not found in the first Basel edition (1602) or the Prague edition of circa 1665, which, together with another edition from Frankfurt an der Oder (c. 1700, title page missing), served as the basis for this Amsterdam edition. The title pages of the Basel, Prague, and Amsterdam editions sum up, more or less, the material contained in the Book of Tales, but each publisher attempted to define the character of his own edition and praised its structure as different. The Amsterdam title page begins with an attempt to expand its potential readership; in order to attract a younger public, tales have been added to appeal to children.[37] In fact, this reveals an essential aspect of Yiddish books. This book was intended to be read both silently and aloud (reading, oral and aural function).[38] Parents, for example, would have read tales from this book to children; it is far less likely that a child would have read them on his own.[39] Indeed, books in the home were controlled by parents and so served the family as a whole.[40]

In order to persuade people to buy the book, the publisher praises it as being based on Jewish tradition, which is of course eminently good; and since it is a Yiddish book designed for a mass audience, people should read it in order not to remain ignorant. A person should learn the Torah (here meaning not the Pentateuch but more broadly Jewish law, tradition, and culture) in Hebrew or Yiddish; both languages are legitimate vehicles of knowledge and wisdom. The title page then advertises the technical details: readable letters, good ink, and decent paper. In a postface, a further explanation of the structure appears:

> Following on from that which is suggested on the title page, three hundred and more stories are not found in this edition. We have based our edition on that of Prague and that of Frankfurt, but we noticed they were mistaken. They have no more than two hundred and fifty odd stories; and two stories are printed twice in the earlier editions. There are some who may think that we dropped stories from the edition, but they can check the earlier editions of the Book of Tales and they will find that it is the truth.

Why did the publisher decide not to change the title page but to add a postface contradicting it? He may not have wished to insult the editors of the previous editions and their endeavor as a whole. Or the title page might have been prepared before the editing and typesetting of the edition was completed, and the publisher may therefore have preferred not to prepare a new title page for financial or other reasons.[41] The compositor and typesetter, Hayyim Druker, was a conscientious man, and two of his publisher's prefaces, below, show a similar attitude.

Yosef Maarssen was another industrious author, translator, and publisher.[42] His *Shene Artlikhe Geshikhtn* was an attempt to present Jewish readers with a Yiddish translation of stories from Boccachio's *Decameron,* based on a Dutch version of the stories.[43] The title page (and preface) attempt to justify this flirtation with gentile literature.[44] Indeed, Maarssen clearly felt the need to explain his project at length, even though some prose publications appeared without a title page or preface and without mentioning the names of the author, translator, or publisher (in fact neither Boccachio nor the *Decameron* is mentioned here). The title page is in the form of a poem composed in two columns (*hemistichon*), as was customary in medieval Hebrew poetry, consisting of twenty-three verses. In it Maarssen explains that this book, translated from *galkhes*[45] and intended for "adults and youngsters," had not as yet appeared in Yiddish, but it was of such beauty that the reader would immediately ask to buy a second, third, fourth, and fifth volume, and he promised his readers to continue translating, provided he had the time.

The tone of the title page text is playful and tries to persuade readers to purchase this secular volume. In the preface that follows, Maarssen abandons this light tenor and expands on his choice of literature and Yiddish: a literary style free of contamination by Dutch idiom, which pervaded the local Yiddish of Amsterdam, as well as Hebraisms, which should not be mixed with a foreign language.[46] He says nothing about the stories or their background, only asserting that people do not always wish to read religious literature, although he is evidently keen to persuade readers that the book is "kosher" and worth purchasing. Maarssen then insures himself against financial debacle by recommending his publishing house to future customers. The preface concludes: "all this is offered to you by your obedient servant Yosef Maarssen from whom you can purchase all sorts of Yiddish books: godly (i.e., religious) and worldly (i.e., secular), at a cheap price."

A justification of a project and a demonstration of its potential benefit to readers might also include words about its practical value. Thus in synagogue men were expected to pray in Hebrew but often had difficulty understanding what they read and recited, so at least two Yiddish prayer books for the High Holidays were published—in 1670 and 1721 (the Krovatz)[47]— the title pages of which contain the following recommendation:

> The text was arranged in a lightweight volume, which will satisfy everyone, especially because the best Hebrew prayer books are printed in quarto. So, we arranged this book in such a way that a person will be able to bind it together with his Hebrew prayer book as a second section. In such a manner both will become one complete prayer book in Hebrew and Yiddish, which has to date never been published under the sun. And, each of you will find it easy to carry this prayer book to synagogue and be able to pray from the bottom of your heart and with full intention.

The publisher was apparently happy to see this volume become an appendix to a Hebrew prayer book, and for two reasons. First, since this book could be combined with another, it might be of interest to a large group of buyers who already possessed a Hebrew prayer book. Second, that the Yiddish text could be attached to a Hebrew volume gave it added legitimacy. The arguments presented in the book's preface emphasize the usefulness of this combination. The subtitle of the preface states: "prayer without full intention [is like] a body without a soul." The Yiddish text provided a commentary that enabled worshippers to understand the Hebrew prayers and allow them to recite them with integrity. Both title page and preface suggest that worshippers read the Yiddish alongside the canonical Hebrew.[48]

5

Genette, following Derrida, prefers the term "preface" to "introduction," since it is phenomenologically connected to the book rather than to its content. An introduction is unique in that it is linked directly to the subject or problem discussed in the book; a preface "obeys an occasional necessity," it is circumstantial.[49] Genette identifies the preface as the central paratextual instrument and discusses it in detail.[50] In fact, the relationship between author and publisher was based on different assumptions in seventeenth- and eighteenth-century Amsterdam from those that pertain today and those discussed by Genette. In Amsterdam it was not the authorial but rather the allographic preface that occupied center stage.

While an authentic authorial preface is the commonest and easiest to understand, the allographic variety needs brief clarification, for it is written not by the author or by an actor (i.e., a character in a fictional work) but by a third person.[51] An allographic preface is therefore by definition separate from the text, and the book in question has, in fact, two senders (to use Genette's terminology): the main text (the book) is sent by its author and the preface by someone else. Allographic prefaces are common, indeed natural, in translations. They are usually original and they may supplement an authorial preface; this practice is rare in fiction but common in nonfiction. Allographic prefaces are meant to provide information: a biography of the author, a discussion of generic questions, the context of the work. All this serves to recommend the book to readers while also offering a critical commentary. But a critical commentary with a theoretical dimension can become a critical essay, turning the paratext into a separate text, a metatext, which has a different role and status and falls beyond the scope of paratexts. Since allographic texts are written by a third person, we would expect most of them to be prefaces, as introductions are the author's province. Nevertheless, the boundaries between preface and introduction are vague, and elements of one may emerge in the other.

The theory of prefaces may be divided into two areas: situation and function. Situation deals with questions relating to form (mostly but not necessarily prose), place (location in the book), time (the moment of publication, delays, and later prefaces, erased prefaces), senders (authorial, allographic, or actorial, whether authentic, fictive, or apocryphal), and readers. Function deals with questions relating to why and how a book is written. Questions about why and how are occasionally interchangeable.[52] In the following examples I scrutinize these parameters and discuss their validity in Yiddish paratexts.

Shtern Shus (1695) is an "ethical book." In general, this genre was intended to support readers in keeping Jewish law and advise them in matters of faith. Authors of ethical books sermonized in print on personal conduct in everyday life, basing their arguments on biblical stories and other pious tales from rabbinic literature. As a medieval genre, these books were originally written in Hebrew, but in the seventeenth century they became a popular Yiddish genre. With their distinctive narrative character and avoidance of the legal jargon of Jewish law, these books were popular with the public while earning the respect of rabbis and scholars. Yiddish ethical books simplified ideas, turning philosophy and jurisprudence into popular ethics.[53] Many of these books, like *Shtern Shus,* were addressed specifically to women:

> Listen, House of Jacob, also known as Israel, who are dispersed all over the world and suffer in bitter exile and wait for the eternal help of God the Almighty, the God of Israel, through the Messiah son of David and Elijah the prophet. I have written here in order to reduce the tremendous licentiousness and to condemn the great arrogance caused by outrage against the holy Torah, Prophets and the holy scholars, just as you find in many books. Therefore, let nobody have in mind to suspect that I wish to hurt and shame a group of women of our true faith, but I have seen that licentiousness has grown in many forms in our hard and bitter times. You cannot accuse a group of people of not knowing it is a great sin, because books are expensive and not everyone can buy them, and because some people are tired of reading large books carefully, when other people find the book *Lev Tov* [Good Heart] to be too big, and especially in our times when many people yearn to read books and tales assembled from gentile literature and do not support the fear of Heaven. Therefore I did what I did for the sake of the God of Israel who holds all souls in his hands and I wrote here about our holy Torah in order to show you that licentiousness is a great sin in our hard exile. It is recommended that each sweet, pious woman read it for the sake of God and rid herself of her arrogance [so] that women's souls will not suffer insults in the world to come. Therefore, I hope that every pious woman who fears God in her heart and is sincere and loyal to Almighty God will accept punishment for her offences with a clear conscience. Her prize will be brilliant paradise forever and ever. And do not accuse me of inflicting punishment on others,

since I support the holy Torah; and anyone can punish people if they
do it in the name of Heaven. God knows that all my thoughts are
derived from His praised name. And He will help us serve Him with
abundant love and loyalty in such a way that we shall soon be
redeemed of our hard exile and He will bring us back to Jerusalem
the holy city.

While the Hebrew portion of the title page identifies women and children
as those to whom the book is addressed and the Yiddish refers to "dear
pious [*frume*] men and women," the preface is dedicated exclusively to
women. It is an original authorial preface and focuses on women's behavior
and sins. The anonymous author writes in the name of God and promises
to present the reader with advice on Jewish religion and customs. The
question of "how" is dealt with in a way typical of many such books. The
author mentions another work that he finds problematic, in this case on
account of its format: *The Book of Good Heart*[54] is too big, too volumi-
nous, for ordinary people, even those who had the book at home, to read.
This flaw has driven them to read gentile literature with no connection to
Jewish ethics.[55] A book's format, therefore, can be a hindrance and may
affect a person's choice of reading matter. In fact, *The Book of Good Heart*
contains ninety folios (180 pages) while *Shtern Shus* has only twenty-nine
(fifty-eight pages); *The Book of Good Heart,* a critically acclaimed Yiddish
best-seller, was often published in folio (2°), whereas *Shtern Shus* was in
quarto (4°).

Instead of adding a publisher's preface, publishers might help fund a book
and support its ideas by placing a rabbinic approbation before the preface.
Rabbi Moshe Yehuda was the chief rabbi of Amsterdam's Ashkenazi community and his text highlights two additional issues. First, his readers are
"the masses of men and women who do not understand the language of
learning, the holy tongue" (i.e., Hebrew), and therefore it would be bene-
ficial to introduce them to a "system in their own language" (i.e., Jewish
law and customs). Second, the rabbi forbade other publishers to publish
editions of the book in or outside the Netherlands for a period of three
years. Not all religious publications contain such an approbation, so this
clearly operated as a recommendation or critical note (or "please-insert"
in Gennette's terminology)[56] of the kind found on covers of modern books,
rather than an instrument of censorship, whereby the printing and distribution of books whose contents had been monitored was approved.
Although rabbis regularly criticized certain books, publishers and authors
of Yiddish books did not always seek rabbinical approbation and were free
of rabbinical shackles, even though for many years Amsterdam's Sephardi
community was subject to censorship.[57] Nevertheless, when publishers of

Yiddish books thought it worthwhile, they solicited approbations from Ashkenazi as well as Sephardi rabbis, who willingly supplied them (presumably for remuneration).

Like *Shtern Shus,* which was designed to encourage women to rejoin the path of righteousness, the prefaces to many of these books reveal that they were preoccupied with the nation's condition. In *Masekhet Derekh Eretz* (1680) the editor, Shabbetai Bass of Prague, discusses the dire economic situation of Ashkenazi Jews: "[It is important] that a man does not sin and especially now when bread winning is so difficult, as if it were the crossing of the Red Sea. A scholar must take care that he has work that also enables him to find spare time in order to study, and it is even truer if a man is not a scholar and he must travel and cross countries in order to earn his bread . . . therefore I initiated the publication of this small book that can be used by businessmen during their travels." The book contains all the prayers a Jew might need on the road, as well as weights and measures, exchange rates, and routes and distances throughout Europe. Bass concludes the preface in a short but playful and rhetorical manner: "Shall I argue why the book is so practical? Let everyone find out for himself. Here then I wish to end this preface." To this he added a blessing and an affirmation that the people are waiting for the Messiah. In *Darkhei Yesharim* (1758), another ethical work, the author, Yosef Dantsiger Oyerbakh, admits that there are many good ethical books in Hebrew and Yiddish. Nevertheless,

> the plan and presentation of these books are based on the local situation and climate in which the authors live. And they correspond to the nature of the people in their own time. Thus, because I noticed that the world and people's nature is constantly and increasingly changing and not everyone follows the path of righteousness . . . and one rabbi cannot work out all the bad habits and ways to punish [people] and also all old ethical books are insufficient [to answer all problems]. So these reasons persuaded me to write this small book . . . because I saw that the present generation is conducting itself in an orderly fashion as far as worldly matters are concerned but in godly matters very unwisely.

Oyerbakh admits that he is not inventing something new: this small, cheap volume provides access to the classics of previous generations, whose titles he mentions. In the preface of *Melamed Siakh* (1710), a glossary of Hebrew words from the Torah and the five *megilot* with Yiddish translations, the writer attacks the inexcusable inadequacy of Torah teachers. The language used in the Yiddish section of the preface is harsh: teachers act as if they never lived in a Jewish community (i.e., as if they have no knowledge of Judaism). Jewish mothers are advised to buy the book to expose the ignorance of their children's teacher and then force him to buy a copy of the book; if he refuses, they should sack him immediately.[58] In *Megilas Esther* (The Scroll of Esther), a Yiddish commentary on this biblical book, designed to be used by men and women as a tool of self-study to understand the Hebrew text, the preface focuses on the position of women: "the order of the world is such that women are not taken seriously and they, old and young, are absolutely neglected and [people] treat them unjustly and with violence." But this, of course, is against God's wishes, and women, like men, should know God's commandments and duties, especially those relating to purity and cleansing. In short, women have duties just as men do: even the Bible has female heroines, among them the prophetess Deborah and Samuel's mother Hannah.

In all these cases, the argument of the preface rests on a lack that justifies the publication of yet another book and explains its contents. They place the publication in context, clarifying the structure of the book, the manner of writing, and what reading the book hopes to achieve. Its practical value was a vindication of the book, while the beauty of its contents was beyond all prosaic reasoning.

Since the justification given for all such books was public demand, the author and publisher depicted as humble servants of the public, even works of prose that had nothing to do with religion, tradition, or Jewish custom adopted a similar approach. *And This Is in Memory,* a sixteen-page poem about the severe winter of 1784 in Amsterdam, contains a mixed title page and preface describing the author's service to the public:[59]

> After I saw several Purim newspapers[60] concerning the winter of the year 544 [1784] containing risqué and foul language, mocking the poor and the insane and other matters that should not be repeated, I decided to write this poetic lamentation on everything that happened during this cold winter to remember in the generations to come. And God will remove his wrath on us and give each what ever he needs in order that they do not need each other. And He will assemble us from our places of dispersion and send us soon the Messiah and we will be able to watch the building of the Temple. Amen.

This small octavo (8°) edition, written by Shlomo ben Itshak Bol, was probably published on the author's own initiative. He decided to record his version of the events of that winter as a correction to the satirical accounts, primarily because he wished to compose something and probably had the money to pay the "widow and orphans of Shlomo Proops" for the printing.[61]

Clearly there was a market for this kind of poem, which belongs to an established tradition of Yiddish historical poems.[62] At the same time, it forms part of a growing group of publications intended for the local market only. At the end of the eighteenth century, Jewish printing presses had reemerged in Eastern Europe, and Amsterdam was losing much of its international market. The list of Yiddish publications clearly reveals this shift to the local market after 1780. While Amsterdam's international publishing industry collapsed, those books that did appear—usually cheap booklets— retained the characteristics of earlier Yiddish books.

The prefaces to such books, by authors, translators, and editors, often attempted to justify their publication. Even when translating from Hebrew, it was apparently vital to justify the undertaking. It was not enough to claim that the Yiddish version was intended for a broader public; this claim had to be explained and argued. In fact, prefaces could be quite long and diffuse, and the argumentation meandering. The following preface by Moshe Frankfurt, translator of Itshak Abohab's *Candelabra of Light* (Amsterdam, 1722), is a good example.[63] The first passage, justifying the publication of Jewish literature in a language other than Hebrew, is particularly diffuse and confusing:

> Moshe Frankfurt says: we find in the Torah that God ordered Moses to provide the Torah in seventy languages so that all the nations would be able to learn the Torah and know how to serve God. But one can also say that God ordered the translation of the Torah into all languages expecting that all nations think that our Torah contains something unjust, which in fact is not the case, and now they see that all that the Torah contains is respectful and these matters lead people into the path of righteousness in order to serve God. Just as it states in the verse that Moses said: the nations will hear Your commandments and law and then they will admit that Israel is a wise people forever. And it is also said: and who is the folk that has such laws and just rules as stated in the Torah. So, we may conclude that God wants all nations to know the Torah and thereafter realize that it is the true Torah, respectful and just. And they know all this because the Torah was translated into all languages. Thus, if we concluded that God ordered the nations who did not receive the Torah [on Mount Sinai], to know it, let alone it is applicable to the sons of Israel, the holy nation, that they must understand the Torah and know how the commandments must be performed, their contents, and that a human being must perform his duties with intention for the sake of Heaven; and a person must accept what the Torah says in order that he may live now and in the world to come

and which cannot be something else because he must grasp the basis of the Torah and commandments. This is of course the reason why books in all languages were produced, the names of which we shall immediately mention. And Jews in all lands of their dispersion should know and understand the Torah, the source of the commandments that God ordered. And he will lead his life in an ethical fashion and with respect to others, and he will be warned to abandon the angry ways and understand that he must follow the good that springs from the Torah. Three reasons, therefore, are there why these matters are written in the general simple language [i.e., Yiddish]: they have the right to understand, consequently the right to know the truth and thereafter they can ensure their eternal life.

He then describes the circumstances that prompted him to translate the text:

And these reasons moved me to take up this exhausting project of translating the famous *Book of the Candelabra of Light* into the Ashkenazi language. Dear Mr Hayyim Druker came to me and said that a couple of hundred people had approached him and asked him to do his best to ensure that the book would appear in the Ashkenazi language. And he also showed me approbations obtained from rabbis of both Ashkenazi and Sephardi communities who were enthusiastic, having learned that the book was to be translated and that many people would be able to study the book and enjoy the light of the candelabra. Hayyim Druker also told me that he had seen that the book had been translated into Spanish by the author Itshak Abohab himself[64] and he appreciated the fact that translating it would enable many more people to enjoy the book. Therefore, I accepted the offer and thought that because I, in my youth, pleased God with a commentary on this very same book, I would like now to offer it to the multitude and translate it into Yiddish in a common language that everyone can understand. Nevertheless, it turned out to be a difficult project and I had to invest much effort and time in order to do justice to the book, especially since there are so many Talmudic passages and legends that needed to be presented in a way that the simple man and women could understand. So, I put my trust in God to give me strength to finish the work as well as the fact that I did it for the general public.

Apparently, unnamed scholars opposed the project and Frankfurt tried to refute their arguments against the translation:

And because of this I composed this preface. I heard that there are scholars who believe it is wrong to translate such books into the language of Ashkenaz and publicize matters that are written in *midrash* and Talmud. Thus, I would like to show them the contrary. It is a duty to publish books in all languages, so that a person who knows no Hebrew can study in his own language and will be rewarded exactly in the same way as students in Hebrew; as the righteous Rabbi Yeshaia writes in his book *The Two Tables* and as Itshak Abohab who translated his book into Spanish immediately (as I already said). And even more, many of our books that are the hardest and most difficult to study were not written in Hebrew but in the language that the simple man spoke. The Palestinian Talmud was written in the language men, women, and children conversed in in the land of Israel and not Hebrew. Also the Talmud, the so-called Babylonian Talmud, contains much that is not Hebrew as well as *midrash,* much of which is not Hebrew but the language of the simple man of the various lands [a series of other books composed in Aramaic and other languages] and many other books that are not mentioned because of lack of space here; all were written in the languages people were speaking in their land [there follow more titles of books written in Arabic, including Maimonides].

Here Frankfurt was prepared to write in Yiddish. He explains his duty to communicate the wisdom of Jewish tradition to the general public: the information he provides about Jewish scholars would lift people's souls. Thus he hopes he has served the people well and will receive their praise in exchange. But Frankfurt felt the need to provide yet another explanation:

I must also inform those who read the book about how I handled matters concerning women. [In fact,] I wished to skip all these questions, since I was afraid that perhaps a frivolous person might dive into these sections, laugh and ridicule them. But Hayyim Druker told me that he published editions of *Lev Tov* (The Book of Good Heart), in which these matters are also discussed. And he asked the chief rabbi how to treat these. The rabbi answered that one should leave out nothing because nothing that stands in our Torah is outrageous, risqué or offensive. But if a person wants to be wicked and turn the living God's words upside down, making them risqué and offensive, his blood will be on his own head. And I also follow the verse: God's ways are correct, the righteous will walk and the wicked will fail on them.

Frankfurt concludes with the hope to be of service to his readers. He asks forgiveness for any mistakes in his text.[65] Unfortunately he did not have enough time to complete his work, for the typesetters rushed him. The publisher Hayyim Druker read his manuscript, since "I was not able to write immediately in correct Yiddish and he knows grammar much better. . . . He put everything in order and I am happy that many persons will gladly read and learn from the book." He closes by appealing to God's mercy, God being the only one able to fully understand the human heart.

Frankfurt's preface is followed by a publisher's "Apology and Preface." Here Hayyim Druker begins by affirming that a person must do his best to serve God. A person can, and must, consult books in Hebrew, Yiddish, and Spanish, as well as in all seventy languages. He mentions that he had been thinking about a Yiddish translation for some years and had noticed its translation into Spanish twice, once by the author and once in Amsterdam, a few years before the current project. He acknowledged that Jewish books were available in the vernacular but pointed out that scholars still rejected such translations. He hoped, however, that all doubts would be dispersed after reading a book so carefully produced: well proofread, written in a style accessible even to a child, printed on high-quality paper in good ink.

This Yiddish edition was a prestigious project and therefore the producers felt a preface or two were necessary. Meticulous attention was paid to every aspect of the book; it was published in folio (2°) rather than octavo (8°) or the even smaller format of many other Yiddish books. Nevertheless, in a city in which Sephardim had a Spanish translation, one may question the need to jusitfy a Yiddish translation. Both prefaces, however, refer to a group of scholars (rabbis) who objected to the project from the outset. They probably had connections with Eastern European rabbinical authorities,[66] and since the book was also intended for sale in Jewish centers in Eastern Europe, Druker and Frankfurt wished to circumvent any problems that might jeopardize the book's sales. In fact, the demands of the international market may have been their main consideration and they may have taken the local market for granted.

Although no specific group of readers is addressed, the book was designed for men who wished to consult an anthology of Jewish traditional literature. The Yiddish book retained its scholarly highbrow character. Indeed, as far as we know, it remained a fruitful source for writers of sermons in the following centuries, and Frankfurt, who wrote a commentary on the Hebrew original, also compiled an abridged version of the *Candelabra of Light* in Hebrew that became even more popular than the original.[67] Nevertheless, the reference to subjects relating to women as a potential problem may indicate how Yiddish was already being regarded as primarily "women's literature."

The writer is also guilty of gross "title dropping." Frankfurt makes many references to books written by Jewish scholars to help justify his own undertaking. In itself, comparison is a logical and practical device used to prove a point, especially where canonical books are concerned. When dealing with subjects relating to women, he mentions the Yiddish book *Lev Tov,* which is also mentioned in the preface to *Shtern Shus,* an edition of which was prepared by Druker in 1706. This shows how thoroughly Yiddish publishers were acquainted with best-sellers and how they used them to their advantage.

In a world in which publishers played an active role in the book production process, Hayyim Druker was an illustrious figure. He had typeset the Amsterdam edition of *The Book of Tales* (1701, see above). By now he was an experienced publisher and probably considered himself the ideal person to publish the Yiddish version of Abohab's *Candelabra of Light:* he had toyed with the idea for some years, solicited approbations, selected and hired a translator and advised him regarding thorny issues (e.g., women's subjects), read and corrected the Yiddish version, and of course organized the production process. This is probably why he felt that he had to add his own preface, which is after all largely a rehash of the ideas and subjects dealt with by Frankfurt. Indeed, Frankfurt says in the preface that he could not complete the work because the typesetters were pressing him to deliver the manuscript. Evidently Druker was the driving force throughout the process.

Both Frankfurt and Druker refer to "the languages of the lands" that Jews spoke. Here they mean Yiddish, not Dutch or some other language. This reference occurs in the context of a comparison of Aramaic and Arabic, vernaculars of other peoples that Jews also spoke and wrote. Nevertheless, in the Ashkenazi Diaspora, at least until the end of the eighteenth century, Yiddish was the vernacular, not the language of the surrounding society, and it remained the almost exclusive vernacular of Eastern European Jews until the end of the nineteenth century. That Yiddish was considered a "language of the land," or indeed a "foreign language" by Jews themselves, indicates that Yiddish books were a vehicle of modernization in a period in which Jews still lived in ghettos. It became the language of the Diaspora, not of a specific Jewish territory.[68]

This paratextual apparatus clearly shows how the reader is led into and beyond the text of the book. It informs the reader of the book's subject and intention: to provide an anthology of texts from rabbinic literature, to assist Jews in their duties and enrich their knowledge of the vast corpus of tradition. It ensures readers that the Yiddish version does no harm to the book's content; on the contrary, the Yiddish text explains and simplifies difficult arguments. At the same time, it informs the reader about other important Jewish books and their role and status; and it compares the book to another Yiddish best-seller as a recommendation. Both translator and publisher are frank about certain problems (scholarly opposition, the treatment of women's subjects, difficulties of translation) and open a window for the reader into the world of Jewish publishing. In a way this approach is modern, since they attempt to put the book in context and do not claim that the text is all that matters. They acknowledge the wider social setting in which the publishing industry operates. No doubt financial factors played a significant role in the publisher's considerations, but these did not detract from his sense of social responsibility; instead, the two things overlapped.[69]

Druker's central role in this project was not only a result of his experience, knowledge, and self-confidence. Sixteen years earlier, in 1706, he was similarly involved in what was probably one of his first publishing projects, an edition of *The Book of the Good Heart*.[70] Elements in the later preface are already evident in the earlier:

> Several times I heard from people who asked to buy it that the book *Lev Tov* is out of print and not available. Accordingly, I thought that I would like to be of service to the multitude and do my best in order that this lovely book be printed again. But it was beyond my capacity to carry out this project. So, I assembled a group of people: religious persons, women, young men, and virgins, and each did his best to check the proofs page by page and with the help of God we completed the work. . . . Now, when I began working I found out that the language of the book could not be compared with the language one hears talking. Thus, I decided to do my best and ceremoniously decided that each child that reads this book, without seeing earlier editions, should understand what is said there. Although the book had already been printed several times (and here in Amsterdam twice), these editions were based on the very old edition. Because of the mistakes, I found the Amsterdam editions worthless. But also the editions that were printed in other locations are full of mistakes as happens in prayer books for daily prayers as well as holidays. Wherever one puts one's five fingers [i.e., one's hand] on a text one finds a mistake and nobody is bothered by the question whether it was correctly proofread . . . but here in Amsterdam it is different. If one wants to print a book, the first duty is to find a good corrector in order to complete this holy task in an accurate manner. . . . Of course it is impossible to erase all mistakes, but one has to do one's best and strive to remove all mistakes. . . . So, every time I reread the first print sheet with a scholar who knew the text well.

Druker correctly mentioned two previous Amsterdam editions (1651 and 1670). These were identical to the first edition, printed in Prague in 1630. All three had the same title page. Druker, however, revised the language, ordered a new title page, and under the author's original he placed his own preface, in which he discussed linguistic as well as publishing issues. Being perfectly competent in Yiddish, both the Yiddish of his own time and that of previous generations, he was able to resolve linguistic problems himself. Indeed, he attempted to modernize the Yiddish and alluded to differences between the spoken language and outdated literary usages. As a typesetter, Druker also expanded on the question of proofreading. Of course, Torah scrolls have to be completely correct, otherwise the parchment is disqualified; editions of the Talmud and other rabbinic literature were usually not amended, since the editor was afraid of introducing even more mistakes. Yiddish, however, was a wide open field and, more important, noncanonical. So it was possible to manipulate the text as required. Naturally Druker and others claimed that they did this in order to help their readers perform their duties in the appropriate way.

As Shlomo Zalman Londen's book *Kohelet Shlomo* shows, a publisher's independence could assume idiosyncratic forms. Written by a Jew from Lithuania and first published in 1722 at Frankfurt am Main,[71] the book contains a compilation of individual prayers to be recited from awakening in the morning to sleeping at night, prayers for men and women for a variety of situations and occasions, supplications for women, customs related to various days, feasts and occasions, a simple method for fathers to teach sons the basics of Hebrew, and two tales: one about Judith to be read during Hanukkah,[72] and another about an evil spirit that entered a woman's body and was exorcised by a cabbalist.[73] Two Amsterdam editions also include a second section incorporating a Passover *Hagada* also edited by Londen.

The first Amsterdam edition appeared in 1744, published by Herts Levi Rofe. In the same year Rofe published a separate edition of the *Hagada*. Bibliographies mention another Amsterdam edition containing only the first section, in 1766.[74] Yet another Rofe edition of the book, including both sections, appeared in 1772. The changes introduced in this edition reflect the tendencies described above. The title page, for example, states that this is the third edition; in fact it is the second, since only the first edition of 1744 included both sections. Indeed, if the other editions were counted—one of the *Hagada* (1744) and the other of the prayers (1766)— the 1772 edition would be the fourth. Moreover, whether this was the third or fourth edition, the publisher was referring only to his own publications, ignoring three previous editions before 1744: the first at Frankfurt am Main and two subsequent printings in Fürth. This may suggest that publishers in

Amsterdam were proud of their work and were not concerned with other publishers. Druker claimed that publishers did things differently and better in Amsterdam.

In the 1772 edition, the order of the paratexts was changed. While the first Amsterdam edition includes a compositor's preface followed by an author's and then a third (including a section in verse) by the publisher, the 1772 edition has the compositor's preface,[75] followed by the text of the first section, while this section closes with the author's preface (!) followed by the "publishers of the first *Kohelet Shlomo* preface," i.e., Herts Levi Rofe. Furthermore, while in the first edition the *Hagada* begins immediately after the first section, the 1772 edition contains a separate title page and a preface by "the author of *Kohelet Shlomo*" before the text of the *Hagada*.

The most radical and curious change is the transfer of the author's preface to the end of the first section of the book. This can only be interpreted as a sign of condescension and contempt for the author and his role in the production of the book. Moreover, while Rofe must have felt in 1744 that the author deserved credit for the book and that it should have helped its sale,[76] the publication of a third edition twenty-eight years later had to be justified on its own merits. The transfer can also be explained by the traditional tendency to focus on the text rather than the author, a tendency that gave publishers ample room to do what they pleased with books and especially with subsequent editions. So the book as a physical object and the text as a creative asset were controlled and practically owned by the publisher. In a world without copyright laws, the publisher had the upper hand.

Publishers might also feel less secure when producing a major book with a particularly prestigious element. In that case they would try to surround the text with a defensive wall of a long series of paratexts, as was the case, for example, with the Yiddish Bible, or indeed two rival Yiddish Bibles of 1678 and 1679. Attempts were made to translate biblical texts into Yiddish throughout the history of the language, with mixed results. Stories and episodes, chapters and single books were all translated into Yiddish; epic poetry and commentaries on biblical themes were written in Yiddish; and a separate Yiddish dialect developed for didactic purposes and was employed in schools to teach children to read and understand Torah.[77]

The two Amsterdam Bibles were the first integral translations of the Hebrew original into Yiddish, and the producers of both claimed to present the public with something new and better: a straightforward version of the Hebrew text rather than an adaptation that did not reflect the original ideas. In fact, only a single translation was originally planned, but because one of the investors (himself a publisher) did not like a section of translation by Yekutiel Blits, he withdrew and launched a second, rival project, hiring Yosef Witsenhausen as his translator. Both publishers, Uri Feibush Halevi and Yosef Athias, refused to abandon their project. In fact, Athias, who launched the rival translation, probably suppressed his own edition for a few years when he saw that Halevi's Bible was not a commercial success, his son eventually republishing it in 1687, after his father's death, as a second edition with a new title page.[78]

Each of the editions consisted of six thousand copies. Investors contributed large sums to both projects in the hope of substantial returns when the book was sold in Central and Eastern Europe. So the publishers surrounded their project with a series of paratexts to persuade the public to buy the book. Each Bible contains a translator's and a publisher's preface, rabbinic approbations from within and outside Holland, and dedications and privileges issued by Christian authorities. The subjects dealt with in the prefaces vary from descriptions of the poor quality of currently available books to questions of editing (the use of parentheses and other typographical symbols), from attacks on rivals (Feibush on his detractors and Witsenhausen's invective against Blits) to praise of the project and the expertise involved in bringing it out.[79] Both Bibles were commercial failures, and the story of their rivalry and the paratexts constitutes a juicy chapter of Yiddish booklore.

6

In early modern Europe the Yiddish book was a cultural article of trade. Ideologically the Yiddish book was written, published, and distributed in order to provide a service to the mass of uneducated people who found it difficult to perform the duties of the Jewish faith as explained in Hebrew literature, which they barely understood. However, publishers had to rely on sound economic foundations. Since literacy was more widespread among Jews than among the surrounding non-Jews, those involved in book production—from author to distributor—understood that Yiddish books would reach a wider readership than Hebrew books and that this potential for growth justified the production of books in many genres and various forms. Indeed, although Hebrew retained its canonical position in Jewish culture well into the nineteenth century, the Yiddish book enjoyed an ever-expanding market and growing popularity.

Having matured under the umbrella of the holy language and having later claimed a more or less parallel existence, while maintaining a division of labor with Hebrew, Yiddish books became a powerful tool in Ashkenazi culture—in Western Europe until the age of Jewish Enlightenment in the

closing decades of the eighteenth century, and in Eastern Europe as a mod-
ernizing force within the religious world of Hassidism and the secular movements of the nineteenth and twentieth centuries. The impact of the Yiddish
book on booklore in general, from authors to readers, through the interim
stages of book production is significant. Moreover, since the Yiddish book
was an international phenomenon from the outset, the development of Yiddish book culture forms an integral part of Ashkenazi history. The Yiddish
book was the cement that united Jews from Frankfurt and Vilnius; it was
a means of communication through which Judaism and Jewish culture
could be transmitted and distributed.

The central position books occupied in Jewish culture makes them a
fruitful area for research, and the investigation of paratexts, as a literary
instrument designed to critically (and economically) enhance the success of
a book, forms a crucial part of this research. As this discussion shows, these
paratexts were an indispensable instrument for promoters of books who
were trying to conquer people's hearts in a deeply conservative community,
where life was still determined by a strict religious tradition. This was
how Yiddish publishers attempted to persuade potential buyers and their
spiritual leaders that books were worthy of their attention. It was therefore
important to present a book in such a way that text and context were in
tune with each other.

Publishers of Yiddish books occupied a central position in the production process and were responsible for the paratextual apparatus. Testimonies reveal that publishers initiated many projects and were the arbiters of
text and form alike. Authors and translators occupied a secondary position,
and so paratexts invariably reflect the publisher's concerns and anxieties.
Publishers like Hayyim Druker intervened in textual, linguistic, and editorial decisions.

It was vital that the subject of a book be deemed correct and legitimate:
it had to be within the tradition and in no way revolutionary. In persuading
readers of this, various paratexts sought to present the author, translator, or
editor as a humble servant of God who hoped merely to be of service to his
people while remaining totally subservient to Jewish tradition. Moreover,
fiction and other narrative prose books tended to be published without even
acknowledging the author. It was in fact in this genre of Yiddish literature
that we find the greatest foreign influences on Ashkenazi culture.

Yiddish books were designed first and foremost to appeal to the "simple
soul," hence the emphasis on women as their primary readers. This was
popular or popularized literature. When tackling subjects relating to tradition and customs, Yiddish books offered an accessible parallel to the intellectual tomes on Jewish law, and so earned a place in every Jewish home.
Indeed, some prefaces praised the book as a family asset. Title pages and

prefaces also frequently gave local and temporal reasons for their publication. Each generation faced its own set of problems, requiring its own literature. Smaller formats, less intimidating to the simple reader, made people more likely to pick them up. As a consequence of reducing the format, texts were also shortened and summarized, and introduced in an abridged form in Yiddish.

Paratexts therefore present a key to understanding the structure of Yiddish books and Yiddish culture. They enable the students of booklore to better grasp the process of book production and to examine its various subdivisions. They allow us to locate the text within a precise context and evaluate its position within a culture that cherished the book and the written word.

Notes

1. See, for instance, A. J. Toynbee, *Greek Historical Thoughts* (New York: Mentors Books, 1952). The first section is a collection of prefaces by Greek historians, from Herodotus in the fifth century BCE to Theophylactus Simocatta the Egyptian in the sixth century CE (29–97).

2. Gerard Genette, *Paratexts: Thresholds of Interpretation,* trans. Jane E. Lewin (Cambridge: Cambridge University Press, 1997) (this is the English translation of *Seuils* [Paris, 1987]); see also Annet Retsch, *Paratext und Textanfang* (Würzburg: Könighausen & Neumann, 2000).

3. These reservations concerning Genette's approach and the expansion of his theory were formulated by Samuel Kinser, "Paratextual Paradise and the Devilish Arts of Printing," in *Paratext: The Fuzzy Edges of Literature,* ed. Carla Dauven et al. (Amsterdam: Institute of Culture and History, University of Amsterdam, 2004), 5–38.

4. On literacy among Jews, see Simcha Assaf, *Sources to the History of Education Among Jews,* 3 vols., rev. ed. (New York: JTSA, 2001–2); on literacy in non-Jewish society, see R. A. Houston, *Literacy in Early Modern Europe: Culture and Education, 1500–1800* (London: Routledge, 1988), esp. 130–54.

5. Yiddish is generally defined as "popular literature," but it is advisable to remember Roger Chartier's reservations as formulated in his *Forms and Meanings: Texts, Performances, and Audiences from Codex to Computer* (Philadelphia: University of Pennsylvania Press, 1995), 83–97. His assertion that "Above all, the 'popular' can indicate a kind of relation, a way of using cultural products or norms that are shared, more or less, by society at large, but understood, defined, and used in styles that vary" (89), is, I believe, essential in understanding the relationship between Hebrew and Yiddish and the ways Yiddish books and culture in general developed.

6. On the history of the Yiddish language, see Max Weinreich, *History of the Yiddish Language* (in Yiddish), 4 vols. (New York: Yivo, 1973) (abridged English translation, Chicago: Chicago University Press, 1980). On the history of Yiddish literature, see Israel Zinberg, *History of Jewish Literature* (in Yiddish), vol. 6 (Vilnius: Tomor, 1936) (English ed., New York: Ktav Publishing, 1975); Max Erik, *History of Yiddish Literature: From the Oldest Times to the Age of Enlightenment* (in Yiddish) (Warsaw: Kultur Lige, 1928); Chone Shmeruk, *Yiddish Literature: Aspects of Its History* (in Hebrew) (Tel Aviv: Porter Institute–Tel Aviv University, 1978) (Yiddish ed., Tel Aviv: Peretz Farlag, 1987); Jean Baumgarten, *Introduction à la*

littérature yiddish ancienne (Paris: Cerf, 1993); on the change from Western Yiddish to modern Eastern Yiddish, see D. B. Kerler, *The Origins of Modern Literary Yiddish* (Oxford: Clarendon Press, 1999).

7. Chone Shmeruk, "Yiddish Prints in Italy" (in Hebrew), *Italia* 3 (1982): 112–75; Chone Shmeruk, "Basic Characteristics of Yiddish Literature in Poland and Lithuania Before 1648–49" in *Yiddish Literature in Poland: Historical Studies and Perspectives* (in Hebrew) (Jerusalem: Magnes Press, 1981), 11–118; M. N. Rosenfeld, "The Development of Hebrew Printing in the Sixteenth and Seventeenth Centuries" in *A Sign and a Witness: 2000 Years of Hebrew Books and Illuminated Manuscripts,* ed. L. Singer Gold (New York: Oxford University Press, 1989), 92–100; Chava Turniansky and Erika Timm, eds., *Yiddish in Italia: Manuscripts and Printed Books* (Milan, 2003).

8. Harm Den Boer, *La literatura sefardi de Amsterdam* (Alcalá de Henares: Universidad de Alcalá, 1996).

9. Leo Fuks and Rena Fuks-Mansfeld, *Hebrew Typography in the Northern Netherlands, 1585–1815,* 2 vols. (Leiden: Brill, 1984–87), which deals with book production until the start of the eighteenth century; further volumes on the eighteenth century were not published up to this date; see also the short evaluation of Yiddish in Amsterdam by Shmeruk, *Yiddish Literature,* 131–34.

10. Christiane Berkvens-Stevelinck, ed., *Le magasin de l'univers: The Dutch Republic as the Center of the European Book-Trade* (Leiden: Brill, 1992); I. H. Van Eeghen, *De Amsterdamse boekhandel 1680–1725,* 2 vols. (Amsterdam: Gemmentelijke Archiefdienst, 1978).

11. It should be noted that Christian publishers also produced Hebrew books, hiring Jewish correctors and typesetters to prepare such editions.

12. Yosef Kaplan, "Jewish Refugees from Germany and Poland-Lithuania in Amsterdam During the Seventeenth Century," in *Culture and Society in Medieval Jewry: Studies Dedicated to the Memory of Haim Hillel Ben-Sasson,* ed. R. Bonfil et al. (Jerusalem: Magnes Press, 1989), 587–622; Yosef Kaplan, "Amsterdam and Ashkenazic Migration in the Seventeenth Century," *Studia Rosenthaliana* 23 (1989): 23–44.

13. A famous example of this trend is found in Yosef Athias's Yiddish Bible (Amsterdam, 1679). He writes in his publisher's preface that he hired a person to correct the text and remove any local Dutch usages of Yiddish, thereby enabling Jews in Central and Eastern Europe to read the Yiddish translation. See also below.

14. Kerler, *Modern Literary Yiddish.*

15. Mirjam Gutschow, *An Inventory of Yiddish Books in the Netherlands* (Dordrecht: Kluwer, 2004)

16. Malachi Beit-Arié, *Hebrew Manuscripts of East and West: Towards a Comparative Codicology* (London: British Library, 1993), esp. 79–124; I. M. Ta-Shma, "The 'Open' Book in Medieval Hebrew Literature: The Problem of Authorized Editions," *Bulletin of the John Rylands University Library of Manchester* 75 (1993): 5–16.

17. As my student, Bart Wallet, currently preparing a Ph.D. thesis on Yiddish historiography in seventeenth- and eighteenth-century Holland, has informed me, this development can be observed, for instance, with the famous Yiddish history book *Sheeris Yisroel* (Amsterdam, 1743). New editions of the book were published with revised and/or new chapters, the name of the author was eventually dropped, and so forth.

18. See Sara Zfatman, *Yiddish Narrative Prose from Its Beginnings to "Shivhei Habesht" (1504–1814)* (Ph.D. diss., Hebrew University of Jerusalem, 1983), esp. 56–103 ("Authors, Addressees, Destinations").

19. See my "Translation as Genre in Pre-Modern Yiddish Literature" (in preparation).

20. It is a verse jotted in a Hebrew prayer book for Passover known as "Makhzor Worms" and now at the University and National Library in Jerusalem. See Shmeruk, *Yiddish Literature,* 9–12.

21. I.e., Yekutiel Blits, translator of one of the Yiddish Bibles (Amsterdam, 1678).

22. Chava Turniansky, *Sefer Massah u'Merivah, 1627* (in Hebrew) (Jerusalem: Magnes Press, 1985), 126–44.

23. Max Weinreich, "Internal Bilingualism in Ashkenaz Until the Enlightenment Period: Facts and Notions" (in Yiddish), *Di Goldene Keyt* 35 (1959): 80–88.

24. See also the discussion of the *Krovats* prayer book below.

25. Roland Barthes, "The Death of the Author," in Barthes, *Image, Music, Text* (New York: Hill & Wang, 1977), 142–48.

26. See also Zfatman, *Yiddish Narrative Prose,* 56–62.

27. Alistair McCleery, "The Return of the Publisher to Book History: The Case of Allen Lane," *Book History* 5 (2002), 161–85.

28. The study of titles is still a desideratum; from my own survey it seems that authors and publishers lacked imagination and occasionally reused existing titles.

29. Genette, *Paratexts,* 32–33.

30. Ibid., 33.

31. Jacob Meitlis, *Das Ma'assebuch: Seine Entstehung und Quellengeschichte* (Berlin: Mass, 1933).

32. Turniansky, *Sefer Masa u'Merivah,* 129–33.

33. On Eliah Bokher, see Baumgarten, *Introduction à la littérature yiddish ancienne,* 201–52.

34. Information about the books discussed can be found in Fuks and Fuks-Mansfeld, *Hebrew Typography* (only for seventeenth century) and Gutschow, *Inventory of Yiddish Books.*

35. See the partial list in Zinberg, *History of Jewish Literature,* 411–13; see also discussion by Zfatman, *Yiddish Narrative Prose,* 79–86.

36. Chava Turniansky, *Between the Holy and the Profane: Language, Education, and Scholarship in Eastern Europe* (Tel Aviv: Open University, 1994), 61–76.

37. Ze'ev Gries, *The Book as an Agent of Culture, 1700–1900* (Tel Aviv: Hakibutz Hameukhad, 2002), 96–99.

38. Robert Bonfil, "Reading in the Jewish Communities of Western Europe in the Middle Ages," in *A History of Reading in the West,* ed. Guglielmo Cavallo and Roger Chartier (Amherst: University of Massachusetts Press, 1999), 149–78.

39. In another book, *Sefer Khen Tov* (Amsterdam, 1756), the editor, Gedalia Teykus, states that he arranged the book to enable the father of the house to assemble his wife and children around the table every evening and read a chapter aloud.

40. In *Brant Shpigl* (Krakow, 1596), chap. 8, the wife is advised to place a book on the table so that her husband will study for at least one hour before he sets out to work; in *Lev Tov,* chap. 5, the wife is told to encourage her husband to learn Torah (as much as possible) when he returns from his day's labor, and in chap. 8 the wife is encouraged to teach her children to read Torah; the preface of the Yiddish section of *Derekh Moshe* (Amsterdam, 1699) urges the wife to read the book and relate its contents to her husband.

41. Postfaces were also added in other books and clarified matters that were neglected in the title page or preface. Avigdor Sofer of Eisenstadt added a postface to the aforementioned prayer book (1650), in which he explained why he did not add a commentary to one of the prayers, this being a particularly difficult text that would require an extra one hundred pages. On other postfaces, see below.

42. Leo Fuks and Rena Fuks-Mansfeld, "Yiddish Language and Literature in the Dutch Republic," *Studia Rosenthaliana* 20 (1986): 34–57; Jacob Shatzky, "The Prefaces of Joseph Maarssen's Compositions," *Yivo Bleter* 13 (1938): 377–89.

43. Marion Aptroot, "'I Know This Book of Mine Will Cause Offence . . .': A Yiddish Adaptation of Boccachio's Decameron" (Amsterdam, 1710), *Zutot: Perspectives on Jewish Culture* 3 (2003).

44. To read gentile books was "dangerous," since "simple Jews" might be led astray. Many efforts were made to produce good Jewish stories in Yiddish in order to divert the masses from this supposedly harmful literature. See also below.

45. *Galkhes* is the Yiddish word for Latin and, *mutatis mutandis,* of any foreign language. It stems from the verb "to shave" and refers to the shaved heads of priests, thus to Latin, the language of the Church.

46. In conversation Professor Marion Aptroot suggested another translation of Maarssen's Yiddish phrase "fremd loshn." Instead of "foreign language," one might read "strange language," so that Maarssen may have rejected the use of Hebraisms because he considered the sort of Yiddish he employed unusual and unconventional.

47. *Krovatz* (in Hebrew characters) is an abbreviation of "the voice of happiness and salvation in the tents of the righteous."

48. This *Krovatz* also contains a postface, a promotional text by the publisher who happened to be a bookseller as well and called himself Shlomo Proops the bookseller. He reminded buyers that he sold other books as well: prayer books, Pentateuchs, prayer books for High Holidays, Selikhot, Mishna, Talmud, Midrash, Commentators, Responsa, Cabbala, "and these kinds of books and any other book one wishes without exception if it is known." The order of these genres of books is not incidental: it starts with the most general and ends with the most specialized. The Proops family ran the largest Jewish book business in eighteenth-century Amsterdam. A study of this family's activity is urgently needed.

49. Genette, *Paratexts,* 161–62 (quoting Jacques Derrida).

50. Ibid., 161–293.

51. Ibid., 263–75.

52. Ibid., 161–236.

53. On Hebrew ethical books, see Yosef Dan, *Hebrew Ethical and Homiletical Literature* (Jerusalem: Keter, 1975); on Yiddish ethical books, Erik, *History of Yiddish Literature,* 207–319; see also Gries, *Book as an Agent of Culture,* 57–64. See also my "From Philosophy to Popular Ethics: Two Seventeenth-Century Yiddish Translations of S. Ibn Gabirol's *Keter Malkhut,*" in *Sepharad in Ashkenaz: Medieval Hebrew Thought in Early Modern Jewish Writings,* ed. Resianne Fontaine et al. (Amsterdam: Royal Academy of Sciences, 2004).

54. On *Lev Tov,* see Zinberg, *History of Jewish Literature,* 182–87; Erik, *History of Yiddish Literature,* 294–301.

55. But compare this with Maarssen's argument that people should not just read religious literature.

56. On "please-insert," see Genette, *Paratexts,* 104–16; on approbations, see the article by Moritz Steinscheider, "Jüdische Typographie und Jüdische Buchhandel," in *Allgemiene Encylopädie der Wissenschaften und Kunst,* ed. I. S. Ersch and I. G. Gruber (Berlin, 1850), part 28, 30ff.; see also Hayyim Leshem, "Approbations" (in Hebrew), *Mahanayim* 106 (1965): 44–51.

57. Den Boer, *Literatura sefardi,* 79–107.

58. Chava Turniansky, "On Yiddish Didactical Literature in Amsterdam (1699–1749)," *Studies on the History of Dutch Jewry* 4 (1984): 163–77; on *Melamed Siakh,* see 168–69.

59. Chone Shmeruk, "'Historical Songs' in Yiddish Printed in Amsterdam in the Seventeenth and the Eighteenth Centuries," *Studies on the History of Dutch Jewry* 4 (1984): 143–61; on this poem, see 149–50.

60. Satirical pieces published during the feast of Purim that turn the community order upside down for the day. In fact, similar publications satirize difficult winters in 1799 and 1802; two others cannot be dated. See Leo Fuks, "Van poerimspelen tot poerimkranten," *Mededelingen over de geschiedenis van joden in Nederland* 1 (1948): 162–76.

61. On the family Proops, see also above.

62. Shmeruk, *Yiddish Literature,* 69–71.

63. On the Frankfurt family, see Avriel Bar-Levav, *The Concept of Death in Sefer Ha-Hayyim (The Book of Life) by Rabbi Shimon Frankfurt* (Ph.D. diss., Hebrew University of Jerusalem, 1997); on the original Hebrew book, see I. M. Ta-Shma, "The Riddle of the 'Menorat Hama'or' and Its Solution," *Tarbiz* 64 (1995): 395–400.

64. This is an erroneous statement; Abohab never translated his composition into Spanish or any other language. The assertion is repeated in Druker's preface.

65. See also his remarks on corrections and proofreading below.

66. Most local chief rabbis were of Eastern European origin and were invited to Amsterdam at the instigation of the local community. They had considerable trouble adapting to the local community structure. See Meyer Sluys, "Ashkenazi Jews in Amsterdam from 1635 to 1795" (in Hebrew), *Studies on the History of Dutch Jewry* 1 (1975): 69–121; on connections with Eastern European Jewish authorities, see Leo Fuks, "The Tensions in the Relationship Between the Council of Four Lands and the Ashkenazi Community in Amsterdam During the Rabbinate of David Lida 1680–1684)" (in Dutch), *Studia Rosenthalaina* 6 (1972): 166–79, Hebrew version in *Michael* 6 (1980): 170–76.

67. On the distribution of the commentary *Nefesh Yehuda* and the abridged edition of the *Candelabra of Light,* which is titled *Sheva Petilot,* see Joshua Vinograd, *Treasures of the Hebrew Book* (Jerusalem: Hamakhon Lebibliografia, 1993), 1:31.

68. Yiddish as a vehicle of modernity is suggested by Ze'ev Gries, "The Book as Cultural Agent in the Eighteenth and Nineteenth Centuries: Printing Books, Reading books, and Book Criticism," *Jewish Studies* 39 (1999): 5–33; Rena Fuks-Mansfeld, "Yiddish as a Means of Cultural Advancement: Moshe Frankfurt and His Yiddish Translation of Isaac Aboab's Menorat Ha-ma'or," in *Speaking Jewish-Jewish Speak: Multilingualism in Western Ashkenazi Culture,* ed. Shlomo Berger et al. (Leuven: Peeters, 2003).

69. It is worthwhile to view such considerations in light of Pierre Bourdieu, *The Field of Cultural Production,* ed. Randal Johnson (New York: Columbia University Press, 1993), esp. 30–73.

70. The same thing happened two years later, in 1708, when he edited another anthology of tales and made decisions on both form and content. See Zfatman, *Yiddish Narrative Prose,* 68.

71. Vinograd, *Treasures of the Hebrew Book,* 1:130.

72. Londen also published this tale (with two others) as a separate book in 1715. See Zfatman, *Yiddish Narrative Prose,* 107–8.

73. According to the title/preface of the story, it was translated from Hebrew, which was written by Yospa Han from Frankfurt am Main.

74. Vinograd, *Treasures of the Hebrew Book,* 1:130.

75. But without the short three-line approbation by Rabbi Aryeh Leib above the compositor's preface, granting Rofe a monopoly on producing the book for six years.

76. Indeed, in his preface Londen thanks the Amsterdam publisher for his efforts in producing the book, since he himself could not travel to Amsterdam to oversee the production process.

77. On Yiddish and the Bible, see Shmeruk, *Yiddish Literature,* 157–210.

78. For a reconstruction of the events involving the production of both Bibles, see Erika Timm, "Blitz and Witzenhausen," in *Studies in Jewish Culture in Honour of Chone Shmeruk,* ed. Israel Bartal et al. (Jerusalem: Merkaz Shazar, 1993) 39*–66*.

79. See also my "Bibles and Publishers: Yiddish Paratexts in Amsterdam," in Dauven, *Paratext,* 127–38.

"... To Collect and Abridge ... Without Changing Anything Essential"

Rewriting Incan History at the Parisian Jardin du Roi

Neil Safier

> My mother's uncle . . . gave me a long account of the origin of [the Inca]
> Kings . . . which I have attempted to translate faithfully from my native
> language, that of the Inca, to a foreign tongue, Castilian, although I have
> certainly not written it with the magnificence [*majestad*] with which the Inca
> spoke nor with all the meaning that the words of that language contain. . . .
> Instead, I have shortened [his account] by taking out some of the things that
> would have made it tedious [*odioso*]. In the end, it will be enough to have
> conveyed the true meaning of [these words], which is what is most important
> for our story.
>
> —Inca Garcilaso de la Vega,
> *Primera parte de los Comentarios reales*

In the early years of the seventeenth century, a Cuzco native named Inca
Garcilaso de la Vega (1539–1616) set out to compose the history of the
origins, customs, laws, and religion of the Inca empire. Boastfully asserting
that he was the only person capable of reproducing "clearly and distinc-
tively. . . . what existed in that [Incan] republic prior to the Spaniards,"
he probably never imagined the extent to which what he called the "true
meaning" (*verdadero sentido*) of his account was to change language,
form, and content in the two centuries that followed its initial publication.[1]

I would like to express my gratitude to Jorge Cañizares-Esguerra for bringing this eighteenth-
century edition of Garcilaso to my attention, and to David A. Bell, Richard Kagan, Anthony
Pagden, and the two anonymous referees for their helpful comments and criticisms on earlier
drafts of this essay.

Garcilaso, commonly referred to as "the Inca" to distinguish him from the homonymous poet of the Spanish Golden Age, became one of the most renowned *mestizo* historians of post-conquest Peru, and his *Comentarios reales de los Incas* (1609) was lauded, when it was not being harshly criticized by official propagandists, as an insider's view of the Andean civilization that had been decimated by Spanish invaders in the sixteenth century. The son of a Spanish conquistador and an Incan "princess of the Sun," Garcilaso had sought to record accurately and unequivocally the traditions of his mother's ancestors by detailing the historical and cultural features of her royal Incan lineage.[2] Aided in his comprehension of Incan tradition by the oral histories to which he had been privy as a child, and profiting from his bilingual upbringing in both "Peruvian" (we would say Quechua) and Castilian, Garcilaso hoped to compensate for earlier Spanish chroniclers who, despite having covered a wide range of topics, wrote about them "in such a terse fashion that I had difficulty understanding even those [customs] that were quite familiar to me."[3] He proclaimed his intention not to attack or criticize historians such as José de Acosta, Francisco López de Gómara, and Pedro Cieza de León, but rather to "provide commentary [to them] and serve as an interpreter for many of the Indian terms which, as foreigners to that tongue, they interpreted outside their appropriate meaning [*propriedad*]."[4] Garcilaso's bilingual abilities allowed him to write the history of his people with a confidence and authority that, as he saw it, were uniquely his own.[5]

Nearly one and a half centuries after Garcilaso staked his claim to having written the authoritative history of the Inca empire, and several editions of the *Comentarios* later, a revised translation of Garcilaso's text was produced in Paris under dramatically different editorial, typographical, and natural historical circumstances. It was at the Jardin du Roi, most probably during the seven-year intendancy of Charles-François de Cisternai du Fay (1732–39), that the project to publish a revised edition of Garcilaso's classic account was conceived and carried out. It was not until 1744, however, that two in-octavo volumes were published whose title pages heralded a text "newly translated from the Spanish" with "an improved organization": the *Histoire des Incas, Rois du Pérou* (Figure 1).[6] The text included two detailed maps of the Andean region, produced in 1739 by Philippe Buache especially for this edition, that were based upon the most recent astronomical observations undertaken by the French and Spanish Academicians who were sent to Quito by the Parisian Académie des Sciences.[7] But the scope of the activities of the Franco-Hispanic expedition's members extended to observing natural phenomena and collecting natural historical specimens as well. The seeds and saplings that they packed into crates and shipped across the Atlantic to Paris expanded considerably the collection of botanical exotica at the Jardin du Roi. These materials, in turn, influenced in no small way the decision to produce a thoroughly revised edition of Garcilaso's *Comentarios reales* in the 1730s and '40s. The editorial movement that would culminate a decade later in the publication of Diderot and d'Alembert's *Encyclopédie* no doubt contributed as well to this zeal for placing extra-European species into a new textual order. This "encyclopedic impulse" was likewise encouraged by the longstanding interest of the French crown (and its metropolitan and colonial institutions) in pursuing the commercial and medicinal benefits of herbs, spices, and medicinal "simples," objects that, since the mid-sixteenth century, had motivated explorers, missionaries, and merchants alike in their quest to pursue the potential remunerative benefits of overseas botanical exchange.[8]

Among those at the Jardin du Roi who participated in this broad editorial project to translate and reconfigure Incan history was Thomas-François Dalibard, a young friend and apprentice to Buffon who demonstrated a keen familiarity with New World travel narratives and who had closely examined natural historical specimens from the Americas in the hope of finding new ways of putting old knowledge to good use.[9] In part owing to their increased access to natural objects brought in from around the world, Dalibard and his colleagues at the Jardin du Roi came to see their role not merely as translators of older accounts—changing terms from one language to another—but rather as active compilers licensed to transform the editorial configuration of previous texts, especially those that dealt with topics about which they now claimed to know far more than the original authors. The epistemological framework within which the editors of the 1744 edition were to interpret, assess, and edit Garcilaso's text had been transformed not only by the arrival in Europe of new information and new material specimens from South America, but also by technical and typographical changes in print culture that allowed for the hierarchical placement of new information through an elaborate system of cross references and complex bibliographical techniques. In addition to the reconfiguration of older material, massive abridgments were effected as well: in some places, entire chapters of Garcilaso's original 1609 text were compressed into two or three lines, and often entire paragraphs were transmogrified into one-line footnotes. Indeed, this last feature of the 1744 edition—the addition of footnotes—was entirely foreign to Garcilaso's original text and to translations prior to this new edition.[10] While few details were added to the historical portion of the text (also condensed, reordered, and compacted into the first volume), some new observations—such as pointing out the literary source of *Robinson Crusoe*, first published in 1688 and translated into French in 1720–21—clearly extended the temporal reach of Garcilaso's text into the eighteenth century. The use of typographical

HISTOIRE
DES INCAS,
ROIS DU PEROU.

Nouvellement traduite de l'Espagnol de
GARCILLASSO-DE LA VEGA.

Et mise dans un meilleur ordre ; avec des Notes
& des Additions sur l'Histoire Naturelle
de ce Pays.

TOME PREMIER.

A PARIS,

Chez PRAULT fils, Quai de Conti, vis-à-vis
la descente du Pont-Neuf, à la Charité.

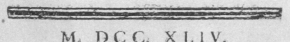

M. DCC. XLIV.

AVEC APPROBATION ET PRIVILEGE DU ROY.

Figure 1. Title Page of the *Histoire des Incas, Rois du Pérou*
(1744). Courtesy of the Bancroft Library, University of California,
Berkeley.

features such as footnotes and brackets facilitated other kinds of additions in the second volume, allowing the editors of the *Histoire des Incas* to give a privileged place within the corpus of the work to details from more up-to-date sources, reference materials, and botanical treasures of the Jardin du Roi recently arrived from overseas.

An analysis of the structural changes wrought in this new edition of Garcilaso's classic text thus provides a conduit through which to assess the material and editorial strategies used by naturalists in France to reconstruct the social, political, and natural history of the precolonial Andes at the midpoint of the eighteenth century. By examining this particular French translation of 1744, a text that used material evidence, academic memoirs, and widely available travelers' accounts to rewrite various portions of Incan history following the Franco-Hispanic expedition's arrival in Peru, this article seeks to reassess a critical moment in the history of the reception and interpretation of the Incas in Europe.[11] This particular conjuncture also happens to be one of the most poorly studied periods in the history of the Parisian Jardin du Roi, largely neglected by recent studies and by some of the more classic accounts of French scientific culture in the early modern period.[12] Remarkably, the conservation and showcasing of Peruvian flora and fauna in the King's Cabinet played a critical role in the textual transformation of the Inca. The editors of the *Histoire des Incas* were able to create a hybrid space within the interstices of a classic text of New World history by bringing specimens of Peruvian natural history into contact with *mestizo* accounts of indigenous culture through the artifice of European editorial and typographical conventions. The Jardin du Roi provided a Parisian theater for collecting and displaying these exotic specimens, a practice that stretched back to the days of Kircher, Aldrovandi, Clusius, and other early Renaissance natural historians.[13] But the housing of a "universal meeting-place for all the productions of nature" within the domain of the royal gardens was also a gesture aimed at centralizing power, a move to extend French knowledge throughout the globe and unite the disparate pieces at the metropolitan center. The production of a new text of Peruvian history provided an ideal opportunity to showcase the superior abilities of French science in capturing and conveying the hidden treasures of botanical knowledge as revealed by indigenous populations in America. It was also an opportunity to vaunt their own capacities vis-à-vis the Spanish, whom they saw as incapable of culling the fruits of indigenous knowledge because of misguided naturalist practices tainted by violence and avarice. The production of a history of the Incas that contained natural historical information from the Jardin du Roi could be seen as a French claim not to possess territory but rather to possess useful knowledge gleaned from an intellectual—and typographical—dominion over the natural world.

I. Editorial (Dis)Order and the
"Ordre Merveilleux" of Inca Agriculture

[N]either his knowledge, nor his experience could provide adequate
preparation for [Garcilaso] to create a methodical Book at a time when even
the best Authors did not write with the precision that one finds today even
in the most mediocre Works.

—From the "Préface du Traducteur," *Histoire des Incas,* 1744, discussing the
original edition of Garcilaso's *Comentarios reales* (1609)

The organizational strategies used by those who cut, arranged, and collated
materials to bring Garcilaso's text "up to date" for an eighteenth-century
audience were revealed to readers in a sixteen-page "Préface du Traducteur." In this preface, the editor explained the historiographical motivations
and methods that were followed throughout the *Histoire des Incas.*[14] Beginning with a brief biographical sketch of "Garcillasso de la Ve'ga, Author
of this History," the "Préface" highlighted particular features of Incan
social, cultural, and economic life and included sections on the enlightened
principles of Inca rule, agricultural practices, and Inca scientific achievements, especially in astronomy. The editor described Garcilaso's mixed
birth, the education he received in a Peruvian school designed especially for
Incan youths, and his encounter with the Spanish chronicles written previously about the conquest of the Incas, the same texts the young *mestizo* had
found woefully inadequate.

But the editor of the 1744 edition also leveled a series of criticisms at
Garcilaso's *Comentarios,* especially concerning the "disorder" and "confusion" of the original text. According to the editor, Garcilaso had failed
to produce a "methodical text," one that evinced a particular historical
logic and a prefabricated and recognizable structure. The editor described
instead the "heaping up" of facts, a disorderly accumulation of details that
drowned the reader in a sea of disorganized, if fascinating, sketches of
Incan life: Garcilaso "heaped the facts together in such a way as to make
it impossible to follow their progression."[15] The "Préface" relied on an
even deeper notion of the perfectibility of historical texts, a positivistic
discourse arguing that the organizational methods employed by eighteenth-
century authors, even those who produced what he called "the most mediocre Works," allowed for greater readability and, ultimately, greater utility
for the public to which the text was being disseminated. The twin pillars
of ever-improving readability and utility were the epistemological underpinnings of this new editorial impulse and encyclopedic orientation, which
was reflected in the explosive increase in the number of natural historical
compendia, geographical dictionaries, and compilations of travel literature

that were becoming available in Europe at mid-century. The celebrated publication of Diderot and d'Alembert's *Encyclopédie* was, in itself, merely a conspicuous example of an emerging tendency to parse knowledge into its component parts and reconstruct the pieces in an abridged form suitable for easy digestion by a broad, learned public.

The "Préface du Traducteur," it should be said at the outset, represented a wholly original contribution of the editor to the *Histoire des Incas*. As such, the preface should be seen not merely as a summary of Garcilaso's original text but also as an explication of the specific reasons why this re-edition was produced for its intended public at precisely this moment. In his prefatory text, the editor discussed the structural transformations undertaken to "remedy" the disorder of the original history and the useful purposes to which, he hoped, the translation would eventually be put. Many of the topics the editor chose to highlight reflected contemporary concerns as much as they did central aspects of Inca life. The subjects discussed, the organizational changes, the editorial conventions, and the stylistic and typographical strategies used to facilitate the expression of particular ideas constitute what the editor called the "principal merit" of this new translation: its "precision" and "exactitude." For the editor, the utility of his "remedied" text lay in its didactic lessons, revealed by certain "great examples" of Incan history: "We thought it could be extremely useful to society because of the great examples which [Garcilaso] presents, of goodness, gentleness, justice, and moderation on the part of the Sovereign, of gentleness, submission, attachment, and respect on the part of the Subjects. The utility of these subjects made us undertake this new Translation."[16] The editor infused his preface with these examples of great moral and political beneficence on the part of the Inca kings, emphasizing aspects of Incan culture that may have resonated with a French audience. For instance, he praised the kings for their generosity, moderation, and benevolence toward their subjects. The preface focused on the figure of Manco Capac, the first Inca and the royal representative who was thought to have descended directly from the sun. The editor portrayed Manco Capac as the most noble monarch possible, explaining that "he steered all the rules he considered toward the general good of the society."[17] Describing the close bonds that linked the people to their sovereign, he went on to explain that the people came to look upon Manco Capac "not only as the direct descendent of the Sun but as the shared Father of all peoples," employing a paternal metaphor about royalty familiar in an Old Regime society accustomed to positive comparisons between politics and family life.[18]

In the course of the brief preface, the editor also drew attention to aspects of Incan religious practices, showing the strong similarities between Inca religion and Christianity.[19] He enumerated some of the Incas' scientific

achievements and offered conjectures about the impact on Incan science of
the lack of an alphabetical script. But the preface dwelt most heavily on the
agricultural innovations of the Incas and their methods for ensuring that
all members of society received adequate provisions through "state" intervention. The editor emphasized how Manco Capac taught his people "the
art of cultivating the Earth, and the means to take from the bosom of this
common mother all the assistance they might ever need to preserve their
lives and their health."[20] While this aspect of Incan life also featured prominently in Garcilaso's original account, the editor gave special attention to
the issue by focusing, in the brief space allotted to him, on the "wise" rules
imposed by the Inca for the betterment of his society: "[E]ach individual
had sufficient provisions each year for himself and his family. If, despite
these precautions, it so happened that some [members of the society] were
wanting, they provided them with free supplies from the public storehouses
with considerable order, since they knew precisely how many needy there
were and the degree of their needs."[21]

This keen attention to Incan agricultural policies may have stemmed
from social conditions just outside the editor's window on the streets of
Paris. Between 1737 and 1741 it would have been difficult to ignore the
sense of social crisis throughout France, especially among the urban poor,
whose pangs of hunger, the result of bread shortages, were increasingly
the subject of critics and observers. On the street as well as in the correspondence of the bourgeois elite, the plight of the destitute was coming to
be recognized as a universal social concern, and the agricultural situation
of 1738–41 was bringing this issue to the fore. In January 1739 a *Mémoire*
on agricultural subsidies was published under the title "on the political and
financial situation in France on the 1st of January, 1739, with [a report on]
the way to bring a prompt solution," indicating that the problem of grain
distribution was urgent enough to attract the attention of the provincial
consuls and the intendants. In May of that year there were reports that
women carrying bread along provincial roads had been murdered for their
victuals, leading the Marquis d'Argenson to comment that a piece of bread
"is more coveted today than a bag of gold was in times past." D'Argenson
went on to recount a story about the Duc d'Orléans having offered the king
a sample slice of bread brought in from the provinces, presumably in poor
condition, and exclaiming, "Sire, look at the kind of bread with which your
subjects feed themselves!"[22]

To understand the editor's effusive praise of the Incas' agricultural, political, and scientific pursuits, the social and political environment of contemporary France needs to be considered. Rather than compare Louis XV's
reign positively with the leadership of the Incan kings, the editor chose to
muffle what would have been a self-evident strategy of patronage by doing

precisely the opposite. In a setting like the Jardin du Roi, unctuous nods to royal support were frequent and natural components of prefaces and forewords. And yet the editor emphasized the singularity of the Incas seemingly at the expense of his own monarch. This kind of foil had several well-known contemporary antecedents. Voltaire set his political satire *Alzire* in the mountains of Peru, far from the palaces of Paris and Versailles, and Montesquieu chose for his *Lettres persanes* another distant venue. The "Préface du Traducteur" concluded with a description of a tyrant, the "last King" of the Incas, who had subverted one of the Incas' fundamental laws by naming one of his youngest sons to the throne. His fate was sealed in a bloody coda by the arrival of the Spanish, "who seem to have been sent to Peru for nothing other than to make this unfortunate [king] suffer the just punishment for his misdeeds."[23] This allegory certainly arrived in print too early to prefigure Louis XVI's violent end on the guillotine, but it may have echoed the frustration felt by many at the monarchy's indifference to the suffering of its people. In the market and on the street, the popular classes had already begun to demand changes and threaten collective action if the king, largely understood to be responsible for the dearth of bread and the price fixing that went along with it, did not do something to ease the crisis. "Unless the government changes its system of dealing with grain," the duc d'Orléans is said to have commented to Louis XV that same year, the monarch would end up alienating "the hearts of all his subjects."[24] In yet another example of the rising tide of urban unrest, the king was greeted in the street with jeers, insults, and threats. Instead of "Long live the King!" the crowd that gathered in the Faubourg Saint-Victor cried, "Misery! Give us bread! Give us bread!"[25]

The frequency of these bread shortages may have given an added degree of urgency to eighteenth-century French naturalists' interest in and experiments with new non-European botanical specimens.[26] Of course, European interest in the salutary medicinal properties of exotic herbs and spices stretched back to the earliest Iberian writings on Asia and the Americas, including the treatises of Garcia da Orta and Francisco Hernández, among others. Extra-European excursions under French auspices, including the transatlantic expeditions of Jean de Léry and André Thévet to Brazil, also set out in the sixteenth century with an eye toward finding new plants and minerals that would benefit the populace in the European metropole. But it was not until the 1620s that religious missionaries were sent under the auspices of the state to explore colonial outposts for potential scientific advantage. The Jesuit Raymond Breton (1609–79) and the Dominican Jacques Du Tertre (1610–87) were sent by Richelieu to Guadeloupe in the 1630s and '40s, and another Dominican, J. B. Labatt (1666–1738), had traveled to Martinique and other islands of the French Antilles at the turn of the century.[27] But it was Guy-Crescent Fagon (1638–1718), superintendent of the Jardin du Roi from 1699 to 1718, who brought botanical exploration together with the burgeoning interest in medical research and made the Jardin du Roi a new center for overseas experimentation.[28] Fagon dispatched two important emissaries to the Antilles in order to carry out long-term research programs: Charles Plumier (1646–1704) and Louis Feuillée (1660–1732). Both returned with detailed descriptions and drawings of the plants of the Americas. And while the work of these religious missionaries was largely aimed at resolving medical problems, they nevertheless provided important details about species that could be transplanted into European soil for both medical and agricultural advantage. Their work did, of course, also require a certain degree of dissemination and experimentation so that the "fruits" of their labors could eventually reach a wider audience and be applied broadly throughout the fields and pharmacies of France. Nevertheless, the correlation between exotic specimens, herbal pharmaceuticals, and domestic subsistence still remained in their day largely unexplored.[29]

Since its inception as the Royal Physic garden in 1626, however, the institution that would later be known as the Jardin du Roi and, following the Revolution, as the Muséum National d'Histoire Naturelle, had taken a deep interest in the medicinal and agricultural properties of exotic plant species. Guy de la Brosse himself commented that the role of the Jardin Royal would be to recognize "all plants by their diverse names and shapes" and to teach "their qualities, faculties, and properties, and their simple and compound usages."[30] But if this were the case, why would a history of the Incas serve as the conduit through which ideas about new forms of botanical and agricultural organization were expressed and considered? The answer lies in the realm of material culture: in 1737, a shipment of natural historical specimens was sent by Louis Godin, leader of the Franco-Hispanic expedition to Quito, to his colleagues back in Paris. This collection of objects of natural historical interest was the first material manifestation of an expedition that had already begun to captivate the curiosity of the Parisian elite since 1735. Once arrived at the Jardin du Roi, these Peruvian specimens caught the attention of Thomas-François Dalibard, who meticulously compared the plants, animals, insects, and minerals with the travel narratives that had been gathering dust on the shelves of the King's Cabinet for decades. It was a perfect opportunity to demonstrate the potential for social improvement that a botanical garden was capable of containing within its walls. It was from comparing these texts with the live specimens that he sought to contribute to a program for social renovation in the mid-eighteenth century. The *Histoire des Incas,* as it happened, became the showcase—a botanical theater—for Dalibard's demonstration.

II. Du Fay's Hothouses and the Footnoted Florilegium of the King's Garden

The Minim priest Louis Feuillée, whom we encountered briefly in the last section, was a prescient man. In 1714, twenty-five years before d'Argenson exclaimed that bread had come to be more valuable than gold in France, Feuillée was already conscious of the figurative (and perhaps literal) riches that might be garnered were Frenchmen to collect, transport, and transplant in France some portion of the botanical bounty growing in abundance on American shores. During his five-year voyage to Chile, Peru, and the Caribbean (1707–12), Feuillée collected, observed, drew, and described a multitude of native plants, cataloguing their uses and later publishing these detailed descriptions as addenda to his *Journal des observations physiques, mathématiques et botaniques*.[31] In the introductory pages to his *Journal*, Feuillée outlined the strategies he used to acquire his information and included a list of instruments and a précis of the overriding scientific concerns that organized his activities. He emphasized that the Comte de Pontchartrain had recommended he "put everything to good use during [his] journey, & . . . send him all the observations and experiments that [he] might accomplish at every possible occasion."[32] Feuillée also drew sketches of the plants and trees whose fruits were unknown in Europe, and attempted to learn about the properties of these specimens through close attention to indigenous knowledge and practices. He took special note of the Incas, whose ninth king, Inca Pachacutec, had ordered that he "would give the name of Doctor to none of his subjects, unless he were fully knowledgeable in all the qualities of Plants, both harmful and salutary." Continuing in his description of the *Tithymalus perennis, Portulacœ folio, vulgò Pichua,* Feuillée lauded the extensive applied knowledge of an entire people: "As this Law was rigorously observed during the reigns of the Incas, all the people of this vast Empire applied themselves diligently to this admirable [field of] knowledge, which being passed from father to son after the destruction of the Incan Empire . . . has been preserved up until today."[33] In a supplement to his *Journal* written in 1725, Feuillée asked rhetorically if it wouldn't be possible to "find similarly effective remedies for other diseases, which for the good that they would provide to the Public, could be regarded as far more valuable treasures than those that are extracted from the mines of Peru."[34] While the precise context of Feuillée's remarks was the many diseases (and botanical cures) he had come across while traveling through the West Indies, his frequent references to the agricultural properties of non-European specimens that could be transplanted into French soil were not lost on subsequent natural historians, who carefully examined his work back in Europe. Neither was his praise for the Incas' botanical knowledge.

One individual who examined Feuillée's printed accounts closely was Dalibard, who we know spent at least a portion of his career as a naturalist at the Jardin du Roi. In the early 1750s Buffon chose Dalibard to translate Benjamin Franklin's treatise on electricity, and it is for this work—and the electrical experiments Dalibard performed both in Marly-la-Ville and before Louis XV with Buffon and Delor—that he was, and still is today, most widely recognized.[35] Earlier in his career, Dalibard had published the *Floræ Parisiensis Prodromus,* a text that confirmed his detailed knowledge of Parisian plant species and that was reputed to be one of the first texts to employ Linnaean terminology in France.[36] Unfortunately, we do not know in what capacity Dalibard was present at the Jardin during the period in question, whether he was merely a knowledgeable visitor or perhaps an official charge of the Jardin itself. What is clear, however, is that the "Préface du Traducteur" refers to Dalibard specifically as having collected previous accounts by travelers to South America and having compared them with more recent "discoveries" made in the realm of natural history. For this reason, the form and content of the revised work probably owe more to Dalibard than to any other individual who participated in the project. Dalibard's collation of descriptions of plant species contained at the Jardin du Roi with accounts from travel narratives to South America, including Feuillée's *Journal,* swelled the second volume of the *Histoire des Incas* and transformed the text into a treasure trove of useful botanical data.

The preparation and publication history of the new translation of the *Histoire des Incas,* to the extent that it can be reconstructed, crossed over a period in the history of the Jardin du Roi that saw the opportunities multiply for the cultivation of exotic plant species within the King's "Cabinet d'Histoire Naturelle," inaugurated as such in 1729. Just prior to Du Fay's intendancy, Pierre Chirac had paved the way for the acclimatization of non-European species by incorporating the Jardin des apothicaires de Nantes under the Jardin's jurisdiction in 1719, privileging thereby "the care and cultivation of plants from foreign countries" through an ambitious program of overseas seed exchange.[37] In 1714 a hothouse had been built especially for a coffee plant imported from Amsterdam, and at some point after Du Fay took over the intendancy in 1732, he ordered the construction of at least two other hothouses.[38] These great bulbous structures transformed the Jardin, in the words of Yves Laissus, into a place "consecrated to the plants of the pharmacopoeia, into an experimental botanical garden, open to all species."[39] They also linked the royal metropolitan institution with the larger French colonial enterprise, a connection that was emphasized in the 1739 "Éloge de M. du Fay," written by Fontenelle, in which the sécretaire perpetuel de l'Académie explained that "Doctors or Surgeons . . . received their instruction at the Garden . . . [and] from there spread themselves throughout the Colonies."[40] With the number of foreign specimens growing at an exponential rate thanks to various overseas expeditions, the hothouses served as artificial but necessary repositories for the increasing botanical store: the hothouses "are constructed in such as a way as to be able to represent different Climates, since the idea is to make these diverse plants forget their natural Climates. Changes in temperature are accomplished in small degrees, from the strongest to the most temperate, and all of the advances that modern Physics has been able to teach us in this regard have been put into practice."[41] Du Fay thus masterminded the production of physical spaces into which these newly arrived non-European botanical specimens would arrive, and saw to their acclimatization in the diverse climactic zones of the Jardin's hothouses. Godin's natural historical specimens, which included insects as well as plant species, may have been some of the first shipments to profit directly from the thick panes of Du Fay's hothouses, and the collection may have been given special attention precisely on this account.

It is clear from the text that the activities of the anonymous editor of the *Histoire des Incas* were intertwined with those of the Jardin. In volume 2, the editor observed that one of the banana trees kept in the Jardin du Roi "flowered and brought forth fruit in 1741," and he was certainly familiar with the materials Godin had sent to the Cabinet in 1737. The *Histoire* was probably begun at some point between 1737 and 1739, augmented over the course of subsequent years, and finally printed and distributed in 1744. This seven-year period not only coincided with the series of social crises discussed earlier; it also corresponded to a moment of great transition in the history of the Jardin du Roi, Buffon having been named intendant of the Cabinet d'Histoire Naturelle late in 1739. Between the period of Buffon's ascension to the post of intendant général and the publication of the first volume of his *Histoire naturelle* in 1749, however, few details about the day-to-day functioning of the King's Cabinet are known. Even less is known about the pre-Buffon period. For these reasons, information gleaned from the *Histoire*'s "Préface du Second Volume" about a shipment of more than 120 "rarities" sent to the "Cabinet d'Histoire Naturelle du Jardin Royal" from the Academicians in Peru deserves especially close attention.

As noted earlier, the hothouses or "serres chaudes" had been constructed at the Jardin du Roi just prior to the arrival of Godin's shipment of Peruvian specimens, making the items from his shipment one of the first collections to be acclimatized within the new setting conceived by Du Fay. In many ways, chapter 28 of the *Histoire des Incas,* the first complete chapter on Peruvian botany, resembles a virtual tour through these newly built hothouses, since Dalibard meticulously recorded the presence at the Jardin of the species sent by Godin, as well as other forms of plant life from the Americas that had preceded his Peruvian rarities. Not surprisingly, the focus of this chapter, "Des Grains," is on those trees and plants that appeared in Garcilaso's text, and Dalibard culled information about these specimens from several chapters of the original edition. But he also augmented Garcilaso's sometimes naïve descriptions with observations made during previous naturalist missions for which easily accessible descriptions existed in the travel narratives and natural historical treatises of Feuillée, Frézier, Marggraf, and Clusius. And, most of all, he described in detail the treasures contained within the Parisian hothouses.

If we were to accompany Dalibard on a tour of the hothouses by peering into the pages of the *Histoire des Incas*'s chapter 28 ("Des Grains") as if they were display cases in the hothouses themselves, we would find a rich collection of plants, shrubs, and fruit trees. From corn and quinoa to the potato and the *palmier,* Dalibard describes these items in detail and always emphasizes whether or not a given species could be found on the grounds of the Jardin or within the collection of the King's Cabinet. The typographical strategies used to construct the editorial edifice of this virtual hothouse in print will be discussed in detail in section III, below. For our immediate purpose—which is to illuminate the hothouse from within—we can divide chapter 28 (and our guided tour) into two discrete sections. The first section is organized around the species enumerated by Garcilaso, only some of which were to be found within the Jardin du Roi. Dalibard begins by listing corn, quinoa, the *papa* (*solanum tuberosum esculentum,* a root-like tubercule closely related to the potato), the potato, and the *inchi,* a sinuous plant that contains bean-like grains "filled with a white interior, which taste like hazelnuts, and are cooked and eaten as dessert" (*Histoire des Incas,* 2:201, note e). Each of these five species, described both in Garcilaso's text and in Dalibard's footnotes, served either as a substitute for bread ("The papa . . . replaces bread [in their diet]") or could be used in some way as a comestible grain or root (2:198). In other words, the entrance to the virtual hothouse is dedicated to plants of an edible variety.

Corn is the first object of study in this first section, described as the "principal food of the Indians." After the initial description of the Spanish and Peruvian names for corn, the editor comments that corn replaced bread in the Peruvian diet. At this point, the first bracketed footnote mark, "[a]," appears. The main text discusses the success of transplanting corn in Spain and the manner in which Amerindian women prepared the grain to be cooked. The vast portion of the text of the footnote, however, which takes up nearly two-thirds of the following page, was lifted from Feuillée's

Journal des observations physiques, mathématiques et botaniques and offers a detailed description of corn's physical characteristics. But at the very bottom of the text, prior to assigning Feuillée authorial credit for these details, the editor adds that the corn seed "grows very well in almost all the Provinces of France, and if we were careful to bring it in to those provinces where it is not cultivated, it could serve as a great resource in the years that are less fertile in wheat" (2:195, note a). This citation appears to have been an editorial addition. Feuillée had written that "few people in France are unaware of what Corn is," but stopped short of declaring it a great resource for confronting agricultural crises. This textual commentary, presumably inserted by the editor, provides proof that those who worked in and around the Jardin du Roi were acutely sensitive to the potential uses to which Peruvian species such as corn might be put in France. The appearance of this commentary in the first footnote on the first species signals the shifting focus to contemporary concerns reflected in the collected material, brought into typographic relief through the use of footnoted brackets within the text, a feature that will be discussed in the third section of this article (see Figure 2).

The next series of specimens in this first section includes the plants and trees described by Garcilaso but specifically emphasizes those species also found in the Jardin. Dalibard includes a note to this effect at the bottom of each description, as in the case of guava: "There are some at the Jardin du Roi" (2:204, note f). Following the guava (*Inga siliquis longissimis: vulgò Pacai*) come the *paltas*, "what are called in our Isles *Avocats*. . . . This tree is at the Jardin du Roy" (2:204, note g); the *lucuma*, a large tree bearing a heart-shaped fruit ("The Lucuma is at the Jardin du Roy"); and the *mulli*, a tree whose fruit "turns black as it ripens, and tastes like pepper. . . . The *Mollé* with jagged leaf is at the Jardin du Roy" (2:207, note i). This section ends with descriptions of the *maugei* and the coca tree, two species for which there were no specimens at the Jardin du Roi. Nevertheless, the *maugei* merited placement within the chapter because of its "utility," and the coca tree deserved to be mentioned because of the "important commerce" which is made of the tree, described as "one of the greatest treasures of Peru" (2:212). We therefore see a progression, within the text and footnotes of this first section of chapter 28, from comestible varietals about which few detailed *in situ* observations had been made—corn, potatoes, *inchi*—to those species represented within the actual soil of the Jardin du Roi's hothouses. Both kinds of descriptions rely primarily on details drawn from travel accounts, but the second category suggests that further observation was possible because of their presence within the hothouse. The link between them was the potential use that could be made of certain species within the agricultural or medical economies of early modern France.

The second section, separated entirely from the first by brackets, describes species at the Jardin *not* listed by Garcilaso in his original text but that nonetheless had been observed empirically by Dalibard. This section extends the discussion of possibilities for further empirical observation by providing specific details of botanical "events" for the specimens described. Notwithstanding an eight-page discussion of the Quinquina tree (as described in detail by Charles-Marie de la Condamine in his 1738 *mémoire académique* on this subject), the section includes descriptions of the papaya,

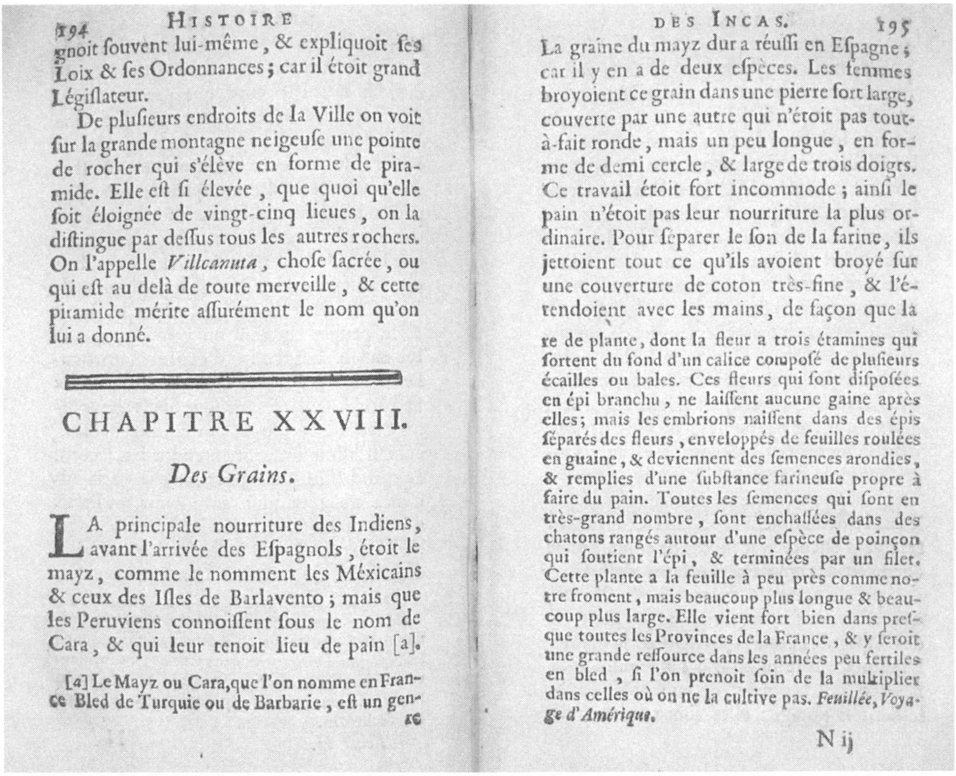
194 HISTOIRE

gnoit ſouvent lui-même, & expliquoit ſes Loix & ſes Ordonnances; car il étoit grand Légiſlateur.

De pluſieurs endroits de la Ville on voit ſur la grande montagne neigeuſe une pointe de rocher qui s'élève en forme de piramide. Elle eſt ſi élevée, que quoi qu'elle ſoit éloignée de vingt-cinq lieues, on la diſtingue par deſſus tous les autres rochers. On l'appelle *Villcanuta*, choſe ſacrée, ou qui eſt au delà de toute merveille, & cette piramide mérite aſſurément le nom qu'on lui a donné.

CHAPITRE XXVIII.

Des Grains.

LA principale nourriture des Indiens, avant l'arrivée des Eſpagnols, étoit le mayz, comme le nomment les Méxicains & ceux des Iſles de Barlavento; mais que les Peruviens connoiſſent ſous le nom de Cara, & qui leur tenoit lieu de pain [a].

[a] Le Mayz ou Cara, que l'on nomme en France Bled de Turquie ou de Barbarie, eſt un genre de plante, dont la fleur a trois étamines qui ſortent du fond d'un calice compoſé de pluſieurs écailles ou bales. Ces fleurs qui ſont diſpoſées en épi branchu, ne laiſſent aucune gaine après elles; mais les embrions naiſſent dans des épis ſéparés des fleurs, enveloppés de feuilles roulées en guaine, & deviennent des ſemences arondies, & remplies d'une ſubſtance farineuſe propre à faire du pain. Toutes les ſemences qui ſont en très-grand nombre, ſont enchaſſées dans des chatons rangés autour d'une eſpèce de poinçon qui ſoutient l'épi, & terminées par un filet. Cette plante a la feuille à peu près comme notre froment, mais beaucoup plus longue & beaucoup plus large. Elle vient fort bien dans preſque toutes les Provinces de la France, & y ſeroit une grande reſſource dans les années peu fertiles en bled, ſi l'on prenoit ſoin de la multiplier dans celles où on ne la cultive pas. *Feuillée, Voyage d'Amérique.*

DES INCAS. 195

La graine du mayz dur a réuſſi en Eſpagne; car il y en a de deux eſpèces. Les femmes broyoient ce grain dans une pierre fort large, couverte par une autre qui n'étoit pas tout-à-fait ronde, mais un peu longue, en forme de demi cercle, & large de trois doigts. Ce travail étoit fort incommode; ainſi le pain n'étoit pas leur nourriture la plus ordinaire. Pour ſéparer le ſon de la farine, ils jettoient tout ce qu'ils avoient broyé ſur une couverture de coton très-fine, & l'étendoient avec les mains, de façon que la

N ij

Figure 2. Chapter 28 of the *Histoire des Incas,* "Des Grains," showing the division into primary and secondary sections using bracketed footnotes. The description of corn in footnote [*a*] makes reference to the potential benefits of cultivating American maize in France during the years when wheat is scarce. Courtesy of the Bancroft Library, University of California, Berkeley.

cotton, and guava trees, the "Floripondio," the banana and palm trees, the "Sang-Dragon," the "Cierge," and many others. These specimens had all been observed empirically at the Jardin and were subsequently described in the text. The first of these species, for example, is the papaya tree, and the description of this species is based primarily on Willem's Piso account in the *Historia naturalis brasilis* (1648). In the paragraph that follows this hundred-year-old description, however, more recent observations about the specific holdings of the Jardin are brought to the fore: "The Papaya trees that have blossomed in the Hothouses of the Jardin du Roi are all females, and have not born fruit, due to the lack of males. We hope that some [male trees] will be found among those that we keep there" (2:229). The flowering of the papaya trees brought a degree of temporal currency to the description offered by Piso and showed that the hothouse could permit useful research far from the papayas' native soil in the Americas.[42] The material presence of these species, and the ability to naturalize them within the hothouse, gave natural historical observers the possibility of placing the on-site study of botanical materials on the same level as those decades-old descriptions provided by travelers to the New World. These recent observations, based on the behavior of material specimens, in turn transformed the identity of the *Histoire des Incas* from a static 150-year-old chronicle into a dynamic vessel for empirically based solutions to contemporary challenges.

This epistemological expansion of both the translator's charge and the very notion of what a translated edition of a classic work could contain were due at least in part to the burgeoning collection sprouting and blossoming within the artificial conditions of Du Fay's hothouses. The blooming trees and ripening fruits allowed the editor of the *Histoire des Incas* to put the empirical observations at the Jardin du Roi on the same plane as the "day-to-day research" undertaken in Peru following the arrival of the Spaniards, thereby shifting the epistemological center of botanical experimentation from Peru to Paris. Typographical mechanisms and editorial layering that highlighted particular pieces of useful information were key elements of the new editorial epistemology that distinguished the *Histoire des Incas* from previous translations of Garcilaso's work. Like the physical hothouse, a virtual hothouse in print required an organizational scheme to guide the observer in examining the name, provenance, and agricultural or botanical properties of its different species. As we shall see, the editor of the *Histoire des Incas* was keenly aware of the structural and typographical stakes of this new translation. The configuration of knowledge on the printed page quickly came to the fore as he revised and reformulated the natural historical information collected from travel narratives, natural historical compendia, and the verdant specimens found within the "elegant edifices" Du Fay had built a decade before.[43]

III. A Peruvian Garden
Enclosed by Parisian Brackets

In addition to a discussion of Godin's shipment of specimens, the revelation of Quinquina's properties by La Condamine, and a special section on Spanish "indifference" to learning about the features of American natural history, the "Préface du Second Volume" presented a detailed account of the contents of volume 2 as well as of the methodology used to put this second volume in order. This second preface outlined explicitly the editor's methodology and the criteria he employed for expanding the range of materials included in the second volume of this new translation. According to the editor, Garcilaso was ill equipped to comment on the natural historical features of his native country. For this reason, the text had been revised "so that the Reader who is knowledgeable about the past of this vast country can also be so about [its] present state."[44] The editor went on to explain the process of collation by which the text was to be transformed: "we will add to what [Garcilaso] says some Notes to better introduce the Vegetables, Animals, and Minerals he mentions. At the end of the Chapters, we will add short descriptions of things he does not speak about."[45] This license to add and abridge according to the interests of the "educated Reader" was an explicit and central feature of the editorial strategy as revealed in the "Préface du Second Volume." That the articles on Inca religion, culture, ceremonies, customs, science, geography, clothing, and industry had been "mixed together in the original with historical facts, and were often confused between the two" added further weight to the editor's call for a new and revised edition. By separating these topics from the historical materials, bringing them together "under the same point of view," and organizing them according to chapters, the editor hoped to "add more order to this work," even though he admitted that much more attention was needed in order to bring the work to the "perfection" it truly deserved.

One of these typographical changes was the addition of footnotes to particular portions of the text, as we saw also in volume 1. But in the second volume another typographical strategy enhanced the readability of the text even further: the employment of a system of brackets to separate material not originally part of Garcilaso's *Comentarios reales* from the principal body of the text. The first twenty-seven chapters of this second volume, which dealt with the religious, cultural, literary, agricultural, and "scientific" features of Inca life, were largely free of bracketed material. Indeed, there were only two uses of brackets, both in the section on astronomy, to which we shall return shortly. But on page 194, which corresponded to the beginning of chapter 28, "On Grains," an extraordinary series of brackets appears. Like a trap door leading to a series of underground chambers, a new sublayer of information emerges from within the original text, splitting the text into two separate but interrelated informational sources. The typographical mechanism that links these upper and lower portions within the text are bracketed footnotes, which begin to appear with regularity throughout this section.

A paragraph in the second preface devoted to typographical technologies suggests the extent to which printing practices—in this case, the insertion of brackets or other editorial mechanisms—were considered an important subject of a preface or foreword during this period. The editor explains that, "In the printing, we have not distinguished additional materials with the use of different characters, which is almost always incommodious, but rather we have marked them with an Asterism, and have added to each article the name of the Author."[46] One can presume that the "different characters" would be italics, employed nonetheless in certain parts of the first and second volumes. But what was meant by an "Asterism"?[47] One finds nothing resembling asterisks signaling or adorning inserted materials. What one does find are brackets, an alternative form perhaps of "asterism" and part of a multilayered system of typographical marks used to indicate new material that had entered the second volume.

The origins of the use of the bracket as a mechanism for showcasing new materials, either within the text or as a footnote, can be traced back to Scaliger, if not further.[48] And yet this particular employment of the bracket seems to have fallen largely into disuse during the eighteenth century. The arguably arcane question of what was to be found between two brackets in the mid-eighteenth century was important enough to merit a section in Martin-Dominique Fertel's typographical manual *La science pratique de l'imprimerie,* published in 1723. Fertel explained that the bracket, a variation on the omnipresent parenthetical mark, had three possible uses:

> Brackets are occasionally used to mark some discourse that should be in italic character or which may be transposed, which often happens in alphabetical Tables or the contents of a Book. . . .
>
> They are also used to enclose things to which the Reader should pay close attention, and this principally in Church-Books like Prayer-books [*missels*], Rituals, &c. . . .
>
> They can also be used to enclose the figures of running titles at the top of the page, where they are placed at the center of the line; this is done when there is no textual material to be placed there; as well as to enclose Alphabetical Letters of a cross-reference [*renvoy*] of Additions in the margins, or at the bottom of the page.[49]

The third definition comes closest to describing the typographical mechanisms on display in the *Histoire des Incas*. What is peculiar about the *Histoire des Incas,* however, is not the insertion of these "Additions" at the bottom of the page but the complex system of footnotes, bracketed footnotes, and bracketed text, all interwoven and layered throughout the second half of the second volume. The struggle between a codified system of typographical rules as described by Fertel and the demands of a text that became a hybrid container for abundant portions of disparate material—animal, vegetable, mineral, and historical—becomes evident as the editor attempts to present information drawn from 150 years' worth of texts in various languages in a smooth and ordered narrative structure.

At the same time, the *Histoire des Incas* seems an ideal candidate for the kind of typographical instructions that Fertel proposed. Print allowed societies to preserve knowledge that would otherwise have been lost, according to Fertel's preface. Without print, "the richest talents would remain buried, the most interesting research would remain unknown, and the most felicitous discoveries would still be unheard of."[50] As such, the *Science pratique de l'imprimerie* served as a technical manual to help control and standardize the use of typographical strategies for organizing printed texts. We do not know whether the editor of the *Histoire des Incas* was aware of Fertel's treatise, but these themes resonated strongly in certain sections of the *Histoire*. Indeed, the opening lines of the section on astronomy might very well have been used as an epigraph for Fertel's text: "Without the use of the alphabet, the Incas were not able to extend their knowledge: and, consequently, their Astrology and natural Philosophy were extremely mediocre. . . . In general, their understanding perished along with its Inventors."[51] It is probably mere coincidence that the editor specifically cited the section from which this quotation is drawn in order to point out the improvements between Baudoin's translation of 1633 and the *Histoire des Incas* of 1744. However, in his "Préface du Traducteur" to volume 1, the editor encouraged the reader to compare these two sections on astronomy in order to observe "the simplicity to which we have tried to reduce each object" and the manner in which each section was designed to be "more pleasant for the Public." But, for the editor of the *Histoire des Incas,* it was not print itself (for, of course, Garcilaso's original text was printed as well) but rather the *configuration* of the printed text that allowed knowledge to be passed on efficiently from one generation to the next. And this was also Fertel's point in writing his treatise. It is perhaps no wonder, then, that the first section to employ brackets to facilitate comprehension and clarity was this very section on astronomy, meant to showcase the improvements between Baudoin's earlier edition and the additional editorial commentary inserted into this new translation by "a man versed in [Astronomy], and well known in the Republic of Letters."[52]

The two instances where brackets are used in the section on Incan astronomy notwithstanding, the first section to employ the bracket as an extended typographical feature is chapter 28, "Des Grains," dedicated to Peruvian natural history. This section recovers a series of chapters originally published by Garcilaso in the middle of book 8 of the *Comentarios reales.*[53] There are several planes of editorial organization within this extended—one might say distended—section, each represented by a different typographical stratum used by the editor to create order in a system where information from a multiplicity of sources was being collated, abridged, transformed, and displayed at once. The first level of textual organization could be called the principal text—that is, the (more or less direct) translation of Garcilaso's *Comentarios reales* itself. As with the first volume, this text was dramatically abridged and reshaped but still follows, by and large, the narrative thrust of Garcilaso's original.[54] This primary level also contains footnotes denoted alphabetically and beginning with (a) on each page where footnotes are found, as opposed to being consecutive (a, b, c, d) over a series of pages. These footnotes, like those of the first volume, oscillate between commentaries inserted *ex post translatio* by the editor and those that are condensations or transplantations of information provided by Garcilaso. An example of the former would be the editor's comment in a footnote on page 207 that the *Huchu,* a kind of piquant pepper, "is our long, or Guinea, pepper" (Figure 3).[55] The latter category of footnote includes page references to classic texts such as Acosta's *Historia natural y moral de las Indias,* lifted from the body of Garcilaso's text, as well as longer commentaries about particular Amerindian customs also pulled out of the earlier text and reinserted using the organizational mechanism of the footnote.[56]

Beyond the material culled from Garcilaso's original text and placed discretely within the parenthetical footnote form "(a)," the second level of editorial reconfiguration consisted of bracketed footnotes injected into Garcilaso's text by the editor, typographical references that pointed to natural historical material based largely on post-Garcilasan travel narratives to South America. The editor employed several texts to make these editorial annotations to Garcilaso's text, including Louis Feuillée's *Voyage d'Amérique* (1714–25),[57] Amédée François Frézier's *Voyage de la mer du sud* (1717),[58] Georg Marggraf and Willem Piso's *Historia naturalis brasilis* (1648), and Carolus Clusius's *Histoire des plantes* (1557).[59] But the text contained within these bracketed footnotes can also be further subdivided, since the commentaries are not only descriptions based on travel narratives but contain occasional indications that certain specimens of these plants could be found at the Jardin du Roi, as we saw above. Additionally, these descriptions sometimes contain details on the current state of attempts to "naturalize" exotic species into French soil.

A third and final level of editorial organization took the shape of an extended, multipage description of the Peruvian natural historical specimens found at the Jardin du Roi, separated from the principal text and enclosed within brackets. This section bears no relation to Garcilaso's original text; indeed, it begins with a statement from the editor that it "should come as no surprise that Garcillasso de la Vega did not know all the plants of his country."[60] Interestingly, this text is separated not only by a line break but also by two closed brackets placed side by side, which indicate

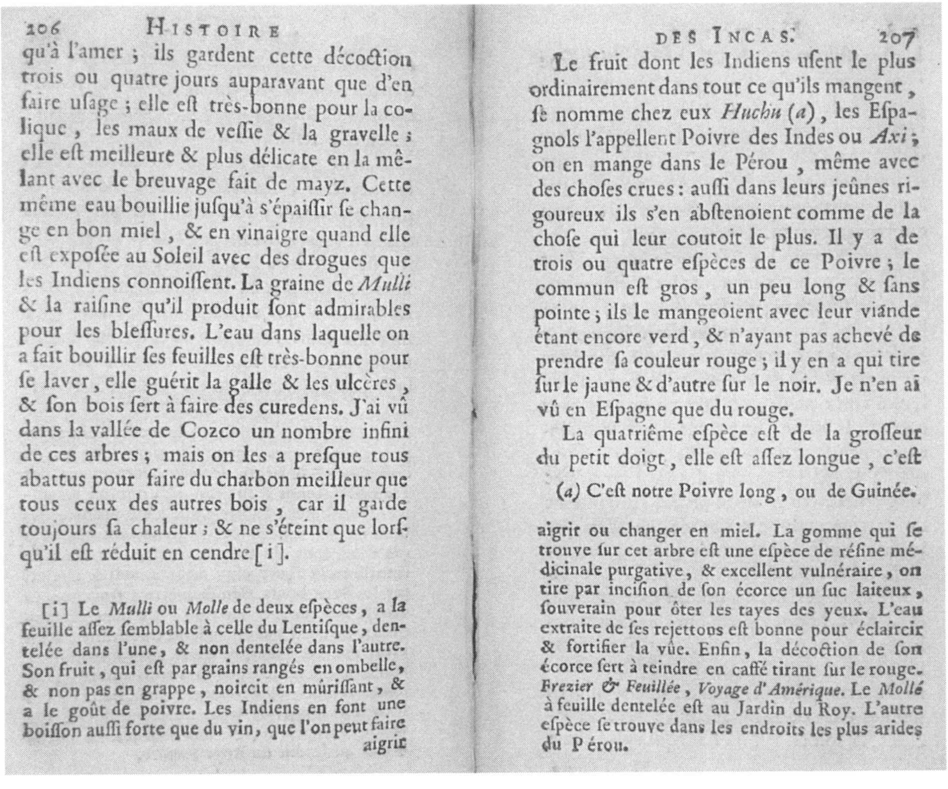
206 HISTOIRE

qu'à l'amer ; ils gardent cette décoction trois ou quatre jours auparavant que d'en faire usage ; elle est très-bonne pour la colique, les maux de vessie & la gravelle ; elle est meilleure & plus délicate en la mêlant avec le breuvage fait de mayz. Cette même eau bouillie jusqu'à s'épaissir se change en bon miel, & en vinaigre quand elle est exposée au Soleil avec des drogues que les Indiens connoissent. La graine de *Mulli* & la raisine qu'il produit sont admirables pour les blessures. L'eau dans laquelle on a fait bouillir ses feuilles est très-bonne pour se laver, elle guérit la galle & les ulcères, & son bois sert à faire des curedens. J'ai vû dans la vallée de Cozco un nombre infini de ces arbres ; mais on les a presque tous abattus pour faire du charbon meilleur que tous ceux des autres bois, car il garde toujours sa chaleur ; & ne s'éteint que lorsqu'il est réduit en cendre [i].

[i] Le *Mulli* ou *Molle* de deux espèces, a la feuille assez semblable à celle du Lentisque, dentelée dans l'une, & non dentelée dans l'autre. Son fruit, qui est par grains rangés en ombelle, & non pas en grappe, noircit en mûrissant, & a le goût de poivre. Les Indiens en font une boisson aussi forte que du vin, que l'on peut faire aigrir

DES INCAS. 207

Le fruit dont les Indiens usent le plus ordinairement dans tout ce qu'ils mangent, se nomme chez eux *Huchu* (*a*), les Espagnols l'appellent Poivre des Indes ou *Axi* ; on en mange dans le Pérou, même avec des choses crues : aussi dans leurs jeûnes rigoureux ils s'en abstenoient comme de la chose qui leur coutoit le plus. Il y a de trois ou quatre espèces de ce Poivre ; le commun est gros, un peu long & sans pointe ; ils le mangeoient avec leur viande étant encore verd, & n'ayant pas achevé de prendre sa couleur rouge ; il y en a qui tire sur le jaune & d'autre sur le noir. Je n'en ai vû en Espagne que du rouge.

La quatriême espèce est de la grosseur du petit doigt, elle est assez longue, c'est

(*a*) C'est notre Poivre long, ou de Guinée.

aigrir ou changer en miel. La gomme qui se trouve sur cet arbre est une espèce de résine médicinale purgative, & excellent vulnéraire, on tire par incision de son écorce un suc laiteux, souverain pour ôter les tayes des yeux. L'eau extraite de ses rejettons est bonne pour éclaircir & fortifier la vûe. Enfin, la décoction de son écorce sert à teindre en caffé tirant sur le rouge. *Frezier & Feuillée*, *Voyage d'Amérique*. Le *Mollé* à feuille dentelée est au Jardin du Roy. L'autre espèce se trouve dans les endroits les plus arides du Pérou.

Figure 3. A sample page from the *Histoire des Incas* (Paris, 1744). The first two levels of editorial annotation are shown here on both pages. The first level is represented on page 207 by the text beginning "Le fruit dont les Indiens usent le plus ordinairement," with the alphabetical footnote marker (*a*) shown underneath. The second level appears in the lower left-hand corner of page 206, represented by the bracketed footnote marker [i] and its accompanying text. Note the reference to the presence of the *Mollé à feuille dentelée* at the Jardin du Roi at bottom right. Courtesy of the Bancroft Library, University of California, Berkeley.

a contained but ultimately limitless display case within which the additional material is allowed to extend for several pages. The section elaborated within the brackets, then, brings together information gleaned from travelers' accounts as well as details gathered by observing the natural specimens *in situ* at the Jardin. This fusion of textual reference and firsthand observation was meant to compensate for Garcilaso's unstudied approach to classifying the natural historical materials of his native land. The editor (probably Dalibard in this case) drew upon several reference texts, citing the appropriate author at the end of each paragraph and extracting various kinds of information to complement Garcilaso's descriptions with more technical observations (Figure 4).

The editor justified these changes to Garcilaso's text by linking his overall editorial project to a positivistic conception of scientific expansion and "commerce" in the New World. According to the "Préface du Second Volume," Garcilaso's sixteenth-century understanding of natural history had been entirely superseded by "day-to-day research and the commerce of Foreigners," including but not limited to those three academicians sent to measure the shape of the Earth: Louis Godin, Charles-Marie de la Condamine, and Pierre Bouguer. This traveling triumvirate makes several cameo appearances within the *Histoire des Incas,* referred to regularly as the "new Argonauts" who would add to "the Collections of the Jardin du Roy, & the Mémoires of the Académie." The bracketed section in chapter 28, for example, includes an eight-page exposition of the Quinquina tree from Loja, written by La Condamine and published in the 1738 *Mémoires de l'Académie Royale des Sciences.*[61] As the editor made clear, much of the impetus behind the editorial reorganization of the *Histoire des Incas* was the arrival of the new materials sent to France by Godin and his colleagues; these "Additions," using Fertel's terminology, required the deployment of brackets as figurative display cases. In this way, typographical markers served as the structural girding for mounting these material specimens within the text, one of the many tools employed by European printers and editors to naturalize exotic flora within the expanded bounds of a historical treatise.

Clearly, the tripartite typographical division of chapter 28 overlaps considerably with the material considerations discussed in section II above, paralleling and facilitating the shifting focus to contemporary concerns reflected in the nature of the information given about the various specimens. The progression, described earlier, from specimens of agricultural interest to those about which material evidence could be drawn from empirical observation was made possible, in fact, by the use of these typographical strategies. The multiple strata of typographically induced divisions within the text provide clear windows onto the state of natural historical knowledge at the Parisian Jardin du Roi. Indeed, the text goes on to describe other viennent fur les bords de l'eau, ils en font provifion pour leur nourriture. [ ]

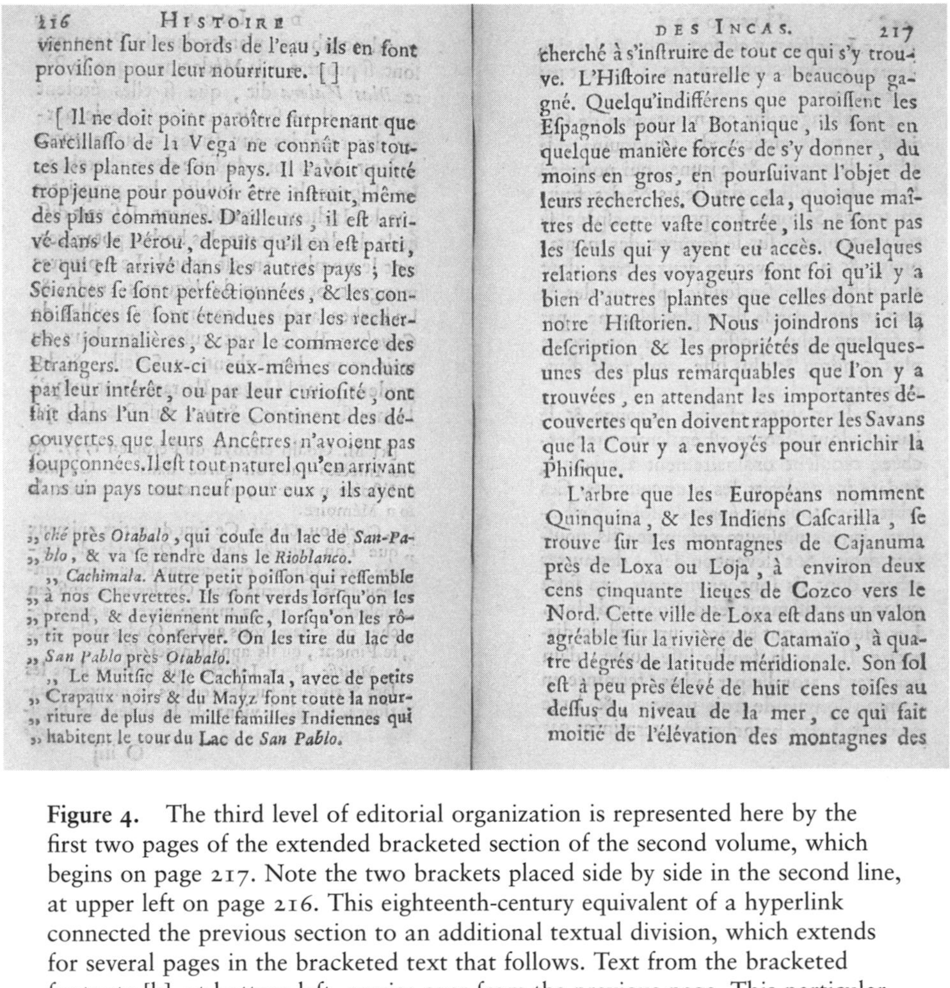

[Il ne doit point paroître furprenant que Garcillaffo de la Vega ne connût pas toutes les plantes de fon pays. Il l'avoit quitté trop jeune pour pouvoir être inftruit, même des plus communes. D'ailleurs, il eft arrivé dans le Pérou, depuis qu'il en eft parti, ce qui eft arrivé dans les autres pays; les Sciences fe font perfectionnées, & les connoiffances fe font étendues par les recherches journalières, & par le commerce des Etrangers. Ceux-ci eux-mêmes conduits par leur intérêt, ou par leur curiofité, ont fait dans l'un & l'autre Continent des découvertes que leurs Ancêtres n'avoient pas foupçonnées. Il eft tout naturel qu'en arrivant dans un pays tout neuf pour eux, ils ayent

,, ché près Otabalo, qui coule du lac de San-Pa-
,, blo, & va fe rendre dans le Rioblanco.
  ,, Cachimala. Autre petit poiffon qui reffemble
,, à nos Chevrettes. Ils font verds lorfqu'on les
,, prend, & deviennent mufc, lorfqu'on les rô-
,, tit pour les conferver. On les tire du lac de
,, San Pablo près Otabalo.
  ,, Le Muitfic & le Cachimala, avec de petits
,, Crapaux noirs & du Mayz font toute la nour-
,, riture de plus de mille familles Indiennes qui
,, habitent le tour du Lac de San Pablo.

cherché à s'inftruire de tout ce qui s'y trouve. L'Hiftoire naturelle y a beaucoup gagné. Quelqu'indifférens que paroiffent les Efpagnols pour la Botanique, ils font en quelque manière forcés de s'y donner, du moins en gros, en pourfuivant l'objet de leurs recherches. Outre cela, quoique maîtres de cette vafte contrée, ils ne font pas les feuls qui y ayent eu accès. Quelques relations des voyageurs font foi qu'il y a bien d'autres plantes que celles dont parle notre Hiftorien. Nous joindrons ici la defcription & les propriétés de quelques-unes des plus remarquables que l'on y a trouvées, en attendant les importantes découvertes qu'en doivent rapporter les Savans que la Cour y a envoyés pour enrichir la Phifique.

L'arbre que les Européans nomment Quinquina, & les Indiens Cafcarilla, fe trouve fur les montagnes de Cajanuma près de Loxa ou Loja, à environ deux cens cinquante lieues de Cozco vers le Nord. Cette ville de Loxa eft dans un valon agréable fur la rivière de Catamaïo, à quatre dégrés de latitude méridionale. Son fol eft à peu près élevé de huit cens toifes au deffus du niveau de la mer, ce qui fait moitié de l'élévation des montagnes des

Figure 4. The third level of editorial organization is represented here by the first two pages of the extended bracketed section of the second volume, which begins on page 217. Note the two brackets placed side by side in the second line, at upper left on page 216. This eighteenth-century equivalent of a hyperlink connected the previous section to an additional textual division, which extends for several pages in the bracketed text that follows. Text from the bracketed footnote [k], at bottom left, carries over from the previous page. This particular text is a "note tirée [du] mémoire" of M. Godin that describes a collection of insects he sent to the Cabinet d'Histoire naturelle in 1737. One of the supposed "insects," the *Cachimala*, is actually a fish. Courtesy of the Bancroft Library, University of California, Berkeley.

categories of Peruvian wonders as well, with chapters on wild animals, aquatic birds, emeralds and other precious stones, horses, fruits, grains, and gold-mining techniques. In each of these sections, pride of place is given to the recent additions to the King's Cabinet, among them the "tail of a rattlesnake [*Serpent à sonette*] that M. Godin sent from Peru in 1737 to the Cabinet d'Histoire naturelle at the Jardin du Roy."[62] Descriptions of snakes such as this were drawn largely from Marggraf and Piso's *Historia naturalis brasilis,* but the ending to chapter 30 became a serpentine coda for the politics of collecting and an overdue *éloge* to the master of the house:

> One can see such well-preserved skins of many of these Serpents in the Cabinet d'histoire naturelle of the Jardin du Roy. This Treasure, which is not at all sufficiently known to the public, contains an unusual abundance of natural products of all genres, assembled with care and great effort from every corner of the world. If these treasures speak to the grandeur of their august Master, the careful attention with which they have been augmented and the order and elegance with which they have been arranged make us admire no less the exquisite taste of their illustrious and zealous Protector, as well as the enlightened precision of [the individual] to whose supervision they have been confided.[63]

What this archaeology of typographical strategies demonstrates is that the tripartite structure of the footnote, the footnoted bracket, and bracketed text helped to bring "order and elegance" to the *Histoire des Incas* as well. But it was not merely a neutral, value-free order these devices brought. Rather, this new epistemology, represented by brackets and material specimens, sought to express the "progress" of natural historical knowledge and, indeed, its ability to confront social problems through botanical solutions imported from outside Europe. Whether in the physical form of the hothouse or the typographical form of the bracket, what we perceive in the end are structures that served to provide stability for hierarchically conceived layers of knowledge. In the specific case of the *Histoire des Incas* and its description of the Jardin du Roi, these units of organization employed editorial mechanisms as forms of centralization and consolidation. When we consider the relationship between knowledge and power, the brackets serve a function similar to that of Du Fay's hothouses: they represent large enclosed spaces where exotic specimens could be planted, cultivated, and made visible while being exploited for social and political purposes.

Several years before Daubenton composed his famous description of the "Cabinet d'histoire naturelle" for Buffon's multivolume *Histoire naturelle,* Dalibard had already performed an initial walkthrough of this burgeoning collection. Godin's shipment of Peruvian specimens probably served as the catalyst for Dalibard's interest in cataloguing and describing the species pertaining to the natural history of a distant land. If so, then the *Histoire des Incas* became the figurative soil into which he transplanted his enthusiasm, combining details gleaned from the travel narratives of the previous century's transatlantic voyages with the material pleasures associated with the objects themselves: collected, cultivated, and displayed in the glittering hothouses that were of such recent vintage. The technical and typographical strategies he later employed to transform these physical specimens into print allowed for the hierarchical arrangement of new information through an elaborate system of cross references and sophisticated bibliographic techniques. In conjunction with the editor, or perhaps *as* the editor, Dalibard gave us an interconnected chain of natural specimens, linked in print by footnotes and brackets that transformed a seventeenth-century chronicle into a revitalized treatise on nature and history.

Whether consciously or not, the three levels of editorial hierarchy that divide the *Histoire des Incas* represent a stadial hierarchy of natural historical progress. The first level, an abridged and translated version of text originally written by Garcilaso, represents pre-Columbian "savage" knowledge, in which native traditions were described "before the arrival of the Spaniards" and an attempt was made to reconstruct these indigenous patterns of culture without reference to the deleterious or salutary effects of European civilization. The second level focuses on those observations of native peoples made after European contact, employing scientific descriptions of plants, seeds, and fruits in tandem with native explanations of remedies drawn from post-contact observation in the New World. But the third level represents the eighteenth-century aspiration to empirically based science, in which on-the-spot discoveries and new systems of natural classification allowed for the determination of universal laws of nature, observable through botanical "events" and specimens drawn from throughout the known world.

This theory of natural historical progress was represented typographically within the pages of the *Histoire des Incas*. The typographical strategies employed by the editor throughout both volumes sought to emphasize the currency and utility of a people's history, even though the Incas had already been decimated some three centuries earlier. The material specimens sent by Godin from the ancient homeland of this destroyed culture made the use of these bracketed footnotes necessary. The brackets, in turn, offered the specimens a unique window in which to be displayed: an ideological space within the margins of a pre-Columbian history where social, material, and typographical interests could be merged and useful objects displayed as novelties to adorn the aisles of the King's Cabinet.

Conclusion: Staking Claims to Incan History

The republication of Garcilaso's text in 1744 shows that intellectual appropriation in a natural historical context was dependent on many factors: material acquisition of new species; the construction of structures in which to house these specimens; an increased reliance on typographical mechanisms to organize and structure printed accounts; and access to books and reports that recounted in print prior natural historical knowledge, including indigenous practices that often formed the basis of European understanding of the utility of a given plant or shrub. In the case of the *Histoire des Incas*, subtle references in the preface to agricultural crisis may have been the clearest hint of the social and cultural conditions under which this translation came to be produced, and why it came to be published in the form that it did. The two prefaces — in fact, the only two portions of the *Histoire* that represent wholly original contributions to the text — also give us a window through which to understand the interrelated stakes of historical (and natural historical) knowledge gleaned from the Americas.

At the opening of the Jardin Royal in 1640, Guy de la Brosse had already lauded the "variety of species of its plants, brought from the two Indies and from all the provinces of the Earth where French intelligence has been able to extend, which is what gives it a large and rich advantage over all the others."[64] Even at this early date the Jardin Royal had already become a *Jardin planétaire*.[65] Bushes from Peru stood alongside other plants and trees transplanted into French soil, blurring the line between the "natural" environments of each and making it possible to think globally about science and applied botany within an institutional setting. But the construction of hothouses in the early eighteenth century provided a structural impetus for the collection of new species and the publication of new texts. The status of the specimens sent by Godin as elements of natural historical interest allowed those specimens to pass unsuspected through the tight cordon of colonial administration put up by the Spaniards to prevent others from profiting from the riches of the Indies. Once in France, seeds, travel logs, and academic *mémoires* provided the ingredients for a potent brew of materials out of which to formulate new configurations of botanical knowledge. Assisted by new typographical methods that allowed a broader range of potential readers to profit from the information contained therein, the texts that resulted from this process served as storehouses for this new knowledge — hothouses in print — that shifted possession from the field to the colonial institutions that these individuals served.

Several years after the publication of the *Histoire des Incas*, Diderot and d'Alembert referred to their project of reorganizing knowledge with an organic metaphor: the tree of knowledge. Diderot considered the *Encyclo-pédie* a "sanctuary wherein human knowledge is sheltered from [the rav-ages of] time and revolutions."[66] What better place to shelter knowledge than the hothouse—an enclosed space where new species could be trans-planted, side by side with older specimens, and encouraged to grow and change according to new soils and new circumstances? Within this figura-tive hothouse, materials could be grafted together in new configurations. In the case of the *Histoire des Incas,* information gleaned from native prac-titioners of the botanical arts was collected by European naturalists, com-pared with specimens sent by scientific explorers, and then molded together into a sourcebook that could be used to address contemporary social prob-lems through agricultural experimentation, all under the protective guise of a natural historical treatise on an exotic region far from Europe. This new metaphorical hothouse was a site of experimentation wherein plants and bushes could provide metropolitan elites with material for projects of social and economic reform, forging a clean and uninterrupted link between the exploration of new worlds and the political ambitions supporting such colonial research.

Halfway through the bracketed section of the natural history portion of the *Histoire des Incas,* between the *Tara* and the *Onagra laurifolia flore amplo, pentapetalo,* the editor inserted the description of a plant that, "because of the beauty of its flower, deserved to have a place in the admir-able Gardens of the Incas": the *Emérocallis floribus purpurascentibus maculatis, vulgò Pelegrina.* When the "perpetual Springtime" of the Peru-vian season finally started to fade and the *Pelegrina* itself began to wilt and decay, the natives took an extraordinary measure to maintain the sun-gilt appearance of their garden: "they substituted in their place new plants cre-ated with gold and silver, which their artistry had imitated with perfection. The trees made out of these precious metals which formed long walk-ways, the fields entirely filled with artificial corn whose flowers and ears were made of gold and whose stalks and leaves were of silver, served as convincing proof of the wealth of this land, the skill of the Indians, and the magnificence of their Sovereigns."[67] These shiny shrubs of silver and gold took their place as monuments to the Incas' artistic prowess, and the description given by Garcilaso and transcribed by Dalibard commemorated in print the metaphorical importance of horticulture to the denizens of an Andean world whose golden treasures had long since been taken from their lands. Feuillée's reference to plants as objects that were "far more valuable treasures than those extracted from the mines of Peru," and the comment by the editor of the *Histoire des Incas* that, had the Spanish been more inter-ested in collecting native botanical knowledge, the mines of Potosi "would certainly not be the only sources from which one would extract riches in

Peru," receive eloquent articulation in this image of a botanical El Dorado perched among the jagged peaks of the Andes. Seeking to profit from the riches of native knowledge as transcribed by Europeans and observed *in situ* by botanists in the metropole, editors and translators employed editorial and typographical techniques to transform this new form of property into a shape they could employ and promote. In the process, Garcilaso's *Comentarios reales* was transformed by an impulse to parse and reassemble. The descriptions and concatenations of new materials offered by Dalibard and the other editors eventually served as a source for new riches extracted from the botanical mines and floral lodes of Peruvian soil, but their legacy as building blocks was a mixed one. The *Histoire des Incas, Rois du Pérou* (1744) was used by the likes of Buffon, Cornelius de Pauw, and others to describe the history of the Incan people, but it was also deployed to denigrate the American continent and the culture of its native inhabitants. In the end, the "important discoveries" brought back to France by the argonauts and their entourage depended both on the *material* conditions in which they traveled and the *typographic* conditions their work was to encounter in print.[68] The bounty of naturalists and their chroniclers, whether sealed in wooden crates or contained within printed brackets, needed protection and preservation in order to make the transatlantic passage from the Peruvian Andes to the *capitale des lumières*.

Notes

1. Garcilaso de la Vega el Inca, *Comentarios reales de los Incas. Primera parte* (Lisbon: Crasbeeck, 1609), "Proemio al Lector." All translations are my own unless otherwise noted.

2. Garcilaso was born to the Spanish military captain Sebastián Garcilaso de la Vega and the Inca princess Ñusta Isabel Chimpu Ocllo. For more on his biography, see Aurelio Miró Quesada, *El Inca Garcilaso* (Lima: Pontificia Universidad Católica del Peru, 1994), and, in English, John Grier Varner, *El Inca: The Life and Times of Garcilaso de la Vega* (Austin: University of Texas Press, 1968).

3. Garcilaso, *Comentarios reales,* "Proemio."

4. Ibid. David Brading has argued, on the other hand, that Garcilaso's *Royal Commentaries* need to be considered "as a carefully meditated, sustained rebuttal of the imperial tradition of conquest history," while José Antonio Mazzotti has reasoned persuasively that "there are textual markers that allow us to understand its internal coherence as derived from multiple discourses," among which indigenous sources form one of the more important threads. See D. A. Brading, "The Incas and the Renaissance: The Royal Commentaries of Inca Garcilaso de la Vega," *Journal of Latin American Studies* 18 (May 1986): 1–23, and José Antonio Mazzotti, *Coros Mestizos del Inca Garcilaso: resonancias andinas* (Mexico: Fondo de Cultura Económica, 1996).

5. Even prior to Garcilaso's celebrated *Comentarios reales,* of course, the Incas had already entered into "universal history" through the treatises of Father José de Acosta, Pedro de Cieza de León, Francisco Lopez de Gómara, and others, as recalled in the title of a recent book by Luís Millones Figueroa: *Pedro de Cieza de León y su Crónica de Indias. La Entrada*

de los Incas en la Historia Universal (Lima: Fondo Editorial de la Pontificia Universidad, 2001). Once Garcilaso's text was published, however, it tended to efface those which had been written previously.

6. Earlier translations of the *Comentarios reales* included *Le commentaire royal, ou L'histoire des Yncas, Roys du Peru,* trans. Jean Baudoin (Paris: Augustin Courbé, 1633); *The Royal Commentaries of Peru, in Two Parts,* trans. Paul Rycaut (London: Miles Flesher, 1688); *Histoire des Yncas, rois du Perou,* trans. Jean Baudoin (Amsterdam: Gerard Kuyper, 1704); *Histoire des Yncas, rois du Perou,* trans. Jean Baudoin (Amsterdam: J. Desbordes, 1715); *Histoire des Yncas, rois du Perou, depuis le premier Ynca Manco Capac, fils du soleil, jusqu'à Atahualpa dernier Ynca* (Amsterdam: J. F. Bernard, 1737).

7. These measurements, carried out under the auspices of the Bourbon kings of France and Spain, were meant to determine conclusively the precise shape of the earth in response to Newtonian theories of gravitation and fluid dynamics. For a more extended study of the Franco-Hispanic expedition to Quito, see my doctoral dissertation, "Writing the Andes, Reading the Amazon: Voyages of Exploration and the Itineraries of Scientific Knowledge in the Eighteenth Century" (Ph.D. diss., Johns Hopkins University, 2003). The dating of these maps is critical for my argument that the *Histoire des Incas* was conceived, researched, and written at least in part during the period leading up to Buffon's intendancy. While the publication date of the *Histoire des Incas* (1744) places it unequivocally within the first five years of Buffon's charge as intendant, it is probable, nonetheless, that portions of the *Histoire des Incas* were actually written and/or researched in the years before Du Fay's death in 1739. The date of these maps confirms that this in fact was the case.

8. For a succinct overview of the early interest of the French crown in the botanical bounty of extra-European territories, see Antoine Schnapper, *Le géant, la licorne, la tulipe: Collections françaises au XVIIe siècle* (Paris: Flammarion, 1988), esp. chap. 4. On the thorny issue of untangling economic, aesthetic, and natural historical motivations in pursuing New World exotica, see the excellent collection of essays entitled *Merchants and Marvels: Commerce, Science, and Art in Early Modern Europe,* ed. Pamela H. Smith and Paula Findlen (New York: Routledge, 2002).

9. Biographical information on Dalibard is quite scanty, especially for the period of his career prior to his experiments with electricity. For the few details that have come to light, see Robert-Gustave-Marie Triger, "Le Collège de Crannes et Thomas-François Dalibard, naturaliste et physicien," *Bulletin de la Société d'agriculture, sciences et arts de la Sarthe* 30 (1885): 189–204. See also "Thomas François Dalibard," *Dictionary of Scientific Biography,* ed. Charles Coulston Gillispie (New York: Scribner's, 1971), 3:535; J. F. and L. G. Michaud, eds., *Biographie universelle, ancienne et moderne* (Paris: Desplaces, 1854), 10:43; I. Bernard Cohen, *Franklin and Newton* (Cambridge: Harvard University Press, 1966).

10. Footnotes did not appear at all in Baudoin's 1633 edition or in the anonymous Amsterdam edition of 1737. Of course, footnotes were gaining increased use over the course of the eighteenth century, most famously by a resident of Geneva whose *Discours sur l'origine et les fondements de l'inégalité parmi les hommes* consisted of an almost equal amount of footnotes and running text. See Jean-Jacques Rousseau, *Discours sur l'origine et les fondements de l'inégalité parmi les hommes,* esp. n. 10.

11. Previous attempts to assess the representation of the Inca in eighteenth-century Europe have tended to paint in broad brush strokes and across genres, rather than focus on transformations and transfigurations within a specific text. See Deborah Poole's chapter, "The Inca Operatic," in her *Vision, Race, and Modernity: A Visual Economy of the Andean Image World* (Princeton: Princeton University Press, 1997). Likewise, Jorge Cañizares-Esguerra's discussion of the 1744 translation of Garcilaso places the *Histoire des Incas* in a broader intellectual context but does not detail the epistemological challenges facing editors and translators

at the Jardin du Roi as they sought to integrate material evidence from the Franco-Hispanic expedition into the printed chronicles of the Inca. See his *How to Write the History of the New World* (Stanford: Stanford University Press, 2001).

12. The recent book by E. C. Spary, *Utopia's Garden: French Natural History from Old Regime to Revolution* (Chicago: University of Chicago Press, 2000), lamentably passes over the period between 1626 and the mid-eighteenth century as if, during these years, there were no history of the institution she discusses. The primary temporal focus of her otherwise excellent study is the period 1750–95, a periodization scheme that is frequently repeated in the historical literature. Charles Coulston Gillispie's classic account of French scientific culture, *Science and Polity in France at the End of the Old Regime* (Princeton: Princeton University Press, 1980), also focuses overwhelmingly on the period of Buffon's intendancy at the Jardin du Roi.

13. Paula Findlen, *Possessing Nature: Museums, Collecting, and Scientific Culture in Early Modern Italy* (Berkeley and Los Angeles: University of California Press, 1994); Krzysztof Pomian, *Collectionneurs, amateurs et curieux: Paris, Venise: XVIe-XVIIIe siècle* (Paris: Gallimard, 1987). For a discussion of the exotic in the context of European print and mercantile culture during this period, see Benjamin Schmidt, "Inventing Exoticism: The Project of Dutch Geography and the Marketing of the World, Circa 1700," in Smith and Findlen, *Merchants and Marvels.*

14. In this article I use the term "editor" as a shorthand to indicate the individual(s) responsible for writing the two prefaces, who presumably maintained some semblance of editorial control over the translation and abridgment of the *Histoire des Incas.* Since it is impossible to say with certainty who may have composed or translated particular sections, with the exception of Dalibard's contribution to the chapters on natural history, the term editor stands in for the multiple tasks (and possibly multiple identities) of these individuals. The term editor, rather than translator, emphasizes the structural changes and organizational modifications that were made to the text. Historians have mysteriously given exclusive credit to Dalibard for carrying out the translation and editorial production. The inclusion of Dalibard's name in the "Préface," and Dalibard's name alone, may have amounted to an eighteenth-century code for the attribution of authorship, or in this case "editorship," of anonymously produced texts. But it is more likely, judging from the inclusion of the anonymous astronomer as a collaborator in the translation project, that the reediting of this text was a collective endeavor, achieved with the assistance of others who collated, translated, and ultimately printed this revised edition of a classic text. On the meaning of anonymity in the context of eighteenth-century authorship, see Mary Terrall, "The Uses of Anonymity in the Age of Reason," in *Scientific Authorship*, ed. Mario Biagioli and Peter Galison (Chicago: University of Chicago Press, 2003), 91–112.

15. "Préface du Traducteur," *Histoire des Incas*, ix.

16. Ibid.

17. Ibid.

18. See Lynn Hunt, *The Family Romance of the French Revolution* (Berkeley and Los Angeles: University of California Press, 1992); David A. Bell, *The Cult of the Nation in France: Inventing Nationalism, 1680–1800* (Cambridge: Harvard University Press, 2001), 19.

19. Among other things, he discussed the shared doctrines of a single God, the deity's eternal and immutable presence, the immortality of the soul, and the notion of resurrection.

20. "Préface du Traducteur," *Histoire des Incas*, xiv.

21. Ibid., xv.

22. René Louis de Voyer de Paulmy d'Argenson, *Journal et mémoires,* ed. E.-J.-B. Rathery (Paris: J. Renouard, 1859), 3:159 (19 May 1739).

23. "Préface du Traducteur," *Histoire des Incas*, xx.

24. Cited in Steven L. Kaplan, "The Famine Plot Persuasion in Eighteenth-Century France," *Transactions of the American Philosophical Society 72*, no. 3 (1982). The link between bread and cultural politics during the early modern period, and the wide-ranging impact of acute subsistence crises that occurred during the years leading up to the Revolution, are recognized as staple features of early modern French society and have also been studied by Kaplan in *Bread, Politics, and Political Economy in the Reign of Louis XV* (The Hague: Martinus Nijhoff, 1976) and *The Bakers of Paris and the Bread Question, 1700–1775* (Durham: Duke University Press, 1996).

25. As Kaplan argues with great conviction and persuasiveness, a "famine plot persuasion" and the social convulsions that accompanied it took "a deep hold of the French consciousness (and unconsciousness) in the old regime and [became] a durable part of the collective memory and mentality." Kaplan, "Famine Plot Persuasion," 62.

26. Marie-Noëlle Bourguet has shown that there was an explicit connection between overseas travel and subsistence problems in the French metropole. See Bourguet, "La collecte du monde: voyage et histoire naturelle (fin XVIIème siècle–début XIXème siècle)," in *Le Muséum au premier siècle de son histoire,* ed. Claude Blanckaert et al. (Paris: Muséum national d'Histoire naturelle, 1997), 184. For a discussion of the importance of alimentary products to the French and Spanish overseas expeditions, see also Jean-Pierre Clément, "Réflexions sur la politique scientifique française vis-à-vis de l'Amérique espagnole au siècle des Lumières," in *Nouveau Monde et renouveau de l'histoire naturelle* (Paris: Presses de l'Université de la Sorbonne nouvelle-Paris III, 1994), 3:131–59.

27. For more on these early expeditions, see Paul Fournier, *Voyages et découvertes scientifiques des missionnaires naturalistes français à travers le monde pendant cinq siècles, XVe à XXe siècles* (Paris: P. Lechevalier & Fils, 1932); James E. McClellan, *Colonialism and Science: Saint Domingue in the Old Regime* (Baltimore: Johns Hopkins University Press, 1992).

28. It was during Fagon's tenure as "médecin du Roi" that the intendancy of the Jardin du Roi came under the médecin's jurisdiction. In 1732 the intendancy was permanently separated from the "médecin du Roi."

29. James McClellan has argued convincingly that as plantation systems expanded during the eighteenth century, European scientific communities, including the French, British, and Dutch, became increasingly interested in cultivating non-European species for incorporation into large-scale production systems. McClellan calls this system "applied" or economic botany, and describes how nations often sought to create applied botanical gardens to wrest control of particular species from other nations that held effective monopolies over certain products. McClellan, *Colonialism and Science,* 147–62. Pierre Poivre, Pierre Barrère, Jean-François Artur, and J.-B.-C. Aublet are among the most important names associated with the implantation of an active network of gardeners and botanists in France's overseas colonies. For a discussion of Pierre Poivre's role in implementing French economic and "environmental" policy in the Mauritius Islands, see Richard Grove, *Green Imperialism* (Cambridge: Cambridge University Press, 1995), esp. 168–263.

30. Guy de la Brosse, *L'Ovvertvre dv Iardin Royal de Paris, Povr la Demonstration des Plantes Medecinales* (Paris: Jacques Dugast, 1640), 16.

31. Louis Feuillée, *Journal des observations physiques, mathematiques et botaniques, faites par l'ordre du roy sur les côtes orientales de l'Amerique méridionale, & dans les Indes Occidentales, depuis l'année 1707. jusques en 1712* (Paris: P. Giffart, 1714–25).

32. Ibid., 3:4.

33. Feuillée, *Histoire des plantes medicinales,* 2:707.

34. Ibid., 2:7.

35. Benjamin Franklin, *Expériences et observations sur l'électricité faites à Philadelphie*

en Amérique, trans. Thomas-François Dalibard (Paris: Durand, 1752). For more on Dalibard's role in the electricity experiments in France, see Cohen, *Franklin and Newton*; Michel Lopez, "La caractérisation de l'électricité dans la foudre du XVIIIe siècle par Thomas-François Dalibard, un physicien français méconnu," *Actes du XIe colloque Forum Industrie de l'Université du Maine* (Le Mans, 1999).

36. Thomas-François Dalibard, *Floræ Parisiensis Prodromus, ou Catalogue des Plantes qui naissent dans les environs de Paris, rapportées sous les Dénominations Modernes & Anciennes, & arrangées suivant la Méthode séxuelle de M. Linnæus* (Paris: Durand, Pissot, 1749).

37. As cited in Yves Laissus, "Jardin du Roi," in *Enseignement et diffusion des sciences au XVIIIe siècle,* ed. René Taton (Paris: Hermann, 1964), 293.

38. Hothouses had already been in existence at the Jardin du Roi prior to 1732, but according to Fontenelle they were in poor shape: "foreign Plants became thin within the poorly maintained Hothouses, and were discarded; when these Plants perished, it was permanent, they were not replaced; even the breaches in the enclosing walls were left unrepaired, [and] large Plots of land lay fallow." Fontenelle, "Éloge de M. du Fay," *Mémoires de l'Académie Royale des Sciences de 1739* (Paris, 1741), 77.

39. Laissus, "Jardin du Roi," 294.

40. Fontenelle, "Éloge de M. du Fay," 78.

41. Ibid., 78–79.

42. The same was true for the banana tree, which first flowered in Paris in 1741, according to the description in the same chapter: "it is the first to which this has happened in France. The fruit even became fairly large, and almost reached maturity, even though it was closed up in the Hothouse." *Histoire des Incas,* 2:242.

43. Fontenelle, "Éloge de M. du Fay," 79.

44. "Préface," *Histoire des Incas,* xxi. The concern for "L'état présent de cette vaste contrée" is yet another indication of the interest in contemporary affairs.

45. "Préface du Second Volume," *Histoire des Incas,* 2:vii.

46. Ibid., 2:viii.

47. "Asterisme. s. m. terme d'Astronomie, Constellation, assemblage de plusieurs estoiles. *Les asterismes sont marquez sur le globe celeste.*" *Dictionnaire de l'Académie Françoise* (Paris: J. B. Coignard, 1694). D'Alembert, in his article "Astérisme" for the *Encyclopédie,* tersely defines it in a similar way: "signifie en Astronomie, la même chose que constellation." Jean Le Rond d'Alembert, "Astérisme," in *Encyclopédie, ou Dictionnaire raisonné des Sciences, des arts et des métiers,* ed. Denis Diderot and Jean Le Rond d'Alembert (Paris: Briasson, 1751–72), 1:776.

48. Anthony Grafton, personal communication, 11 July 2002.

49. Martin-Dominique Fertel, *La science pratique de l'imprimerie. Contenant des Instructions Tres-Faciles Pour se Perfectionner dans cet art* (Saint Omer: Martin Dominique Fertel, 1723).

50. Ibid., "Préface."

51. *Histoire des Incas,* 2:33.

52. There are several possible candidates for the authorship of this revised section on Inca astronomy, including Etienne-Simon de Gamaches (1672–1756), who published his *Astronomie physique, ou, Principes généraux de la nature appliqués au mecanisme astronomique, et comparés aux principes de la philosophie de M. Newton* (Paris: Jombert, 1740) around this time; Maupertuis, who in 1732 had published his *Discours sur les differentes figures des astres* (Paris: Imprimerie Royale, 1732); and Pierre Bouguer, who had published a set of texts entitled *Entretiens sur la cause de l'inclinaison des orbites des planetes* in 1734, although his absence from Paris during the period 1735–43 makes him the least likely of the three.

53. This section corresponds roughly to chaps. 9–15 of book 8 in Garcilaso's original text. While the placement of this section seems random, organizational schemes that do not conform to our own cultural expectations often seem disorderly and in great disarray, as Robert Darnton has shown. See his "Philosophers Trim the Tree of Knowledge: Epistemological Strategies in the *Encyclopédie*," in *The Great Cat Massacre and Other Episodes in French Cultural History* (New York: Vintage Books, 1985). A plethora of literary scholars have addressed the issue of organization in Garcilaso's *Comentarios reales,* among them Margarita Zamora, *Language, Authority, and Indigenous History in the* Comentarios reales de los Incas (Cambridge: Cambridge University Press, 1988), and Mazzotti, *Coros Mestizos.*

54. There are, of course, important exceptions that lie outside the purview of this essay, focusing as it does more on the internal organization of the 1744 translation than on the method used for converting seventeenth-century Spanish syntax into eighteenth-century French prose.

55. *Histoire des Incas,* 2:207, footnote (*a*).

56. One such example includes a discussion of how the "Indiennes" dyed their hair dark by literally boiling it in a cauldron filled with herbs, part of the section that describes the *Maugei* tree. Footnote (*a*) on p. 210 of the *Histoire des Incas* notes that "Cette coutume n'est cependant pas générale, car les femmes des Collas ont la tête couverte à cause du froid de leur pays," a portion of text that Garcilaso had originally included in his primary text: "Las indias del Perú todas traen el cabello largo y suelto . . . si no son las Collas, que, por el mucho frío que en la tierra dellas haze, la traen cubierta." Garcilaso, *Comentarios reales,* book 8, chap. 13.

57. In fact, the *Voyage d'Amérique* consists of three separate volumes, which together make up the *Journal des observations physiques, mathematiques et botaniques.* The first two volumes were published in 1714, the final volume in 1725. The second volume contains the two *Histoires des plantes medicinales.*

58. Amédée François Frézier, *Voyage de la mer du sud* (Paris: Jean-Geoffroy Nyon, Etienne Ganeau, Jacque Quillau, 1717).

59. Carolus Clusius, *Histoire des plantes en laqvelle est contenve la description entiere des herbes cest a dire, leurs especes, forme, noms, temprerament, vertus & operations: non seulement de celles qui croissent en ce pais, mais aussi des autres estrangeres qui viennent en vsage de medecine* (Antwerp: Jen Loë, 1557).

60. *Histoire des Incas,* 2:216.

61. La Condamine, "Sur l'Arbre du Quinquina," *Mémoires de l'Académie Royale des Sciences* (1738): 226–43.

62. *Histoire des Incas,* 2:270.

63. Ibid., 2:274.

64. Brosse, *L'Ovvertvre dv Iardin Royal de Paris,* 7.

65. The term is Gilles Clément's. See Clément, *Le jardin planétaire* (Paris: Albin Michel, 1999).

66. Denis Diderot, "Prospectus," reproduced in *Discours préliminaire des éditeurs de 1751 et articles de l'Encyclopédie,* ed. Martine Groult (Paris: Champion, 1999).

67. *Histoire des Incas,* 2:250.

68. Ibid., 2:217.

Recovering
The French Convert

Views of the French and the Uses of
Anti-Catholicism in Early America

Thomas S. Kidd

Historians today know a great deal more about the history of the book in the Atlantic world than they did twenty years ago, particularly with the publication of the first volume of the American Antiquarian Society's magisterial *History of the Book in America* series, *The Colonial Book in the Atlantic World*. Although our knowledge has increased dramatically, the eighteenth-century book *The French Convert* still languishes in almost total obscurity. This widely reprinted chapbook, which eventually ran in more than forty editions in Britain and America, has received scant attention from historians, perhaps partly because of difficulties in assigning it authorship, date, or even initial location of publication. But these qualities make *The French Convert* significant and interesting, even beyond its obvious attractions as a largely forgotten colonial best-seller. A book like *The French Convert* is not text alone but an unpredictable interplay among authors, readers, and printers/publishers. Though textual analysis has a place in book history, it alone does not suffice to explain the historical uses of a book.[1] Thus both this book's text and the history of its many printings reveal important trends in Anglo-American print domains and consumer interests during the eighteenth century.[2] This article offers a case study of *The French Convert* and its career in print in order to consider two larger topics of interest: the changing but enduring influence of anti-Catholicism in early American culture, and the ways in which American views of the French conditioned *The French Convert*'s uses.[3]

The French Convert told the story of the French noblewoman Deidamia's conversion from Catholicism to Protestantism, and its anti-Catholic tropes proved an excellent complement to the growing hostility among Britons toward French Catholicism, first during the early eighteenth century and then later during the era of the American and French Revolutions. Protestantism had been implicitly anti-Catholic since the Reformation, but British anti-Catholicism became much sharper beginning in 1689, with the coming of the imperial wars between Catholic France and Protestant Britain. The deposal of the Catholic king James II by William of Orange had secured Britain's official commitment to Protestantism, which in turn had set the stage for a generation of world war between the nascent French and British empires. These were not simply wars for political or mercantile hegemony, but the Protestant and Catholic powers saw the fate of world Christianity hanging in their balance. On both sides, the print trades helped create and service an apocalyptic hostility between them with hosts of anti-Catholic tracts, sermons, and stories such as *The French Convert*.[4] Later, in the 1770s and '80s, the French alliance with American revolutionaries no doubt complicated Anglo-American anti-Catholicism, but nonetheless many remained culturally anti-Catholic and rejoiced to see the French throw off the shackles of "priestcraft" in the French Revolution. Many Americans saw Catholicism as the inveterate enemy of republicanism and liberty, which helps explain the resurgent popularity of *The French Convert* in the 1790s. Understanding the historical context and various uses of anti-Catholicism in early America goes a long way toward explaining the enduring popularity of Deidamia's story.

Though *The French Convert* underwent some revisions during its two hundred years of printing history, the basic narrative remained the same: it told the story of the noble French woman Deidamia, "a Young Lady of Quality . . . , whose Beauty and Vertue were equally attractive." Beautiful, intelligent, and chaste, Deidamia was lacking in only one respect: knowledge of the true religion.[5] In fact, though anti-Catholic literature did not lack for misogynist tropes, Deidamia represented the French woman as innocent heroine, waiting only to be liberated from the clutches of priestcraft.[6]

Deidamia learns about Protestantism from her Huguenot gardener, Bernard. Her husband is away in the military, and while one might expect an absent husband and a present gardener to lead to more salacious activities, Bernard remains utterly innocent: he is the vehicle of Protestant doctrine and little more. This contrasts sharply with the role played by the book's Franciscan priest, Antonio, who burns "with Lustful desires to enjoy the tender Beauties of the fair Deidamia" (34). Antonio fills the stereotype of the lecherous, conniving predator, a role priests often played in English anti-Catholic literature and would continue to play in American nativist anti-Catholicism. As the popular British anti-Catholic tract *A Protestant's Resolution* (printed in Boston, 1746) put it, "the Popish doctrine forbidding [priests] to marry, is a devilish and wicked Doctrine . . . it leads to much Leudness and Villany, as Fornication, Adultery, Incest, Sodomy, Murder, &c. Because this Doctrine is a Badge of Antichrist."[7] In the Protestant stereotype, priests like Antonio used their clerical authority to prey sexually on innocents like Deidamia. This standard anticlerical characterization represents an earlier version of the "seducer motif" that became central to the moral lessons of early American novels such as Charles Brockden Brown's *Wieland* (1798) and Susanna Rowson's *Charlotte Temple* (1791).[8]

Ignorant of Antonio's predatory designs (or similar ones by her household steward, Fronovius), Deidamia sets out on the path to Protestantism after she overhears Bernard reading from the book of Romans and praying. He thanks God that he has been saved from the "Ignorance and Superstition" that holds much of Europe in its sway. Deidamia listens with interest, but her yet-strong "Zeal for the Romish Religion" leads her to rebuke Bernard for disparaging Catholicism. Bernard replies that he does not fear exposure and tells her that the Church forbids reading Scripture only because the Bible would expose "their Worldly Interest, plainly discovering their Errors, gross Idolatries." She rebukes him again but retires, contemplating what he has said (17–20).

On their next meeting, Deidamia begins to question Bernard about his religion, and here the book moves into what amounts to a Protestant catechism against Catholicism. Anglo-American Protestants had ready access to these sorts of catechisms in many forms: the Westminster Confession of Faith, the standard confession used by British dissenters, identified the Pope as the Antichrist, for instance. But the American colonists also had access to anti-Catholic texts such as *A Protestant's Resolution,* mentioned above, and Cotton Mather's *The Fall of Babylon. A Short and Plain Catechism which Detects & Confutes the Principles of Popery* (Boston, 1707). When Deidamia asks Bernard what he considers the foundation of his religion, he responds that Scripture alone "can Warrant the Truth of any Profession." The Catholic Church, by contrast, teaches that the laity should have no access to the Scriptures and should heed only the hierarchy's testimony as to God's truth. He argues that this has led the Church into all manner of errors and heresies, including "Divine Adoration" of angels and saints and the doctrines of transubstantiation and purgatory. Bernard convinces her of the hypocrisy of the Catholic Church and "the Cheat of pretended Miracles, and Relicks, the imposing on People with Pardons and Indulgences to get Money; the Whoredoms, Murthers and Incests of many Popes, Cardinals and Prelates of the Romish Church; their Unreasonableness in prohibiting Priests Marriage, which is immediately appointed by God, and the allowing them by Canons and Decrees the Embraces of Concubines, or to commit adultery" (22, 30).

After Bernard leaves, the priest Antonio arrives, right on cue, and tries to seduce Deidamia. She promptly throws Antonio out of her house, convinced now that Bernard is correct in his evaluation of priests (30–32). In the classic Protestant liberatory trope, Deidamia secures her own French Bible and begins to read it with Bernard's assistance.[9] Protestant treatises against Catholicism routinely argued that plain study of the Scriptures would always reveal the truth. As Cotton Mather wrote in *The Fall of Babylon,* "by the Judgment of the Sacred Scripture only (not by any Man, or Church pretending to Infallibility) must all Doubts in Religion be determined."[10]

Antonio continues to spy on Deidamia, hoping to catch her in an affair with Bernard, but instead he overhears her praying, thanking God that he has delivered her from "those Antichristian Errors wherein I have lived since my Child-hood." Antonio is delighted, thinking that he can use her conversion to coerce her into submitting to his lustful designs. Deidamia still refuses to give in, however (40–41). Antonio reveals to Deidamia's horrified parents that she has become a Protestant and proposes that she be detained in a nunnery. The steward Fronovius and Antonio then arrange for two criminals to kidnap Deidamia, but the kidnappers decide to rape and murder her instead. "Heaven interposed," however, and when the two rapists begin to fight over who will go first, one is killed and the other wounded, giving Deidamia her chance to run away (53–54). Deidamia is saved by a generous Huguenot couple and convinces her returning husband to convert as well. Fronovius is hanged for raping a woman, and Antonio falls "Distracted" with guilt, being sure that he will be damned to hell for what he has done. He eventually commits suicide by bashing his head against a wall (79). Here, as in other early American novels that employ the seducer motif, the predators fall prey to the consequences of their own sin.[11]

To further connect the account of Deidamia to the real-life sufferings of French Huguenots, printers of *The French Convert* often appended "A Brief Account of the Present Persecution of the French Protestants." In the colonies and in New England particularly, the news was regularly filled with updates on the condition of these fellow Protestants, from the 1685 revocation of the Edict of Nantes onward. After Boston's John Campbell inaugurated domestic newspaper publishing with the *Boston News-Letter* in 1704, the Huguenots' troubles were standard fare in his publication. In 1704, for instance, Campbell printed a letter from a Huguenot leader reporting a victory against the royal army and demanding that "the Protestant Religion should be re-established in Languedoc, and that those who are in the Galleys or in Prison for that Religion, should be set at Liberty." The writer thought the Camisards' defeat of the Royalists was providential, noting that they lost few men in the latest battle because "God fought for us; He overthrew our Enemies with all their Devilish Devices."[12] Colonial ministers also regularly reminded their congregants of the fate of the Huguenots. The fictional account of Deidamia, along with the details of the persecution, helped meet an ongoing demand for such information.[13] The "Brief Account" appended to *The French Convert* attributed the Huguenots' troubles to "the restless Malice of the Great Enemy of Mankind against the Church of God," and noted that no other Protestant group in Europe had suffered more at the hands of "Blood thirsty Papists" (80). The account described how some were thrown in the galleys, while others were put in "nasty Dungeons and Holes, full of Mire and Dirt." Despite their terrible circumstances, these courageous Protestants "glorify'd GOD in their Sufferings," making them a heroic example to the world Protestant movement (81–82).

To portray the book as directly produced by the courageous French Protestants, *The French Convert*'s publishers always advertised it as having been penned by a French Protestant pastor, one A. D'Auborn, and it was probably first published in London in 1696. Scholars have doubted both points, and have speculated that an English or even a colonial American writer might have written it. It is not clear whether D'Auborn was a real person or an invented pseudonym. Furthermore, though always listed as having been published originally by London's John Gwillim, some have argued that the appearance and construction of the earliest version available hints at a Boston manufacture and publication.[14] In any case, there can be no doubt as to *The French Convert*'s popularity and its distinguished publication record. It almost certainly was printed in Boston as early as 1708, and it became noted New York printer John Peter Zenger's first independently printed book in 1725. By 1897 it had gone through at least twenty-one American and twenty-five British editions.[15] We know then a good deal not only about the text of *The French Convert* but also the locations and years of printing, and from these we may ascertain some of the text's uses. As is often the case, we know little about what readers thought of the book, but the printing record suffices to show that *The French Convert* played on pervasive anti-Catholic sensibilities to entertain readers not only in metropolitan London and provincial Boston, New York, and Philadelphia, but in outlying towns such as Walpole, New Hampshire,[16] and even Buffalo, New York, where it seems to have become the first locally printed book in 1812. A survey of the book's printing record will help us understand the local conditions under which the book became popular, and will also help introduce us to colonial and Atlantic print domains in which authorship was often indeterminate and in which local printers responded to changing interests to sell their wares.[17]

The French Convert's publishing history lies in the interstices between premodern and modern publishing practices, and this is particularly evident from the author "D'Auborn," who appears to exist only within the book itself. One can see here a striking example of the lack of emphasis on authorial rights and profits under the premodern patronage system, especially if one assumes that the author of the book was English and took no profits whatsoever from the many American editions. In fact, the standard presentation of the book (as seen in the earliest edition, ostensibly 1696) subordinates "D'Auborn's" role in the production of the book to the bookseller's and reader's roles. Gwillim (if he was the original publisher) constructed a narrative to explain his own reception of the text, which he claimed to have received from one "R. D.," who received it from D'Auborn. R. D. wrote to Gwillim that he was looking for an English bookseller of integrity to take control of the manuscript, not knowing whether he should just circulate the manuscript or actually print it. He suspected that putting it in print would be "most for God's Glory," and he assured Gwillim that D'Auborn's account was reliable.

This explanation of source and authorship lends an air of providence to the text, a sense that God had ordained its emergence in the print market, obscuring the profit motive of the bookseller, whether he was Gwillim or one of the many British and American peddlers who sold editions of it. The book's producers downplayed the author function to add divine sanction to the story and allow the author-to-printer transmission to seem only a continuation of the purposes God had for the narrative. Books could gain credibility not only through their antiquity or the credibility of the author but through the appearance of divine agency in bringing them to print, so that the market fades from view and God's hand comes to the fore, sanctifying the transmission of the narrative into print and then into the bookstores and peddlers' hands.[18]

Whether or not readers believed that *The French Convert* was a "true" story, as it asserted, the book clearly served in the colonies and early republic not only to entertain but also to confirm existing impressions about the heroic Huguenots, lecherous Catholic priests, and damnable French Catholics. Combining these types with an adventure story featuring treachery, lust, and Protestant heroism made *The French Convert* a great marketing success throughout the British Atlantic world.

Beginning in the 1680s, American readers learned how Catholic France had begun vicious persecution of the Huguenots, quartering dragoons in

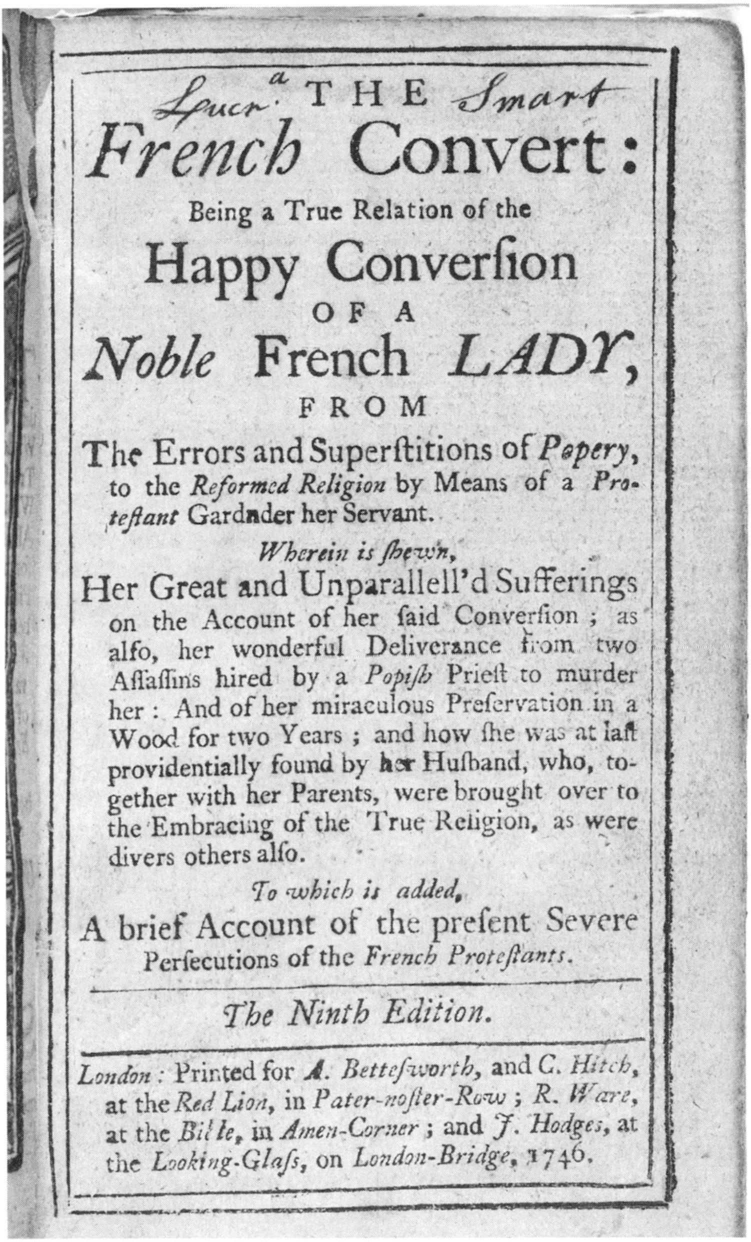

Leuer[a] THE *Smart*

French Convert:

Being a True Relation of the

Happy Conversion

O F A

Noble French *LADY,*

F R O M

The Errors and Superstitions of *Popery,*
to the *Reformed Religion* by Means of a *Protestant* Gardner her Servant.

Wherein is shewn,

Her Great and Unparallell'd Sufferings
on the Account of her said Conversion ; as
also, her wonderful Deliverance from two
Assassins hired by a *Popish* Priest to murder
her : And of her miraculous Preservation in a
Wood for two Years ; and how she was at last
providentially found by her Husband, who, together with her Parents, were brought over to
the Embracing of the True Religion, as were
divers others also.

To which is added,

A brief Account of the present Severe
Persecutions of the *French Protestants.*

The Ninth Edition.

London : Printed for *A. Bettesworth,* and *C. Hitch,*
at the *Red Lion,* in *Pater-noster-Row* ; *R. Ware,*
at the *Bible,* in *Amen-Corner* ; and *J. Hodges,* at
the *Looking-Glass,* on *London-Bridge,* 1746.

Figure 1. Title page of *The French Convert* (London, 1746), by
permission of Harry Ransom Humanities Research Center,
University of Texas at Austin.

Protestant homes and trying to force conversions to Catholicism. Eventually Louis XIV's anti-Protestant crusade culminated in the revocation of the Edict of Nantes, a 1598 decree that had protected the rights of religious dissenters. French Protestantism, already desperately weakened by persecution, almost completely collapsed after 1685. Beginning in 1695, however, war began between the holdout Camisards and the French government forces, who were trying to stamp out Protestant resistance once and for all, and this resistance movement proved highly interesting to American observers. The dissenters of New England, who considered themselves in common cause with the persecuted Protestants of Europe, watched with particular interest. Reverend Nicholas Noyes of Salem argued in his 1698 election sermon that "It were Infidelity to conclude that God hath done with the Protestant People, and his Witnesses in Germany, Bohemia, Hungarra, France, the Valleys of the Piedmont; and many other places in Europe: where for his Name and Gospel sake they have been Killed all the day long."[19] The prospect of a French Protestant remnant held considerable attraction, representing persecuted martyrs of the world Protestant cause.[20] Surely not coincidentally, the first edition of *The French Convert* probably appeared in London in 1696, and the first American edition appeared in 1708.

Reports from France concerning the Camisard revolt and the Huguenot persecutions were regular fare in Campbell's *Boston News-Letter*. As prospects for French Protestants looked increasingly bleak and increasing numbers fled France, New Englanders also followed accounts of their movements in London and America, including New England.[21] Colonial pastors regularly called for prayer and sympathy for the Huguenots, warning the people that they could easily become the next victims should the French succeed in their North American ambitions. John Danforth, pastor at Dorchester, Massachusetts, told his congregation and reading audience in 1716 to thank God they had not yet met the fate of the French Protestants, that "Our ministers are not Banished, nor our Children (excepting a few in Captivity) forced from us, and brought up in Soul-Destroying Popery; Nor our Assemblies broken up, nor Dragoons let in upon us, to Torture us a thousand ways, to Compel us to Blaspheme & Abjure our Holy Religion. . . . Do we Escape the Woful Day, because of our Godliness and Righteousness, that is greater than theirs? No verily."[22]

New Englanders and New Yorkers also had firsthand experience with Huguenots for a generation after the revocation of the Edict of Nantes, as thousands made their way to Boston, New York, and smaller settlements such as Oxford, Massachusetts. Many Bostonians appreciated the beneficence of Huguenots in Massachusetts such as Andrew and Peter Faneuil.[23] The French Protestant pastor Andrew Le Mercier became a figure of some considerable influence in Boston and led the French church there until its dissolution in 1748.[24] As Jon Butler has noted, however, the Huguenots' numbers in America were overall not very large and their communities quickly assimilated religiously and ethnically. But the image of the persecuted French Protestant remained powerful enough to help sustain printings of *The French Convert* through the mid-eighteenth century.

A survey of the printing record of the chapbook also reminds us, however, that local printers' marketing decisions are often the key element in the survival of a book, much more so than authorial credit or reliability. The story of the uses of *The French Convert* also shows the nuances of a book's "fixity" in the colonial context: although the narrative and packaging were essentially the same from place to place, interest in the book changed from a fascination with French Huguenots to an anti-Catholic celebration of the French Revolution. Following its publishing record is like following a map of the progress of print markets in the colonies and early republic, as the "village Enlightenment" not only made outlying townspeople more conversant with the produced knowledge of the Atlantic world, but made them cosmopolitan consumers of, among other things, books sold by the peddlers and publishers representing that broader market.[25] And so it was that residents in Hudson, New York, or Amherst, New Hampshire, could buy or hear Deidamia's enduring story.

The first known publisher of *The French Convert* in the American colonies was Boston's John Phillips, who was also a major publisher of Cotton Mather's and Benjamin Colman's works and therefore a promoter of two of Boston's leading pastors and advocates of Protestant internationalism. Phillips's printing of *The French Convert* in 1725 fed the existing interest in Boston concerning the French Huguenots.[26] Likewise, Boston bookbinder and dealer Thomas Rand arranged for the prolific printers Daniel Fowle and Gamaliel Rogers to print a 1744 edition, supplying the same market that bought titles by Jonathan Edwards, Benjamin Colman, and George Whitefield, leading evangelicals and internationalists in the 1730s and 1740s. It is not clear from this catalogue of imprints that Rogers and Fowle themselves were evangelicals; they also printed works by opponents of the religious awakenings such as Charles Chauncy. But *The French Convert* fit well into their strategy of making profits from the evangelical book and pamphlet trade.[27]

Later, *The French Convert* seems to have been published to serve new markets and interests. It was sometimes paired with various accounts of the persecution of not only French but also Scots-Irish Protestants, or with other religious pieces. In 1758 the "12th edition" of *The French Convert* came from Philadelphia publisher William Dunlap. Dunlap, an Anglican from Ulster who had married Benjamin Franklin's wife's niece, took over for Franklin as Philadelphia's postmaster and a bookseller when Franklin departed for England in 1757.[28] His edition of *The French Convert* came at the height of the Seven Years' War in North America, which saw France, Britain, and their respective Native American allies fight for imperial domination of North America. The fall of Quebec, the key moment of the North American theater of the war, came in 1759 and led to new heights of American anti-Catholicism. Timothy Green Jr. also published an edition in the same environment of anti–French-Catholic sentiment in New London, Connecticut, in 1762, and Zechariah Fowle, brother of Daniel and patron of Isaiah Thomas, printed an edition even in the postwar depression of 1766.

After the Seven Years' War, *The French Convert* declined in popularity but then reemerged in the 1790s as a response to the French Revolution. Colonists, and particularly New Englanders, had taken various paths of justifying that which previously would have been unthinkable: the French alliance during the Revolution. Anti-Catholicism waned in some circles, while others explained that the spirit of Antichrist could live even in British Protestants, especially in those who sought to destroy the liberty of the American colonists. Some argued that God could deliver the colonists even through the agency of an evil state such as France, just as God had used Cyrus to deliver Israel from the Babylonians. Still others explained that France was no longer all that Catholic anyway, and that association with the Protestant colonists might help bring about the downfall of the rotten edifice of French Catholicism, making France open finally to the spread of the true gospel.[29] In any case, hostility to French Catholicism persisted and was transformed into a strain that celebrated the anticlericalism of the French Revolution. And, as Gary Nash has shown, the American clergy and the presses that gave them public voice were nearly unanimous in their celebration of the Revolution as the destroyer of French popery. This sentiment would persist until 1795, when fears of Deism, French corruption, and social chaos began to turn many clerics toward a Federalist critique of the Revolution's excesses.[30] The early enthusiasm for the Revolution also proved welcoming to *The French Convert,* which went through at least nine new printings in three years between 1793 and 1795.

Samuel Hall, who specialized in sermons, catechisms, chapbooks, and children's literature, and published the first Boston edition of Samuel Richardson's *Clarissa* (1795), also sold *The French Convert* in 1793, with another edition following in 1794. Hall had earlier supplied interest in French culture by publishing the weekly *Courier de Boston* for J. Nancrede, who taught French at Harvard, evidence of the growing print market for things French.[31] New York also saw editions in 1793 and 1795, while the third Timothy Green of the New London printing family brought out another edition for that port town in 1794.

Most striking, however, in this spate of new editions were those coming to inland towns and villages that could support printing presses only after the revolutionary diaspora. Haverhill, Massachusetts, Exeter, New Hampshire, Amherst, New Hampshire, and Hudson, New York, all saw editions between 1794 and 1796. Isaiah Thomas arranged for a Walpole, New Hampshire, edition in 1794 as well. New Haven and Hartford, Connecticut, Brookfield, Massachusetts, and Catskill, New York, all produced editions in 1798.[32] These revealed the trend toward local "country printing" along the rivers and thoroughfares connecting the interior towns to the large port cities and the broader Atlantic world beyond. The country printers facilitated the transformation of the northwestern Revolutionary frontiers into significantly commercialized regions with newly integrated communication networks.[33] The development of local markets for printed goods more fully integrated these towns with the Atlantic trade systems, which in the early republic increasingly siphoned through the large national publishing houses of Boston and New York. But in the transition period between the Revolution and the rise of the large-scale publishing house, agents and peddlers like Isaiah Thomas brought the outlying towns into the print market by selling imprints of *The French Convert* and similar texts.[34]

It is instructive to compare this reemergence of *The French Convert* with the simultaneous popularity of James Bicheno's two-part *Signs of the Times; or, The Overthrow of the Papal Tyranny in France, the Prelude of Destruction to Popery and Despotism; but of Peace to Mankind.* Susan Juster has described Bicheno as a "republican prophet" in England and a defender of the French and American Revolutions. He and other more radical writers, such as Richard Brothers, gained circulation in the 1790s in America among many of the same peddlers and readers who bought *The French Convert*, a market anticipating the divinely ordained destruction of priestcraft. Providence, Rhode Island, saw Bicheno's first American edition in 1794, while Hudson and Catskill, New York, among others, saw printings of the first volume in 1795, and Philadelphia received another run of the book in 1797.[35] Bicheno's popularity lay in his interpretation of prophecy in simple, accessible language, and he believed that reason made prophecy clear to his wide audience. In fact, he believed, a reasonable and simple approach to prophecy would destroy the hold of priestcraft.[36] The literary climate in Britain and America in the 1790s, inclined to see in the French Revolution the destruction of popery by reason, could also find literary heroes for that cause in Deidamia and especially in Bernard, the simple Bible-reading gardener.

The French Convert did not disappear in the nineteenth century, either, as editions came out in New York and New Hampshire in the 1830s. In 1863 *Harper's New Monthly Magazine* printed a book inventory from a newly discovered pastor's will of 1711 in the Connecticut valley. The editors used the occasion to lament the Puritans' reading habits and to wonder at how the dour Puritan of the early eighteenth century became the enlightened New Englander of the mid-nineteenth. In the inventory, among forty-one other books that were almost exclusively theological, was *The French Convert.* "The Puritan was an uncharitable Christian," the editor noted, who "would have burnt a Romish priest with the same solemn zest that he hung a Quaker."[37] Colonial hostility toward French Catholicism, born of centuries of conflict between Protestant and Catholic but newly energized by the imperial wars of the eighteenth century, found its most widespread literary expression in *The French Convert.* The publishing history of this book demonstrates that increasing engagement with the book in the Atlantic world also generated increasing interest in the ongoing world contest for the fate of Christianity. Among the issues of greatest interest in this battle was the question of religion in France. If Protestantism could win out there, as it did, in microcosm, with Deidamia's conversion, then the greatest military power behind the Roman Church would fall, and, ultimately, Protestantism would win the war for Christianity in Europe and the world, a victory with millennial implications.

In the late eighteenth century, this global conflict was transformed into a war between reason and tradition, liberty and slavery, democracy and monarchy. This does not necessarily mean, however, that for the new American democrats the matter had become "secular." In the revolutionary climate of the late eighteenth century, *The French Convert* served a reading public interested in the liberating effects of the French and American Revolutions. Many Americans believed that the destruction of corrupt priestcraft of the sort represented by Antonio, and the empowerment of the people, figured in the simple Protestant gardener Bernard, were crucial to the success of the American and French Revolutions. For those influenced by both Jeffersonian democracy and evangelicalism, *The French Convert* may have served to narrate the impulse that the revolutions unleashed: a great and perhaps apocalyptic flood of liberty, democracy, and Protestant freedom.[38]

Neither sacred nor secular, fact nor fiction, *The French Convert* and its career tell us a great deal about the categories of literature that might become best-sellers in early America. How did this book function in the print market? We can draw several conclusions: first, it was clearly meant to entertain, and its narrative of heroic Christian womanhood against Romish licentiousness and treachery met this demand well. Second, it was meant to edify, in the tradition of *Foxe's Book of Martyrs,* as the story reinforced Protestant ideology and assured readers that with a fair hearing Protestantism would win over Catholicism. Finally, *The French Convert* helped personalize the ongoing struggle between Protestant and Catholic powers as seen in the wars from 1689 to 1763. Later it helped fix the issues at stake in the American and French Revolutions, which were often couched as wars against priestcraft and, in the case of the French, against Romanism specifically.

That this book's uses were so pliable and instructive makes its current obscurity all the more undeserved. *The French Convert* was uniquely suited to take advantage of the developing print market of eighteenth-century America, which was becoming more integrated with Atlantic world trade systems. This trade increasingly demanded tales of adventure and virtue, which helped Britons and Americans categorize the ongoing violence and ideological conflict between them and the French empire, or between them and the enemies of democracy. Despite the changing views of the French and the uses of anti-Catholicism, the story of Bernard and Deidamia persisted in popularity, revealing again how books cannot be taken out of context but must be understood as they are written, produced, sold, and read in ever-shifting print domains.

Notes

1. Roger Chartier, *The Order of Books: Readers, Authors, and Libraries in Europe Between the Fourteenth and Eighteenth Centuries,* trans. Lydia Cochrane (Stanford: Stanford University Press, 1994), 7–10.

2. On the concept of print "domains," see Adrian Johns, *The Nature of the Book: Print and Knowledge in the Making* (Chicago: University of Chicago Press, 1998), 59–61.

3. The question of print's role in history has been a matter of vigorous debate, especially between Adrian Johns and Elizabeth Eisenstein, "AHR Forum: How Revolutionary Was the Print Revolution?" *American Historical Review* 107 (Feb. 2002): 84–128.

4. W. R. Ward, *Christianity Under the Ancien Régime, 1648–1789* (New York: Cambridge University Press, 1999), 6. On British anti-Catholicism generally, see among others Raymond Tumbleson, *Catholicism in the English Protestant Imagination: Nationalism, Religion, and Literature, 1660–1745* (New York: Cambridge University Press, 1998); Linda Colley, *Britons: Forging the Nation, 1707–1837* (New Haven: Yale University Press, 1992), 11–54; Francis Cogliano, *No King, No Popery: Anti-Catholicism in Revolutionary New England* (Westport, Conn.: Greenwood Press, 1995).

5. *The French Convert,* 2d ed. (London: Gwillim, 1699?), 2. I use this edition, contained in *Early English Books,* with the understanding that some doubt the place and date of publication. I do believe that it was written by an English author, not the French pastor "D'Auborn," as it advertises. Further citations of this edition appear parenthetically in the text.

6. Frances Dolan has shown that anti-Catholic English literature in the seventeenth century tended to portray women as more easily duped by Catholicism than men because of their illiteracy and ignorance. Frances E. Dolan, *Whores of Babylon: Catholicism, Gender, and Seventeenth-Century Print Culture* (Ithaca: Cornell University Press, 1999), 27–28.

7. *A Protestant's Resolution* (Boston, 1746), 18–19, cited in Cogliano, *No King, No Popery,* 10–11. *A Protestant's Resolution* was apparently printed first in late seventeenth-century London but saw editions in Edinburgh and Dublin. An 1831 printing in London

is listed as the thirty-seventh edition. See also Dolan, *Whores of Babylon,* 85–94; Jenny Franchot, *Roads to Rome: The Antebellum Protestant Encounter with Catholicism* (Berkeley and Los Angeles: University of California Press, 1994), 122–25.

8. Cathy Davidson, *Revolution and the Word: The Rise of the Novel in America* (New York: Oxford University Press, 1986), 136–37.

9. Hugh Amory and David Hall, eds., *The Colonial Book in the Atlantic World,* vol. 1 of *The History of the Book in America* (New York: Cambridge University Press, 2000), 2–3.

10. Cotton Mather, *The Fall of Babylon* (Boston, 1707), 4.

11. Davidson, *Revolution and the Word,* 137.

12. *Boston News-Letter,* 9 Oct. 1704, no. 10.

13. On news of the Huguenots in provincial Boston, see Thomas S. Kidd, "'Let Hell and Rome Do Their Worst': World News, Anti-Catholicism, and International Protestantism in Early Eighteenth-Century Boston," *New England Quarterly* 76 (June 2003): 265–90.

14. For details on these questions, see Mary Daniels, ed., *French Literature in American Translation: A Bibliographical Survey of Books and Pamphlets Printed in the United States from 1688 Through 1820* (New York: Garland, 1977), 484–88.

15. On Zenger's edition, see Linda M. Kruger, "The New York City Book Trade, 1725–1750" (D.L.S. diss., Columbia University, 1980), 77–79. Thanks to Joyce Goodfriend for sharing this reference with me. An 1897 American version published by J. & M. Robertson is listed as the twenty-first edition. A 1795 version published in Blackburn, England, by J. Waterworth is listed as the thirteenth edition, but it was published at least nine more times in Britain after this version.

16. On Walpole, books, and the "Village Enlightenment," see David Jaffee, "The Village Enlightenment in New England, 1760–1820," *William and Mary Quarterly,* 3rd ser., 47 (July 1990): 333, 339; William Gilmore, *Reading Becomes a Necessity of Life: Material and Cultural Life in Rural New England, 1780–1835* (Knoxville: University of Tennessee Press, 1989), 59.

17. Johns, *Nature of the Book,* 30, 59.

18. Chartier, *Order of Books,* 58–59.

19. Nicholas Noyes, *New-Englands Duty and Interest* (Boston, 1698), 67.

20. On the Camisard revolt and the Huguenot persecution, especially in their international context, see among others Ward, *Christianity Under the Ancien Régime,* 14–20; Marco Sioli, "Huguenot Traditions in the Mountains of Kentucky: Daniel Trabue's Memories," *Journal of American History* 84 (March 1998): 1313–23; Linda Frey and Marsha Frey, *Societies in Upheaval: Insurrections in France, Hungary, and Spain in the Early Eighteenth Century* (Westport, Conn.: Greenwood Press, 1987), 37–60; Jon Butler, *The Huguenots in America: A Refugee People in New World Society* (Cambridge: Harvard University Press, 1983), 13–40; Clarke Garrett, *Spirit Possession and Popular Religion: From the Camisards to the Shakers* (Baltimore: Johns Hopkins University Press, 1987), 15–34; Ronald Knox, *Enthusiasm: A Chapter in the History of Religion,* reprint ed. (Notre Dame: University of Notre Dame Press, 1994), 356–71.

21. See, for instance, *News-Letter,* 1 Sept. 1707, no. 177, on Huguenots in London, and March 6, 1709, no. 257, on French Protestants in Oxford, Massachusetts. Sometimes the French Protestant presence in New England could be unsettling, as Marco Sioli explains in "Huguenot Traditions," citing a General Court resolution from 1692 that suspected that some of the refugees only "pretend to be Protestants" and were actually Catholics (1322).

22. John Danforth, *Judgment Begun at the House of God* (Boston, 1716), 42–43.

23. On the Faneuils, see Jonathan Beagle, "Remembering Peter Faneuil: Yankees, Huguenots, and Ethnicity in Boston, 1743–1900," *New England Quarterly* 75 (Sept. 2002): 389–93.

24. Butler, *Huguenots in America,* 71–90.

25. Jaffee, "Village Enlightenment," 334; T. H. Breen, "'Baubles of Britain': The American and Consumer Revolutions of the Eighteenth Century," *Past and Present,* no. 119 (May 1988): 73–104.

26. Benjamin Franklin V, ed., *Boston Printers, Publishers, and Booksellers: 1640–1800* (Boston: G. K. Hall, 1980), 406–7.

27. Ibid., 181–85, 421, 426–31.

28. Amory and Hall, *Colonial Book in the Atlantic World,* 272–73; Isaiah Thomas, *The History of Printing in America* (reprint, New York: Weathervane Books, 1970), 386–87.

29. Cogliano, *No King, No Popery,* 74–78; Charles Hanson, *Necessary Virtue: The Pragmatic Origins of Religious Liberty in New England* (Charlottesville: University Press of Virginia, 1998), 119–53.

30. Gary Nash, "The American Clergy and the French Revolution," *William and Mary Quarterly,* 3rd ser., 22 (July 1965): 392–412. Nash noted *The French Convert* as evidence of sympathies for the Revolution (394).

31. Franklin, *Boston Printers,* 271; Thomas, *History of Printing,* 177.

32. Other extant American editions include Philadelphia (1801); Burlington, N.J. (1802); New York (1804); Wilmington, Del. (1806); [Unknown] (1812); Buffalo, N.Y. (1812); Utica, N.Y. (1831); Concord, N.H. (1833); [Unknown] (J. & M. Robertson, 1896). Extant British editions besides the advertised London 1696 and 1699 editions include London (1719, c. 1725, 1740?, 1746, 1757, 1784?); Glasgow (1762, 1808); Bolton (1786); Berwick (1795); Burslem (1808); Tewksbury (unknown); London (c. 1780, 1785, 1790?); Blackburn (1795?); Leeds (1806, 1808, 1809, 1812); Edinburgh (1811); Manchester (1823, 1828).

33. Gilmore, *Reading Becomes a Necessity,* 17–18.

34. Amory and Hall, *Colonial Book in the Atlantic World,* 316.

35. Other American editions are Baltimore (1794); Albany (1795), which was then sold in Lansingburgh, Cooperstown, and Schenectady in addition to the above New York locations; West Springfield, Mass. (1796). Part II was sold in Philadelphia (1797).

36. Susan Juster, "Demagogues or Mystagogues? Gender and the Language of Prophecy in the Age of Democratic Revolutions," *American Historical Review* 104 (Dec. 1999): 1568–70.

37. *Harper's New Monthly Magazine* 27 (Oct. 1863), 711–12.

38. Nathan Hatch, *The Democratization of American Christianity* (New Haven: Yale University Press, 1989), 184–85.

"*JANE EYRE* FEVER"

Deciphering the Astonishing Popular Success of Charlotte Brontë in Antebellum America

Cree LeFavour

On 4 September 1848, Charlotte Brontë wrote her friend Mary Taylor to report that "*Jane Eyre* had had a great run in America." This was good news, of course, and yet it created a complication that required immediate attention. As a result of the success of *Jane Eyre,* Charlotte wrote, an American publisher, Harper & Brothers, "had consequently bid high for the first sheets of the next work by 'Currer Bell' which they [Brontë's publisher, Smith & Elder] had promised to let him have." These "first sheets" would have secured for Harper, for a small fee paid to the British publisher, the proofs of the next manuscript, enabling them to issue the first edition of the novel in the American market if not "courtesy of the trade" rights to its "exclusive" publication there.[1]

The problem arose when Harper & Brothers wrote back to complain that they had been cheated; the new work by "Currer Bell" was being issued in America by their main rival in publishing, T. B. Peterson. Harper & Brothers "asked to know the meaning of such false play." Enclosed in the letter was a note from Acton and Ellis Bell's rather shady British publisher, Thomas Newby, "affirming that 'to the best of his belief' *Jane Eyre, Wuthering Heights—Agnes Grey—*and *The Tenant of Wildfell Hall—*(the new work) were all the production of one writer." As Charlotte wrote,

"This was a lie, as Newby had been told repeatedly that they were the productions of three different authors."[2]

In fact, of course, the novel in question, *The Tenant of Wildfell Hall*
(1848), was written by Charlotte's sister, Anne (Acton), and thus could not
possibly be promised to Harper & Brothers as "the next work by 'Currer
Bell.'" Newby, it seems, "wanted to make a dishonest move in the game—
to make the Public & 'the Trade' believe he had got hold of 'Currer Bell'
and thus cheat Smith & Elder." This attempt to confuse the American publisher not only deprived Charlotte's publishers of their rightful claim to a
share in the profits of her next work, but enabled Newby to take advantage of Currer Bell's success in the United States by selling her sister's work
under her name there. And while the Brontës' representation of themselves
as "gentlemen" is well known, the confusion over the author's identity in
this incident takes the mixing of the Brontës' identities a step further. It
thus sets the stage for my discussion of *Jane Eyre*'s reception in the United
States, a reception characterized by the novel's widespread popularity, by
critical ambivalence, and by a remarkably public conflation of the author
and her fictional subject, Jane. I suggest that the circumstances surrounding the novel's reception in the United States exemplify the fluidity of literary genres and the relationship between that fluidity and the value and
significance of reading for women. Finally, I argue that the epistemological
confusion arising from the combined effects of the genre's, protagonist's and
author's ambiguous status conspires to place the reader in a particularly
charged and intimate relation to the first-person narrator of *Jane Eyre*.

The fierce competition between the two rival American publishers illus-
trates the level of their interest in securing the first rights to publish any
new work by the author of the smashingly successful *Jane Eyre,* but it also
underlines the extent of these publishers' investment in reprints and their
desire to secure for themselves a central position in the reprint game. The
incident involving *Jane Eyre* thus provides an opening for a broader discussion of the centrality of British reprints in the American market during
the immediate antebellum period and how this previously neglected segment
of print culture alters our understanding of popular "American" fiction of
the period.[3] While critics in recent years have revised and widened the
scope of "popular" fiction in the United States, departing from the static
image long dominated by "sentimental" women's writing, a crucial piece
is still missing—British reprints.[4] As the critic David Reynolds notes, "the
sentimental-domestic fiction that is thought to have conquered the popular
market [in the 1830–60 period] actually ran a distant second to more sensational genres."[5] Without disputing Reynolds's point, I want to add that
British reprints—and I take *Jane Eyre* as a representative example—necessarily shift our understanding of the composition, balance, and tenor of all

genres of popular fiction during this period, including the still significant "domestic" or "women's" fiction Reynolds wants to place in proper perspective as a portion of the market. British reprints must be included in any consideration that claims to account for popular reading or to characterize the popular writing of the period. And if British reprints are counted, as they must be in American popular cultural history, this history needs to be rewritten insofar as their presence alters the frame and the foundation of the field.

While I hope to complicate antebellum print culture by adding this crucial British dimension, I use the text and reception of *Jane Eyre* to demonstrate this point and at the same time to show how the ambiguity surrounding the author and the text's genre place the novel's particular engagement in the American literary market in a highly charged relation to its readers.[6] The two points cannot be separated because the reception of *Jane Eyre* in the United States was, at least in part, dependent on the novel's British origins and its status as a reprint. In other words, *Jane Eyre* is useful in making a broader point about British reprints and their significance to American literary history precisely because of the initial ambiguity surrounding the author and because, as a reprint, the novel was available in a range of inexpensive editions, making it possible for the widest range of readers to gain access to it. In particular, *Jane Eyre* is useful in analyzing the cultural status of novels and the often fuzzy boundaries separating them from other genres because Brontë's early death (1855), and Gaskell's subsequent biography of her (1857), provide additional, immediate evidence of how Jane and Charlotte were perceived by the public. Because *Jane Eyre* is represented as an "autobiography" and narrated in the first person by a protagonist who uses books and reading to great effect, the text invites the reader into a particularly close identification with it. For these reasons, *Jane Eyre* provides an exemplary study of the ambiguous and rapidly shifting status of imaginative prose in the United States during this period, while at the same time demonstrating the centrality of reprints and the effect one novel's status as a reprint had on its reception.

The porous borders between fiction and nonfiction demonstrated by the scope and tenor of *Jane Eyre*'s critical reception in the United States (was it truth or fiction? autobiography or novel? moral? immoral?) help to explain white middle-class literary culture's virtual obsession with the ideological work of reading and the unformed boundaries between the subject reading the text and the subject *in* the text. A literary culture in the process of negotiating the boundaries between fiction and nonfiction is exemplified by the identification with character inside and outside texts in the case of *Jane Eyre,* and with a confusion between the two and their ontological status. Discerning these borders, as I will show, was important

to the novel's reception and to its perceived moral value for female readers. *Jane Eyre,* as a feminine/feminist coming-of-age story, invites a close
identification with the text's protagonist, Jane, just as Brontë's representation of Jane's process of self formation lends the novel to a particularly
intense and productive reading practice that occurs both inside and outside
of the text. *Jane Eyre* is one example of "women's intense engagement
with books," an engagement central to female subjectivity—and I submit
that reading and representations of reading or "figuring" (reading/writing/
drawing) inside and outside of texts are crucial to understanding female
subjectivity in this culture.[7]

I am certainly not the first to argue that books and reading were absolutely central to antebellum culture, just as I am not alone in pointing out
the tentative status of the novel during this period. Yet our understanding
of these issues remains one-dimensional in the absence of British reprints
that formed such a crucial part of the fiction market.[8] Thanks in part to the
disciplinary orientation of American literary history, the history of British
reprints during the crucial "American Renaissance" years has scarcely been
investigated.[9] *Jane Eyre,* in part because of its insistence on implicating
readers in its formation of subjectivity through reading, and in part because
of the institutional and material conditions surrounding its reproduction
in the United States as an inexpensive reprint, provides an opening into
the complex dynamics of how books were positioned as pedagogical tools,
and into precisely how that pedagogy was perceived. At the same time, the
novel sheds light on the status of British fiction in the American market and
on its undifferentiated place as a key part of popular reading.

The conflict between the American publishers Harper & Brothers and T. B.
Peterson over reprint rights to the next work "by the author of *Jane Eyre*"
was quickly resolved by an adventure Charlotte details in her letter as
altogether ridiculous, in which she and Anne "set out ourselves after tea"
to walk "through a thunderstorm" to Leeds. The two then "whirled up
by the Night train to London with the view of proving our separate identity to Smith and Elder and confronting Newby with his lie." Charlotte
describes "Mr. Newby being anathematized, I fear with undue vehemence"
for his attempted deception.[10] And while this surprise presentation may
have ended the confusion and doubt over the author(s) in question in
Britain and affirmed Smith & Elder's right to Charlotte's work, confusion
reigned in America for at least as long as it took the news to travel by ship.
As *Godey's Lady's Book* remarked in an October 1848 announcement of a
new edition of *Poems* by Currer, Ellis, and Acton Bell: "Another mysterious book by these mysterious authors. When we have positive evidence
that the three names above mentioned do not pertain to one and the same

individual, we will announce the fact, and not before."[11] In the notice for the Harper edition of *The Tenant of Wildfell Hall, Godey's* announced, in mild complaint, that "the author, or authors, of *Jane Eyre* and *Wuthering Heights* seem determined to keep up the mystery surrounding them," while the reviewer for the *Harbinger* (1848) wrote provocatively, "we think we see 'a beard under the muffler.' Jane Eyre, rare and excellent though she may be, is not to our mind a genuine woman."[12] The *North American Review,* in its wide-ranging survey of "Novels of the Season" in October 1848, speculated on the various admixtures of male and female, whether Acton, Ellis, or Currer Bell, who had produced *Jane Eyre:* "The work bears the marks of more than one mind and one sex, and has more variety than either of the novels which claim to have been written by Acton. The family mind is strikingly peculiar, giving a strong impression of unity, but it is still male and female."[13] And while "the mystery" of "the Bells" was clarified in the United States sometime in the next year, not until the early 1850s did the Brontës begin to appear under their correct names, works, and genders.

While American publishers were competing for advance sheets of new works by the Brontës, *Jane Eyre* had been secured by none. As a result, the novel was reprinted in the United States in the late 1840s and throughout the 1850s by multiple publishers. And while only the printings by Harper & Brothers and by Wilkins, Carter & Co. are listed in O. A. Roorbach's *Bibliotheca Americana* through 1858, many other editions were available, as evidenced by extant dated copies, by the *National Union Catalog,* and by advertisements in the back pages of novels, in popular magazines and newspapers, and in the book-trade paper *American Publishers' Circular.* The dated printings listed in the *National Union Catalog* include two from the German firm Tauchnitz (1848, 1850); three from Derby & Jackson (1857, 1858, 1860); the initial printing from Wilkins, Carter & Co.; and multiple Harper & Brothers printings.[14] The Harper reprint history is compelling in establishing the popularity of *Jane Eyre,* as it includes five dated printings, in 1848, 1850, 1855, 1857, and 1859.[15] But the geographical range of publishers that reprinted *Jane Eyre* is perhaps most compelling, for it includes not only the initial rivals from New York (Harper) and Philadelphia (Peterson) but also a one-volume edition from Boston's William D. Ticknor & Co. that served as the review copy for *Graham's Magazine* in May 1848, and another from the Cincinnati publisher, H. B. Pearson, which advertised *Jane Eyre* for sale at its "Great Western Cheap Publication Depot" in Cincinnati in 1854.[16] Evidence from *Godey's* and the *National Era* also shows that the New York publisher Derby & Jackson issued *Jane Eyre* in 1856 and 1860, although these copies have not survived in the library system and are thus not listed in the *National Union*

Catalog.[17] The steady demand for the novel is indicated by its extensive reprinting in the United States, although the size of each print run is not known.[18]

Unlike W. M. Thackeray's popular *Vanity Fair,* however, which was secured under the custom known as "courtesy of the trade" by a single publisher, there is strong evidence that the popularity of *Jane Eyre* should be understood in market terms.[19] For, unlike many American novels of the period, *Jane Eyre* was available for twenty-five cents in the Harper and Pearson editions.[20] Estimated by a contemporary source to have sold 80,000 copies by 1853, *Jane Eyre* continued to sell well through the 1850s, in no small part because it was available from multiple publishers at competitive prices.[21] Indeed, as the prominent Philadelphia publisher Henry C. Carey argues in his antiprotectionist polemic *Letters on International Copyright, Jane Eyre* sold for less than a quarter of the price of another popular book of the era, Fanny Fern's *Fern Leaves* (1853).[22] *Fern Leaves,* however, was protected by American copyright law, and consequently sold for $1.25, a price that reflects the publisher's obligation to pay the author at least a minimal fee. The low price of books not limited in reproduction under the "courtesy of the trade" practice made reprints widely available to the expanding American reading public. Carey, one of the leading spokesmen for the democratic virtues of freely reprinting foreign books, argued in favor of the interests of American readers in his *Letters on International Copyright:* "The common school makes a great demand for school-books, and both make a great demand for newspapers. All of these combine to make a demand for cheap books among an immense and influential portion of our community, that cannot yet afford to pay $1.25 for *Fern Leaves* or for the *Reveries of a Bachelor,* although they can well afford 25 cents for a number of *Harper's Magazine,* or for *Jane Eyre.*"[23] As Carey's comment indicates, even five years after the first appearance of *Jane Eyre,* the novel remained in the public consciousness. This is also reflected in the way *Jane Eyre* was repeatedly invoked as the standard by which to judge new novels by "the Bells."

While the conservative women's magazine *Godey's* compared *The Tenant of Wildfell Hall* (1848) to the "rare attractiveness of the best portions of *Jane Eyre,*" its 1848 announcement of *Wuthering Heights* took the comparison further by attributing *Wuthering Heights* to Charlotte and, not surprisingly, expressing a certain consternation at the differences between the two novels: "*Wuthering Heights.* A Novel. By the author of *Jane Eyre.* . . . If the title-page tells the truth, the author of *Jane Eyre* is wonderfully versatile, for no two books are more dissimilar in style and sentiment. There seems to be as much mystery about the author as there was about the Great Unknown. But, man or woman, Currer Bell or Harriet Martineau, he or she is the novelist of the hour."[24] In the early notices, among them the 1849 announcement of *Shirley* in the *National Era*, the author was praised as "possess[ing] extraordinary power and originality," while the reviewer noted that "as a novelist, *he* stands alone the imitator of nobody—and yet he has plenty of faults" (emphasis added).[25] A year later the same newspaper compared *Agnes Grey* unfavorably to *Jane Eyre* and *Shirley*, writing that "to us it seems to fall short of the writer's acknowledged ability."[26]

By 1848 *Jane Eyre* was widely noticed in the press. Critics praised the novel's distinctive voice almost unanimously. Charles Dana, writing for the Brook Farm paper *The Harbinger* in January 1848, noted "a freshness and originality, a manly vigor of style, a penetration into the secrets of human character . . . which fully justify the high and unanimous praise it has received from the British press."[27] As this comment indicates, the American response to the novel was, at least in part, predicated on the British response; many British reviews were reprinted in the American press and American reviews responded implicitly to the British reaction to the novel. The flow of print in both directions across the Atlantic, that is, was so free that to draw a hard distinction, even by the 1850s, between British and American literary cultures is to superimpose a far more developed literary and cultural identity on Americans than they possessed. This is not to say that Americans were unaware of reprinting as a practice or that they didn't distinguish between British reviews and their own when reprint information was made available to them.[28] The evidence shows quite the opposite; readers were very much aware of the mechanisms of cultural production, including the availability of multiple editions and their relative merits. As a writer for *Graham's Magazine* noted in an 1848 review of the Ticknor & Co. edition, "Few novels published within the last ten years have made so great a stir among readers of all classes as this. The Harpers have sold a vast number of their cheap reprint, and we have here to notice its appearance in the old duodecimo shape, with large type and white paper. That the work bears unmistakable marks of power and originality cannot be questioned."

And yet the reviews were not all favorable; as the writer for *Graham's* put it, "there has been a great deal of discussion about the morality of this part [Rochester and scenes at Thornfield] of the novel."[29] While these reservations about the morality of the book were fairly widespread, as we shall see, the dominant reaction to the novel is best captured by *Peterson's Ladies National Magazine* (1848), whose reviewer wrote: "Who is the author of this original and most powerful novel? There is something fresh in the style and in the plot, that would bespeak the first outbreak of genius upon the world. It is a story that once read is never forgotten; the heroine with her history is so original, so out of the common way in all she thinks, says, and does, that nothing could drive her from the mind. Gentle reader, get *Jane Eyere* [*sic*] before you are a day older, it is worth your while we assure you."[30] Charlotte and her novel were indeed American favorites and remained so in later years. While novels by the other Brontë sisters were greeted with enthusiasm, none surpassed *Jane Eyre,* which consistently served as the standard by which their work was judged. As a writer for *Putnam's Magazine* commented in 1853, "A new work by the author of *Jane Eyre* is announced, a novel of course,—but whether of the *Jane Eyre,* or the *Wildfell Hall* School, is not told. How many readers who were thrilled by that thrilling series of romances put forth by the 'Bells,' will look forward with eagerness to this forthcoming volume. A new *Uncle Tom's Cabin* could not produce more sensation in the literary world."[31] While this was perhaps hyperbolic, *Jane Eyre* was, as the writer put it, a "sensation" that did not fade from the public's consciousness. As E. P. Whipple humorously noted in the *North American Review* in October 1848, "the New England States were visited by a distressing mental epidemic, passing under the name of the 'Jane Eyre fever,' which defied all the usual nostrums of the established doctors of criticism."[32]

Jane Eyre did not simply provide the standard of popularity prior to the proverbial best-sellers of the early 1850s by Susan Warner and Harriet Beecher Stowe, or merely the measure by which new novels by "the Bells" or "the firm Bell & Co." were judged. It was also frequently the standard by which to measure the importance of new American and British novels, in terms of both potential sales and cultural or literary significance.[33] Throughout the 1850s and into the 1860s, British and American novels were repeatedly referred to as reminiscent of *Jane Eyre* and were "recommended as equal to *Jane Eyre*" or found "not so interesting as *Jane Eyre*."[34] A *Boston Post* writer proclaimed Jedediah Huntington's scandalous 1849 novel *Lady Alice: or, the New Una* "decidedly a work of genius . . . both peculiar and original. Nothing since *Jane Eyre* is more so."[35] A critic for the *Springfield Daily Republican* declared in 1851 that "No novel published in this country since *Jane Eyre* has been read more universally, and with more universal approval than *Frank Farleigh*."[36]

Jane Eyre, and to a lesser extent the Brontë sisters as a group, became shorthand for a certain narrative style. Other novels were referred to as being of "that school," "like that of the *Jane Eyre* novels," or of "the *Jane Eyre* school."[37] Although it is not clear precisely how to characterize this "style" or "school," the comments seem to refer in equal parts to content (an orphaned girl coming to a romantic end in marriage) and to a somewhat direct or unsentimental style used as a selling point. In other words, when advertisers or reviewers referred to other novels as being "like" *Jane Eyre,* they were in part, I think, attempting to capitalize on the minor scandal the novel caused with its unvarnished style, and on its useful straddling of the line between what was perceived as moral and immoral fiction.[38] When a reviewer used *Jane Eyre* as an adjective in a review of a new novel by Caroline Chessbro—it had "*Jane Eyre* earnestness"—or when another novel, "edited" by Charles J. Peterson (*The Valley Farm; or, the Autobiography of an Orphan*) was advertised as "a companion to *Jane Eyre*," these references may have loosely identified the content and style of these books, but, perhaps more to the point, these books benefited by their association with the popular Brontë novel.[39] As one writer, in a letter to the *National Era* inquiring about the serial of the *Autobiography of a New England Girl*, explained, "It is creating quite a sensation in this city, and I predict for it a large sale. It is certainly the finest thing we have had since the days of *Jane Eyre*."[40] *Jane Eyre*'s penetration of the market was so widespread that even the madwoman Grace Poole entered the American vernacular, with a mysterious boarder in Thomas Gunn's *Physiology of New York Boarding Houses*, "generally" known "by the soubriquet of 'Grace Poole,' after the twin Mystery in *Jane Eyre*."[41]

Jane Eyre's currency as a literary referent perhaps helped to keep the novel in the public consciousness and certainly improved its sales throughout the 1850s. As late as 1864 a new novel by Amelia Edwards was said to "remind" the writer "strongly of *Jane Eyre*." "This announcement alone is a sufficient assurance for the interest of its pages."[42] But the cultural and literary durability of *Jane Eyre* over the course of the decade can be explained not only as a reflection of the novel's cheapness and widespread availability as a reprint but as a result of the not uncommon conflation of Charlotte Brontë the person with Jane Eyre the literary character. In fact, I want to suggest that the novel's widespread popularity was entangled in this confusion, and that readers' identification with the "autobiographical" subject explains a great deal about the particularly powerful appeal of the novel in the United States.[43] The confusion about the literary status of the novel, which was encouraged by its subtitle, "an Autobiography," reflects the unstable borders separating fiction, biography, and autobiography during this period.[44] As Barbara Hochman has argued, the desire to identify the text with the author may be understood as a specific reading practice of the antebellum period. What she calls "reading for the author" or "friendly reading"—that is, a mode of reading in which "the idea of continuity between literary discourse and authorial presence" is a given—helps explain the identification of Jane with Charlotte.[45] But there is more to the identification of Jane with Charlotte than a conventional assumption of authorial presence; the commingling of the two indicates a degree of closeness to books and to the process of reading that is at once specific to a female reader's experience of *Jane Eyre* and indicative of broader trends in female culture that made the experience of books of all kinds particularly important instruments for the development of female subjectivity. The tension between the positive moral effects of reading and the potentially negative ones underlines the extent to which reading, domesticity, and femininity were in tension. And the onus was on books and their authors to demonstrate that the dangerously sympathetic modes of reading in which women engaged (a kind of sympathetic reading practice fueled by the ambiguous genre identification of various texts) be undertaken for moral purposes and with the edification of family, comfort, and the domestic sphere in mind.[46]

In Brontë's novel, reading is a trope that gathers the multiple selves within and outside the text by calling on the pleasure of vision, language, and marking (drawing and writing) as an expression of a specifically female freedom.[47] "Reading," as I use the term, is thus a metaphor for diverse modes of production and reproduction that denies the historical construction of the metaphysical split between language and image, deploying instead the two registers simultaneously so as to disrupt the values attached to each.[48] To identify Charlotte with Jane, then, is to enter into the logic of the novel's narration of the way that, within the text, Jane reads and writes and draws herself into existence.[49]

Even after the author had been publicly identified as Charlotte Brontë and not as Currer Bell, an identification that took place in 1850 at the latest with the explanatory preface to *Wuthering Heights,* the public was nonetheless encouraged, if encouragement was needed, to read *Jane Eyre* as "autobiography." This reading was encouraged not only by the subtitle but by the first-person narration and, most significantly, by the very bookish qualities of Jane's coming of age, discussed below. *Jane Eyre* both fueled and frustrated identification with its intriguing, perhaps scandalous, disembodied author. The conflation of Jane and Charlotte was encouraged by the ambiguous information about the author at her debut, and was refueled by the coincidences in circumstance between Charlotte's life and that of her character, Jane, the most notable of these being that both Charlotte and Jane attended a rather unhealthy girl's boarding school and that each served briefly as a governess.[50] This confusion between the author and her literary character, simultaneously an indication of particular reading conventions and a result of the book's ambiguous status, was not confined to the United States. Indeed, many of the reports linking Jane and Charlotte originated in the British press and were reprinted in the American.[51] But it is worth noting that as a British reprint in the United States, the author and the book were one step further removed, and that the novel was kept a mystery somewhat longer under the guise of Currer Bell. More important, the book and its author remained dislocated throughout publication, with multiple editions and reprintings in various cities, from Boston to New York to Philadelphia. Lacking a body and a fixed location, the circumstances of the novel's publication in the United States in multiple editions and under varied titles and authors only heightened the interest in and confusion over the novel. Some editions were simply titled *Jane Eyre* and others *Jane Eyre: An Autobiography*, the early editions listing "Currer Bell," as the author or editor and later editions naming "Charlotte Brontë," or both.[52] And while Scott Casper argues that "readers and certainly critics understood biography as a distinct literary form," they did not necessarily so easily recognize the difference between autobiographies and novels.[53]

It was not only "unsophisticated" readers who identified Jane with Charlotte. Far from it, in fact, as the example of the author Catharine Maria Sedgwick indicates. In a letter of 1853 Sedgwick wrote that she greatly admired *Vilette* and asked if it was not "one of the great books of the time." Seeing "nerves of such delicate fineness of edge" in the protagonists of both *Vilette* and *Jane Eyre*, she amalgamated the two and equated their characters with Brontë's, declaring, "Whether she calls herself Jane Eyre, or Lucy Snowe, it does not matter—it is Miss Brontë."[54] *Vilette* provided another opportunity to replace Jane with Brontë. As *Frederick Douglass' Paper* speculated in 1853, in an announcement of the Harper edition of the novel, "It is rumored that the authoress was once a governess in the family of a distinguished literary man in England, whose wife (we have heard) is deranged. Perchance *Jane Eyre* is not all fiction."[55] Indeed, as *Godey's* noted in its 1855 obituary, "'Jane Eyre' was naturally and universally supposed to be Charlotte herself."[56]

Not surprisingly, given the overwhelming popularity of *Jane Eyre* and the undue interest in the true identities of all three Brontës, discussion of *Jane Eyre* and Charlotte herself was renewed at her death in 1855. The American response to the news of Charlotte's death underscores the cultural and literary significance her novel and its protagonist had achieved. As *Godey's* "Editor's Table" announced in 1855: "Charlotte Brontë, or Currer Bell, author of *Jane Eyre, Shirley,* and *Vilette,* is dead! This sad event has touched the hearts of American women as for the death of a dear sister."[57] *Frederick Douglass' Paper* ran two long obituaries in 1855, the first reprinted from the *London Morning News* and the other from *Sharpe's London Magazine*.[58] *Godey's* dedicated half of a lengthy retrospective on the three previous years' "literary losses" to her. And although the piece eulogized five other authors, Brontë was "most lamented of all."[59] As the writer of the *Harper's* feature "Easy Chair" asked his readers in 1855, "Have we not a tear for Charlotte Brontë? Shall that short, sad, solitary life end so soon—shall the promise and hope of noble and earnest books perish suddenly and forever—and we fling no flower on the grave? Who has read Jane Eyre? who has not? and shall that eye be closed and we not feel the darkness?"[60] The outpouring of grief for Charlotte provides some idea not only of her importance in the United States but of the centrality of fiction in the social and cultural life of the period.

Charlotte's death, life, and work were reassessed with the publication, in 1857, of Elizabeth Gaskell's *Life of Charlotte Brontë.*[61] Gaskell's book was widely reviewed and reprinted in the United States and large portions of it were excerpted in magazines and newspapers, including *Godey's, Putnam's,* and the *National Era.*[62] And yet the biography seems to have complicated, and even reinforced, the mixing of Charlotte and Jane in the public mind. As a writer for the *Democratic Review* commented in a brief 1857 review of Gaskell's biography:

> Any biography of Charlotte Brontë that could fail to interest us would be a curiosity of literature more strange than any preserved by the Disraeli in his collection of literary wonders. The authoress of *Jane Eyre, Vilette,* and *Shirley* has left a monument more enduring than adamant—as mysterious as the Egyptian sphinx—in the eye and memory of an admiring world; and the reader who has perused those weird and sybilline romances, must be either more or less than human if he experience no desire to acquaint himself with the character and modifying circumstances of the fountain from which those enigmatic streams were poured.[63]

As this comment suggests, the interest was widespread and the explanation or "modifying circumstances" much sought after. Another critic wrote in *Littell's Living Age,* "It is as if the churchyard-air they breathed, and the strong cold breezes from the moor, had entered into their very nature, and made them what they were." In other words, while "all had strong imaginations, not one of them had the power for a moment to get rid of her individuality. It permeates with its subtle presence every page they write." The writer added, in discussing Charlotte's desire for society, "Jane Eyre speaks for her in this as in many things."[64] And a British review noted, "ordinary readers and critics have not failed to discover for themselves that the painful and unnatural isolation of the Brontë family powerfully affected the development of their character, and that Jane Eyre is as faithful a transcript of Charlotte Brontë as an individual can give of herself."[65]

Certainly Gaskell's work removed certain kinds of speculation about Jane as Charlotte or Charlotte as Jane, but it is also worth noting that Gaskell's work is thrown into question by the still contingent status of biography during this period. As Casper writes, "as 'literature,' biographies were always part of a constellation of genres with overlapping conventions, goals, and markets," sharing borders with both novels and history.[66] Thus the same genre ambiguity that fueled speculation about the "real" *Jane Eyre* may have undermined Gaskell's truth claims, particularly given Gaskell's closeness to her subject and her own fictional impulses, as evidenced by her own novels.[67] The assumption of a link between the author's character and experience and those of her characters was explicit and, according to the reviewer for the *North American Review,* even more relevant given Brontë's sex than it otherwise would have been:

> We propose, in the first place to examine the memoirs which Mrs. Gaskell furnishes us, with special reference to those portions which tell most powerfully upon the development of Miss Brontë's mind and heart, and then to turn, with the light thus thrown upon the author, to a scrutiny of her works. We believe that this knowledge of the individual — always more necessary in judging of a woman's comparative position than of a man's, since her sphere of feeling is less rounded by external action — is in a peculiar degree necessary to a full comprehension of Currer Bell's romances. We also believe that many of the criticisms made in times past, in the total absence of such knowledge, would now, were it possible, receive very decided modification, and the general judgement in regard to her works become even more favorable than their popularity proves it to be already.[68]

Indeed, the ongoing "sensation" of *Jane Eyre* the novel and "Jane Eyre/ Charlotte Brontë" the person, and even *Jane Eyre* the play, was focused around American interest in the pathetic figure herself, real or imaginary.[69] As the popular American author Fanny Fern asked in 1857 in *Fresh Leaves:* "Who has not read *Jane Eyre*? And who has not longed to know the personal history of its gifted author?"[70] This history included the details of the controversy surrounding Charlotte's depiction of Chasterton School (both as repeated in Gaskell's biography and as insinuated by the depiction of Lowell School in *Jane Eyre*), which were followed and reprinted in the United States, as well as the criticism of Gaskell's (and Charlotte's) representation of the Rev. Patrick Brontë, Charlotte's father, and the press's response to it.[71] Indeed, the publication of Gaskell's biography provoked a reassessment of Brontë and her work and provides an overview of how she was viewed from a perspective that is still within the era of her popularity, and not from the perspective of twenty or thirty years later, as would have been the case had she not died so young. This reassessment tended to place Charlotte more fully into her fictional world, rather than extricate her from it. As the critic Margaret Sweat wrote of Gaskell's biography in the *North American Review:*

We find in it, not only the satisfaction of an urgent curiosity upon many points of personal history, but a key to Currer Bell's fictions, which sends us to their reperusal with a new and more tender interest. . . . We find the atmosphere of the novels predominating in the "Life,"—the "counterfeit presentment" of persons and incidents known personally or by tradition, placed before us in the romances. . . . The most repulsive and the most contradictory of her fictitious characters prove to be but the careful elaboration of outlines sketched from her own circle of experience.[72]

The biography perhaps softened the reception of *Jane Eyre,* prompting sympathy for Charlotte, who was mourned and pitied for the secluded life she led in "the dreary wilds," as represented by Gaskell, while at the same time excusing, to some extent, the crudeness of some of her incidents and characters. And while nearly ten years after the publication of *Jane Eyre,* she and her novel remained irresistibly appealing and intriguing to many, both Charlotte and Jane remain during this period, particularly in the "female" press, as undeniably significant but nonetheless vaguely objectionable, troublesome figures. Explaining this contradiction is in fact helpful in situating the cultural position novels occupied during this period, and how they, and the practice of reading them, were so deeply implicated in the culture's preoccupation with feminine virtue.

In September 1857 *Godey's* published a lengthy appraisal of Charlotte's life and work, in part excerpted from Gaskell's biography, with an explanation that "the short notice of this in the July number was hardly sufficient to satisfy the readers of our Book." Giving some hint of what is to come, the writer began, "Since the appearance of the Waverly Novels, no work of fiction seems to have seized on the public mind like *Jane Eyre.* The genius which has effected such an impression is undeniable, and is acknowledged by these [*sic*] who offer the strongest objections to the authoress's productions." Charlotte's life was then detailed, using short pieces from Gaskell's biography, until her death in 1855. The writer noted that "Mrs. Gaskell's biography of the author of *Jane Eyre* will be widely read in our country. . . . We do not, therefore, like to notice this work without remarking on the unhealthy tone communicated by the subject." Although they were not affluent, the Brontës "were by no means needy," "nature had endowed them with uncommon abilities," and "they were never without kind and substantial friends." And yet, despite all of this,

The moral conformation of both father and children is undeniable. Each one acted on the others and rendered it impossible for them to be comfortable themselves, or the agents of comfort to others. . . .

Indulging unsocial eccentricities of life, cherishing sick fancies and nervous feelings . . . they neglected the cultivation of that cheerfulness and hopefulness which every Christian should feel bound, in duty to others, if not for his or her own happiness, to strive for. . . . They suffered like martyrs; but they did not try to make themselves amiable.[73]

Somewhat incongruously, Charlotte is accused here of a failure to achieve happiness and, more to the point, of failing to strive to make those around her happy—to be sufficiently "amiable." And while in part the writer seems to be complaining that Charlotte and her family simply failed to conform to normative behavioral standards of the day, there is far more to the complaint than too many rainy walks on the moors in defiance of the rules of health and decorum. I would suggest that the writer's use of the term "comfort" is central to the comment as a whole, insofar as it alerts us to what is really at stake in the criticism.

During the antebellum period, "comfort" represented an idealized state of being as envisioned by white female sentimental culture. The word expressed, but encompassed much more than, an acceptable level of material and/or spiritual well-being. The power of "comfort" as an ideological concept stems from the way it signals a moral and spiritual state marked by stasis.[74] To achieve "comfort" is to cease desiring. As the critic Gillian Brown convincingly argues, feminine self-sacrifice imbues the idealized feminine of the period with an economy that denies desire but grants a "superabundance" of possession. The virtuous woman, according to this logic, is fully self-possessed. "Lack of desire," Brown writes, "reflects the imagined state of possession, that is, the condition of satiety and fulfillment, the goal of the pursuit of happiness. . . . In her self-sufficiency she escapes the fluctuations attendant upon desire and achieves the ideal of the masculine economy: complete self-possession and satisfaction."[75]

Part of what is objectionable about Charlotte (*and* Jane, since the commingling of the two is inescapable) is her failure to be self-sufficient—free of desire; she has failed to achieve comfort (stasis) by failing to seek and attain happiness. This idea is best developed by pairing the *Godey's* reviewer's objection to Charlotte with some of the criticism of *Jane Eyre* the novel and the character, as I think the two converge to reveal the qualities that rendered them both slightly offensive to the dominant sentimental women's culture represented by *Godey's*. Not only does some of this fairly mild criticism explain the objection, it helps us understand the novel in the context of American domesticity and the Christian reform movement, and will bring us at last to a discussion of the novel itself and the broader American literary context.

As we have seen, the initial critical response to *Jane Eyre* was generally positive, with an emphasis on the freshness and originality of the work. And yet, while it served as the standard of comparison for other books, there was controversy over its morality. A reviewer signed T. C. C. in the *American Whig Review* noted this controversy while defending *Jane Eyre*: "Both *Wuthering Heights* and *Jane Eyre* have been reviled for their immoral tendency; the first deservedly enough; the latter, for no good reason that we can see . . . in *Jane Eyre*, every thing tends to the side of virtue. As we read, our breasts are filled with the sombre dogged spirit that chained the maiden to her duties."[76]

Other critics were less forgiving. As Lady Eastlake (Elizabeth Rigby) famously wrote in her exceptionally harsh appraisal of the novel in the *Quarterly Review* (reprinted in the United States anonymously by *The Living Age*): "Jane Eyre is throughout the personification of an unregenerate and undisciplined spirit. . . . It is true Jane does right and exerts great moral strength, but it is the strength of a mere heathen mind which is a law unto itself. No Christian grace is perceptible upon her. She has inherited in fullest measure the worst sin of our fallen nature—the sin of pride. Jane Eyre is proud, and therefore she is ungrateful too."[77] To some extent echoing this comment, another reviewer wrote in *Littell's Living Age* (1848): "Never was there a better hater. Every page burns with moral Jaobinism. 'Unjust, unjust,' is the burden of every reflection upon the things and powers that be."[78] Significantly, Jane Eyre was accused of self-sufficiency, or pride, but not of particular moral transgressions. She failed to submit to conventional authority, relying instead on her own resources as she wandered the moors in search of her own unconventional brand of spiritual salvation.

Because of her failure to submit, the character, the author, and the novel itself were perceived as lacking a certain moral fiber—the resolutely independent spirit of self-making embodied by Jane put her outside the bounds of conventional Christian morality. A notice in the *National Era* cautioned readers against the book for this reason, in a review of the popular American E.D.E.N. Southworth's novel *Retribution* (1849): "*Retribution* reminds us of *Jane Eyre*, and the later productions of that school. It has their strength and sustained intensity, while it embodies, as they can scarcely be said to do, an important moral lesson."[79] Or, as Fern noted in *Fresh Leaves*, "a Boston paper" had called *Jane Eyre* "an immoral book," while she accused the press of making Brontë "the target for slander, envy and misrepresentation."[80] These comments and accusations may also reflect the text's resistance to interpretation on many levels; indeed, the novel offered no easily accessible model for moral behavior or religious belief. As a writer for *Godey's* cautioned in a review of a novel by Elizabeth Stoddard: "It is not such a book as we would place in the hands of the young, whose taste for reading is just forming. Though not precisely of the *Jane Eyre* school, yet, like that and similar novels, there is a morbid tone about it, which is apt to have an unhealthy effect upon the mind, to say nothing of the morals of the reader."[81] Again, the complaint centers on morality but, like the criticism of Charlotte herself, the writer's objection is to something dark and "unhealthy" that remains unexplained. Indeed, the "morbid tone" to which the writer refers is explicitly linked to the "unhealthy effects" on the mind and morals of the reader, indicating again the potentially negative possibilities of exposure to the novel without giving an explicit explanation for their cause.

Of course, novels had been condemned for their baleful influence on the morals of readers at least since Samuel Richardson's *Pamela* (1740).[82] As Nina Baym has argued, the protagonists in many popular novels by female authors "represent instances of character that the authors want their readers to become, while the grippingly affective reading experience is meant to initiate or further the resolve of readers to change themselves."[83] I think Baym is correct that many readers and critics understood novels as an intimate means of implicating readers in a particular moral or philosophical doctrine through their plots and narration. As the editor of the *Harper's* "Easy Chair" column put it in 1855, "When the unavoidable influence of literature is considered, when you remember for a moment that all the young girls cannot devote the leisure of their girlhood to reading tales of life, and character, and feeling, without in some manner confessing their power in their own lives and characters, it will be seen how remarkable a position the female writers hold."[84] The possibilities and the dangers inherent in this process, given the range of reading available, were highly visible in the culture; as such, the impulse to shield female readers from the potentially dangerous effects of such a powerful influence formed an integral part of literary commentary in most forums.

The incentive to police female novel reading is also demonstrated by the debates in advice books, magazines, and newspapers of the period.[85] Reviewers typically offered their judgment of whether a novel was appropriate reading for "ladies" or "young girls," and beginning in 1847 *Godey's* ran a lengthy series of articles entitled "Course of Reading for Ladies." In explaining the purpose of these essays, *Godey's* showed how the internal logic of domesticity was bound up with reading choices, making explicit the link between domestic ideology and reading:

> The foregoing observations are intended as a sort of preface to the counsel we shall give, from month to month, concerning the books we consider most appropriate for our sex. We must never lose sight

of the grand truth, that the development of the human mind and the direction of public opinion are both committed to women. The books we read our children will read also; the sentiments we imbibe from our reading we shall transmit to them. . . . This power is only good so far as it is based on moral and religious truth.[86]

Women were largely responsible for reproducing moral and religious doctrine in the home and, according to *Godey's,* it was this work that ultimately guided the "development of the human mind and the direction of public opinion." From this perspective, very few forms of leisure could be more important or more serious than reading, as it was through reading that the moral sense was developed. Indeed, given their role as the molders of children's minds and morals, women "require that their moral and religious feelings should be early and constantly cultivated."[87]

The central function of moral and religious instruction in domestic ideology helps to explain how and why the role of literature shifted during the antebellum period. White middle-class domesticity and the social practices surrounding its reproduction were constructed as a safe enclave that remained untainted by the marketplace. As literacy expanded, and as women gained access to more and more inexpensive fiction by British and American authors, the sanctity of the home was simultaneously sustained and breached. As women read more prolifically, their exposure to the world outside the home increased exponentially, while at the same time reading and writing played a central, if inconsistent, role in the construction of domesticity as a set of material practices and ideological beliefs. This conflict was by no means resolved during this period, nor was it confined to it. But that these tensions were being worked through over the course of the antebellum period with a particular intensity is shown, in part, by representations of writing and books in the pages of the period's novels.

The anxiety over this conflict, and the stress exhibited in discussions about the influence of reading on feminine character, indicate a cultural shift in the place of books and "fictitious writings." Not only, as Reynolds argues, did religious tracts and sermons begin to take on the narrative contours and generic traits of imaginative literature in the 1830s and 1840s, but, as Richard Brodhead and others have pointed out, fiction and books generally assumed "a newly central place" in the culture in the antebellum period. Novels (and other books) were prominently and conspicuously displayed in the carefully constructed home, which represented "a new place *for* literature among its organizing habits and concerns."[88] The shift in the cultural category to which novels and other "literature" belonged made books newly visible both as revered objects of the domestic home and as objects of use and value within the pages of domestic fiction.[89] As literature and reading emerged as prominent physical and ideological features of the home, books as instruments of instruction became central to maintaining the domestic landscape both inside *and* outside their pages. And while novels remained contested territory, books of all kinds gained in prominence.

I would argue that representations of reading demonstrated the problematic centrality of reading and books in antebellum culture. Because reading was an integral part of the way women constructed themselves, the doubling of the inside/outside relation between reading and representations of it was played out in the pages of novels. The virtual obsession with books, reading, writing, and their uses as the foundation for identity in *Jane Eyre* makes the novel an exemplar of this point, from the opening scene, in which Jane sits "cross-legged, like a Turk," reading Bewick's *History of British Birds*, to her induction into the pains and pleasures of reading through a hateful book such as *The Child's Guide*, and through an intriguingly sophisticated novel such as *Rasselas*. While I lack the space to undertake a full account of the way the text demonstrates this point, let me briefly focus my reading of it with a crucial scene that begins with the salvation Jane finds at Marsh End in the bookish company of Mary and Diana Rivers.

That books, letters, and language(s) fill chapters 30–35 of the novel serves to foreground the centrality of reading in forming Jane's steely but feminine individualism in the final section of the novel. From Jane's first sight of Mary and Diana through the window, "each bent over a book" and comparing "two great volumes between them" as if "consulting a dictionary," Jane is introduced to a new world of intellect, one far more sophisticated than that offered to her by Helen Burns at Lowood (358). Not only does Jane find pleasure in these pursuits, she secures her claim to language—to genteel culture—in the company of two women who are "ladies in every point" (358). "I liked to read what they liked to read" and to "devour the books they lent," Brontë writes of her protagonist (358, 376–77). Of a whole other order than the childhood reading that opens the novel, different even from her education at the hands of Helen Burns, Jane's literary pursuits at Marsh End seem to quell and distract her imagination for a time, rather than fuel it. There are few ghosts or fairies in these chapters, and the decisive one that does appear is the one that carries Jane away from Marsh End to the fairy-tale forests of Ferndean.

Marsh End is important as the final stage of Jane's self-development because it is only at Marsh End, with Diana and Mary, that Jane finally secures herself as a full-fledged individual subject; it is the culmination of a process of claiming the self through literacy. In these chapters Jane prepares for her eventual marriage to Rochester as she acquires more of the education proper to a lady of his (and, soon, her) class. Jane's engagement with books in this phase reconciles the tension between her love for Rochester and her class status. But, far more important, books and reading in these chapters enable the return of the self that repeatedly has been nearly lost, first in the red room, then to Rochester as "idol," and then on the moors to all-devouring Nature, a "self" rescued and strengthened each time by the various technologies and practices of literacy—books, reading, writing, and drawing. Jane's extended stay at Marsh End restores not only her bodily health but the spiritual, mental, and intellectual confidence necessary to a fully developed independent subject. Jane's fresh consciousness of a self that must be preserved, and her firm conviction that there is something to preserve, are all that keep her from the ravages of St. John's cold desire and returns her to where her passion and sexual impulses lead her, to Rochester. Jane's self-conscious knowledge of the importance and delicacy of her internal self—the same self that she has long "communicated" with in solitary contemplation—marks a mature knowledge that has been painfully produced and is finally, jealously guarded by her.

In the context, then, of Brontë's representation of Jane's coming of age through books, Baym's argument that "the protagonists represent instances of the character that the authors want their readers to become" needs to be further developed and perhaps modified insofar as the evidence for this process is to be found in the pages of the novels themselves. Through representations of reading, and the related registers of writing and drawing, women's subjectivity was developed and explored in concert with their moral and intellectual independence. In the case of the reception of *Jane Eyre* in the United States, it is the exchange between the subject *of* the text (Brontë/Jane) and the subject *in* the text (Brontë/Jane/the reader) that simultaneously disperses and authorizes the "I" of *Jane Eyre*. By claiming a distinctive place for the feminine with this "I," one that lies outside and yet works within the masculine literary traditions of autobiography and Romanticism, Brontë's text challenges the passive construction of the female and explicitly encourages the reader to model *her* reading after Jane's.[90] The first-person narrator of *Jane Eyre* thus becomes the source of an intelligible female history of self that belongs not only to Brontë and Brontë's fictional other, Jane, but to the reader of the novel as well. For this self is an active articulation of the female subject that seeks, rather than avoids, language, the literary tradition, and reading/writing as reproduction. By engaging authoritative male discourse without becoming its object, the novel/autobiography claims this authority for the female self by explicitly rejecting female submission to desireless absence.

That *Jane Eyre* did not always sit well with the guardians of female moral development, who viewed their duty as having national significance, is hardly surprising given that Brontë did not load her narrative with the pabulum of religious piety and self-sacrifice that so neatly concealed the substance of Susan Warner's and others' novels, with which it shares so much. And while I think *Jane Eyre* is exceptional in many respects, Jane Tompkins is surely right that "a novel's impact on the culture at large depends not on its escape from the formulaic and derivative, but on its tapping into a storehouse of commonly held assumptions, reproducing what is already there in a typical and familiar form."[91] Brontë's keen articulation of Jane's spiritual and intellectual growth resonated with American readers, whose familiarity with a range of narrative styles, from the sensational writing of E.D.E.N. Southworth to the gloomy reaches of Hawthorne, from the piety and realism of Warner to the gritty sentimentality of Dickens, would have prepared them for Brontë's strangely feminist coming-of-age tale. Perhaps ultimately it was an inkling of Brontë's radical revision of feminine subjectivity that made the guardians of women's culture justifiably nervous about *Jane Eyre*. The often problematic "feminine individualism" that has been so central to contemporary criticism of the novel, and arguably central to *Jane Eyre*'s appeal to female readers since the book's publication in 1847, can best be understood through a reading of Brontë writing Jane that attends to the ways Jane writes herself.[92] For, on separate ontological levels, each explicitly takes possession of language (the first person "I") through a dialectical practice of reading/writing in which writing, by making speech visible, makes the subject legible—literally and metaphorically through the practice of reading. The popularity and reception of *Jane Eyre*, Jane Eyre, and Charlotte Brontë taken together demonstrate an Anglo-American world of reading and books that is far more complicated, and far richer, than a narrowly national consideration would have it. *Jane Eyre* helps us to complete the picture of this period's American literary history, placing both British and American books in more accurate perspective as elements of a materially grounded literary culture.

Notes

1. In the absence of an international copyright law to control the intellectual property of either British or American authors in their respective nations (the law finally passed in 1891), British texts of all kinds were reprinted in the United States, often by many publishers simultaneously. The only restraint on this widespread practice was the "courtesy of the trade," a kind of gentleman's agreement not to infringe on the initial publisher's right to reprint a work. This informal system, which was unevenly implemented and adhered to, served the economic interests of American publishers, since prices and demand fell in a market flooded with multiple editions of a single text. For a detailed discussion of the controversy over copyright and of the political economy and politics of the reprint business in America, see Ezra Greenspan, *George Palmer Putnam: Representative American Publisher* (University Park: Pennsylvania State University Press, 2000); see also Sidney P. Moss, *Charles Dickens' Quarrel with America* (Troy, New York: Whitston Publishing Co., 1984). For an account of this period's efforts to pass a copyright law, see James J. Barnes, *Authors, Publishers, and Politicians: The Quest for*

Anglo-American Copyright Agreement, 1815–1854 (Columbus: Ohio State University Press, 1974).

2. Charlotte Brontë to Mary Taylor, 4 Sept. 1848, Haworth, England, in *The Letters of Charlotte Brontë: With a Selection of Letters from Family and Friends,* vol. 2, ed. Margaret Smith (London: Clarendon Press, 1995), 111–12.

3. T. B. Peterson did not give up its pursuit of the Brontës' works. *Godey's Lady's Book* notes in an 1850 announcement of *Agnes Grey* that "something was due to the enterprise of Mr. Peterson, who received it in proof impressions from the London press, in advance of its publication in that city." See *Godey's Lady's Book* 40 (March 1850): 221, available at http://www.accessible.com/. Accessible Archives is a for-profit database containing, among other things, the full text of *Godey's Lady's Book* (1830–80), as well as a range of African American and abolitionist newspapers, including the *National Era* (1847–60). Like many other databases, including Proquest (*New York Times*) and NAWLD, Accessible Archives requires a password or access through a library subscription. *Godey's,* it is worth noting, was the leading women's magazine in the United States during this period. It was published in Philadelphia from 1830 to 1880.

4. Some extremely interesting work has been done on the links and affinities between British and American writers, although little has been done on reprinting, with the exception of Meredith McGill's *American Literature and the Culture of Reprinting, 1834–1853* (Philadelphia: University of Pennsylvania Press, 2003). Other works focus primarily on British Romantics and American Transcendentalists, most notably Richard Gravil, *Romantic Dialogues: Anglo-American Continuities, 1776–1862* (New York: St. Martin's Press, 2000), and Paul Giles, *Transatlantic Insurrections: British Culture and the Formation of American Literature, 1730–1860* (Philadelphia: University of Pennsylvania Press, 2001). Also of interest but less sophisticated in method are Robert Weisbuch, *Atlantic Double-Cross: American Literature and British Influence in the Age of Emerson* (Chicago: University of Chicago Press, 1986), and Benjamin Lease, *Anglo-American Encounters: England and the Rise of American Literature* (New York: Cambridge University Press, 1981). Other relevant studies of British-American literary relations include Stephen Fender, *Sea Changes: British Emigration and American Literature* (New York: Cambridge University Press, 1992); Frank Thistlewaite, *The Anglo-American Connection in the Early Nineteenth Century* (Philadelphia: University of Pennsylvania Press, 1959); Stephen Spender, *Love-Hate Relations: A Study of Anglo-American Sensibilities* (London: Hamish-Hamilton, 1974). By "reprints" I mean all kinds of British novels, not simply bound books, including serialized editions in magazines and newspapers, as well as the "supplements" so popular in the 1840s. See John W. Tebbel, *A History of Book Publishing in the United States,* 4 vols. (New York: R. R. Bowker, 1972–81), 1:248.

5. David S. Reynolds, *Beneath the American Renaissance: The Subversive Imagination in the Age of Emerson and Melville* (Cambridge: Harvard University Press, 1988), 338.

6. I am using "domestic fiction" and "women's writing" in their broadest sense, primarily as a way of designating fiction that was widely understood to be written for and read by women and young girls. And while I am using these categories for the purposes of my discussion here, I don't construe them as rigid or impermeable.

7. This is Barbara Sicherman's phrase. I should note that I am not arguing, as she does in the late Victorian context, that reading of this kind provided the foundation for Progressive politics. See Sicherman, "Sense and Sensibility: Women's Reading in Late Victorian America," in *Reading in America: Literature and Social History,* ed. Cathy Davidson (Baltimore: Johns Hopkins University Press, 1989), 202.

8. The foundational study of the novel in early America is Cathy N. Davidson, *Revolution and the Word: The Rise of the Novel in America* (New York: Oxford University Press, 1986). Davidson is careful to acknowledge British reprints when she writes, "I must also

emphasize that most books Americans read, even after the Revolution, still came from abroad." Yet Davidson does in the end gloss over the problem reprints pose because the very framing of her work makes reprints more essential than she is willing to concede, even as she writes, "I do not assess how British fiction shaped American fiction."

9. The most thorough treatment of this orientation and its limitations is in William C. Spengemann, *A Mirror for Americanists: Reflections on the Idea of American Literature* (Hanover: University Press of New England, 1989).

10. Charlotte Brontë to Mary Taylor, 4 Sept. 1848, Haworth, England, in Smith, *Letters of Brontë*, 2:112.

11. "Editor's Book Table," *Godey's Lady's Book* 37 (Oct. 1848): 249, available at http://www.accessible.com/.

12. Ibid.; *Harbinger* 6 (15 April 1848): 189. The writer for the *Harbinger*, at least in the brief January 1848 notice of *Jane Eyre*, is quite determined that Brontë is a man. As he writes, "In the author of *Jane Eyre*, we welcome a man destined to take a decided and important position in English literature." See *Harbinger* 6 (22 Jan. 1848): 95.

13. "Novels of the Season," *North American Review* 67 (Oct. 1848): 356, available at http://cdl.library.cornell.edu/moa/.

14. Fales Library at New York University holds a copy of the 1850 Tauchnitz edition in two volumes, half morocco, with a copyright date of 1850, Leipzig. Tauchnitz distributed its books widely in the United States. For a complete listing of Tauchnitz printings of *Jane Eyre*, see William B. Todd and Ann Bowden, *Tauchnitz International Editions in English, 1841–1855: A Bibliographical History* (New York: Bibliographical Society of America, 1988).

15. This does not include a Harper edition dated only by the preface copyright, 1847.

16. See *Graham's Magazine* 32 (May 1848): 299; see also the front-page advertisement in William Linn Tidball, *Olinda, or, the Mexican's Daughter* (Cincinnati: H. B. Pearson, 1854), 6, available at http://www.letrs.indiana.edu/web/w/wright2/. The Pearson edition underscores the fact that the phenomenon of *Jane Eyre*, and of British reprints in the American market more generally, was not limited to the northeastern, or even the eastern, United States. Pearson advertised a range of other British novels as well as the works of popular American women writers. For more on the book trade in the western and midwestern states, see Michael Winship, "Ticknor and Fields: The Business of Literary Publishing in the United States of the Nineteenth Century," Ninth Hanes Lecture (Chapel Hill: Rare Book Collection, University of North Carolina Library, 1992).

17. Derby & Jackson advertised *The Works of Charlotte Brontë (Currer Bell)* in 1860, including *Jane Eyre*, *Shirley*, and *Villette*, ranging in price from $3.00 in cloth, $3.75 for sheepskin library style, and $6.00 for half-calf extra or antique. See back-page advertisement in Charles Burdett, *Margaret Moncrieffe: The First Love of Aaron Burr, A Romance of Revolution* (New York: Derby & Jackson, 1860), 440–41, available at http://www.letrs.indiana.edu/web/w/wright2/. In 1856 Derby & Jackson announced in *Godey's* the availability of their "beautiful, uniform editions" of *Jane Eyre*, *Shirley*, and *Villette*. "These celebrated novels by Currer Bell (Miss Brontë)" were listed without price, available by mail from the publisher. See *Godey's Lady's Book* 53 (July 1856): 82, available at http://www.accessible.com/. Derby & Jackson's price for *Jane Eyre* ($1.00) appears in an advertisement in the *National Era* that lists Derby & Jackson's best-selling novels. See *National Era* 10 (12 June 1856): 95, available at http://www.accessible.com/. The same price ($1.00) is listed in a Derby & Jackson advertisement for 1858. See *Godey's Lady's Book* 57 (Dec. 1858): 561, available at http://www.accessible.com/. Another edition is listed with an incomplete date (185?) and no publisher in the *National Union Catalog*, which very much seems to belong to the early period, as there is no mention of Brontë, only "Currer Bell." This partially dated copy is held by the University

of Illinois at Urbana. Analysis of it may enable me to determine whether it in fact dates from the early 1850s and constitutes another early printing of the novel in the United States. I include it here in part because the author is listed as "Currer Bell" with no mention of Charlotte or any other Brontë, which according to the extant early printings would suggest a publication date sometime in the early 1850s.

18. Two pioneering historians of nineteenth-century popular literature, Frank Luther Mott and James Hart, back my contention that *Jane Eyre* was one of the most popular books of the decade. See James D. Hart, *The Popular Book: A History of America's Literary Taste* (Berkeley and Los Angeles: University of California Press, 1950); Frank Luther Mott, *Golden Multitudes: The Story of Best Sellers in the United States* (New York: Macmillan, 1947).

19. For a good example of the tenuous nature of the courtesy of trade agreements during this period, and of negotiations over reprint rights, see Greenspan's discussion of Thomas Carlyle's fate in the United States in *George Palmer Putnam*, 122–28.

20. Eugene Exman claims, in his history of Harper & Brothers, that the initial Harper edition, part of its Library of Select Novels, sold for twenty-five cents. See Exman, *The Brothers Harper* (New York: Harper & Row, 1965), 262. For the other reference to this price, see Henry C. Carey, *Letters on International Copyright* (Philadelphia: A. Hart, 1853), 57. Carey is comparing the price of books in England with their price in the United States. He lists *Jane Eyre* as a book selling for $7.50 in England and for twenty-five cents in the United States. Carey notes his source for the information as the New York *Daily Times*. Evidence that the Harper edition price for *Jane Eyre* rose to thirty-seven cents by 1857, if not earlier, is suggested by a listing at this price in a back-page advertisement for Catharine Maria Sedgwick's novel, *Married or Single* (New York: Harper, 1857), 289. H. B. Pearson listed its price for *Jane Eyre* as twenty-five cents in 1854. See front-page advertisement in Tidball, *Olinda*, 6. T. B. Peterson may have offered *Jane Eyre* at twenty-five cents, but I have no evidence for this beyond the fact that Peterson advertised *Agnes Grey* at this same price in 1852. See the back-page advertisement in Caroline Lee Hentz's novel, *Eoline; or, Magnolia Vale* (New York: Charles J. Peterson, 1852), 288, available at http://www.letrs.indiana.edu/web/w/wright2/.

21. For the estimate of sales see Carey, *Letters on International Copyright*, 60.

22. As noted, many editions of the novel were on the market simultaneously, with the quality of the print and binding affecting price. It was a common practice for a single publishing house to issue two or more editions of a book, the cheaper edition in paper and the more expensive in "boards" or leather, with or without gilt edges, as Derby & Jackson did in 1860. On multiple editions and their prices, see also Orville A. Roorbach, *Bibliotheca Americana: Catalogue of American Publications including Reprints and Original Works, from 1820–1852, inclusive: Together with a List of Periodicals Published in the United States* (New York: O. A. Roorbach, 1852), and Roorbach's supplements to this work of 1852–1855 and 1858–61, as well as his *Addenda: 1855–1858*. Roorbach's work is useful, but incomplete.

23. Carey, *Letters on International Copyright*, 66.

24. *Godey's Lady's Book* 37 (Oct. 1848): 249, and (July 1848): 56, available at http://www.accessible.com/.

25. *National Era* 3 (6 Dec. 1849): 194, available at http://www.accessible.com/.

26. Ibid., 4 (3 Jan. 1850): 3, available at http://www.accessible.com/.

27. Charles A. Dana, *Harbinger* 6 (22 Jan. 1848): 95.

28. Many reviews from the British press were reprinted without attribution of the original source. See note 53 below.

29. *Graham's Magazine* 32 (May 1848): 299.

30. "Review of New Books," *Peterson's Ladies National Magazine* 13 (March 1848): 126.

31. *Putnam's Monthly: A Magazine of Literature, Science, and Art* 1 (Feb. 1853): 233, available at http://cdl.library.cornell.edu/moa/.

32. Edwin Percy Whipple, "Novels of the Season," *North American Review* (Oct. 1848): 355, available at http://cdl.library.cornell.edu/moa/. Published anonymously. For author, see web database *Nineteenth-Century Masterfile*, Poole's database, at http://poolesplus.odyssi.com.

33. *North American Review* (Oct. 1848): 355, available at http://cdl.library.cornell.edu/moa/.

34. *National Era* 3 (20 Sept. 1849): 150, available at http://www.accessible.com/; *Godey's Lady's Book* 41 (Oct. 1850): 250, and 39 (Dec. 1849): 464, both available at http://www.accessible.com/. In addition to the 1850 *Godey's* mention of a new novel "equal to *Jane Eyre*," roughly the same phrase is quoted in comparison with another work in a front-page advertisement in T. S. Arthur, *The Two Wives: Or, Lost and Won* (Philadelphia: Lippincott, Grambo & Co., 1851), 3, available at http://www.letrs.indiana.edu/web/w/wright2/.

35. See back-page advertisement in Talvi, *Life's Discipline* (Philadelphia: Appleton, 1851), 185, available at http://www.letrs.indiana.edu/web/w/wright2/.

36. See back-page advertisement in M. M. Huet, *Silver and Pewter* (Cincinnati: H. B. Pearson, H. Long, 1852), 104, available at http://www.letrs.indiana.edu/web/w/wright2/.

37. *National Era* 2 (20 Sept. 1849): 150, *National Era* 6 (1 April 1852): 55; *Godey's Lady's Book* 65 (Sept. 1862): 301, all available at http://www.accessible.com/.

38. The scandal surrounding *Jane Eyre* was caused by its perceived autobiographical qualities, discussed below. Similarly, the autobiographical qualities of Fanny Fern's novel, *Ruth Hall*, were used as a selling point by Mason Brothers, who ran advertisements to fuel the controversy—"IS RUTH HALL AN AUTOBIOGRAPHY?" See Susan K. Geary, "The Domestic Novel as a Commercial Commodity: Making a Bestseller in the 1850s," *Papers of the Bibliographical Society of America* 70, no. 3 (1976): 389.

39. *National Era* 10 (11 Sept. 1856): 147, available at http://www.accessible.com/. The *National Era* was an abolitionist broadsheet published in Washington, D.C., from 1847 to 1860. It was famous for serializing Harriet Beecher Stowe's *Uncle Tom's Cabin*. The new novel by Caroline Chessbro was *Victoria: Or, the World Overcome*. While the description of the book's "*Jane Eyre* earnestness" may refer to the novel or to its protagonist, the relevance of the cultural reference and its meaning is not significantly altered. The comparison to Peterson's novel is in a front-page advertisement in Bennett Emerson, *Viola; or, Adventures in the South-West* (Philadelphia: T. B. Peterson, 1852), 6, available at http://www.letrs.indiana.edu/web/w/wright2/.

40. *National Era* 11 (6 Aug. 1857): 126, available at http://www.accessible.com/.

41. Thomas Butler Gunn, *The Physiology of New York Boarding Houses* (New York: Mason Brothers, 1857), 292–93, available at http://www.letrs.indiana.edu/web/w/wright2/. All punctuation in original. Rochester also entered into usage, with Ella Gertrude Thomas noting that her "Piney Woods place was named Rochester by me just after having read *Jane Eyre*." Ella Gertrude Clanton Thomas, 27 Sept. 1848, in *Secret Eve: The Journal of Ella Gertrude Clanton Thomas, 1848–1889*, ed. Virginia Ingraham Burr (Chapel Hill: University of North Carolina Press, 1990). See *North American Women's Letters and Diaries* at AlexanderSt.com, http://colet.uchicago.edu/cgi-bin/asp/nawld.

42. *Godey's Lady's Book* 69 (Aug. 1864): 176, available at http://www.accessible.com/.

43. I do not mean exclusively in the United States, since the critical response to *Jane Eyre*, speculation about the identity of the author, and interest in her life and works as exhibited by the response to Elizabeth Gaskell's biography occurred in England as well as America. However, the novel was not only far more expensive in England but literacy rates, distribution, and lending libraries all made the material conditions surrounding the widespread popular reception of the novel there somewhat different and, I would suggest, muted the effects of reading on women that I describe here.

44. Of course, these borders remain unstable, becoming more so, in fact, in postmodern

literature. However, the point I want to make here is that the novel as a category of writing linked to a particular kind of pedagogical reading practice was in flux. This created a renewed confusion about the definition of novels in the culture.

45. Barbara Hochman, *Getting at the Author: Reimagining Books and Reading in the Age of American Realism* (Amherst: University of Massachusetts Press, 2001), 12, 15.

46. On female readers and empathetic reading practices, see Kate Flint, *The Woman Reader, 1837–1914* (1993; Oxford: Oxford University Press, 2002).

47. Asserting that Jane "claims" language is, of course, not a simple, self-evident move for either Brontë or myself, given a critical tradition that more often than not has understood subjects as always already inside language, there being no outside. Without ignoring this problem, I am working in an alternative critical discourse that *has* been able to find a space for "emancipatory" strategies within and through language. See Patricia Yaeger, *Honey-Mad Women: Emancipatory Strategies in Women's Writing* (New York: Columbia University Press, 1988), 239.

48. See W. J. T. Mitchell's second chapter, "Image versus Text: Figures of the Difference," in Mitchell, *Iconology: Image, Text, Ideology* (Chicago: University of Chicago Press, 1986), 47–52, for an explanation of the historical construction of the metaphysical difference between image and text.

49. Nina Baym makes a similar reader-text identification but does not develop the concept at great length, except insofar as she extensively documents the centrality of plot and "interest" in defining the genre. "In sum, the formal principle of the novel was plot, and the basic principle of reader response—interest—also derived from plot. The 'novel,' in a basic sense, existed only when the distinction between it and the reader disappeared, when the novel initiated and the reader completed a single experience." Baym, *Novels, Readers, and Reviewers: Responses to Fiction in Antebellum America* (Ithaca: Cornell University Press, 1984), 81.

50. Helen Burns is also said to be a virtual copy of Charlotte's younger sister Maria, who died at a school not unlike Lowood, the same attended by Emily and Charlotte. See Charlotte Brontë, *Jane Eyre*, ed. Q. D. Leavis (New York: Penguin, 1985), 483n6. Page citations in the text are from this edition.

51. These include the infamous review of *Vanity Fair, Jane Eyre*, and the report on the *Governesses' Benevolent Institution* for 1847 by Elizabeth Rigby (Lady Eastlake), originally published in the *Quarterly Review* 84 (Dec. 1848): 153–85, and reprinted in the United States in *Living Age* 20 (17 March 1849): 497–511, available at http://cdl.library.cornell.edu/moa/. Mysteriously, *Living Age* attributes the article to the *Edinburgh Review*. Also notable are a lengthy review of all the Brontës' works and of Elizabeth Gaskell's biography of Charlotte, reprinted from the *National Review* in *Littel's Living Age* 693 (2 Sept. 1857): 577–98, available at http://cdl.library.cornell.edu/moa/, and a response to Charlotte's death written by W. M. Thackeray, "Charlotte Bronte's Last Sketch," *Harper's New Monthly Magazine* 20 (May 1860): 824–25, available at http://cdl.library.cornell.edu/moa/.

52. As late as 1860 the complete edition of Brontë's novels published by Derby & Jackson lists the title simply as *Jane Eyre*, with "Charlotte Brontë as the author but with "Currer Bell" added in parentheses after her name. See back-page advertisement in Charles Burdett, *The First Love of Aaron Burr: A Romance of Revolution* (New York: Derby & Jackson, 1860), 440, available at http://www.letrs.indiana.edu/web/w/wright2/. Three years earlier, however, the order was reversed and the emphasis on the novel as an autobiography was heightened. "The Brontë Novels" was given as a header and the title was listed as *Jane Eyre: An Autobiography*, followed by "*Edited* by Currer Bell (Charlotte Brontë)" (emphasis added). See back-page advertisement in Sedgwick, *Married or Single?* 2:289.

53. Or perhaps, as Casper argues, they "elided its purposes and effects with those of other genres," as they did with biography. See Scott E. Casper, *Constructing American Lives:*

Biography and Culture in Nineteenth-Century America (Chapel Hill: University of North Carolina Press, 1999), 9.

54. Letter from Catharine Maria Sedgwick, April 1853, in *Life and Letters of Catharine M. Sedgwick,* ed. Mary E. Dewey (New York: Harper & Row, 1871), 349, available at http://www.alexanderstreet2.com.NWLDLive/.

55. *Frederick Douglass' Paper* (18 March 1853), available at http://www.accessible.com/. *Frederick Douglass' Paper* was an African American newspaper published in Rochester, New York, from 1851 to 1859.

56. *Godey's Lady's Book* 51 (Sept. 1855): 273, available at http://www.accessible.com/.

57. Ibid.

58. *Frederick Douglass' Paper* (4 May 1855) and (31 Aug. 1855), available at http://www.accessible.com/.

59. *Godey's Lady's Book* 51 (Sept. 1855): 273, available at http://www.accessible.com/. The five other authors included in the obituary, all British, were Amelia Opie, Caroline Southey, Sara S. Coleridge, Susan E. Ferrier, and Mary Russel Mitford.

60. *Harper's New Monthly Magazine* 11 (June 1855): 128, available at http://cdl.library.cornell.edu/moa/.

61. Published in book form by New York's D. Appleton & Co., in 1857, with additional dated editions in 1858 and 1862. Tauchnitz also issued two editions in the United States during the 1850s, the first in 1857 and the second, "revised" and "corrected," in 1859. See the *National Union Catalog,* vol. 192. For the advertisement of the Appleton edition, see the *National Era* 11 (4 June 1857): 90, available at http://www.accessible.com/.

62. These reprints include but are by no means limited to *Godey's Lady's Book* 55 (Sept. 1857), *National Era* 11 (28 May 1857), 85, (4 June 1857), and (9 July 1857), 109, all available at http://www.accessible.com/; and *Putnam's Monthly* 9 (June 1857): 648–54, available at http://cdl.library.cornell.edu/moa/.

63. "Our Books Table," *United States Democratic Review* 40 (Aug. 1857): 191, available at http://cdl.library.cornell.edu/moa/.

64. "Miss Brontë," *Littell's Living Age* 693 (2 Sept. 1857): 579, 586, available at http://cdl.library.cornell.edu/moa/.

65. "Notices of Books," *English Woman's Journal* 1 (1 May 1858): 197, available at http://gerritsen.chadwyck.com/.

66. Casper, *Constructing American Lives,* 9.

67. It is perhaps worth noting that this conflation of the two, and the identification of Charlotte with Jane, is not limited to the period. My copy of *Jane Eyre,* from Penguin Classics, 1985, edited by Q. D. Leavis, features a reproduction of a chalk drawing of Brontë on the cover.

68. *North American Review* (Oct. 1857): 297, available at http://cdl.library.cornell.edu/moa/.

69. The advertisement for the play, sold for twenty-five cents, is in the back pages of Osgood Bradbury, *Alice Barber: or, The Adventures of a Young Woman* (New York: Samuel French, 1853), 104, available at http://www.letrs.indiana.edu/web/w/wright2/.

70. Fanny Fern [Sara Parton], *Fresh Leaves* (New York: Mason Brothers, 1857), 332. Fern might have been particularly eager to defend Brontë as she was widely attacked for being "unladylike" and for other infractions of the feminine code of genteel conduct, in particular because of her willingness to expose her brother's treatment of her in *Ruth Hall.* The novel uses a first-person narrator to tell a story that is perhaps more fact than fiction, documenting as it does Fern's rise to literary success. On women's writers' difficulty in maintaining their femininity as public figures, see Mary Kelley, *Private Woman, Public Stage: Literary Domesticity in Nineteenth-Century America* (New York: Oxford University Press, 1984).

71. See, for example, a notice in the *National Era* 11 (2 July 1857): 107. See also a long explanation of the controversy by Harriet Martineau in *Living Age* 55 (27 Oct. 1857), available at http://cdl.library.cornell.edu/moa/.

72. Margaret Jane Mussey Sweat, "Charlotte Bronté and the Bronté Novels," *North American Review* (Oct. 1857): 295–96, available at http://cdl.library.cornell.edu/moa/. Review published anonymously. Author identification from web database, *Nineteenth-Century Masterfile,* database Northhamer, *North American Review Index 85,* at http://poolesplus. odyssi.com.

73. *Godey's Lady's Book* 55 (Sept. 1857): 274, available at http://www.accessible.com/.

74. Anyone who has read many nineteenth-century texts (both fiction and nonfiction) will need little convincing of the word's prevalence.

75. Gillian Brown, *Domestic Individualism: Imagining Self in Nineteenth-Century America* (Berkeley and Los Angeles: University of California Press, 1990), 31, 32.

76. T. C. C., "Shirley, Jane Eyre, and Wuthering Heights," *American Whig Review* 2 (March 1850): 234, available at http://cdl.library.cornell.edu/moa/.

77. "Review of *Vanity Fair, Jane Eyre, and Governesses Benevolent Institution—Report for 1847,*" *Living Age* (17 March 1849), 505, available at http://cdl.library.cornell.edu/moa/. As noted, the review was originally published anonymously in the *Quarterly Review* but later became famously known as having been written by Lady Eastlake (Elizabeth Rigby). See note 51 above.

78. *Littell's Living Age* 213 (10 June 1848): 481, available at http://cdl.library.cornell.edu/moa/. Reprint from the *Christian Remembrancer.* A British reprint, as indicated also by the review copy, which is the Smith, Elder & Co. second edition, Cornhill.

79. *National Era* 3 (20 Sept. 1849): 150, available at http://www.accessible.com/.

80. Fern [Parton] is quite indignant at the accusation, exclaiming, "Donkey! It is vain to hope that his life has been as pure and self-sacrificing as that of 'Charlotte Bronté.'" The quotation marks around the name may indicate the still-tentative status of Bronté as the author of *Jane Eyre.* See Fern [Parton], *Fresh Leaves,* 249, 333.

81. *Godey's Lady's Book* 65 (Sept. 1862): 301, available at http://www.accessible.com/. The novel reviewed is *The Morgesons,* published by Harper & Brothers.

82. The most thorough treatment of the history of female reading is Flint, *Woman Reader.*

83. Nina Baym, *Woman's Fiction: A Guide to Novels by and About Women in America, 1820–70* (1978; Urbana: University of Illinois Press, 1993), xix.

84. "Easy Chair," *Harper's New Monthly Magazine* 11 (June 1855): 128, available at http://cdl.library.cornell.edu/moa/.

85. Popular advice books typically contained sections on novel reading, as does Catherine E. Beecher's popular *Treatise on Domestic Economy for the Use of Young Ladies at School and at Home* (Boston: Marsh, Capon, Lyon and Webb, 1841), 256. The book was reprinted frequently throughout the 1850s. Beecher hedges her advice, not banning all reading of "fictitious writings" but calling for the careful supervision of young girls' reading.

86. *Godey's Lady's Book* 34 (Jan. 1847): 51, available at http://www.accessible.com/.

87. Ibid.

88. See Reynolds, *Beneath the American Renaissance,* 7; Richard Brodhead, *Cultures of Letters: Scenes of Reading and Writing in Nineteenth-Century America* (Chicago: University of Chicago Press, 1993), 43, 44. While Brodhead is certainly correct in arguing that books took on a new importance and that their cultural significance underwent a change during this period, I think he is mistaken in limiting this development to women and children, just as I think many of his conclusions are skewed because they fail to account for the popularity of British reprints and their dilution of what he understands as a market dominated by American sentimental novels.

89. As Mary Poovey points out, "the historical emergence of 'literature' as a distinct body of culturally valued texts belongs to the late eighteenth and early nineteenth centuries; its social and ideological functions during this formative period were extremely complex, as were its relations to other emergent social institutions, such as literacy, the daily press, and public education." Poovey, *Uneven Developments: The Ideological Work of Gender in Mid-Victorian England* (Chicago: University of Chicago Press, 1988), 89.

90. The Western masculine autobiographical tradition into which Brontë inserts herself is, of course, defined by St. Augustine's foundational *Confessions* and extends through Rousseau's *Confessions* and Wordsworth's *Prelude*. The Romantic tradition shares a great deal with the autobiographical impulse but defines its project differently. In this tradition I include the major British poets, Keats, Coleridge, and Wordsworth.

91. Jane Tompkins, *Sensational Designs: The Cultural Work of American Fiction, 1790–1860* (New York: Oxford University Press, 1985), xvi.

92. "Feminist individualism" is the term Gayatri Chakravorty Spivak uses in her still influential essay on *Jane Eyre* to describe the subject of Western historical discourses. Spivak explains that she uses the term to underline what is at stake in the "making of human beings, the constitution and 'interpellation' of the subject not only as individual but as 'individualist'" in the age of imperialism. The term is useful here as it invokes the language of feminism in the context of my discussion of the domestic woman, at the same time drawing attention to the discursive links between self-possession/production, property, and subjectivity. See Spivak, "Three Women's Texts and a Critique of Imperialism," in *Race, Writing, and Difference,* ed. Henry Louis Gates Jr. (Chicago: University of Chicago Press, 1986), 262–80. For a reading of Lockean individualism, see C. B. MacPherson, *The Political Theory of Possessive Individualism: Hobbes to Locke* (New York: Oxford University Press, 1962); and Brown, *Domestic Individualism.*

Uncle Tom's Cabin in the National Era

An Essay in Generic Norms and the Contexts of Reading

Barbara Hochman

How we can become accustomed to anything!
—Harriet Beecher Stowe[1]

Surprisingly little attention has been paid to the interplay between *Uncle Tom's Cabin* and the material that surrounded it when it first appeared as a series of installments in the free-soil weekly the *National Era*.[2] Publishing in that context, Stowe faced a formidable challenge: how to shape an account of slave culture that would have a greater impact than the antislavery discourse already typical of the abolitionist press. In representing slavery during the 1840s, writers of slave narratives, sermons, poems, and other texts often sought to elicit empathy from their readers. But it was *Uncle Tom's Cabin* that established sympathetic identification as a widespread reading practice for consuming the story of slavery. How did Stowe's tale accomplish that end?

Stowe was well aware that neither her facts nor her arguments would be new to readers of the *Era*. Indeed, in a sense they were all too familiar. By 1851 every edition of the *National Era* included images of fugitives as well as political discussions, religious appeals, and other well-rehearsed attacks on slave culture. William Lloyd Garrison and other abolitionists

Research for this essay was conducted with the generous support of a Gilder-Lehrman Fellowship and an NEH Fellowship for University Teachers.

complained that this flood of print was often greeted only by the "apathy of the people."[3] In designing her narrative, Stowe took up the rhetorical challenge that the Russian formalist critic Victor Shklovsky later called "defamiliarization": how to tell a well-known tale so as to "make it new."[4]

As we know from recurrent scenes of violence in today's news, outrages that cannot easily be remedied can often be ignored. "The best we can do is to shut our eyes and ears and let [slavery] alone," St. Clare remarks in chapter 19 of *Uncle Tom's Cabin*.[5] Earlier in the novel, when Haley the slave trader is unmoved by "the wild look of anguish" on the face of a slave mother whose child he has sold, Stowe's narrator adds, "You can get used to such things too my friend" (208). The numbing of sensibility required to "let [slavery] alone" is a recurrent emphasis in the novel; it was a specific obstacle to response that Stowe set out to overcome.

Abolitionist discourse itself unwittingly contributed to the making familiar that allows one to "get used to" atrocities. In composing *Uncle Tom's Cabin,* Stowe was determined to break through what she saw as the defenses of readers who could hear about slavery every day and never "listen." In the novel's own words, Stowe asked herself what the point was of telling "the story, told too oft,—every day told . . . the weak broken and torn for the profit and convenience of the strong! It needs not to be told" (202). Stowe may have felt that the story of slavery was "told too oft" to bear repeating, but she was still impelled to publish her own version of the tale. While composing her novel, Stowe gave careful thought to the problem of rhetoric: how could she subvert the complacency of contemporary readers, indifferent to sentimental appeals on the one hand and abolitionist arguments on the other?

Discussions of Stowe's novel over the past twenty-five years have emphasized the common ground between *Uncle Tom's Cabin* and other sentimental forms of middle-class culture. As the common ground has become increasingly visible, some significant differences in emphasis have been lost.[6] *Uncle Tom's Cabin* echoed, even epitomized, the ubiquitous themes and images of sentimental print culture;[7] but at the same time it modified firmly established rhetorical conventions. The unprecedented success of *Uncle Tom's Cabin* implies that there was a great deal of pleasure for readers in finding their generic expectations not only confirmed but also upset and remade.[8]

Stowe wanted her readers to see slavery with "new eyes."[9] We might say that she tried to do for her readers what Eva does for Ophelia and what Tom begins to do for St. Clare: she offers them a new way of seeing.[10] To this end, Stowe recast well-known sentimental motifs (such as the beautiful moribund child) and reshaped the conventional images of fugitive slaves that dominated the news reports, political commentaries, and poetry of the abolitionist press. If we examine *Uncle Tom's Cabin* in the context of the abolitionist and literary material that appeared alongside it in the *National Era,* we will be in a better position to understand how Stowe's narrative often challenged well-worn interpretive norms.

Although the *National Era* is not a faithful mirror of antebellum literary culture as a whole, its potpourri of "high" and "low" genres was typical of abolitionist newspapers as it was of periodicals that ranged from mass-circulation dailies to literary "annuals." A disparate array of texts, laid out side by side, was designed to attract a readership of men, women, and even children.[11] The *Era's* format—four large pages, seven columns each—characterized many weeklies and dailies. But the place of "literature" in the *Era* was unusual. Garrison's *Liberator, Frederick Douglass' Paper,* the *National Anti-Slavery Standard,* and even the *New York Tribune* tended to print poetry, and sometimes fiction, on the last page of the paper. By contrast, the *Era* placed poems and serialized fiction in a prominent position on page one. Spread out over two, three, and even four columns, the fiction and poetry of the *Era* was not separated from the news in a clearly labeled column at the back; it was interlaced with readers' letters, congressional debates, political speeches, and news reports.

What was the aesthetic and political function of literary discourse in the *National Era?* While its poetry sometimes took slavery as a subject, its fiction more often gave readers a respite from the highly charged issues of the day. Within the abolitionist press generally, fiction played only a minor role in addressing the problem of slavery. In the *Era* itself, as we shall see, fiction assiduously avoided the subject—until installments of *Uncle Tom's Cabin* began to appear.[12] Stowe's novel altered the horizon of expectations for sentimental tales by creating a dialogue with the texts that surrounded it; *Uncle Tom's Cabin* reshaped the relation between fiction and the network of ideas and images within which it was embedded.

The *National Era* had clearly defined ambitions as both a literary and a political paper. These aims coexisted but did not merge. In November of each year, Gamaliel Bailey, the editor of the *Era,* published an "Annual Letter" encouraging readers to renew their subscriptions. In 1851 Bailey's letter noted that "[i]n conducting the *Era,* I have aimed to give it a two-fold character—that [of] a high-toned Literary paper, and that of a firm, consistent advocate of Human Rights."[13] To judge by the subjects of the "literary" discourse in the *Era,* Bailey's two aims had very little to do with each other. To be sure, lofty poetry about the value of freedom was a staple of the paper; and satiric poems occasionally addressed the hypocrisy of the church on the fugitive question. Fiction, however, paid attention to "human rights" only within the context of family relations: parents or stepparents who are cruel to their children; children who break the heart of a parent by secretly meeting a lover, by running off to sea, or just by being untruthful or lazy.

Slave issues gained prominence in the *Era* during and after 1850. In the issue dated 3 January 1850, the first number of the paper for that year, slavery was not mentioned until page 2, but attention to slavery steadily increased as the debate about whether and how to admit new territory to the Union intensified and as the Fugitive Slave Law was debated, passed, enforced, and resisted. Nonetheless, the fiction of the *Era* did not address and rarely even reflected social or political realities. Stowe's decision to make her antislavery work a fictional one deserves particular attention in this context.

Fiction was not an inevitable choice for Stowe. She herself had produced several kinds of writing by 1851—a children's geography, poetry, parables, and sermons. Stowe had also given considerable thought to the persuasive potential of imaginative texts. An introductory essay she wrote for Charles Beecher's fictionalized account of *The Incarnation* (1849) affirms the use of fiction in the service of religious and historical truth. Stowe's effort to justify her brother's imaginative recasting of Scripture anticipates one of the biggest problems she herself would encounter while writing her novel: how to treat serious issues of religious faith and historical reality in a narrative form widely presumed to encourage romantic fantasy, passivity, and idleness.[14]

Stowe was keenly aware of the stigma attached to reading fiction at mid-century. Like many middle-class women of her generation, Stowe had been forbidden to read novels during much of her childhood. When her father made an exception for Sir Walter Scott, Stowe read him avidly—only to feel "constantly pursued and haunted" by a sense of her own frivolity.[15] In her introduction to *The Incarnation,* Stowe defended her brother's "blending together of . . . truth and fiction,"[16] supporting Beecher's invention of incident, dialogue, and descriptive detail. Stowe's essay, like other discussions of fiction that she wrote in the 1840s, became an occasion for her to articulate her criteria of literary value. Several of her early pieces explore the pros and cons of fictional modes, from Beecher through Bulwer to Dickens.[17] Stowe gradually prepared herself to write a novel informed by religious, political, and social concerns.

If we consider *Uncle Tom's Cabin* in relation to the fiction typical of the *Era,* innovative and neglected features of Stowe's text become visible. With few exceptions the *Era*'s serialized fiction was set in a domestic space, implicitly in America but generally in an undifferentiated, unnamed locale. Cabins in "the woods," a little farm, or an elegant mansion provide the background for tales of saintly children, headstrong youth, and treacherous stepmothers. The fiction is didactic: it tells the reader to be diligent and patient, to obey one's parents and trust Providence. It stresses the efficacy of individual will and the importance of emotional moderation, whether in love or death. To act impulsively is to court trouble. To mourn excessively is to forget that the dead parent, child, or lover has gone to a better world.

Such stories endorsed piety while suggesting that the realm of the family, like an individual's moral life, could remain untouched by ongoing political turmoil.[18] When the fiction of the *Era* did engage a social problem—such as poverty—it stressed the value of perseverance and humility.[19] If a story mentioned the situation of an immigrant or an abandoned woman, it always implied that the intemperate, careless, or otherwise culpable victim got what he or she richly deserved.[20] If a tale made a passing reference to slavery (which was extremely unusual), the institution was taken for granted as a given.[21] Since the *Era*'s abolitionist views were explicit and pervasive, their absence from fiction is an anomaly that repays consideration.

Until the appearance of *Uncle Tom's Cabin,* a reader of the *Era* could turn to fiction for escape from complexity or doubt. "There is much loose talk about an overruling Providence" Stowe wrote in 1850.[22] Nowhere is such "loose talk" more evident than in the fiction (and poetry) of the *National Era,* where Providence is regularly seen to "work . . . all things well."[23] *Uncle Tom's Cabin* directly challenged the moral messages of the *Era*'s "high toned Litera[ture]"; it ushered religious doubt, political conflict, and the problem of human rights into installment fiction. But it did so in a style so familiar and disarming as to create a popular sensation that obscured the depth of the challenge it posed to both social and generic norms.

Fictive Norms: Representing the Death of a Child

Untimely death is a recurrent motif in the *Era;* stories and poems repeatedly render a young person's death and offer a clear set of directives for making sense of it. This theme provides a particularly useful lens through which to reexamine Stowe because it enables us to see how she recast ubiquitous popular clichés.

The good and preternaturally wise child who dies young was represented in obituaries as well as in poems and stories. The child who dies is always remarkable: "a child of rare beauty and unusual precocity."[24] She (the child is generally a girl) is imagined as a precious "gem,"[25] a shining star, or, more often, a flower: "the fairest, purest, / the heavenliest flower of all."[26] This flower is "blighted"[27] and doomed, but the reader is encouraged to see that the death of the child is for the best: she will be "glad to go where pain is o'er"[28] and will partake of heavenly glory. Mourning is represented as an inappropriate response in this context.[29] The fact that the victim has achieved "immortal youth" in Paradise[30] is easily borne in upon the bereaved family (or childhood friend).

The very repetition of the dying-child motif suggests that it had wide appeal. One need go no further than the obituaries of the *Era* itself to see that the stories and poems dealing with this theme drew on a common reality.[31] Stowe's image of beautiful, innocent Eva conformed to a well-known model. But Stowe reworked this popular image for new ends: unlike her analogues, Eva dies of slavery, and her death has significant consequences.[32] Stowe's exploration of the reason for Eva's decline constituted a challenge to common assumptions about the appropriate subject matter for fiction. Her emphasis on the impact of Eva's death further complicated the sanguine moral messages of the serials published alongside *Uncle Tom's Cabin* in the *Era*.

The fourteenth installment of the novel introduces Eva with an epigraph that emphasizes her youth, freshness, beauty, and general superiority to the world in which she resides: "A young star! which shone / O'er life— too sweet an image for such glass! / A lovely being scarcely formed or moulded; / A rose with all its sweetest leaves yet folded" (226). A star, a rose, "too sweet" for this world, Eva, like many contemporary heroines, is not expected to live. Yet Stowe gives the figure of the moribund child additional resonance by raising a question never asked by the other fiction of the *Era:* how do wider social conditions participate in shaping the fate of this "scarcely formed or moulded" being?

From the beginning, Eva has the characteristic marks of a rare and otherworldly child whose "dreamy earnestness" and "spiritual gravity" (230) would have made her approaching death obvious to any informed reader of the period.[33] Eva exhibits the typical features of the exceptional child, untouched by her surroundings: "[D]ressed in white, [Eva] seemed to move like a shadow through all sorts of places, without contracting spot or stain" (231). But the similarity between Eva and the *Era*'s other saintly children comes to an end when Stowe shifts her attention from Eva as "unstained" by earthly things to Eva as shaped by events in this world. This "rose" is "formed and moulded" by a social "blight." She is doomed by slave culture, the cruelties of which she is repeatedly required to witness.

The symbolic implications of Eva's illness have been noted by Philip Fisher, Richard Brodhead, and others.[34] The point to be emphasized here is that Stowe gives Eva's death a derivation unheard of in the stories from which she might seem to emerge. Moreover, while Stowe may have believed that a dying child was indeed going to "a better country" (416), she knew from her own experience that there was no death without suffering.[35] The fiction of the *Era* tended to note a child's suffering only to emphasize that death would bring welcome release. It never dwelled on pain. Stowe, on the contrary, makes Eva's anguish a central focus. With pale cheeks and "her hands on her bosom," Eva listens to tales about brutally mistreated slaves and "sigh[s] heavily." As she tells Tom, in the recurrent formulation that explicitly links her approaching illness to slavery, "'These things sink into my heart . . . they sink into my heart'" (326, 347).[36] When, after hearing one such story, Eva "bursts into tears, and sob[s] convulsively" (347), St. Clare responds that "This child . . . ought not to hear any of this kind of thing"; but it is too late. Slavery, Stowe implies, cannot be kept away from Eva. And it should not be kept out of fiction.

Stowe adapts the image of the dying child to new ends by giving Eva's death a social matrix; she also uses the figure of Eva to modify other typical features of the female child in popular tales of the period. Unlike many of her fictional antecedents—"sweet [and] frail," "dreamy, retiring . . . modest"[37]—Eva is tough-minded when it comes to the most difficult subjects. She speaks frankly of her own death, though no one (except Tom) is willing to listen; and her questions are not "dreamy" or hesitant but clear and sharp. When her mother complains about how much trouble the slaves cause her ("'as if we did it for our *convenience*,' said Marie. 'I'm sure if we consulted *that,* we might let them all go at once'" [260]) Eva responds: "'What do you keep them for, mama?'" (260). This simple question, like the comment of the little boy in "The Emperor's New Clothes," calls attention to a bald fact, which an entire society attempts to deny.

The popularity of *Uncle Tom's Cabin* as a whole, and the figure of Eva in particular, suggest that Stowe's emphasis tapped a widespread desire to move beyond familiar stereotypes. Many readers must have welcomed the chance to hear more about the dying child than her humility and fortunate escape from this world. Stowe's perspective on the question of mourning deserves further attention in this context. For in representing the moment of death, as in shaping the figure of Eva, Stowe radically revised familiar terms of discourse.

Just as Eva is initially presented to the reader in the conventional imagery of the too-beautiful flower, so her death is rendered in language that would have been perfectly familiar to any regular reader of sentimental fiction. Chapter 26 (installment 25),[38] which describes the death of Eva, is preceded by an epigraph that exemplifies a characteristic perspective on death—there is good reason not to mourn: "Weep not for those whom the veil of the tomb / In life's early morning hath hid from our eyes" (412). Here as elsewhere the finality of death is redefined as a temporary removal from the sight of the living. In representing Eva's end, however, Stowe again recasts familiar tropes, shifting the focus from theoretical consolation to the problem of what remains to the living after the death of a child.

By 1850, as Ann Douglas, Karen Halttunen, and others have shown, representations of mourning often deflected attention from the stark fact of death itself. The fiction and poetry of the *Era*, like the visual iconography of the contemporary graveyard, stressed the regenerative potential of mourning and projected optimistic visions of the hereafter. In rendering the St. Clare household, however, Stowe explores the drama inherent in the very story that the fiction and poetry of the *Era* never pursued. Instead of tying up the loose ends of the episode with reassuring words about immortality, Stowe offers a sharp distinction between the blissful dead and the tortured survivors.

In the *Era*, stories and poems about premature death always ended on the upbeat with a benign plot development to balance the represented loss, or with a consoling message, akin to Stowe's epigraph. In the final lines of one typical poem about a dead girl: "When she wakes another morning / Angel hands will take her up."[39] By contrast, although chapter 26 of *Uncle Tom's Cabin* begins by instructing the reader to "weep not" for one who has died young, it ends by underscoring the difficulty of accepting this advice. "Woe for them who watched the entrance into heaven," Stowe writes, "when they shall wake and find only the gray sky of daily life, and thou gone forever" (428). The exceptional nature of this emphasis can be seen if we compare it to the final words of a story that shared a page with Stowe's description of Eva's death.

"James McCary and His Boy" was a tale in two installments. At the end of the final episode the hero and heroine of the story find a poor young orphan who has been abused and abandoned to the cold. He dies in Molly's arms, the word "Mother" on his lips, and in the last lines of the story, "when the morning dawned cold and gray, it was over plighted lovers, whose hope stretched goldenly down the future and the dead untimely perished."[40] The concluding image of love, consummated in the presence of death, emphasizes "hope" and a "golden" future. This finale provides a sharp contrast to the "gray sky of daily life" that ends Stowe's episode. *Uncle Tom's Cabin* emphasizes that for those who remain behind, the sting of Eva's death is unrelieved. In the chapters that follow, moreover, Stowe questions the notion that conventional words of religious solace can be effective at such times.

Uncle Tom's Cabin suggests that Eva's own equanimity in dying will not easily compensate those who survive her. For St. Clare, after Eva's death, "the whole world is as empty as an egg-shell" (435). As the narrator notes, only "the cold mechanical habit of living remain[ed] after all vital interest in it [had] fled" (439). Such words must have come as a relief to many readers for whom—as for St. Clare—reassuring formulas about the immortality of a dead child were less than persuasive. Like contemporary mourning manuals, tales of "consolation" in the *Era* often emphasized that affliction "naturally . . . make[s] us Christians."[41] Stowe's narrative, on the contrary, asserts the lack of any such "natural" or easy quid pro quo. Although St. Clare's spirit begins to heal before his own sudden death, the installment format itself ensured that readers would linger with his pain and doubt. Stowe missed the deadline for 11 December 1851, and the *Era* appeared without an installment of her novel. As a result, readers found themselves with an additional week to contemplate the previous episode: St. Clare full of doubt and unable to pray while reading the Bible with Tom. It is tempting to speculate that Stowe purposely missed her deadline in order to intensify the effect of this installment.[42]

Uncle Tom's Cabin encouraged its readers to feel that despair at the death of a child was a natural rather than a self-indulgent response. If Stowe's representation of Eva's illness and death gave mortality a social frame, her representation of mourning reexamined the advice, at once so facile and so stringent, not to give way to grief. Tears had acquired considerable legitimacy in fiction, sermons, and mourning manuals by 1850; yet the imperative of restraint and resignation remained central, not only in the fiction and poetry of the *Era* but in such widely read texts as Susan Warner's *The Wide Wide World*. Tears flow copiously in that novel, but the injunction to master one's emotions is emphatic.

Death is a great leveler, but antebellum mourning practices played a major role in middle-class self-definition. As a cultural form, mourning consolidated class distinctions, marked certain kinds of behavior as genteel, and served as a visible barometer of a mourner's moral condition. Unlike middle-class mourners, of course, slaves—who were dying or threatened with death every day—remained outside the loop of conventional behavior associated with burial, consolation, and other polite forms. Ritualized practices shaped the experience of white middle-class death in the antebellum United States. In this, as in so much else, slaves were different.

Generic Norms/Moral Norms: Representing Slave Mothers

Stowe's representation of bereavement goes well beyond the Eva plot. It is central to her delineation of slave mothers. In depicting the experience of slave women in particular, *Uncle Tom's Cabin* makes the threat to or loss of a child the occasion for radical action. Such action ranges from escape to suicide and even infanticide. Stowe challenged both the generic conventions and moral norms of installment fiction with regard to this issue; in doing so she raised questions about the relation between black and white experience. *Uncle Tom's Cabin* thus fused the disjointed aims of Gamaliel Bailey's paper and opened a literary space for the meaningful representation of social and political turmoil.

Stowe's representation of mourning in *Uncle Tom's Cabin* addressed aspects of bereavement that most sentimental fiction avoided. St. Clare's dry eyes and lack of faith challenged religious clichés. Black characters whose responses to death were marked by a lack of restraint challenged social norms. Extreme behavior on the part of bereaved black characters also drew attention to the extraordinary circumstances of slave death. Stowe's rendering of unconventional mourners, especially African American ones, enabled her to defamiliarize mourning as she defamiliarized the moribund child, and as, most radically, she would defamiliarize the figure of the fugitive.

Chapter 12 of *Uncle Tom's Cabin* ("Select Incidents of Lawful Trade") begins with the following epigraph: "In Ramah there was a voice heard—weeping and lamentation, and great mourning; Rachel weeping for her children and would not be comforted." This citation from Jeremiah gains its full resonance only in the context of what precedes and follows it, both in the adjacent columns of the paper and within *Uncle Tom's Cabin* itself. On 21 April 1851, for the first time since Stowe's novel began to be serialized, the *Era* appeared without an installment of *Uncle Tom's Cabin*.[43] Occupying the first three-and-a-quarter columns of the paper, in place of Stowe's tale, was the fifth installment of "Ill-Starred," by Patty Lee. This episode of "Ill-Starred" included the death of a baby, accompanied by the narrator's comment: "I marvel sometimes when I see mothers who will not be comforted, mourning for the deaths of their children. They forget that the beauty of immortal youth is theirs."[44] In the next issue of the paper, the epigraph to *Uncle Tom's Cabin* ("Rachel weeping for her children") created a sharp comment on the moral bromides of "Ill-Starred." Stowe's citation implies that under certain conditions there is plenty of reason to be disconsolate.

The installment that begins with the reference to Rachel's grief presents two cases of children lost to their mothers—not through death, but through slavery. While pursuing the fortunes of Tom and his new owner, Haley, Stowe introduces two distraught slave women: Hagar (whose name, with its biblical source, links her to Rachel) and Lucy. Early in chapter 12, Haley separates Hagar from "her only remaining son" (194) by purchasing the boy at auction. As bystanders strive in vain to comfort her (198), the scene shifts to the boat that will transport Haley and his cargo to New Orleans. Here Haley sells Lucy's sleeping infant while her back is turned. As Lucy sits down dizzily, Haley philosophizes: "'I know this yer comes kinder hard, at first, Lucy, but such a smart, sensible gal as you are, won't give way to it. You see it's *necessary,* and can't be helped!'" When Lucy pleads with him to stop talking ("'O! Mas'r, if you *only* won't talk to me now,'" [209]), Haley cannot fathom Lucy's feelings. He does not anticipate her subsequent suicide. For J. P. Jewett's gift edition of 1853, the celebrated abolitionist illustrator Hammatt Billings amplified the resonance of this scene with an engraving of Tom trying to comfort Lucy (see Figure 1).[45]

Stowe's representation of Lucy complicates two common themes of the period: optimism about God's design and fortitude in the face of "necessity." The figure of Lucy justifies extreme behavior born of despair. As we have noted, representations of black children and mothers were conspicuous by their absence in the fiction of the *Era;* when Stowe made them central to her text, she suggested that reality was not fully represented in contemporary tales. She also extended her attack on facile images of suffering, death, and white mourning.

Figure 1.   Tom trying to comfort Lucy. Courtesy of Special Collections, Alderman Library, University of Virginia.

By sympathetically representing slave women who are driven to defy both moral conventions and the law of the land, Stowe presents despair and defiance as acceptable responses to injustice and pain. Like Eliza's famous escape over the ice, Hagar's or Lucy's inconsolability gains justification from the fact that slave children and mothers were more likely to experience prolonged suffering than death; even the theoretical comfort of heaven was denied them. In the story of Lucy, or that of Cassy, who kills her child to prevent him from remaining a slave (chapter 34), Stowe goes much further than she could have gone in representing white characters.[46]

Much attention has lately been given to the potentially voyeuristic, even pornographic, satisfactions of white middle-class readers who consumed narratives about the sexuality and abused bodies of black slave women. Given the religious and literary conventions of the period, narratives of African American experience indeed opened windows on aspects of life that were rarely represented in relation to the white world. It would surely have been impossible in 1850 to publish a sympathetic portrait of a white woman stripped naked and beaten.[47] Neither a genteel periodical nor an inexpensive story paper would have been likely to print a tale that justified suicide (not to speak of infanticide) among white mothers. Stowe's emphasis on what black mothers could be driven to do needs to be seen in the context of generic expectations and middle-class reading conventions.

Stowe designed such figures as Lucy and Cassy to suggest—and to affirm—the intensity of violent emotional states. It is eminently likely that middle-class readers, schooled in faith and restraint, derived multiple satisfactions from Stowe's representation of slaves expressing anger, pain, despair, and aggression. From alphabet books and conduct manuals through sermons and sentimental fiction, antebellum print culture endorsed the virtues of self-control and self-regulation, especially in women. Images of slave experience invited readers to identify with modes of behavior that were beyond the pale of white middle-class life, or at least prescriptions for it.[48] The pleasure derived from such identifications would necessarily be multiple and complex; but *Uncle Tom's Cabin* encouraged white mothers to try circuiting themselves through black ones in order to imagine states of feeling systematically forbidden to them.

If slave characters like Hagar, Lucy, Prue, Emmeline, and Cassy dramatize the disjuncture between black and white experience, some of these characters also imply a continuum of experience by striking a balance between the extreme and the normative. Such a balance may have been designed to deflect the potentially prurient pleasures of voyeuristic identification. The extremes suggested by the most dramatic actions of Lucy or Cassy are contained by other aspects of their behavior. These characters take to drink, die, even kill, but they tend to remain highly self-possessed. Lucy is exemplary in her restrained and dignified mode of expression. Emmeline is exemplary in her modesty. Cassy speaks of having "raved and cursed" when her children were sold (519), but she shows no traces of madness while relating her life history to Tom. Her rhetoric is carefully modulated, often elegant. The most extreme actions are offset by proper language. The figure of Eliza provides another counterweight to the unruliest implications of experience among Stowe's slave women. Eliza, intermittently present in the narrative from beginning to end, rarely sheds a tear and altogether behaves like the perfect model of true womanhood. Nevertheless, she too breaks the law: she runs away from her legitimate owner. Stowe's portrait of Eliza and other slave mothers both fulfilled and challenged the moral norms of white women's behavior as represented in the *Era* and throughout sentimental print culture.

Reportorial Norms: Representing Runaways

Uncle Tom's Cabin revised not only the sentimental themes and images of installment fiction but also the conventions for representing slaves elsewhere in the *National Era*. Although the Fugitive Slave Law was a common point of reference for reporters, editors, and other commentators in 1851, fugitive slaves were skimpily portrayed in the pages of the paper. Stowe believed that the truth about slavery resided in its concrete particulars; these were rendered invisible by the legalistic arguments, heavy-handed irony, and sweeping generalizations characteristic of much abolitionist rhetoric.

In the news reports, letters, and political articles of the *Era*, "fugitives" were constituted by a few fleeting details—the name of the slave's alleged owner, his or her place of capture, passing mention of the slave's activity prior to being arrested. These fugitives are abstract, barely adumbrated figures. They are often as stereotyped as the visual images in advertisements for runaway slaves that could be found in plenty on standardized specimen sheets.[49] Even when the case of a specific fugitive was discussed in the *Era* over a number of weeks—like a story in installments[50]—the case was not presented as the experience of a differentiated human being capable of love, pain, or reflection. Legal issues and the larger moral questions displaced individuating detail about a specific man or woman.[51]

Occasionally, to be sure, a news report offered a more detailed account of a specific fugitive, real or imaginary. But with few exceptions, these accounts remain brief, generalized scenarios that hurry to make a moral point: a Christian nation should not treat human beings as chattel; a "higher law" should be acknowledged. Even when a specific incident was given extended coverage, the figure of the slave who was the occasion for the story remains anonymous, blank, a mere outline. Whether the report involves "a handful of poor negroes" "thirty or forty negroes" or "five persons, two white, Lewis and Hanaway, and three [nameless] blacks"[52] the terms of reference effectively deprive the fugitives of all personality.

The choice of sentimental fiction afforded Stowe a battery of rhetorical devices for defamiliarizing slavery. Central to this project was her effort to endow slave characters with voices and feelings—in short, with subjectivity. Readers have become increasingly sensitive to the racist assumptions that inform Stowe's slave portraits and to sympathy itself as a coercive dynamic that appropriates and demeans its object.[53] But we underestimate Stowe's courage and originality if we fail to take account of the initial publication context within and for which she designed her plot and characters.

While fugitive slaves were often mentioned in the pages of the *Era*, their voices were never heard there any more than in the legal system. *Uncle Tom's Cabin*, by contrast, suggested that slaves had thoughts, feelings—and voices. Stowe's effort to attribute emotional depth and moral consciousness to the slaves she created relied heavily on white middle-class conceptions of subjectivity, moral norms, and family relations. Still, it is worth underscoring the difference between the fugitive slaves of *Uncle Tom's Cabin* and the representation of anonymous fugitives not only in runaway ads but in the news reports and political commentaries of the *Era* itself.

"Mr. Rust, who knocked the alleged slave Daniel down, and then chained him as a fugitive, is not yet in possession of 'his property' in spite of all aid rendered by Mr Commissioner Smith and the Police Justices."[54] This sentence from the *Era* refers to "The Buffalo Fugitive" (or "The Buffalo Outrage" [140]), an incident in which a fugitive was beaten senseless before being captured. The episode was the focus of considerable attention in the abolitionist press. The report in the *Era* consistently refers to the "alleged slave" in question ("the negro by the name of 'Daniel'" [140]) using italics and quotation marks. These devices are intended to suggest the injustice of his treatment and the problems created by his legal status. The quotation marks around the term "property," and around Daniel's very name direct irony against a law that defines a man as a thing. Yet these rhetorical ploys also have the effect of denying the fugitive all particularity, not to mention subjectivity.

The case of the "Buffalo Fugitive" raised the question of whether a slave who escaped after being brought into a free state by his master could be legally reclaimed, or whether, having disappeared from a free state, the man is already free by rights. The editors of the *Era* believed that there were no grounds for returning such a slave to captivity: "undoubtedly by law [this slave] had a right" to leave the boat that had brought him to a free state (140). The issue that deserves attention here is the surprisingly limited arsenal of rhetorical weapons that had become conventional in such reports: to assert the slave's "undoubted" right to freedom in this instance would not have persuaded anyone who (like Commissioner Smith) believed that "*a master has a perfect right to take his slave into or through a free state, and we as citizens of Free States are bound to protect the rights and the property of people in the South*" (140). The *Era* italicizes this statement by the commissioner in order to ridicule it—as if its absurdity is patently obvious. But its absurdity was obvious only to those who already agreed with the *Era*'s view of the case.

The tactical use of quotation marks and italics as well as other modes of punctuation became routine in attacks on the legal commonplaces of slavery.[55] Another passage about "The Buffalo Fugitive," quotes Commissioner Smith as follows: "'A man has a perfect right to bring his slave into a free state and it does not enfranchise him (!)'" (140). The exclamation point, placed in parenthesis after the commissioner's statement, is designed to mock his claim. Such devices implied irony; they were to trigger a familiar set of associations in like-minded readers. But the limited range of punctuation marks the *Era* employed as a kind of shorthand for this purpose had little power in shaping an argument, and still less in creating the sense of a fugitive as a particular person.

We "are alternately shocked by the inhumanity of the commissioner and amazed by his ignorance of the law which he undertook to administer," the article notes. "The common reader will at once confess the inhumanity. The barefaced ignorance we shall easily expose" (140). Presuming the "inhumanity" to be self-evident (apparent "at once"), the article soon passes over it and proceeds to make a detailed case for the idea that local and municipal law should determine relations between owner and slave. "Daniel" himself, having been given no words, thoughts, or actions to begin with, now disappears from the report.

Stowe attempted to grab the attention of jaded readers by reshaping the horizon of expectations for fictions of black experience. Just as she created a new function for the image of the moribund white child and bereaved parent, so she transformed the perfunctory representation of slaves typical of the abolitionist press. Many images of slaves were clichés by 1850—the male fugitive with a bundle on his back, the female fugitive with a child in her arms, the dogs in pursuit of a slave at bay.[56] Stowe urges her reader to become acquainted not with a "handful of negroes" or a silent, depersonalized "fugitive named Daniel" but with "our old friend Eliza," and "our humble friend Tom." On the whole, the black characters who are given the greatest amount of attention in *Uncle Tom's Cabin* sooner or later embody ideals of white middle-class behavior, including gratitude and self-control.[57]

However, many of these characters invite the reader's identification precisely where white norms of behavior are abrogated.

Poetic Norms: Fugitives and Others

One additional framework for representing slavery in the *Era* is worth examination. Well before 1851, poetry had become a forum for rendering imaginary scenarios that involved fugitives as well as slave-catchers and other representatives of the white community. The poetry of the *Era* was often as flowery, didactic, and pious as installment fiction; yet the subject matter of poetry was broader. As the "highest" of the literary genres, poetry was widely presumed to be suited to lofty subjects—such as freedom. Poetic celebrations of freedom are frequent in the pages of the *Era* between 1850 and 1852, but these texts generally confine themselves to abstractions. Many a "Liberty Ode" castigates "foul oppression's night" and praises "freedom" without mentioning slavery at all.[58]

As Susan Belasco Smith has noted, one recurrent focus for the theme of liberty in this period was the revolution in Hungary, which brought Louis Kossuth to New York and stimulated much discussion of America as a haven for Hungarian exiles ("Ho! to the brave and noble band, / To Hungary's cause so tried, and true, / Columbia stretches forth her hand— / There's room for each, for all of you").[59] This theme became so pervasive in prose as well as poetry that some commentators, including Stowe herself, noted the ironic distance between the image of the noble European fugitive and his persecuted American counterpart (see *Uncle Tom's Cabin*, 299). More often, however, this analogy was not emphasized. Indeed, most of the *Era*'s poetry, like its fiction, refrained from addressing contemporary social problems directly, unless (as with events in Hungary) they could become the occasion for an expression of exemplary moral, spiritual, or patriotic ideals.[60]

For the purposes of the present argument, it is the exceptions to this ritual of avoidance that should be noted. The *Era* did publish some poetry that (unlike its fiction) directly addressed the problem of slavery. Such poems took a variety of forms. They ranged from urgent appeals to the North for political action ("Ho! . . . New England's sons! / . . . Come forth! ye chosen ones, / . . . to rend the curtains / Of slavery's brooding night" [4 April 1850, 52]) to satires of hypocritical clergymen. Poems in the former mode were often dominated by abstractions ("freemen," "battle for the right," "redemption drawing nigh"). Satiric poems, on the other hand, were often so coy or so broad that (like the rhetoric of news reports) they would only appeal to the already convinced. In John Greenleaf Whittier's "A Sabbath Scene," for example, a minister throws a Bible at an escaped fugitive to trip her in the aisle of a church: "'Of course I know your right divine / To own and work and whip her; / Quick deacon, throw that Polyglott / Before the wench, and trip her!'"[61] This turns out to be a nightmare from which the speaker of the poem awakens at the end; but the dream conceit made it all the easier for a proslavery reader to dismiss the represented events as exaggerated.

The antislavery poetry of the *Era,* whether exhortatory or satiric, formed a relatively repetitive array of verse. From within this array, however, a few texts stand out. Occasionally, poetic narratives created slave figures capable of thought and action. Some poems in this category even attempted to render a black character's voice. Such texts helped prepare the ground for Stowe, directly or indirectly.

The speaker of "The Slave—A Tableau" is a slave-parent, on the verge of running away. He (or she—the speaker's gender is not clear) declaims a series of reflections as follows:

> The stream is free, that courses through our vales
> The waves whose music breaks upon the shore—
> Why should I be thus doomed to wear a chain? . . .
>
> What hopes and fears now crowd my aching brain?
> As by our sleeping breasts our children lie!
> To make us free, does Night now pour her strain,
> For which the stars are beckoning in the sky? . . .
>
> We snatched our babes, so young and fair. . . .
> O! keep the bloodhounds from our tear-stained track![62]

If this poem attempts to create the feel of spontaneous speech it is hamstrung by the literary convention of dramatic monologue and the constraints of its rhythm and meter. The poem's elaborate focus on the backdrop of benign Nature further disrupts any sense of immediacy in the speaker's voice. Still, unlike news reports, such poetry did attempt to motivate the action of a fugitive from within. Relying on the sentimental image of a threatened domestic idyll, the poem invites the reader to contemplate an analogy between black and white experience, to identify with the speaker's situation, to believe that a slave has words and feelings.[63] The elevated language itself makes a claim for the slave speaker as human and literate.

Occasionally, a poem about a fugitive went further in the direction that Stowe herself would soon take. One such poem was published in the *Era* on 24 April 1851, ten weeks before the first installment of *Uncle Tom's Cabin.* A forceful text in its own right, it deserves special attention here because both its language and its themes may have inspired Stowe as she began to write her novel. "The Wanderer," by M. Hempstead, was a narrative poem in twenty-one verses.[64] It creates an effect quite different from the *Era*'s bitingly satiric portraits of white hypocrisy or its occasional poetic efforts to render a fugitive's voice. Unlike poems such as "The Slave—a Tableau," with its literate speech, high-flown rhetoric, and elaborate imagery, the language of "The Wanderer" is colloquial, its rhyme scheme simple. Its primary speaker briefly sets the scene and proceeds to represent a conversation between a minister and his "little daughter." "'Father,'" she asks, "'When you told us about Daniel, / How he would not cease to pray, / Tho a law was made against it— / It was righteous, did you say?'" (lines 7–12). The girl's question leads her father to affirm the notion of "a higher law than human" (line 25)—a familiar argument to opponents of the Fugitive Law. The child in the poem bows her head in silent understanding, and her voice disappears from the text at this point. But when a servant enters the room to tell the father that "'there is a stranger woman / Wants to see you at the door; / So forlorn a human being / Never did I see before'" (lines 37–40), the little girl presses her cheek "close against the window pane" (line 44) in order to observe the stranger. This child is more marginal to the action than the figure of Eva in *Uncle Tom's Cabin,* but, like Eva, she is a witness to many of the subsequent events and provides a kind of "natural" morality against which to evaluate them.

The minister sends for the stranger ("'None have ever sought in vain / At my hand,' replied the master" [lines 46–47]). It soon turns out, however, that the stranger is a fugitive: "'Save me! for the love of Heaven, / Save me!'" (lines 61–62) the woman cries, as her "searching glance" discerns "moving figures in the distance" (lines 65–66). The minister now refuses to help her: "'God protect you,' said the pastor, / 'For I cannot grant you aid; / Evil times are fallen upon us, / When such brutal laws are made; / But it is the will of Heaven / That our rulers be obeyed'" (lines 73–78). Unlike the self-righteous figures often mocked by the *Era*'s satiric pieces, this minister is torn: "O, the gaze of speechless anguish! / O the heart-wrung woman's wail! / As the hunted slave flew onward, / Made his very heart to quail— / Made his very hair to stiffen / And his face turn ashy pale!" (lines 77–84). The narrative now pursues the fugitive, introducing two additional characters and adding another moral level with a few economical strokes: "When the moon arose that evening / On the evil and the good / Two poor tenants of a hovel, / That beside a forest stood, / Found the hunted woman lying / Where they went to gather wood" (lines 91–96). This couple takes the fugitive in and tends her until she dies. The parish then provides a coffin and a grave. The pastor presides at the funeral but "his language fail[s him]" (line 110). In the last three verses, the narrator celebrates the actions of the poor couple and adjures the reader to have sympathy for the minister:

> In his ear a wail is ringing
>   And he hears it everywhere
> Hears it in his quiet parlor
>   Hears it on the pulpit stair
> O, entreat this pastor kindly
>   For he has enough to bear!
>
> But for that poor hovel's inmates
>   When they thither turned again,
> Well they knew it was an angel
>   That upon their bed had lain
> For it lighter seemed, and softer
>   To their weariness and pain.
>
> And their frugal bread seemed sweeter
>   To their hunger than before—
> Warmer was the sullen hearthstone,
>   Smoother was the broken floor,
> And they loved each other better,
>   Loved their God and neighbor more.

Stowe was already working on *Uncle Tom's Cabin* when this poem appeared in the *Era* on 24 April. In a letter to Bailey, written on 9 March, Stowe explained that she had begun work on an antislavery sketch for his paper.[65] Bailey announced the forthcoming serial on 8 May (though the first installment did not in fact appear until 5 June).

Whether or not Stowe read "The Wanderer," its innovations for representing slavery point in the direction of her text. Like *Uncle Tom's Cabin*, "The Wanderer" stresses the moral consequences of slavery for everyone involved. With its evangelical emphasis, it attempts to create an empathetic perspective not only on the fugitive, but also on the minister and the poor couple. Stylistically, is has a simple and dramatic narrative line; its story is told alternately through dialogue and through the words of an omniscient narrator who (like Stowe in *Uncle Tom's Cabin*) sometimes exhorts the reader ("O, entreat this pastor kindly" [line 125]), sometimes heightens the drama with vivid descriptions ("Made his very hair to stiffen / And his face turn ashy pale!" [lines 83–84]), and sometimes renders an action in succinct and prosy language ("but the door was shut and bolted / And the fugitive was gone" [line 85–86]). The emphasis on the minister's failure of language suggests that the poet had given considerable thought to the question of rhetoric.

This poem anticipates many of the structural imperatives Stowe was in the process of grasping: the need to strip the slave situation of lofty generalities; to situate the action in a recognizable America rather than in Africa, Europe, or a dreamscape; to eliminate unrelieved caricature when representing those who upheld the Fugitive Law; to give ample time and space for developing the portrait of human relationships and dramatic conflicts; to differentiate between the voices of the actors in the tale; to leave certain problems unresolved, encouraging the reader to ponder.

"The Wanderer" challenged some conventional images and rhetorical strategies characteristic of the abolitionist press. Nonetheless, like most fiction and poetry of the *Era,* this versified drama is set in an unnamed locality, not a specific village or state of the Union. Moreover, the fugitive here remains a victim, dependent on others and unable to achieve her goal at any level. She is an occasion for demonstrating the appropriate behavior of the white world on which she is dependent.

It remained for Stowe to make the figure of the fugitive both more radical and more attractive in a work of fiction, thereby engaging the attention not only of already convinced readers but also of undecided ones. Stowe elicited the sympathetic responses of a complacent reading public by making slavery "new" in multiple ways. In the course of an unusually long serialized narrative (*Uncle Tom's Cabin* ran for more than ten months when a two- or three-month serial was common), Stowe created a framework for complicating a set of political, religious, and literary norms. Devoting ample attention to the desires, pain, and doubts of her black characters, Stowe modeled her African American figures on an idea of human beings. If many of the slaves she imagined exemplify widely accepted ideals of white middle-class behavior, some also violate civic laws and social conventions.

Uncle Tom's Cabin ultimately affirms many of the moral and rhetorical norms that it challenges along the way. But it also gave its initial readers ample time and imaginative space to try out a fresh perspective. Stowe's emphasis on middle-class altruism and evangelical Christianity kept the most radical implications of her vision in check. But in representing slave bereavement, language, and action, Stowe both catered to and radically revised the expectations of sentimental readers. It was this complicated balancing act that made Stowe's novel such a paradoxical accomplishment: a popular sensation with a revolutionary impact.

Notes

1. Stowe used these words to describe the cholera epidemic that would later claim her infant son among its victims in Cincinnati. Charles E. Stowe, *The Life of Harriet Beecher Stowe Compiled from Her Letters and Journals* (Boston: Houghton, Mifflin and Co., 1889), 121.

2. For discussions that address the serialization of *Uncle Tom's Cabin,* see E. Bruce Kirkland, *The Building of Uncle Tom's Cabin* (Knoxville: University of Tennessee Press, 1977), 61–149; Susan Belasco Smith, "Serialization and the Nature of *Uncle Tom's Cabin,*" in *Periodical Literature in Nineteenth-Century America,* ed. Susan Belasco Smith and Kenneth Price (Charlottesville: University Press of Virginia, 1995), 69–89; Michael Winship, "The Greatest Book of Its Kind: A Publishing History of *Uncle Tom's Cabin,*" *Proceedings of the American Antiquarian Society* 109, part 2 (1999): 309–32.

3. Moira Davison Reynolds, *Uncle Tom's Cabin and Mid-Nineteenth-Century United States: Pen and Conscience* (Jefferson: McFarland and Co., 1985), 76.

4. Victor Shklovsky, *Theory of Prose.* The term "defamiliarization" is commonly used in English to represent Shklovsky's Russian expression. It appears in Lee T. Lemon and Marion J. Reis, *Russian Formalist Criticism* (Lincoln: University of Nebraska Press, 1965). Shklovsky's term is retranslated as "enstragement" by Benjamin Sher (Normal, Ill: Dalkey Archival Press, 1991), xviii–xix.

5. Harriet Beecher Stowe, *Uncle Tom's Cabin* (New York: Penguin, 1987), 328. Further references to this edition are given parenthetically in the text.

6. David Reynolds explores the balance between subversive and conventional elements in *Uncle Tom's Cabin.* Reynolds's emphasis on the "dark" undercurrents in Stowe's novel has been overshadowed by the critical preoccupation with sentiment. See his *Beneath the American Renaissance: The Subversive Imagination in the Age of Emerson and Melville* (New York: Knopf, 1988).

7. See especially Jane Tompkins, "Sentimental Power: *Uncle Tom's Cabin* and the Politics of Literary History," in Tompkins, *Sensational Designs: The Cultural Work of American Fiction, 1790–1860* (New York: Oxford University Press, 1985), 130, 135.

8. According to the reception aesthetics of Hans Robert Jauss, a popular success is created when a work fulfills—rather than disturbs—generic expectations. Jauss seeks a way to differentiate between major and minor works. For him, popularity is at odds with the possibility of "greatness." The great work disrupts convention, while the popular one merely fulfills it. As I will argue, however, *Uncle Tom's Cabin* both fulfilled and disrupted interpretive norms.

9. Stowe uses the phrase "new eyes" in her pamphlet *Earthly Care: A Heavenly Discipline* in order to emphasize the difficulty of both perceiving and representing God's involvement in everyday life (Boston: American Tract Society, 1850), 14.

10. Ophelia comes to "view . . . [Topsy] through the softened medium that Eva's hand had first held before her eyes" (443). "'I wish I had your eyes,'" St. Clare tells Tom, when reading the Bible after Eva's death (437).

11. On the balance of fiction and news in antebellum newspapers, see Ronald Zboray, *A Fictive People: Antebellum Economic Development and the American Reading Public* (New York: Oxford University Press, 1993), 126–29. On the penny press, see Frank Luther Mott, *American Journalism: A History of Newspapers in the United States Through Two Hundred and Fifty Years: 1690–1940* (New York: Macmillan, 1947), and Michael Schudson, *Discovering the News: A Social History of American Newspapers* (New York: Basic Books, 1978), 12–60. For a succinct discussion of the difference between the "story papers" and the "penny press," see Michael Denning, *Mechanic Accents: Dime Novels and Working-Class Culture in America* (New York: Verso, 1987), 10–11. Ann Douglass argues that in the 1840s and 1850s

the religious press tried to compete with popular women's magazines by a judicious use of fiction "designed to precipitate religious sensibility" (*The Feminization of American Culture* [New York: Knopf, 1977], 234). On the role of periodicals in antebellum literary culture, see also Isabelle Lehuu, *Carnival on the Page: Popular Print Media in Antebellum America* (Chapel Hill: University of North Carolina Press, 2000), and the introduction to Belasco Smith and Price, *Periodical Literature in Nineteenth-Century America.*

12. The closest thing to an exception in the year before *Uncle Tom's Cabin* began is Stowe's own "Freeman's Dream," which appeared in the *Era* on 1 August 1850. This brief "parable" engages the problem of fugitive slaves in a fictionalized form. But its brevity, combined with the dream motif and "parable" aspect, makes it quite different from *Uncle Tom's Cabin.* E.D.E.N. Southworth's *Retribution,* serialized in 1849, attempted to address the subject of slavery but, as Lyde Cullen Sizer notes, Southworth represented slaves "only marginally" (as well as reductively). See Sizer, *The Political Work of Northern American Women Writers and the Civil War, 1850–1872* (Chapel Hill: University of North Carolina Press, 2000) 52–54.

13. "Our Annual Letter," loose sheet inserted into the *National Era,* 13 Nov. 1851.

14. For a discussion of Stowe's essay, see Barbara Hochman's introduction, *PMLA* 118 (Oct. 2003): 1320–22.

15. "I am reading Scott's novels in their order. . . . I shall begin *Kenilworth* next week; yet I am constantly pursued and haunted by the idea that I don't do anything," Stowe wrote in a letter (cited in Charles Stowe, *Life of Harriet Beecher Stowe,* 139). On the persistence of the antifiction prejudice, see Nancy Glazener, *Reading for Realism: The History of a U.S. Literary Institution, 1850–1910* (Durham: Duke University Press, 1997), 93–146, and Barbara Hochman, "The Reading Habit and 'The Yellow Wallpaper'" *American Literature* 74 (March 2002), 89–110.

16. Harriet Beecher Stowe, "Introduction" to Charles Beecher, *The Incarnation: or, Pictures of the Virgin and Her Son* (New York: Harper, 1849), iv.

17. See especially Harriet Beecher Stowe, *Literary Epidemics* 1 and 2, *New York Evangelist* 13 and 14 (28 July 1842, 13 July 1843), 235, 109.

18. As Gillian Brown suggests, *Uncle Tom's Cabin* represents the family not as a refuge from but as an index to contemporary economic and political issues. See "Domestic Politics in *Uncle Tom's Cabin,*" in Brown, *Domestic Individualism: Imagining Self in Nineteenth-Century America* (Berkeley and Los Angeles: University of California Press, 1990), 13–37.

19. "The Poor Boy," an exhortatory piece, presents the typical moral found in fiction about "the poor": "Don't be ashamed, my lad, if you have a patch on your elbow. It's no mark of disgrace. . . . No good boy will shun you, because you cannot dress as well as your companion; and if a bad boy sometimes laughs at your appearance say nothing, my lad, but walk on. . . . Be good my boy; and if you are poor you will be respected a great deal more than if you were the son of a rich man and were addicted to bad habits" (18 Sept. 1851), 151.

20. In "Ill-Starred," by Patty Lee, for example, a well-matched pair of good-for-nothings die in poverty and disgrace. "Ill-starred" was serialized in the *Era* between 17 July and 9 October 1851. Lee was a frequent contributor to the *Era.* See also "Be Patient," by Mary Irving (18 Dec. 1851, 201, and 25 Dec. 1851, 203).

21. The only example I have found of a fleeting reference to slavery in the fiction that shared the pages of the *Era* with *Uncle Tom's Cabin* is in the following lines from "Ill-starred": "Mrs. Bates said she . . . had come to say something that would have been . . . to Mr. Claverel's advantage, and that she would rather be to the advantage of a black slave than to the disadvantage, but that if he was not of a mind to have an advantage" (25 Sept. 1851, 153).

22. Harriet Beecher Stowe, "Earthly Care: A Heavenly Discipline," 60. Stowe's pamphlet was frequently reprinted over the next nineteen years.

23. Irving, "Be Patient," 20.

24. Obituary of Mary Osgood (10 July 1851, 110). Cf. obituary of Isabella Rose (31 July 1851). "Death loves a shining mark," says the narrator of "Light and Shade," by Patty Lee, which appeared on the same page as installment six of *Uncle Tom's Cabin* (10 July 1851, 109).

25. "Guard Thy Trust," poem by "Meta" (28 Aug. 1851, 137).

26. "The Lost Child," poem by Jane Kavenaugh (19 June 1851, 98). As another typical poem puts it, "Oh she was choicer, sweeter far / My lovely fragrant rose / More beautiful, beyond compare / Than thy broad garden knows" ("Meta," "Guard Thy Trust," 137).

27. Kavenaugh, "Lost Child," 98; cf. the "smitten bud" in "Thoughts at a Grave," a poem by "Constance" (25 Sept. 1851, 153).

28. "Annie Clayville," by Alice Carey (12 June 1851, 94). In "Bessie" by Phoebe Carey, she is "hushed away from mortal pain" (13 Nov. [misprinted 31 Nov.] 1851, 183).

29. On the shifting norms of mourning in antebellum America, see Douglass, *Feminization of American Culture;* Karen Halttunen, *Confidence Men and Painted Women: A Study of Middle-Class Culture in America, 1830–1870* (New Haven: Yale University Press, 1982), 125–52; Mary Louise Kete, *Sentimental Collaboration: Mourning and Middle-Class Identity in Nineteenth-Century America* (Durham: Duke University Press, 2000).

30. As one characteristic poem puts it, "Immortal youth crowns him who 'died young'" (Caroline Chessbro, "Finis," 4 Sept. 1851, 141); or, in the final stanza of another, "Oh! many a blossom, blighted / Drooping on Earth's cold sod, / Transplanted blooms in beauteous life, / In the Paradise of God" (Kavenaugh, "Lost Child," 98). Cf. "She blooms in brighter bowers" (Constance, "Thoughts at a Grave," 25 Sept. 1851, 153).

31. Children's obituaries provide additional emphasis, as do multiple ads for products that claim to cure bronchitis, consumption, and other "diseases of the lungs." Such ads, which sometimes appeared in the same column as obituaries, often included testimonials from patients, "statistics" stating (for example) that "one sixth of the whole population die annually of consumption" (5 June 1851, 91), and reminders of the danger in neglecting even "a slight cough" (advertisement for Dr. Wister's Balsam of Wild Cherry, 31 Jan. 1851, 123).

32. Some critics have claimed that Eva's death achieves nothing (Douglass, *Feminization of American Culture,* 3–4; Philip Fisher, *Hard Facts: Setting and Form in the American Novel* [New York: Oxford University Press, 1985], 104–10), but this claim is overstated. At the level of the plot Eva converts and thus redeems Topsy; she has a profound effect on Ophelia, who sets Topsy free as a result. Eva's death also begins to work spiritual changes with practical implications in St. Clare.

33. On some specific reading conventions typical of antebellum fiction readers, see Nina Baym, *Novels, Readers, and Reviewers: Responses to Fiction in Antebellum America* (Ithaca: Cornell University Press, 1984); James L. Machor, "Fiction and Informed Reading in Early Nineteenth-Century America" *Nineteenth-Century Literature* 47, no. 3 (1992): 320–48. On communally agreed upon norms as a shaping force in interpretation generally, see Stanley Fish, *Is There a Text in This Class? The Authority of Interpretive Communities* (Cambridge: Harvard University Press, 1980), esp. the title essay, "Is There a Text in This Class?" 303–21.

34. Fisher, *Hard Facts,* 103, 106–7; Richard Brodhead, *Cultures of Letters: Scenes of Reading and Writing in Nineteenth-Century America* (Chicago: University of Chicago Press, 1993), 35; Athena Vrettos, *Somatic Fictions: Imagining Illness in Victorian Culture* (Stanford: Stanford University Press, 1995), 99–101. Stowe gives Eva the symptoms of consumption as well, of course—persistent cough, hectic flush, misleading remissions. But this "realistic" motivation does not make the symbolic implications less emphatic.

35. When her infant Charley died of cholera in July 1849, Stowe wrote to her husband, "Many an anxious night have I held him to my bosom and felt the sorrow and loneliness pass out of me with the touch of his little warm hands. Yet I have just seen him in his death agony,

looked on his imploring face when I could not help nor soothe nor do one thing, not one, to mitigate his cruel suffering, do nothing but pray in my anguish that he might die soon." Cited in Joan D. Hedrick, *Harriet Beecher Stowe: A Life* (New York: Oxford University Press, 1994), 191.

36. The notion of children's impressionability—their susceptibility to impressions that literally "sink into" the heart—became central to educational theory early in the nineteenth century. See Nancy F. Cott, *The Bonds of Womanhood: "Women's Sphere" in New England, 1780–1835* (New Haven: Yale University Press, 1977), 46, 84–87; Halttunen, *Confidence Men and Painted Women*, 3–4, 40, 49–50; Patricia Crain, *The Story of A: The Alphabetization of America from the New England Primer to* The Scarlet Letter (Stanford: Stanford University Press, 2000), 57–60, 128.

37. "Dora's Children," by Grace Greenwood (12 June 1851, 93). Typically the sentimental child is "meek and gentle and patient"—unlike her "wayward and petulant and fretful" sister, rival, or stepparent. "Light and Shade," by Patty Lee (10 July 1851, 109).

38. Chapter 26 of the book is numbered as chapter 25 in the *Era*. Such discrepancies occurred sometimes because of an error, sometimes because installments contained more or less than a single chapter. Stowe made corrections and occasional changes before the serial was published in book form.

39. "Bessy," by Phoebe Carey, appeared on 13 Nov. 1851, 183. The same number of the *Era* included the famous scene from *Uncle Tom's Cabin* in which Eva, reading the Bible with Tom beside Lake Pontchartrain, tells Tom of her approaching death (installment 22).

40. Patty Lee, "James McCary and His Boy" (4 Dec. 1851, 193). In the episode of *Uncle Tom's Cabin* that was published on 25 Dec., St. Clare himself dies saying "Mother," but, characteristically, Stowe's text soon shifts attention to the chaos St. Clare leaves behind.

41. Cited in Douglass, *Feminization of American Culture*, 129.

42. The reason for the missed deadline is unknown. (Only three times after the serial began did the *Era* appear without an installment of *Uncle Tom's Cabin*.) On 18 December Bailey printed the following announcement: "We regret as much as any of our readers can regret, that Mrs. Stowe has no chapter in this week's *Era*. It is not our fault for up to this hour we have nothing from her. As she is generally so punctual we feel constrained to make this apology, so profound is the interest taken in her story by nearly all our readers" (203). The episode that appeared in the following number of the *Era*—on Christmas day—included St. Clare's death.

43. The following announcement appeared instead: "Chapter XII of *Uncle Tom's Cabin* reached us at too late an hour for insertion this week and Mrs Stowe having requested that it should not be divided our readers may look for the entire chapter in the next *Era*" (21 April 1851, 134).

44. "Ill-starred," by Patty Lee (21 Aug. 1851, 133).

45. Billings had designed the masthead for William Lloyd Garrison's abolitionist newspaper *The Liberator* and illustrated a volume of poetry with many verses on the subject of slavery by John Greenleaf Whittier. Whittier, *Poems* (Boston: Benjamin B. Mussey & Co., 1849). On Billings's career, see James F. O'Gorman, *Accomplished in All Departments of Art: Hammatt Billings of Boston: 1818–1874* (Amherst: University of Massachusetts Press, 1998).

46. From sentimental fiction through the dime novel, popular heroines conformed to norms of gentility. Henry Nash Smith discusses the figure of the Indian girl who can ride and shoot as an alternative to the heroine as "passive sexual object" in *Virgin Land: The American West as Symbol and Myth* (New York: Vintage Books, 1950), 126. In temperance fiction, nongenteel women characters demonstrate violent behavior but, like the mildly erring heroines of the *Era*, they are always punished or converted at the end. Even in such outrageous

crime fiction as George Thompson's *The Housebreaker: or, the Mysteries of Crime,* the vital and sexually active Anne Mobray is, at the end of the story, relegated to a permanent place on the social margins. Another alternative to the genteel heroine is the figure of the prostitute — "the erotically deviant body." On this recurrent image in nineteenth-century fiction, see Peter Brooks, *Reading for the Plot: Design and Intention in Narrative* (Oxford: Clarendon Press, 1984), 154. Brooks's discussion of Eugene Sue's serial, the popular *Mysteries of Paris* (which Stowe read), directly engages the paradox by which a sensational novel that offers "melodramatic contrasts" to titillate a bourgeois audience may also provide "an inquest into the system responsible [for those contrasts]" (151–52).

47. On the conventions of representing the female body in this period, see Sanchez-Eppler, *Touching Liberty: Abolition, Feminism, and the Politics of the Body* (Berkeley and Los Angeles: University of California Press, 1997), 14–49, and Joy S. Kasson, "Narratives of the Female Body: The Greek Slave," in *The Culture of Sentiment: Race, Gender, and Sentimentality in Nineteenth-Century America,* ed. Shirley Samuels (New York: Oxford University Press, 1992), 172–90.

48. For an emphasis on the "transgressive pleasures" of reading *Uncle Tom's Cabin,* see Marianne Noble, *The Masochistic Pleasures of Sentimental Literature* (Princeton: Princeton University Press, 2000), 141–43.

49. See Marcus Wood's fine analysis of the visual semiotics for representing fugitives in *Blind Memory: Visual Representations of Slavery in England and America, 1780–1865* (New York: Routledge, 2000). Wood notes but does not pursue the difference between Stowe's text and the visual images that often deformed her initial emphases (143).

50. See, for example, discussions of the "Christiana Case" or "Christiana Tragedy," which ran intermittently from 2 Oct. 1851 through 1 Jan. 1852.

51. In the antebellum period most people got their political information from newspapers. In the decades before the Civil War, the development of the telegraph and wire services helped stimulate the interest in "hard" news. As Menahem Blondheim puts it, the public "developed a taste for ever more and ever faster news. . . . It was the telegraphic columns the public craved, bought the newspaper for, read first, if not exclusively." Blondheim, "Public Sentiment Is Everything: The Union's Public Communications Strategy and the Bogus Proclamation of 1864," *Journal of American History* (Dec. 2002): 875. The function of the abolitionist weeklies was different from that of the mass-circulation dailies in many respects. The abolitionist press printed proportionally more editorial commentary, more correspondence, more "literature." Yet, as Stowe seems to have perceived, the growing availability of "facts," in the *Era* as elsewhere, would seem to have left other readerly desires unfulfilled.

52. "Philadelphia Correspondence: The Christiana Tragedy" (2 Oct. 1851, 158, 159); "Commitment for Treason" (2 Oct. 1851, 158).

53. On the tensions informing sympathy and sentiment, see Fisher, *Hard Facts;* Samuels, *Culture of Sentiment;* Glenn Hendler, *Public Sentiments: Structures of Feelings in Nineteenth-Century American Literature* (Chapel Hill: University of North Carolina Press, 2001).

54. "The Buffalo Fugitive" (18 Aug. 1851, 139). Further references to this article are given parenthetically in the text.

55. William Lloyd Garrison's *Liberator* was more innovative than the *National Era* in using "attention-getting visuals, such as capital letters, bold face, and italics" for emphasis. On the *Liberator's* typographical strategies, see Augusta Rohrbach "'Truth Stronger and Stranger Than Fiction': Reexamining William Lloyd Garrison's *Liberator,*" *American Literature* 73, no. 4 (2001): 739. Nonetheless, the norms of representing fugitives in the *Liberator* do not differ significantly from those of the *Era.* For characteristic examples, see the report of the Henry Long Case (*Liberator,* 17 Jan. 1851, 10); or "A Remarkable Decision in the Supreme Court" (*Liberator,* 31 Jan. 1851, 17).

56. The official seal of the Society for the Abolition of the Slave Trade in London (1787) represented a "kneeling enchained male African beneath the question "Am I not a man and brother?" This image "was reproduced as the heading to a great number of anti-slavery publications appearing as stationary, in books, prints, oil paintings, newspaper headings and as a ceramic figurine" (Wood, *Blind Memory*, 22). As Marion Wilson Starling notes, "The figure of the fugitive slave, panting in a swamp, with the slave holder brandishing a whip and surrounded by bloodhounds . . . became so popular as a symbol [after 1835] that dinner plates were made with the scene for a center motif; the handles of silverware were embossed with the story . . . and the fad even extended to the embellishment of transparent window blinds." Starling, *The Slave Narrative: Its Place in American History* (Washington, D.C.: Howard University Press, 1988), 29.

57. On self-control as indispensable in marking slaves as deserving of white sympathy, see Christopher Castiglia, "Abolition's Racial Interiors and the Making of White Civic Depth," *American Literary History* 14, no. 1 (2002): 37, 45–49.

58. "Liberty Ode," (21 Nov. 1850, 188). See, for example, "Reform Verses," by Charles J. Smith (31 Jan. 1850, 20). This poem envisages "a better time for all" and stresses the speaker's "feeling for my fellow / In his most degraded state / Whom his Father in the heavens / In his image did create, / Whom his earthly brother visits / With so devilish a hate." But the poem does not refer to slavery directly. *Frederick Douglass' Paper* and the *Liberator* more regularly addressed slave issues in poetry. These poems expressed a range of ideas that included the evils of the Fugitive Law; the ironic contrast between a nation once committed to liberty but now a "land of vile oppression" (*Liberator*, 3 Jan. 1851); the freedom of mind and soul even when the body is enslaved; the importance of extending sympathy to victims of slavery, seen as a persecuted group. Only toward the end of 1851 and the beginning of 1852 did the *Liberator* begin to publish poetry that attempted to capture the slave's point of view. Perhaps *Uncle Tom's Cabin* played a role in this shift of emphasis.

59. "The Fall of Hungary" (15 Aug. 1850, 132). See also Belasco Smith, "Serialization and *Uncle Tom's Cabin*," 79–80, and Larry J. Reynolds, *European Revolutions and the American Literary Renaissance* (New Haven: Yale University Press, 1988), 52–53.

60. For some exceptions, see Mary Irving, "To Daniel Webster" (4 April 1850, 55); John Greenleaf Whittier, "On the Portrait of a Celebrated Magazine Publisher who has Lately Saved the Union and Lost a Contributor" (ibid., 54); George W. Putnam, "To the Workingmen of America" (17 April 1851, 61).

61. "A Sabbath Scene" (27 June 1850, 102).

62. S. H. Lloyd, "The Slave—A Tableau" (16 Jan. 1851, 9).

63. For other poetic attempts by the *Era* to give speech to slave women, see "The Slave Mother to Her Child" (1 Aug. 1850, 12), where a mother uses familiar sentimental terms to express satisfaction in the death of her child ("Thou art sleeping calmly dearest") but departs from the typical emphasis in child-death poetry by stressing that she can bear her own pain now: "For the dregs of slavery's chalice / *Thou* wilt never drink." Cf. "The Free Negro Girl's Message" (17 Jan. 1850, 12). Written in the voice of the "Free Negro Girl" herself, this poem tries to establish a link between the emotions familiar to a "gentle lady" who has loved someone with her "whole soul" and the love of this girl for a man who has been "torn from [her] and sold! / Sold to the land of whips and chains / For gold! For paltry gold!" A strategy that had been used by Margaret Fuller, Lydia Maria Child, and other abolitionists is evident here: humanizing the black woman and elevating her moral and emotional standing by making it similar, if not superior, to that of white women. Here, its dramatic effect is lessened by the speaker's high literary style, which undercuts the naturalness if not the credibility of the girl's speech. The drama is attenuated as well by the fact that the first half of the poem does not

mention the slave issue and relies on a lengthy, generalized, and conventional narrative of lovers who are parted.

64. M. Hempstead, "The Wanderer" (24 April 1851, 68). A "Martha Hempstead" contributed a poem called "Liberty Bells" to *The Liberty Bell* of 1851 (Boston: National Anti-Slavery Bazaar), 1–3; "Who Is Free?" by "M. Hempstead" appeared on the fourth page of *Frederick Douglass' Paper* on 14 Jan. 1853.

65. See Winship, "Greatest Book of Its Kind," 312.

ANOTHER LOOK AT "THE LIFE OF 'DEAD' HEBREW"

Intentional Ignorance of Hebrew in Nineteenth-Century Eastern European Jewish Society

Iris Parush

> The study of language had always stood at the forefront of every Jewish movement of revitalization and cultural renewal. It served as bridesmaid as each new spiritual period began, accompanying it along up to its full ascendancy.
>
> —Reuven Fahn (1937), 31

The Hebrew Language—A "Lost Tongue"

One hundred and fifty years of arduous attempts to revive Hebrew as a modern literary language preceded its revival as a spoken language. Yet, from its incipience to the end of the nineteenth century, modern Hebrew literature could barely gain itself a narrow circle of devoted readers. One of the more acute expressions of the distress of Hebrew authors in the last third of the century was voiced by Yehudah Leib Gordon (1830–92), the greatest of the *Haskalah* (Jewish Enlightenment) poets.[1] In 1871 Gordon published the poem "For Whom Do I Labor?" out of a sense that, lacking an audience, he was perhaps the last of the Hebrew poets:

This article is an expanded version of a lecture given at the Hebrew Language Academy for a session held in honor of Professor Ya'akov Elerhand in 1996. I would like to thank all those who read earlier drafts of the paper and offered helpful comments, especially Professor Menachem Brinker, Mrs. Brakha Fishler, and Professor Luis Landa. It was originally published in Hebrew in *Alpayim* 13 (1996): 65–106, and appears here in modified form. The translation into English is by Dr. Saadya Sternberg.

For Whom Do I Labor?

Whilst poesy's muse upon me comes stealing
Whilst heart conceives and with right hand composing
Poems composing and in a language forgotten
Where triumph, what bliss, may ever prevail
And for whom do I spend my best years in travail
Depriving my person of quiet and gain?
My parents—adhering to their Lord and nation
Commerce, Commandments, their life's occupation
Reason revolts them, good taste never found
"Deathly is poetry, and rhetoric heathen!
"To lodge near a poet is strictly forbidden!"
Thus do they taunt us, viciously hound.[2]

Gordon avers that his best years have been devoted to composing poetry in a "language forgotten"—a language in demand by no one. His lament is that the traditional Jewish society of his day treats writing poetry in Hebrew as an act of apostasy and attacks and isolates those engaged in it.

This lament may strike the modern reader as odd. Scholarship on the origins of Hebrew, like research on the traditional Jewish educational system, rejects as superficial the characterization of Hebrew as a "dead language." Yet if Hebrew was not dead, why were there no readers for modern Hebrew texts? The conventional view can accommodate this difficulty: traditional education indeed prepared potential readers in the Hebrew language, but the community also imposed strict social sanctions on those who read the new Hebrew literature.[3]

Indeed, many researchers dwell on the preservation mechanisms that sustained the Hebrew language over the generations and kept it in continual use.[4] Benjamin Harshav's "Essay on the Revival of the Hebrew Language" is a case in point. Harshav expounds on "the life of 'dead' Hebrew" and claims that explication of Hebrew texts, a central activity in religious life, served to sustain "awareness of the meanings of words and of the parallels between various texts in the Hebrew library."[5] In his opinion, such "Education emphasized the *understanding* of texts" (his emphasis), both in the *heder* and in the *yeshivah*. Language comprehension was reinforced by the methods of study employed within the education system, which included reading and translating the Torah in the *heder,* quoting texts and interpreting them as part of Talmudic studies, and the dialogic method of study employed in the *yeshivahs*. Hebrew, furthermore, was the language used in religious literature, in responsa, in rabbinic decisions, and in community documents. All these, along with the Hebrew component of Yiddish, show,

in Harshav's opinion, that "unlike Latin, which the common folk did not
know and whose primary students were monks, all Jews were required to
study texts in the Holy Tongue. . . . Even if in the lower classes of society
the level of study was not advanced, in fact every male knew—or was
supposed to know—how to read. Hebrew texts served also for daily prayer,
blessings and so forth. Hebrew was understood well in every community
and understood at least partially within each family."[6] Yet this description
of "the life of 'dead' Hebrew" emphasizes only one aspect of the story of
Hebrew while obscuring another. The attitude of the traditional educational
establishment in nineteenth-century Jewish Eastern Europe was much more
complicated. The very instructional methods that contributed to the preservation of Hebrew also made it a "half-dead" language. These methods
reserved the full knowledge of Hebrew to a narrow elite and excluded large
sectors of the reading public. The traditional community did not merely
erect barriers to modern Hebrew literature by denigrating its "heathenish"
authors; it also deprived students of the linguistic capacities needed for
proper understanding of biblical idiom and of the emerging literature. The
literacy policy employed in the traditional educational establishment[7]—
whose students were the potential readers of modern Hebrew literature—
further restricted such literature and thus diminished its potential audience.[8]

This article reconsiders the rift between modern Hebrew literature and
its readers and traces its roots to the politics of literacy in nineteenth-
century Eastern European Jewish society. My thesis is that this society
deliberately withheld instruction of Hebrew, and thus prevented Hebrew
literature from taking root among a much broader potential readership.
This withholding was not a matter of neglect, nor was it a symptom of an
educational system in disarray, but in many respects the opposite. The literacy policy employed in the traditional educational system reflected the
express importance the rabbinic leadership gave to controlling language
and knowledge as a means of shaping the beliefs and ways of life of the
population. The educational system controlled access to linguistic knowledge, determining who would read and what he or she would read. The
traditional elite thus sought to prevent the infiltration of undesirable ideas,
and to reinforce its authority and maintain the existing social order.[9]
Hebrew texts did play a central role in religious life, but Harshav's conclusion that "Education emphasized the *understanding* of texts" is true only
in part.

The withholding of systematic instruction in Hebrew was not unique
to nineteenth-century Eastern European Jewish society. The gradual with-
drawl of Ashkenazi Jewry from the Hebrew language was a continuous process begun long before the Haskalah.[10] Yet it was only during this period that
the attitude toward the Bible and the Hebrew language became a matter of

major, explicit dispute between an emerging *maskilic* elite and the rabbinical authority. In the fierce cultural war that took place during the Haskalah, marked by wrenching processes of secularization, modernization, and Europeanization, the main battle for the soul of Jewish society was waged on the fronts of language, literacy, and education. The *maskilim* returned to the biblical text and struggled to legitimize the acquisition of biblical Hebrew. Their decision to introduce Hebrew (and particularly the pure biblical language) into the Jewish cultural discourse at this particular historical moment was a subversive act that released an immense amount of secularizing energy. The rabbis, for their part, used every available means to deter their adherents from following the *maskilim* and impede the *maskilic* enterprise. As we shall see, the deliberate control of the Hebrew language was clearly one of these measures.

The status of two bodies of knowledge in nineteenth-century Eastern European Jewish society—Hebrew grammar and the biblical text—supports my contention. The acquisition of Hebrew, which was not a spoken tongue, depended entirely on systematic instruction in these two areas.[11] Yet, for reasons I will adduce later, the rabbinic leadership approached the engagement with grammar and the biblical text with reservations and hostility. As a result, an intentional ignorance of the Hebrew language evolved. This situation, in turn, had a decisive influence on the readership of modern Hebrew literature and on the linguistic options that this literature had available to it. An examination of the sociolinguistic background of the rise of modern Hebrew literature is therefore essential for understanding both the formation of this literature and its later development. The autobiographical work of Avraham Baer Gottlober (1810–99), *Childhood Memories*, provides a good starting point, for Gottlober's memoir reflects the traditional attitude toward grammar.

The Memoirs of Avraham Baer Gottlober

The opening chapter of Gottlober's *Childhood Memories* has three parts.[12] The first part depicts his father's personality; the second, in the style of Haskalah autobiography, deals with the education of the author, and the third describes his induction into married life. Thus this first chapter is highly compressed, emphasizing the author's key childhood experiences up to the period of his adulthood and marriage. It is noteworthy that, in such a compressed account of the first part of his life, Gottlober describes his introduction to grammar in great detail; it dominates the story of his education.

Gottlober portrays his studies in the *heder* as a short and traumatic experience that ended when, after vigorous beatings from the *belfer*, he fell sick, at which point his alarmed father hired a *Melamed*—a private tutor— to instruct him at home. The *Melamed*, says Gottlober, taught him after his own way, "and his way was all dark and devious, for he knew not even the grammar of the letters and the vowels and other punctuation marks." The *Melamed*'s deficiencies were compensated for by Gottlober's much-admired father, who studied with his son each night.

Of all his hours in the company of his father, Gottlober selects one episode for special mention:

> In those days I was studying [Talmud] Tractate *ktubbot* with my father of blessed memory, and upon reaching the end of chapter 6 (folio 69b) my father skipped over the commentary of Rashi and sought to conceal it from me. And when I inquired thereupon what fault was to be found with these words of Rashi, that he would not read them aloud as was his manner, my father responded saying: Know, son, that we have no share and portion in these words of Rashi and futile will it be to approach to understand them, for these statements concern grammar, which we are not to know.[13]

His father's concealment only sharpens Gottlober's interest.

> This occasion was the first time I had heard the word Grammar. And dumbfounded was I at what mine ears heard, knowing not the meaning of the word, and over me the impression arose, that surely this single word embraces a subject vast and wide-reaching, of which my soul longed to know, and hastily I asked my father and beseeched him to explain the meaning of this word and its significance, yet in vain, my father could explain it not. And he replied: "I know not son!" and his face grew pale. And upon seeing how frightened was I from his manner of response, he said in apology: Know, son, that the wisdom of Grammar is large and wide, and hard it is for a man to master it by himself from books without a guide, and moreover books of Grammar are not to be found in all places as are books of the Talmud and the rabbinic verdicts and books of the devout, and in the towns I have dwelt in since my youth I was never able to find books of Grammar, or perhaps they existed in some of these places yet I never inquired about them nor sought to obtain them, for a man can not learn all the forms of wisdom, and it sufficed me to study the books which every man in Israel is obligated to learn, and I had not time enough to peer into books

inessential for the worship of the Lord or for the perfection of my
soul. (74)

Still, confronted with his son's evident passion, the father relents and presents him with the grammar text of Shlomo Zalman HaCohen Hanau
(1687–1746), *Tzohar ha-Teivah.* The first encounter with grammar is described by Gottlober as a deeply moving experience:

> To whom shall I speak and recount my feelings of that moment,
> when I opened the book and began to read in it? Who may under-
> stand me? . . . I will not be fathomed except by one who likewise
> dwelt in darkness as did I then, and suddenly beheld a great light.
> To whom may I speak and recount and be fathomed? I shall keep
> mute and leave it to a great soul, to a wise man who understands
> on his own, to him shall I describe my emotions upon first opening
> mine eyes to read the book. (75)

Gottlober describes the texts he has read up until then, books that fired
his imagination and encouraged his first youthful efforts to write, then
remarks:

> All these books were as naught and void compared with this *Tzo-
> har ha-Teivah,* which lit mine eyes in the laws of the Lord and taught
> me discernment, for until then texts of the Bible I could not rightly
> read, even the names of the vowel-marks I did not rightly know, even
> the remainder of the pronunciation marks such as hard and soft
> stresses, explicit and implicit 'o' marks, cantillation signs, etc. . . .
> which stole sleep from mine eyes the first night, when my father
> brought me the book, which I set not down until the lamp oil ran
> out and burnt away entire and left me covered in darkness, and then
> I reclined another hour and two yet sleep came not to mine eyes nor
> rest to mine brows, as the new knowledge I had gained left me not
> to sleep, and when at last I had fallen into slumber surrounded was
> I round by [diphthongs and sibilants and virgules] which rose in
> dance before me till dawn. (77)

Gottlober's difficulties of self-instruction in grammar using *Tzohar ha-Teivah*
cause him to turn again to his father for help. This time the father seeks
the advice of a knowledgeable Hebrew *maskil* and the *maskil* recommends
the *Talmud Leshon Ivri,* by Yehudah Leib Ben-Ze'ev (1764–1811), which
in his opinion is more systematic and more amenable to self-instruction.[14]
The book, says the *maskil,* "is to be found at so-and-so's, and although its

author was a man with whom the divine spirit does not lodge and is suspected of being an infidel and heretic, yet seeing as the text deals only with the Wisdom of Grammar and not with any of the interrogations of the faith there can be no harm in it." The father decides to give the book to his son but warns him not to spend too much time on it and to temper his interest in it. Gottlober is again overcome: "as I opened the book *Talmud Leshon Ivri* I seemed as if dreaming whilst awake. Like first fruits before summer I drank in his words which were sweet as honey in my mouth, and I put it not down until completing the entire first section" (78).

Talmud Leshon Ivri, however, had its grammatical terms translated into German, a language Gottlober had not mastered, and the difficulties of self-instruction cause him once again to appeal to his father for assistance. The Hassidic father has refrained until then from forming contacts with *maskilim,* yet seeing the distress of his son he departs from practice and turns to another *maskil,* named Wizner. Wizner, amazed that this Hassid has come to him with so strange a request, agrees to tutor Gottlober. It is from this man that Gottlober learns for the first time about the laws of logic: "his words arrived as oil to mine bones and lit mine eyes and I became nearly another man. . . . It seemed as if I had suddenly arrived in another land: for mine eyes had opened and new sights I did see" (80). Here a new chapter in Gottlober's intellectual development begins. For the first time he tackles Maimonides' *Milot ha-Higayon* in Mendelssohn's commentary, identifying "logic" not with the principles of rational thinking alone but also with grammar, as exemplifying logical principles.

Gottlober describes the study of grammar as a sort of stage in a spiritual apprenticeship. He is initiated into a secret world, a process accompanied by dread and other extreme emotions. He sees an opening to "another land" and experiences revelations of a "great light" that amount to a form of re-birth: "I nearly became an other man."[15] In recounting his personal experience Gottlober supplies us with a rich panoply of ethnographic details. He describes the *heder* and his teachers, the "heretic" *maskil* living on the fringes of the town, the rarity of grammar texts, and the difficulties of an autodidact forced to use one text with a defective method and another that uses German terms. His description is more than a personal account of a youth on the road to enlightenment, for it also portrays the attitude toward grammar as a central point of dispute between the *maskilim* and the *Haredi-*orthodox community.[16]

Gottlober's experience was not unusual. The educational process he describes is echoed in the autobiographies and memoirs of numerous *maskilim* that create an impression of a shared literary convention. Often the teacher is portrayed as an ignoramus in grammar and Scripture; the practice of skipping over the Rashi commentaries when they involve grammar appears countless times; and authors like Mordechai Aharon Ginzburg, Y. L. Gordon, Moshe Leib Lilienblum, Mendele Mocher Sfarim, and others, who were lucky enough to have instructors in grammar and Bible, heap infinite praise on the open-minded father or educated teacher, and wonder at their own rare good fortune.[17]

There is a certain *maskilic* tendentiousness in these accounts, yet it is hard to doubt the core of truth they contain. Evidence of a different sort, showing the inferior status of Hebrew grammar, may be found in the responsa of Rabbi Ya'akov Ben-Zvi Emden (1697–1776), in which Emden must decide whether it is permissible to "study the verb cases and tenses in the bathroom."[18] In his responsum Emden points to the practice of allowing the "external wisdoms" to be perused only in the bathroom. The mere question whether one may behave likewise with books of Hebrew grammar reveals the problematic status with which this field of knowledge was regarded in broad circles of Jewish society.[19]

Indeed, in nineteenth-century Jewish Eastern Europe, grammar instruction was not part of the curricula of the *heder* and the *yeshivah*,[20] and anyone examining the source materials for Simchah Assaf's history of Jewish education, or the scholarship of Eliezer Meir Lifschitz, Zvi Sharfstein, Nathan Morris, Emanuel Gamoran, Shaul Stampfer, and others will find ample evidence to that effect. As I shall try to show, the status of grammar instruction—and even the peripheral status of Scripture studies—was not the product of neglect but part of a broad policy of the traditional elite to create deliberate illiteracy in Hebrew grammar and Scripture and hence also in the Hebrew language.[21]

Intentional Ignorance

I am borrowing the concept of "intentional ignorance" from *The Sociology of Ignorance*, by Amos Funkenstein and Adin Steinsaltz.[22] The term "ignorance" connotes lack of knowledge in certain fields, reading not necessarily among them, although the ignorance treated here is closely bound up with illiteracy. "Intentional ignorance" is ignorance deliberately created and maintained by particular authorities. It is created in diverse ways and is effectively maintained by various institutions and social and educational mechanisms, and may be openly acknowledged and justified or generated via vilification or neglect. *The Sociology of Ignorance* exposes such concealed mechanisms and analyzes their causes, and it distinguishes between societies that maintain an ideal of "closed knowledge" and others that seek an ideal of "open knowledge." "Closed knowledge" conceals its method of delivery and is itself opaque in its characteristics and in the critical standards that may apply to it, whereas "open knowledge" is knowledge, in principle at least, accessible by all—it is transparent, its standards of criticism are generally agreed upon, and it can be criticized by anyone who shares in such knowledge.

Funkenstein and Steinsaltz claim that ever since Raban Gamliel was impeached from the presidency of the Sanhedrin, Jewish society has embraced the ideal of "open knowledge" with regard to religious law and Jewish philosophy, and that this ideal "has not been entirely rejected, except in recent generations—and then only with regard to esoteric doctrines" such as the Kabbalah. Yet, as I shall try to show, traditional Jewish society in nineteenth-century Eastern Europe treated grammar, Scripture, and therefore also the Hebrew language as realms of knowledge reserved to the few. In this it continued an educational policy first formulated in the Middle Ages in the communities of France and Ashkenaz. Nonetheless, this intentional ignorance was not the product of some particular institution's decision, nor was it even the result of any explicit ideological opposition to grammar, Scripture, or Hebrew as such. The withholding of knowledge in these realms from the broad public and its maintenance in the hands of a narrow elite derived from a desire, conscious or not, to protect certain beliefs, ideas, and social practices from the threatening elements viewed as associated with these realms of knowledge.

Eastern European Jewish society in the nineteenth century maintained ignorance in grammar, Scripture, and Hebrew in several complementary ways: first, by excluding grammar from the curriculum;[23] second, by abridging instruction of the Bible and by the methods used for such instruction; and third, by presenting rabbinic language as the sole model worthy of imitation.

Exclusion of Grammar from the Curriculum

That systematic instruction in grammar was not part of the educational program was of far-reaching social and cultural significance.[24] The inclusion or exclusion of subjects in curricula is generally evidence of sociocultural change. Thus, for instance, the term "humanism," which denotes the cultural transition from the Middle Ages to the Renaissance, arose from changes to the curriculum and a strengthening of the *Studia Humanitatis*, which included grammar, rhetoric, poetry, and history, and was a reaction to the scholastic curricula, which emphasized logic and metaphysics. This change in curriculum reflected one of the most significant social shifts produced by the humanistic culture of the Renaissance.[25] One can only hint here that there are more than a few parallels between this shift and those that the Haskalah movement sought to achieve in the traditional Jewish educational system.

We may be tempted to conclude that the reason for the exclusion of grammar from the traditional curriculum came not from ideological motives but from difficulties involved in its instruction. Yet this explanation does not seem reasonable. Consistently in the educational system, from the lowest level in the *heder* to the higher *yeshivahs,* the subjects considered important were studied, without hesitation or reservation, regardless of the difficulties involved.[26] Alternatively, one may suppose that Hebrew grammar was excluded simply because it was considered unimportant. This is the opinion of Eliezer Meir Lifschitz, who describes the *heder*'s educational programs from a manifestly apologetic stance. Lifschitz concedes that some two-thirds of *heder* pupils graduated without knowing Hebrew and says:

> In the old *heder,* Hebrew was not among the subjects taught, and the road to its attainment by means of the other studies was long and arduous. . . . The old *heder* was able to persist in this manner because it could depend on the fact that most of its students would remain in its framework until graduation, except for a very few: it gave up on the weakest ranks, accepting that the lower classes of the nation would not know Hebrew, which, in the Diaspora, only mattered to the book-learned. And there was no damage caused, as they were not taught another language either.[27]

Yet this explanation, too, appears inadequate and contrived. In a society where Hebrew was not a spoken language and had to be acquired outside the framework of the formal educational system, avoidance of systematic instruction in grammar functioned as a real barrier to acquiring proficiency in that language. The assumption that in these circumstances knowing Hebrew was deemed insignificant requires a belief that comprehending the words of the prayer books and of the Bible was considered unnecessary. And while many contemporaries indeed believed that this viewpoint reflected the establishment position,[28] their belief makes this explanation no more plausible, given the central importance of the Bible to this society.[29] Had the literal understanding of the text not been perceived as problematic, had the approach to comprehension of Scripture been merely a neutral affair, it is doubtful whether the society would have systematically acted to limit the linguistic facilities needed to study it. It is more reasonable to suppose that the understanding of Hebrew by the broad public was indeed *represented* as unimportant but was in fact regarded by the traditional elite as undesirable and even as dangerous.[30]

This explanation seems especially plausible because—among other reasons—the grammar barrier was not the only obstacle placed by the keepers of the faith on the road to proficiency in Hebrew. The educational system also cut back the amount of instruction in Scripture and limited the methods used for such instruction.

Instructional Methods of Teaching Scripture

The status of Bible instruction in the traditional educational system was, naturally enough, better than that of grammar. Unlike grammar, instruction in reading texts such as the Torah was part of the *heder* curriculum, although the time allocated to Torah study was short and the focus was primarily on the laws set forth in Leviticus.[31] Once study of the five books of Moses was concluded, pupils went on to study the Talmud, and with that the period of formal Bible study typically came to an end.

The encounter with the scriptural text, though brief, might have offered its students access to the linguistic model of biblical Hebrew and its grammar. Yet the pedagogic methods used in the *heder* largely foreclosed this possibility. Torah instruction was carried out using a translation, sometimes after the biblical verse was read out in Hebrew and sometimes before. The translated words were taught in singsong and were learned by heart. The translation into *Yiddish-taytsh* (ancient Yiddish, used in the translations of the books of the Torah and printed for popular use) became canonical, and the sacred nature of the Hebrew original was transferred to this text[32]—so much so that any effort to amend it was considered heresy. Not only did the differing Yiddish dialects obscure the ancient Hebrew words—frequently rendering them incomprehensible—but the method of instruction created further difficulties of comprehension, for the Hebrew words were translated one by one, without regard for comprehensible grammatical order. Thus both understanding of the scriptural text and the learning of Hebrew from the Bible were effectively limited.[33]

A further obstacle was the fragmentary way in which the Torah was taught. Every week, usually only on Thursday evening and Friday, the first part of the weekly Torah portion was studied; the following week the Torah was picked up not where it had left off, but at the beginning of the next portion, before the previous portion had been completed. Thus large sections were skipped, creating gaps in narrative continuity that increased the difficulty of learning Hebrew through Bible study.[34]

Finally, the Torah was read in the *heder* accompanied by the commentary of Rashi, which presented students with rabbinic methods of text analysis and the Midrashic worldview.[35] Yet, even in this framework, the widespread practice was to skip over those of Rashi's commentaries that dealt with grammar, commentaries that many of the instructors themselves could not understand.[36] This practice was extended into the higher *yeshivahs,* as Gordon, for instance, attests, speaking of his comrades at the *yeshivah:* "These young men, in training since early infancy to be Leaders of Israel, did not understand Scripture and could not read verses in the original. This was occasionally the source of embarrassment during their Talmud reading classes. Though the Talmudic stories were full of 'Bible-passages' we used to skip past them in front of our Rabbis or run through them in a single breath, yet when there was some tough unavoidable verse inside a legal passage it stuck like a bone in their windpipes."[37]

Each of these obstacles, taken by itself, may seem innocent enough, an accidental disorder, an expression of conservatism or didactic inexperience, or the sign of a decaying educational system.[38] But taken together they reveal a consistent tendency to conceal the language of the Bible and keep it from serving as a linguistic model. Since Hebrew was not a spoken tongue, restriction of this linguistic model blocked the acquisition of grammar very effectively. Wisely did Rabbi Emden make this point when he prohibited the study of grammar in the men's room on the grounds "that there is no way to arrive at knowledge of the Holy Tongue except by using quoted Bible passages which can serve to illustrate the grammatical rules. For there is not left in our hands a knowledge of the ways of the Holy Tongue except by their means. And thus since one can not peruse them without also murmuring biblical phrases and verses, it is prohibited."[39] This prohibition, then, was no accident, a fact borne out by the failure of attempts to reform the methods of instruction in the *heder,* such as those made by the Prague Maharal (Yehudah Liva Ben Betzal'el 1512?–1609) and his successors, Rabbi Shlomo Ephraim Luntschitz (d.1619), Rabbi Yeshayahu Horowitz (author of *Shnei Luhot ha-Brit,* 1565–1630), and others.[40]

The Model Set by Rabbinic Language

The rabbinic language also played a role in restricting knowledge of Hebrew grammar to an elite few. Boaz Shahevitch sums up the characteristics of rabbinic language:

> A large part of its vocabulary derives from the Talmud and later sources, and intermixed in it is a large number of Aramaic idioms—

words, concepts and sayings. It has few linguistic elements drawn from the Bible, especially in the quotations; its morphology is largely that of the Talmudic idiom, the syntax is chiefly Talmudic, and one finds numerous standard legal expressions from Hebrew and Aramaic: abbreviations, initials, and complex concepts.

The impression it makes is that it is untidy, neglected almost as to its grammar: it is *anarchic* in its use of Hebrew and Aramaic suffixes and in the conjugations of nouns, adjectives, and verbs, as well as in its use of gender, number, and the definite article. . . .

Anyone assessing this language using literary measures . . . finds it to be abbreviated to the point of extremity: heavily dependent on the reader's deep knowledge of the *Halakhic* sources (to the point where anyone not versant in them is likely not to be able to make sense of what is written).[41]

The grammatical "untidiness" of rabbinic language contributed to the fact that even the most advanced scholars lacked a model of a pure and correct Hebrew language. The features Shahevitch describes, including the carelessness toward grammar, were clearly ideological. The complications, the abbreviations, and the complexity of the professional concepts suggest that rabbinic language intended to address only a select and qualified audience.[42] The scholarly elite's special language thus combined with the other measures to foster ignorance of Hebrew.

In these circumstances it was not surprising that there was such a dearth of masters of Hebrew, not only among the majority of students but even among some genuine scholars. It must be stressed that there were differences on this score between Hassidim and Mitnagdim. Among the Hassidim grammatical ignorance was widespread, whereas among the Lithuanians there were students, teachers, and rabbis who knew grammar.[43] But this in no way diminishes the extent of ignorance of Hebrew among the broad public, nor does it undermine the explanation being offered for it here. Indeed, the existence of an elite that *did* maintain this knowledge is itself evidence that there was a social and ideological purpose to keeping it hidden from the "masses." Had there not been such an elite, Hebrew grammar would have been a sort of "nonexistent knowledge," and there would have been no social or other significance in the effort to keep it hidden.

Thus Hebrew was indeed "half-dead," not only because it did not develop through the generations as a living language but because of the small number of people who had full mastery of it. The high degree of literacy among Jewish males in nineteenth-century Europe was in most cases limited to an ability to read the Bible mechanically in order to fulfill their religious obligations; it did not extend to deep comprehension of the Bible or of modern Hebrew texts.[44]

Why Was Knowledge of Hebrew Restricted?

The conclusion that all the factors listed above combine into a single express effort to withhold knowledge is not one that can be immediately drawn. For it may still be asked: was the restriction of access to Hebrew grammar part of a coherent plot or strategy on the part of the rabbis? Prevention of knowledge with the aim of forming intentional ignorance is generally explained or excused in several ways: (1) the particular body of knowledge is not relevant to a profession, or to society as a whole; (2) the body of knowledge interferes with the society's intellectual life; (3) such knowledge is unsuitable to an intellectual man; (4) such knowledge corrupts those who possess it; (5) the knowledge, and the opinions or habits of mind to which it gives rise, threaten to upset the public order and undermine the authority of the leadership.[45] Typically, the first four justifications are supplied explicitly by the established authority and are generally accompanied by the voluntary assent by those who have internalized the leadership's norms. The fifth justification, by contrast, is rarely acknowledged openly.

If we look again at the attitude of Gottlober's father—and he was relatively liberal—we shall see that most of the justifications I have noted were present in traditional Jewish society. Gottlober's father claimed that grammar was of "no use to a person like him, for whom the Torah is his trade," that it was "unnecessary for the worship of the Lord and the perfection of the soul," and that "valuable time should not be wasted on it." But behind these reasons we hear echoes of his first reaction to his son's request: *"We have no share and portion in these words of Rashi and futile will it be to approach to understand them, for these statements concern grammar, which we are not to know."*

Gottlober's father's basic attitude to the study of grammar thus combines two almost opposite ideas: first, that this knowledge is insignificant for attaining religious completeness, and second, that grammatical knowledge is so significant as to be confined to the privileged few. This contradiction is itself evidence that the subject was sensitive and that voluntary ignorance like Gottlober's father's grew from a social norm that served the interest of an elite in keeping such knowledge to itself.

It is no coincidence that all of these justifications address the knowledge of grammar rather than knowledge of the Bible. For the Bible was studied, if only slightly, and its standing as a body of "open knowledge" was not really damaged. Thus the link, which may seem obvious to us, between ignorance of grammar and the shoddy methods of Bible instruction was hidden, repressed. One gets the impression that traditional society found no fault with the accepted methods of instruction in Scripture and believed that knowledge of the Bible among the masses was adequate. That anyone who read the Bible (especially the prophets) outside the framework of devotional obligations was suspected of apostasy contemporaries generally explained as a reaction to the ways in which the *maskilim* engaged the biblical texts, or as an effort to prevent *yeshivah* students from taking up with *maskilim*.[46] Modern researchers, meanwhile, have regarded the "Bible problem" as perplexing but have tended to treat it in isolation, obscuring its close connection with the "Grammar problem."

Scholars have explained the inferior status of the Bible in traditional education in two ways. One view stresses the idea of neglect, even criminal neglect. Zvi Sharfstein goes further and claims that "this practice—not to teach Bible at all or not in a sufficient quantity—was not only a national sin, but also an enormous educational defect," yet he does not delve into the causes of this practice, which he attributes to "a widespread perspective" that "ruthlessly ruled over public opinion." Sharfstein devotes a chapter of his *Ha-Heder* to Bible instruction, and he follows this with another chapter entitled "The Grammar and Geography of the Land of Israel—Which Was Not Studied."[47] Thus Sharfstein associates the neglect of grammar with the lack of education on the geography of the Holy Land, yet he downplays the tighter link between the abridged and defective modes of instruction in Scripture and the withholding of instruction in grammar.

The second explanation for the inferior status of the Bible in the traditional educational system—and the more current one—has to do with "priorities." In this account the priority given to oral tradition is what pushed instruction in Scripture to the sidelines.[48] A more refined version of this account emerges in the claim of Shaul Stampfer, who finds that the traditional educational programs were calculated to preserve the stability of the social structure and cement the status of the elite. Since this was an elite not of income or aristocracy but of scholarship, the educational system had to safeguard the prestige and value of education. And since open access to knowledge was liable to diminish the prestige of learning, the system chose to create the appearance of equality (everyone learned to read) while in practice dividing its resources of knowledge unequally. In this way the educational system created a clear class division between "simple Jews" and Talmudic scholars and rabbis. In this account, the *heder* curriculum was designed to pass by the "simple Jews" and leave only the "refined Jews," those talented enough to become scholars. Scholars were trained for their main task—study of Talmud—whereas "simple Jews" were equipped with enough reading skill in Hebrew to satisfy their religious obligations, but no more than that.[49]

Yet the explanatory power of this account, however true and important the account may be, is limited. It may help us to understand the preference given to study of the Talmud and its commentators, but it does not sufficiently explain the persistence of pedagogical methods that systematically blocked the way to deep engagement with the biblical text in its entirety. Moreover, both explanations—one emphasizing neglect and the other the superiority of the Talmud—blur the connection between the lack of instruction in grammar and the method of teaching the Bible, and between both of those things and the literacy policy concerning Hebrew. This obfuscation hides the deliberate nature of the propagation of ignorance and ignores its social and ideological causes.

Indeed, the approach that traditional society took to Hebrew literacy was fundamentally instrumental. The level of literacy promoted by the system was determined according to the social role each person was destined to fill, and while everyone was given some instruction in reading so as to suggest the appearance of equality, the society had in fact an interest in maintaining *unequal* levels of literacy. It is important to note that the lack of instruction in grammar kept the biblical text hidden, that the method of teaching the Bible concealed its grammar, and that the two in combination served to keep the Hebrew language obscure.[50]

The rabbinic leadership kept the biblical text hidden and maintained grammatical ignorance so as to assure that all would accept the midrashic worldview and to prevent anyone from reading the Bible unguided by the authorized interpreters, for this might lead to questioning of the received interpretations. This stance is rather clearly expressed in the exegesis offered by Rabbi Zvi Elimelech of Dinov (1785–1841) for the dictum of the sages, "U'min'u bneichem min ha-higayon" (And may your sons desist from reason):

> That is to say that as minors they must not study Scripture in its literal form; without the homilies of the Rabbis in the Bible commentaries they will find it strange to overlay the rabbinic commentaries upon the texts, and easily will they be led (heaven forbid) to apostasy. And I as an adult have seen the poor of our nation in this age, which is on the threshold of the Messiah, I saw an event and recalled a ruling and well appreciated the practices of our ancestors in these lands, who directed that as soon as the babe can recognize verses of the Five Books directly he is begun with instruction in Talmud. . . . So that routine in the mouth of the babe will be the words of the Rabbis in the received form of Torah from Sinai in the version of the oral transmission, which preserves the soul of man from all evil.[51]

At the root of the refusal to teach grammar and Hebrew, and of the prohibition against reading Scripture without intermediaries, were fears relating to the literal meaning of the Bible and the possible damage that reading it might do to rabbinic and Halachic authority.[52] Rabbi Shaul Levin (1740–95), who presented a defense of *Divrei Shalom ve'Emet* (1782) by Naphtali Hertz Wesseley (1725–1805), described this position in his satirical *Ktav Yosher* (1894):

> And the study of grammar is the first step on the road to apostasy, for that is the way of temptation, today it tells him study grammar, and once equipped with the wisdom of grammar it incites him to compose verse and poetry in a pure language, and once acquainted with the pure language, he will tolerate no commentary or homily on the Bible text that distorts its literal truth, and will resist and rifle through all the commentaries and innovations which the texts seem to require as substance, as well as the endless books composed about them; and as sin draws sin in its wake, he will afterward rebuff the prayers and the wonderful sacred liturgical poems and condemn their lack of grammatical composition.[53]

Yet the rabbinic fears were not entirely without foundation. Moshe Leib Lilienblum (1843–1910), for example, describes in his book *Hat'ot Ne'urim* an argument he had with his uncle: "He would say that all the interpretations which the exegesists give as to all the Scriptures, they all have a foundation in the text, and the author of that interpreted verse intended that very interpretation when he wrote it—for there are seventy faces to the Torah. . . . I who acquired knowledge of grammar in the house of my Rabbi, said, that most of the interpretations do not accord with the rules of grammar, and it is impossible that they may be true."[54] Even Rabbi Yitzhak Baer Levinsohn (1788–1860), one of the first Haskalah authors in Russia to propose sweeping reforms to the traditional education system, handled this matter cautiously. The first question posed in the introduction to his book *Te'udah be-Yisrael* (1824) is "whether it is necessary for a member of the Jewish faith to study the holy Tongue according to grammar to attain perfection." He answered decisively that "Knowledge of the Holy Tongue for every member of the Jewish faith is of the utmost necessity." He called for changing the typical modes of study in the *heder,* connected the need to learn grammar to the study of language and of the Bible in its entirety, and called on the "honorable of our nation" and its scholars to become familiar with the language in "its pure, perfected form."[55] And yet, in a response to an epistle brought before him, Levinsohn took pains to note: "But there is no need for the entire nation from youngest to oldest to all be Rabbis. . . . It suffices for a man of Israel of the masses to know the Bible with adequate commentary, with a smattering of grammar . . . and knowledge enough to read in the books of morals and qualities in the Holy Tongue, also to write in the Holy Tongue somewhat."[56]

"And May Your Sons Desist from Reason"

The *maskilim*'s criticisms of traditional education reveal that they recognized not only the deeper reasons behind inadequate Bible instruction but also how this was related to the rejection of modern Hebrew poetry and fiction. In the critiques of traditional education woven into Mendele's *Ba-Yamim ha-Hem*, there are more than a few insightful remarks on this subject:

> And among the learned in those days were only included those who studied the subjects fit for a Jew. . . . A person who had sated of bread and meat, that is, of Talmud and *Poskim,* and who had acquired for himself also some knowledge of the Bible and a bit of the rules of grammar as supplement to the body of the Torah—so much the better: *he* is a wise man, *he* a scholar, *he* is perfected with all the virtues and all else is just the world's vanity and unnecessary. Yet would anyone in those days teach his sons Bible beyond the first fragment of the weekly portion? The fathers withheld from their children not only reason, but also the Bible, and those who studied it were suspected of heresy. The matter is most perplexing, and of the hundred and fifty excuses given for it not a one justly resolves this issue in Israel's favor. And while many will not believe this, yet thus it was in fact and thus—in our sins—it remains among many Jews even today. In the past the rabbis were not versed in the Bible and even today many rabbis do not understand the written Scripture. And nevertheless one must not question them, God forbid, doubtless they have reasons which the simple soul cannot accept; and perhaps it is possible to be a certified expert in Torah and a teacher of teachers even without knowing a verse of the Holy Writings. . . . And Rabbi Hayim is the one who sought to change the coin, minted by the Sages in education, and as an experiment to teach his sons the whole Bible—including also the [Aramaic] translations—from "In the beginning" up to "And he arose," in proper sequence and as it appears. Rabbi Hayim himself was a master of the Bible and a great poet in his day. Sweeter than honey were his biblical verses, say those who knew him, who spoke of him as a master of language.[57]

Mendele's critical and ironic description of the traditional educational approach ties the question of the status of grammar and Scripture to the problems modern Hebrew literature faced in gaining acceptance. Mendele makes it apparent that the traditional approach to grammar and Scripture was bound up with the delegitimization of poetic expression, and that the attempt of the *maskilim* to make poesy acceptable was viewed as a dangerous deviation from "the coin minted by the Sages in education." Mendele even suggests that both the fear "that those who study it may become heretics" and the suspected atheism of those engaging in grammar and poesy have the same source: they relate to the commentary, in his opinion mistaken, given to the saying of the sages, "and may your sons desist from reason."

This is not the place to review the evolution of the exegesis of this phrase, or even to weigh the ideological and educational attitudes reflected in its various interpretations. It suffices for our purposes to note that Rashi offered two lines of interpretation. First, "do not give them excessive training in the Bible, as it is seductive," and second, "alternative version: from children's chatter." Following Rashi's lead, numerous other commentators pondered the meaning of this phrase. Some took it as a warning against too deep a reading of Scripture; others took it as a caution against a literal reading of the Bible, which could lead to heresy; still others viewed it rather as an admonition against mechanical and superficial readings, such as those of the "whistlers and reciters." There were also some who claimed that the phrase warns against study of the laws of reason, understood as the "external wisdoms" or part of them, while others maintained that the admonition against studying "reason" was intended for youth alone—after all, it says "your sons"—and that the pursuit of wisdom was permissible in adults.[58]

The various interpretations drew on the multiple meanings of the root letters HGH (reason, logic, speech) and reflected the different attitudes then current to the study of grammar, Scripture, Hebrew, and the "external wisdoms." Mordechai Breuer reviews the exegetical history of this phrase from the twelfth century on down and finds that the communities of Spain and Italy gave it a "mild" interpretation and tended to provide instruction in grammar, Bible, and Hebrew; whereas the communities of France and Ashkenaz on the whole took a harsher line, with the result that the Bible was pushed to the sidelines and grammar education was eliminated almost entirely.[59] Jewish society in nineteenth-century Eastern Europe was thus carrying on an educational tradition of long standing, and it worked to maintain ignorance in those fields of knowledge that it included under the heading "reason."[60]

What stands out in the writings of the *maskilim* is the repetition of this phrase of the sages in various polemical contexts. In order to achieve legitimacy and act by rules acceptable to traditional society, the *maskilim* stressed the "milder" interpretations in an effort to prove that their preoccupation with wisdom, grammar, Scripture, and Hebrew did not contradict the saying of the sages or its interpretation by Rashi.

I will cite two illustrations of this point, one from the *maskilim* of Berlin, which deals with Hebrew, and the other from the *maskilim* of Eastern Europe, whose subject is the "external wisdoms."

In his preface to Mendelssohn's *Kohelet Musar,* part 2,[61] Tuvia Bock uses the style of lamentations to characterize the abandonment of Hebrew and attributes it to the interpretation—in his opinion erroneous—given to the dictum of the sages "And may your sons desist from reason": "I did behold and see our brethren the children of Israel who have departed from our Holy Tongue: and verily ill it is to me, I know not how the evil came about. What purpose they saw and what came over them—to cast off the crowning glory and pride of their grandeur. For it is the fairest of tongues." Bock blames the mistaken interpretation of the dictum of the sages:

> And there are those of brazen temper who appeal to the Holy One of Israel he is Rabbi Shlomo [Rashi] in his commentary (Tractate *Brachot* 28:2) on the expression of the Sages "and may your sons desist from reason," which he says refers to the study of Scripture. Here they have erected a barrier of deceit and have hidden behind falsehood. Not only have they turned their eyes from the interpretation of Maimonides who explains that reason is the study of eternal truths. But also Rashi's words they have viewed mistakenly and falsely interpreted. The thrust of his idea is that we ought not spend all of our days in study of Scripture and the tradition, in the manner of those who delight when they find some letter or punctuation mark which escaped the notice of the First Ones. For so He of Blessed Memory himself said, that excessive exercises in Scripture should be avoided. And better it is for us to study the Torah as transmitted to us via the rabbis for this is our life and the length of our days. Yet to withhold oneself from the craft of language altogether? Heaven forbid a righteous man should do such a thing. On the contrary it is a religious obligation.[62]

Whereas Bock appeals to the commentary on the sages' dictum to sanction the return to the Hebrew language, Shalom Ya'akov Abramovitch, i.e. Mendele Mocher Sfarim, appeals to the same source to legitimize *belles letters.* In his book *Ein Mishpat* he assembles numerous proof texts to support his position and says:

> And the dictum May your sons refrain from reason (*Brachot* 21:b) here is the interpretation of all the great commentators, such as the author of the *Aruch* and Rashi and the author of *Ein Ya'akov* and their like, that the meaning is to refrain from interpreting the text

by its literal form, instead of by its intent. And what is meant by "reason" [*higayon*] is mere chatter, such as those of the reciters and the elaborators. Even the author of *Menorat ha-Ma'or,* who thought that the passage cited indeed refers to the Wisdom of reason, even he says explicitly (illum. 4 rule 3 sec B): "Where it is said Let your sons desist from reason, perhaps their intent was this: when they said your sons they mean when they are small and that is why they did not say you yourselves, for our rabbis would never have prevented any man from studying all the forms of wisdom.[63]

It emerges from the polemic of Bock and Abramovitch that their opponents had extended the range of the sages' dictum and enlisted it to denounce, as needed, either the preoccupation with grammar, Scripture, or Hebrew or the engagement with the "external wisdoms." Rabbi Yehezkel Halevi Landau of Prague (1713–93), who led, with his son-in-law Rabbi David Tevle of Lissa, the campaign against Naphtali Hertz Wesseley and Moses Mendelssohn,[64] interprets "and may your sons desist from reason" as referring "to any part of the Wisdom of nations":

And it is said let your sons desist from reason and I have seen written in *Ein Ya'akov* that one must not interpret reason as the Wisdom of reason for that is indeed a wisdom essential also for study of the Torah. And I say so what that it pertains also to the study of the Torah since from the first it was established as a basis for the "external wisdoms," and one ought to keep oneself far from it, using the formula "in emergencies for the Lord," etc. . . . The Wisdom of reason brings in its train the study of philosophy which continues with pressures inch by inch to displace the entire doctrine of the Torah, so much the more must one stay far away from it, and anyone who even comes near may find the barest shred there and so as to secure this distance from philosophy our rabbis issued the warning let your sons desist from reason. Yet also with regard to the Torah their sons should be trained in genuine studies and not be led astray in the manner of the misguided who use the wisdom of reason, therefore he gave honest counsel that they must sit at the lap of wise scholars from whom they will hear the proper manner of Torah study and the straight and true explanations, and the teachers will instruct them in the true study and keep them far from the philosophers thus "May your sons desist from reason."[65]

The position of Rabbi Yehezkel Landau, who "a thousand great students instructed," was very similar to that of the Hatam Sofer (1762–1839), for whom the concept "reason" also refers to the "external wisdoms."[66] Unlike Rabbi Landau's, however, the Hatam Sofer's rejection of the "external wisdoms" is not merely a necessary temporary measure, a reliance on the formula "In emergencies for the Lord thy laws may be broken." It was, rather, grounded in an atemporal principle according to which the nation of Israel was unique among the peoples of the world and had its own proper sequence of studies that had to be adhered to. In a commentary on the Torah portion of *Be-Shalah* written in 1811, the Hatam Sofer refers to the liturgical phrase "Blessed be our Lord who created us for his glory and distinguished us from the misguided and gave us the true Law and life everlasting." The Hatam Sofer sees this verse as hinting at why the sages "made it essential to instruct their sons etc. in Talmud and Bible according to approved commentary without informing them of the simple interpretations, for a scriptural passage is not to be divorced from its direct literal meaning . . . and there is no doubt that it was thus transmitted father to son and that fathers and forefathers saw fit to act thus since eternity." Later in the homily the Hatam Sofer directly associates study of the "external wisdoms" with the study of Torah in its literal form and scathingly attacks the trend taking shape in his generation to give such studies primacy over the oral tradition: "Our son and our seed should they study at the outset of their education the literal Scripture and the 'external wisdoms' which are external to the Torah when yet immature, when they arrive to some of the commentaries and the oral law which is the principle object . . . they will have already chosen apostasy and will renounce the Lord and his law just as our eyes have seen in this evil age." If the boy interprets Scripture literally and begins his education by studying the "external wisdoms," he will end up such that "in his acts he will denounce his Father in Heaven and will not desire the Name and his laws." Accordingly the Hatam Sofer concludes with the unequivocal verdict "And from this the moral will be drawn that one must not heed the novices who have just arrived, to distance us from the Lord using the Torah of God and who seek to overturn the plate and teach us in the manner of reason to enlighten our sons in order that there shall remain neither name nor trace to the Talmud God forbid— approach it not and heed it not."[67] Both the Hatam Sofer and Rabbi Landau were careful to avoid explicitly prohibiting the study of grammar.[68] Yet it is no coincidence that the warning against literal study of Scripture and the broad admonition against the "external wisdoms," taken together, were understood also to prohibit involvement in grammar.

This, for example, is how Rabbi Shlomo Kluger (1786–1869) understood Rabbi Landau's pronouncements when asked explicitly about grammar: "A question from the leaders of one community regarding several people who set up a study group to learn *Talmud Leshon Ivri* and the compositions of

R. Moshe Dessauer and tempers flared and they were excommunicated and the books were taken from them and burned and I was appealed to so as to decide who was right in this matter." As to the burning of the books, Rabbi Kluger says in his responsum that "there might be cause for culpability by law but they are not to be blamed for this . . . and given that they were incited into this action and acted from passion doubtless they did well." Later Rabbi Kluger turns to the heart of the matter; he disagrees with the author of *Ein Ya'akov*, used by Bock and Abramovitch to legitimize engagement in the wisdoms, and relies instead on the statements of Rabbi Landau quoted above:

> For owing to the requirements of the age it is proper to enact laws and to increase our distance from even the slightest sin . . . and therefore certainly for the study of Grammar or reason, in the early days when the philosophizers and atheists had not yet taken hold of these subjects then certainly it was proper to study them yet now that they have taken hold of them one must keep as far from them as the arrow flies. . . . And here I am told that also the righteous Rabbi Hirsch Melech wrote in this vein, for we have seen with our own eyes that study of grammar leads to exclusive involvement in the Bible and the Bible leads to German translation and the translation to German leads to apostasy and the author of *Talmud Leshon Ivri* I did know him in his youth . . . and observed that he was a great sinner . . . and we must uphold only the Six Books [of *Mishnah*] and the *Poskim* may the light that shines from them return us to the true course.[69]

Indeed, some communities viewed the prohibition against reason as proscribing also any involvement with grammar and Hebrew. I. H. Weiss, for instance, attests that in Hungary [*Ungern*], the land of the Hatam Sofer, it was believed that "the Wisdoms were sinful and the rabbis also steered their pupils away from involvement in the 'external wisdoms' . . . and even the knowledge of the Wisdom of the Holy Language, its grammar, and literature was treated as an 'external wisdom.'"[70]

No less important than the rabbis' interpretation of the dictum of the sages was the way in which the broad public understood their position and the way in which it was practically implemented, both within the traditional educational system and outside it. In this regard it is worth noting the testimony of the autobiographers and memoir writers, who repeatedly point out that the expression "and may your sons desist from reason" was often used to justify attacks against voluntary reading of the Bible as well as against systematic instruction in Hebrew and its grammar.[71]

As we have seen, Bock and Abramovitch attempted to resist such claims and put forward a narrower interpretation of Rabbi Eliezer's phrase. One observed that the dictum does not speak about the Bible or Hebrew, nor does it order that they be neglected; the other sought to show that the dictum does not refer to the "external wisdoms" or prohibit their study. Yet both concede that Rashi intended to forestall some of the dangers inherent in literal readings of Scripture and preferences of the Bible over oral law, and both insist that their concern does not imply any doubts about the validity of the *Midrash* or the authority of the *Halachah*.

It must be conceded that these positions contained no small measure of innocence or at least of pretense to it. Without inquiring here which of the *maskilim* honestly believed that their preoccupations did not constitute a threat to *halachic* authority, no one denies that the *maskilim* tried to sharpen the distinction between the literal text and its commentary, or that they advocated literal readings of Scripture.[72]

The Sages' Injunction and the Status of Modern Hebrew Literature

Modern Hebrew literature's beleaguered status within the traditional community had much to do with the link between interpretations of "reason" and of *melitzah*. A brief glance at the connotations of *melitzah* as used by the *maskilim* reveals that before it acquired its derogatory sense, around 1860, the word had referred to sublime poetic language based on biblical phrases and proper grammatical Hebrew. The *melitzah* was to be an expressive poetic form with a logical structure that enabled persuasive rational argument while at the same time employing rhetorical and figurative flourishes that lent to texts a pleasing aesthetic format.

In their definitions of the term *melitzah* and the practical use they made of the concept, the *maskilim* stressed the close bond between the *melitzah* and classical rhetoric, grammar, logic, and poetics[73]—relying, in one way or another, on the humanistic divisions (the seven "external wisdoms") common in the Middle Ages, or those common during the Renaissance.[74] Naphtali Hertz Wesseley, who finds correspondences between "the roots of language," i.e., grammar, and "the *melitzic* sentence," speaks also of the "clarity of the Holy Tongue and its grammar, and the phrasing of its *melitzah*."[75] *Melitzah* is often equated with clarity, and the words "clear" and "clarity," in the phraseology of the *maskilim,* connote a high idiom or rhetoric: some go further and associate rhetoric with grammar and logic. Clarity, furthermore, refers to the biblical purism of the *melitzah*. Thus, for example, Yitzhak Satanov (1732–1804) writes: "Every adept scribe will do well to ornament his *melitzah* materially, preserving purity; that is to say, the words which are the material of the *melitzah* should be based on grammar according to the rules and there should not be linguistic hybrids. I have seen certain *melitzot* whose authors knew nothing of grammar. Moreover, their *melitzot* half-spoke the Talmudic language; they do not speak the Jewish tongue. And a mixture of linguistic layers underwrites them."[76] It should be stressed that the *melitzah* was valued not merely for its figurative expression but also for its logic, order, and freedom from grammatical error and foreign terms. These aspects of its aesthetic appear in the discussions of both authors and grammarians: the latter viewed the *melitzah* as an integral part of the grammar books and devoted entire chapters to the *melitzah* and to poetic composition. Thus, for example, in *Talmud Leshon Ivri* Ben-Ze'ev notes that the *melitzah* must "speak metaphorically, imaginatively, and indirectly, and its ideas must be so exalted as to waken and exalt the spirit";[77] and Shlomo Zalman HaCohen Hanau writes in his *Tzohar ha-Teivah*: "The *melitzah* must be such that it conveys its message in an orderly form and with a beauty of arrangement that accords with what is appropriate to introduce it to a soul attending to the depth of the speaker's thoughts. Among the requirements of the high form of the *melitzah* is a contentment with neither superfluity nor deficiency; an awareness of the dangers of the obstructing gaze which restricts the rhetorical flow; and an elimination of double meaning."[78] These applications of the concept *melitzah* indicate that its essential attributes are its close tie to scriptural idiom and grammar on the one hand and to the "external wisdoms" of grammar, logic, and rhetoric on the other. Because of these associations, a reassessment is required of the factors involved in the campaign of the traditional society against the *melitzah* of the *maskilim*.

"The Bane of the *Maskilim*"

Conventional wisdom has it that the principal reason for the traditional community's rejection of modern Hebrew literature was that it infringed upon the sanctity of the Hebrew language. In this account, the traditional community viewed Hebrew functionally, as serving the uses of prayer and Torah study, and saw these uses being perverted by the *maskilim* for secular ends. In the concise formulation of Immanuel Etkes, the *maskilic* attitude was characterized by

> a romantic approach which elevated the Hebrew language as a linguistic lone and precious residue of a glorious past, and therefore one worthy of conservation and care. Hence the considerable

importance of treating the Hebrew language as a subject of research and investigation. Hence also the excitement and emotionalism accompanying efforts to compose modern Hebrew poetry, and the high regard for the biblical poesy as a source of inspiration and an aesthetic model worthy of imitation. This new approach, which removes Hebrew from the exclusive realms of Torah study and worship of God, and which turns it into a research topic and a means of intrinsically valued poetic creation, is one of the clear expressions of the secularizing trend which marks the Haskalah.[79]

In this account the *maskilic* secularization of Hebrew had to do with the functional shift the *maskilim* applied to the language, and it was this change that called forth the traditional community's opprobrium. This language, intended for sacramental purposes alone, was being removed from the exclusive realm of religious devotion, was being treated as possessing intrinsic worth, and was being prepared for use for secular purposes and for the creation of poetry. Yet, given the associations we have noted between the *melitzah* and Scripture, grammar, and the "external wisdoms," we can see that this functionalist claim was little more than a smokescreen for undeclared, and sometimes even unconscious, motives. The claim that Hebrew, because it is a sacred language, must not be used for secular ends or be ascribed an independent value scarcely reflects the profound reasons for the disparagement of the *melitzah* of the *maskilim*. Similarly, the claim that the shift the *maskilim* were seeking to effect through language was limited to their use of the holy tongue for secular ends vastly underrates the scope of the revolution the *maskilim* were hoping to bring about through language. The functionalist view of the language and the insistence on its sacredness were meant to serve larger purposes, goals left hidden by these inadequate explanations.

The hostility toward poetry, literature, and the *maskilic melitzah,* like the hostility toward the "external wisdoms," Scripture, and Hebrew, was bound up first and foremost with the problem of grammar. A striking insight into this effect is given by Buki Ben Yogli (Yehudah Leib Katzenelson, 1846–1917) at the end of his autobiography:

> Falsely did they accuse the first *maskilim* of excessive preoccupation with the grammar of the Hebrew tongue. A great deed those men did at that time, something whose value was appreciated neither by Kovner nor his opponents. Although it is possible that his opponents understood this, yet they held it back behind their tongues. And in truth, what was the threat from the *maskilim* which so frightened the zealots of those days? Why did they set upon them in rage and

in fury? Did [the *maskilim*] not persevere in all the customs practiced by the nation? Was it because they wrote poetry? But since when was poetry prohibited from reaching the public? . . . In the Middle Ages there were great Jewish poets, and no one attacked them. All the great Torah-learned Rabbis wrote poetry and no one attacked them. Grammar was the bane of the *maskilim,* it was Grammar that undermined the foundations of the oral law, according to the zealots: and in this they were very right, for indeed Grammar weakened the authority of the Talmud over the people. Someone who has even a little knowledge of Talmud knows that the oral law, as it says in the Talmud, "the *Halachah* supplants Scripture." The Sages of the *Prushim* [anti-literalists] of yore saw that already in their day it was no longer possible to live according to the laws of the Torah of Moses; so they rose and enacted various emendations. . . . The Sages of the Talmud who succeeded them, observing the contradiction between the two bodies of law and seeking to reconcile them, sought to move from the literal sense of the Bible and interpret it in such a way that it would not be opposed to the *Halachah.* They would not worry if their commentaries always contradicted the grammatical rules. For in Talmudic times the language of the Bible had already ceased to be current, and Hebrew was differently viewed and had a different grammar; the ancient tongue was not understood by most of the nation, and therefore it was comparatively easy to give non-literal commentaries. . . . Those in power sensed the danger the Talmud faced from Grammar and condemned all those engaging in it. Yet the questioner will still ask, weren't there great Jewish grammarians in the Middle Ages, and how is it that Grammar didn't threaten the Talmud in any way then? Neither is that the full truth. Grammar even then posed a threat to the Talmud; then too the Karaites felt that the *Halachah* was based on a false interpretation of Scripture, and they were banished from the House of Israel.[80]

Buki Ben Yogli is correct that in prefaces to medieval grammar books, just as in prefaces to grammar texts of the *Maskilim,* one repeatedly finds the defensive claim that mastery of Hebrew grammar leads not to apostasy but, on the contrary, strengthens faith as it aids in comprehension of Scripture. In the author's preface to *Sefer Ha-Rikmah,* which deals with scriptural grammar, Jonah Ibn Janah set out to defend grammar from those who denigrated it and vilified its devotees. In his opinion, jealousy[81] is what motivated the persecution of students of grammar and the wisdoms. Ibn Janah condemned the use of linguistic ignorance as a means of intimidating the masses and withholding wisdom from them:

> Many of those who are jealous of the wise ones of our time, and in our country, their zealotry and boorishness cause them to assail [the wise ones]. How wonderfully do they innovate, and how charmingly do they interpret, except in matters relating to religious obligations; their words differing from what is said in the *Midrash* and *Aggadah*. [So that the zealous] say: "This differs from what our rabbis taught us," and the accusation is fanned, and the person is singled out, and defects are sought in him, and he is held as an example to frighten off the common uneducated men, until they are prevented from seeing the truth of things, and they are incited to loathing, from their jealousy of the wise men and their ignorance of what our rabbis of blessed memory said: "A scriptural passage is not to be divorced from its literal meaning," and further: "The literal meaning of Scripture is one thing, and the *Halachah* is another."[82]

Jonah Ibn Janah was perplexed by his generation's attitude toward grammar, when "our rabbis of blessed memory knew it and insisted on it and took pains with it," "and most perplexing of all is their dismissiveness of this wisdom and denigration of its adherents and their limited recognition that fulfillment of the religious obligations as they are written and their proper observance is impossible unless grammar is relied upon."

Like Ibn Janah, Shlomo Zalman HaCohen Hanau was convinced that grammar aids comprehension of the ancient commentaries on Scripture, and is "a great tool for analysis of the oral law." Statements in this spirit are to be found in his preface to *Tzohar ha-Teivah:*

> And I did settle upon the wisdom of grammar because much of the Torah is bound up with it after I did see that this wisdom has been cast into a corner no suitor has She and no inquirer blessed be She and blessed her cause. She it is who delivers correct reading of our precious Torah it is She who directs a person to gain knowledge and gives the boor insight and clothes the youth in wisdom and virtue. She it is who clarifies all the verses of Scripture with its roots and its rules and its punctuation and cantillation marks.[83]

Yet these assertions did not improve the traditional society's attitude toward grammar in particular or toward Hebrew more generally. In the preface to his *Otzar ha-Shorashim,* Yehudah Leib Ben-Ze'ev avers that since the death of Mendelssohn the status of grammar has worsened:[84]

> Those who grasp the Torah and serve as our eyes, they have become its persecuted ones. For an old plague has sprouted anew in the

nation, the name of wisdom has become hateful to her sister religion, and the Talmudic rabbis will not allow the tent of wisdom to be pitched alongside the tent of Torah, although the First Ones made her handmaiden to the mistress, religion. And now even as a cook or servant she will not do. Banished is this handmaiden and her son, knowledge of language; no dowry or inheritance will she find among all the Great Ones of Israel. And many there are whose tongues have moved to pour scorn and wrath upon the devotees of wisdom and the students of language.[85]

In a still more forceful allegation the poet Adam HaCohen (1794–1878) describes the attitude of the traditional community toward Hebrew as an enmity that led to a campaign to destroy it: "[Hebrew] is now being exterminated. . . . [S]he is abandoned alone and humiliated, both she and her suitors, but not at the hands of some other nation but by her own people . . . for she has no greater enemy than these of her own people."[86] And in his lament for Mordechai Aharon Ginzburg, he says: "For behold all nations and observe all peoples: does any nation on earth so abhorr its language? For so precious is their language in their eyes that they greatly revere its sages and admirers, whereas we, the nation of God, despise our native tongue and persecute its scholars with everlasting hatred."[87] Buki Ben Yogli offers an explanation of what Adam HaCohen presented as a campaign of annihilation against the Hebrew language and its literature. He begins by explicitly declaring that "grammar was the bane of the *maskilim*," and concludes by hinting at an analogy between the contemporary *maskilim* and the Karaites of yore. In fact, Buki Ben Yogli hints that the danger threatened by the study of grammar was that of approaching the Karaite worldview. And, indeed, Ya'akov Halevi Lifschitz, who takes the side of the *haredim* in its campaign against the Haskalah movement in Poland and Russia, seems to support this idea. Lifschitz notes the similarity between the *Maskilim* and the Karaites, and views this as justifying the *haredi* suspicion of the Haskalah's emphasis on Scripture and Hebrew:

> And therefore with every reverence that the guardians of the Torah and the keepers of its commandments esteem the Bible, still they do not refrain from casting aspersions at those who cry endlessly: Bible! Bible! As if God forbid no Torah in Israel existed except for the literal portion of the Bible, when this position had already been taken by the Karaites, and moreover the Bible in their hands is just a means to expand the Hebrew tongue, and the Hebrew tongue was not so much an end in itself, but rather served the purpose and goal which they found in it for some other end. Which is the opposite

not only of the sacredness of the Bible but also the sanctity of the Holy Tongue. . . . The intent of these lovers of Hebrew becomes more explicit in the letter of Minister Uvarov to Tsar Nicholas II . . . published in St. Petersburg in 1871 . . . which runs as follows: "There is no better means or more appropriate device for eliminating the Talmud from Israel, than by introducing study of the Holy Scriptures and the Hebrew language, its grammar and literature into the general curriculum."[88]

Moreover, the intensive involvement of *maskilim* such as Shlomo Levisohn (1789–1821), A. B. Gottlober, Rashi Fuenn (1818–90), and others who researched the language and history of the Karaites, as well as the broad relations pursued by *maskilim* such as Rabbi Nachum Krochmal (1785–1840), Levinsohn, Gottlober, and Gordon with leading figures in the modern Karaite community, suggests that the possible analogy between the Haskalah and Karaism preoccupied, and perhaps also worried, the *maskilim* themselves.[89] In his explicit statements and veiled hints Buki Ben Yogli uncovers the link between the threats the rabbis felt, from grammar on the one hand and from the writers of modern Hebrew literature on the other. The rabbis rejected the *melitzah* first and foremost because it was founded on the model of a grammatical and pure scriptural Hebrew. It was not the use of the language for secular functions that threatened rabbinic authority but the scriptural purity itself. The revitalization of Hebrew on the basis of a scripturally pure grammar and a platform of equal public availability, even had it been done for purely religious ends, would have potentially threatened the hold of the oral tradition and hence of the traditional rabbinic elite—which took pains to defend its supremacy.

Who Is Master of the Language?

The intentional cultivation of ignorance for the purpose of controlling language thus served traditional leadership as a powerful instrument for fortifying its religious authority and reproducing the existing social order. This ignorance successfully kept broad circles of society from direct knowledge of grammar, Scripture, and Hebrew. It stunted the critical reasoning power of the general populace and ensured that the traditional sources of authority would be obeyed. Arrayed across the battle lines were the Haskalah authors and literary critics active in Eastern Europe in the second half of the nineteenth century, and they vigorously assailed the dependency of the Jewish culture on—in their words—these "authoritarians." In the spirit of the Haskalah posture, and under the influence of the radical Russian critics,[90] they demanded free critical thinking and strove to democratize language and knowledge. In his 1867 book *Ein Mishpat* S. Y. Abramovitch dealt with this subject at length. "Since time immemorial," he wrote, "this has been the way of the wise of all nations: to hide the wisdoms and sciences from the eyes of the people and to use hints and a special scholarly language, so as to have their speech understood by the erudite alone . . . and not by the masses."[91] Yet Abramovitch also found that the age of restriction of knowledge to a scholarly elite had ended, and that the time had come to follow the example of other nations and make knowledge and enlightenment available to all. In a similar vein, Avraham Ya'akov Paperna (1840–1919) lambasted the rabbinic tendency to "write in such a way so as not to be understood" and demanded the democratization of language and writing.[92]

The battle over grammar between the *maskilim* and the rabbis was thus a battle over control of the language. It was meant to answer decisively who would be "master of the tongue" and who would thus be able to shape the consciousness of society. In order to wrest this mastery from the hands of the traditional leadership the *maskilim* set out, consciously or not, to put together a "counter-discourse,"[93] a subversive language, that would undermine the authority of rabbinic language and offer an alternative that would shape anew the consciousness of those using it.

In the particular historical circumstances under which the *maskilim* worked, pure biblical language had clear subversive potential, because it brought to the fore the repressed, repudiated native language and its grammar. Moreover, Haskalah thinkers considered biblical language a referential and transparent idiom oriented toward the "real world" and representing it faithfully. In this it stood in direct contrast to rabbinic language, which they viewed as oriented toward the language of canonized texts.[94] The return to a scriptural idiom and the emancipation for the public of a biblical Hebrew founded on its grammar was meant, among other things, to present a language reoriented toward the world and a tool for revolutionizing the attitudes of those employing it. Its purpose was to shape a new conception of reality and to alter the character of the culture and the society.

Paradoxes of Scriptural Purism

Given all of this, conventional wisdom concerning the repressive influence of the purist scriptural ideal on the development of Hebrew and its literature must also be reassessed.[95]

The debate over purism accompanied Hebrew literature from the out-set. In the first half of the nineteenth century numerous authors and critics viewed the ideal of purism as one of the great barriers to the development of Hebrew literature. The main points of the criticism of the purist ideal were articulated by Israel Hayim Taviov (1858–1920) in his essay "Our Fine Literature and Its Future," published in *Pardes* in 1891: "The *melitzic* style (the style of biblical phrases) which has ruled in our literature to its detriment . . . has removed authority from the author and turned him into a willing slave of biblical verse—the style that yielded whole volumes of quotes of scriptural rhyme, . . . this style has not allowed our literature to develop naturally, surrounding it as it has with a biblical wall."[96] Taviov explains the return of the Berlin *Maskilim* to scriptural purism as a wish to ennoble the dead language by drawing on the glories of the biblical idiom. Yosef Klausner, who also sharply attacked scriptural purism, explained this process as a "living protest" against "the great corrupt state into which our language has fallen . . . from the days of the Kalir up to the period of the *Me'asfim*." In his opinion, Hebrew "had become a sort of gypsy dialect . . . and for their goal of counteracting . . . this corrupted style, they [the Berlin *Maskilim*] found no better means than to adopt the Hebraic style—with-out noticing that this stifled our language at a time when it most needed to be simplified and expanded."[97]

Unlike Taviov, who stressed the goals toward which scriptural purism strove, Klausner dwelled on what this choice attempted to overcome. Still, he did not disagree that building a scripturally pure Hebrew as an alterna-tive to rabbinic idiom and a platform for a modern language and literature was a project fraught with difficulties. For, notwithstanding the image of biblical idiom as a mimetic, transparent, world-oriented discourse, many *maskilim* wrote in an exegetical style that stuck to the conventions of rab-binic discourse. They tended to cite verses, to use expressions centered on canonical texts, and to avoid describing concrete realities. Their pseudo-rabbinic style angered *melitzah* critics such as A. U. Kovner, A. Y. Paperna, and Mendele, who demanded a halt to phraseology and a realization of the mimetic potential of scriptural idiom, one in which nouns and concepts would refer to "the real world."[98]

Without denying the validity of such criticism, one must also keep in mind that the historical circumstances made the *maskilim*'s choice of bibli-cal purism a necessary move that went beyond the mere correction of "styl-istic corruption," first, because only such a language could have shaken the traditional worldview, and, second, because grammatical biblical purism, despite its problems and limitations, was a necessary move toward forming a linguistic standard. Only on the basis of such a linguistic standard could the Hebrew language synthesize all its layers into one organic whole.[99] Only such a standard could provide a sturdy foundation for a language that was lucid, grammatical, and accessible to everyone.

Nonetheless, the turn toward a pure biblical language was full of paradoxes. The hope of revitalizing the language conflicted with a narrowing of the scriptural vocabulary, and the desire to develop Hebrew literature on the model of European realism conflicted with the pathos and nobility of the scriptural idiom. The preoccupation with grammar and philology, necessary though it was, invaded literary creation and damaged it,[100] and meanwhile the desire for linguistic democratization was contradicted by the unfamiliar style of biblical discourse. The constraints within which the *maskilim* operated forced them to use elitist language in order to establish a popular and equitable language. This paradox was revealed in the Haskalah of Eastern Europe in the second half of the nineteenth century, for, by contrast with the more aristocratic Berlin *maskilim*,[101] many of the Eastern European *maskilim* favored democratization of language and knowledge.[102]

Then too there was the extended detachment of Hebrew literature from its readership. Distrust of the Bible and its high priests "stained" texts written in biblical style, marking them as texts not to be read or printed.[103] Paperna, for example, says in his memoirs that "The Shapira Sons printers . . . never accepted for publication in their print house in Salavita and Zhitomir any book written by one of the *maskilim*, which is why the authors of Vohlyn and Podolia, RiBal, Lerner, Abramovitch and the rest had to publish their works in Vilna or abroad. As fervent *Hassidim* they detested grammar and eliminated the hard-consonant marks and left it only in the letters *Bet, Kaph, Pey,* and *Tav.* And they never bothered to proofread any text they set to type."[104] Still more serious was the fact that modern Hebrew literature could not find a broad audience fluent in the language, a consequence of the traditional elite's successful control of linguistic knowledge. Thus, despite many efforts to expand its circle of readers, until the end of the nineteenth century Hebrew literature continued to develop as an elitist literature whose readership wasn't much larger than the handful of authors who composed it.

Many explanations have been given for the return of the *maskilim* to the biblical language and to the purist ideal it represented. Some have asserted that the national language of the Bible symbolized the unity of the nation scattered in the Diaspora. Others have noted that Hebrew, perceived as a relic of a glorious past, was approached with a romanticizing attitude. There are those who believe that this choice reflected a preference for biblical values over the supposedly exilic values of the Talmud. Another camp has stressed that there was a pursuit of classicist aestheticism in the quest for a pure language, and they have offered an apologetic explanation that this was a means of erasing the "shameful Yiddish jargon," and a way to show to the nations the language of the ancient and sublime culture of the Jews.[105]

To all these arguments we must add yet another. In the historical circumstances in which the *maskilim* acted, the choice of a pure biblical language was subversive.[106] It was a necessary part of their long struggle over control of language and knowledge, for at stake were the means of altering the character and values of their society and the role of the individual within it.

For all that, the choice of an ideal of biblical purism also had a confining aspect, which slowed the development of modern Hebrew literature and created a rift between it and its readership. The linguistic strategies put forward to heal this rift will require separate treatment.

Glossary

Aggadah	Talmudic legends, homiletic expositions of the Bible, stories, folklore, anecdotes or maxims, the content of which is not considered to be legally binding
Ashkenazi (pl. Ashkenazim)	German or Western, Central, or Eastern European Jews
Belfer	Instructor's aid in *heder*
Bi'ur	German translation of the Pentateuch with Hebrew commentary
Halachah	Traditional Jewish law
Haredim	Adherents of Jewish religious orthodoxy
Hassidim	Adherents of religious social movement founded by the Ba'al Shem Tov in the eighteenth century
Haskalah	Jewish Enlightenment
Heder	Religious elementary school, generally for boys
Maskil (pl. Maskilim)	Adherent(s) of the Haskalah
Melamed	Teacher in a heder
Melitzah (pl. Melitzot)	Biblical verse, poetry, in modern usage florid style
Midrash	The body of rabbinical writings concerning the interpretation of biblical texts
Mishnah	Early rabbinic legal code, compiled by Yehudah ha-Nasi in the second century
Mitnagdim	Opponents of the Hassidic movement
Responsa	Written replies given by rabbis to questions related to Jewish law

Talmud	Compendium of discussions on the Mishnah by scholars and jurists in the Babylonian and Jerusalem academies, canonized in the early sixth century
Torah	The Pentateuch; also the entire body of traditional Jewish teaching and literature
Yeshivah	Jewish traditional academy devoted primarily to study of the Talmud and rabbinic literature

Notes

1. For readers unfamiliar with Jewish life, culture, and religion, a glossary of Hebrew terms is provided at the end of the essay.

2. Yehudah Leib Gordon, *Kitvei Yehudah Leib Gordon (Shirah)* (Collected writings of Yehudah Leib Gordon [poetry]) (Tel Aviv: Dvir, 1956), 27, translated by Saadya Sternberg.

3. It should be noted that, among the causes of the limited audience, Gordon also notes the contempt in which the *maskilic* supporters of Russification held Hebrew and its literature. Ibid., 27; Shmuel Yosef Fuenn, *Safah le-Ne'emanim* (Language for the faithful) (Vilna, 1881), iii–vii; cf. note 45 below.

4. See, e.g., Shlomo Haramati, *Ivrit Hayah bi-Merutzat ha-Dorot* (Living Hebrew throughout history) (Rishon-le-Zion: Massada, 1992). Conversely, Shimon Halkin says two contrary things on the subject. On the one hand he says, "The idea that the Bible was alien to the curricula of the *heder* pupil and *yeshivah* student of the 18th century may have been overstated. It reveals great ignorance to assume that a man may be conversant in the Talmud without having knowledge of the Bible. A Jew who studies the Bible, Talmud, *Midrash,* Rashi (and via it, grammar) and who reads acrostics and attempts to understand the verses—such a Jew's mind would be full of bits of scriptural texts." See Shimon Halkin, *Zramim ve-Tzurot ba-Sifrut ha-Ivrit ha-Hadashah* (Trends and forms in modern Hebrew literature) (Jerusalem: Mossad Bialik, 1984), 101. But elsewhere he says: "To Jewish children it was forbidden to learn the fundamentals of secular education, Hebrew and grammar included. . . . Bible only a very few knew. The majority had a taste of something—from Torah reading, from the sermons of the rabbis and the interpreters, but not from genuine study. Such was their education." Shimon Halkin, *Muskamot u-Mashberim be-sifrutenu* (Conventions and crises in Hebrew literature) (Jerusalem: Mossad Bialik, 1980), 61–62.

5. Benjamin Harshav, "Masah al Techiyat ha-Lashon ha-Ivrit," (An essay on the revival of the Hebrew language) *Alpayim* 2 (1990): 23–26. See also Harshav's "The Life of 'Dead' Hebrew," in his *Language in Time of Revolution* (Berkeley and Los Angeles: University of California Press, 1993), 116–17.

6. Harshav, "Masah al Techiyat" 23.

7. "Literacy" is a general term denoting various levels and types of reading and writing ability, beginning with basic literacy (as in the ability to sign a name or read mechanically) and ending with complete reading comprehension and writing capability. Research into literacy and its social impact must therefore consider not merely elementary name-signing abilities but the variety of levels and the sociocultural context of literacy acquisition—in other words, the purposes and uses for which such capacities are acquired. Carl F. Kaestle, "The History of Literacy and the History of Readers," *Review of Research in Education* 12 (1985): 12–13. In

this article the literacy policy of nineteenth-century Jewish Eastern European society is treated in light of these distinctions (cf. note 9, below).

8. This article, which focuses on Hebrew instruction within the traditional Jewish educational system, deals with the literacy of males only. The female half of the Jewish population did not study Hebrew until the end of the nineteenth century, and the vast majority of women were thus not even potential readers of modern Hebrew literature. Eliyahu Eliezer Friedman, for example, attests that "The Hebrew tongue was barely taught to boys and still less so to girls." See Friedman, *Sefer ha-Zichronot* (Book of memoirs) (Tel Aviv, 1926), 25. Literate women learned to read Yiddish. See Shaul Stampfer, "Gender Differentiation and Education of the Jewish Woman in Nineteenth-Century Eastern Europe," *Polin* 7 (1992): 71–72; Yosef Yitzhaki, "De'Oteihem shel Sofrei ha-Haskalah al ha-Lashon ha-Ivrit ve-Dracheihem be-Harchavatah" (The views of Haskalah authors on the Hebrew language), *Leshonenu* 35 (1970): 290–91. Those few women who did know Hebrew acquired it well outside the formal educational settings. See Iris Parush, "The Politics of Literacy: Women and Foreign Languages in Jewish Society of Nineteenth-Century Eastern Europe," *Modern Judaism* 15 (1995): 190–99; Iris Parush, *Reading Jewish Women—Marginality and Modernization in Nineteenth-Century Eastern European Jewish Society* (Hanover: University Press of New England, 2004); Shmuel Feiner, "Ha-Ishah ha-Yehudiyah ha-Modernit: Mikreh Mivchan be-Yehasei ha'Haskalah ve-ha-Moderna" (The modern Jewish woman: A test case in the relationship between Haskalah and modernity), *Zion* 58 (1993): 484–97.

9. This argument is based on Pierre Bourdieu's concepts of "culture," "symbolic Power," and "symbolic violence," and on his analysis of the ways by which educational institutions serve to maintain the elite's interests in the reproduction of the existing social order. See Pierre Bourdieu and Jean-Claude Passeron, *Reproduction in Education Society and Culture* (London: Sage, 1997), 3–31. "Symbolic violence" is practiced, among other ways, through an unequal distribution of the "linguistic capital" among the various social classes, as a result of which entire populations find themselves outside the circle of readers and writers. See Pierre Bourdieu, *Language and Symbolic Power* (Cambridge, UK: Polity Press, 1991), 43–116, 137–70. See also notes 24 and 50, below.

10. In this respect nineteenth-century Eastern European traditional society was only carrying on a longstanding practice that had originated in the communities of France and Ashkenaz and that was markedly distinct from the educational tradition that had developed in the Spanish and Italian Jewish communities. Simchah Assaf, *Mekorot le-Toldot ha-Hinuch be'Yisrael A* (Sources for the history of Jewish education) (Tel Aviv: Dvir, 1954), 18–26. More on this point below.

11. Rabbi Ya'akov Emden (1697?–1776) claimed that as Hebrew was not a spoken language it was not possible to learn its grammar without use of the biblical model. Accordingly, study of grammar was bound up with thoughts about biblical verses and thus one was not permitted to engage in such study in the bathroom. See Ya'akov Emden, *She'elat Yavetz* (Yavetz's response) (New York: Grossman, 1976), 17, question 10. Likewise Yosef Klausner, who dealt with the lack of knowledge of grammar among Hebrew authors of his day, asserted: "Our language is not a spoken one and we acquire proficiency in it by means of Bible study." Klausner, "Sfat Ever Safah Hayh" (The Hebrew language—a living tongue), *Otzar ha-Sifrut* 5 (1896): 89.

12. My essay relies heavily upon several kinds of source materials. Among them are ethnographic descriptions drawn from autobiographies and memoirs of *maskilim* and of representatives of the Jewish traditional community, works of literature by major *Haskalah* writers, and responsa and statements by rabbis. I chose to follow the practice shared by most contemporary anthropological studies and cite many of these passages in their original form, often without abbreviation or ellipsis. I had several reasons for this: first, I sought to present the experiences of both *Maskilim* and *Haredim* with maximum transparency; second, any attempt

to paraphrase these accounts in my own words, or to select individual details from the wealth of particulars every account contains, runs the risk of distorting the description and detracting from the concrete picture I wish to convey; and third, the language of the quoted passages is the source of much of their special appeal, and the only way for the reader to taste the flavor of nineteenth-century Hebrew is to read them in an adequate translation.

13. Avraham Baer Gottlober, *Zichronot u-Masa'ot* (Memoirs and travels) (Jerusalem: Mossad Bialik, 1976), 73–74 (hereafter cited parenthetically in the text). Gottlober first published these remarks in *Ha-Boker Or* (1880): 1109–13, which he edited. In a footnote there he deciphered the relevant statements of Rashi dealing with grammar, concluding, "And this is the meaning of Rashi and the *Tosafot* in my opinion, as I came to understand them later, once I had studied the wisdom of grammar and recalled that this very passage in the Talmud and the commentary upon it by Rashi and *Tosafot* had been the original cause of my aroused interest in knowing our language thoroughly. That tiny cause has been the source of all my ways and all of my life's effort" (1111).

14. For a similar transition from self-instruction in grammar using *Tzohar ha-Teivah* to study using Ben-Ze'ev's *Talmud Leshon Ivri* (The study of Hebrew language), see also Yitzhak Nissanboim, *Alei Heldi* (My life) (Warsaw, 1929), 49, 77; Hayim Leib Zuta, *Be-Reshit Darki* (Jerusalem: Tal-Hermon, 1934), 31–34; Moshe Leib Lilienblum, *Ktavim Autobiography'im I* (Autobiographical writings) (Jerusalem: Mossad Bialik, 1970), 121.

15. It may be worth noting that "other" also carries connotations of apostasy.

16. For my purposes the term *Haredim* refers to orthodox Jews in nineteenth-century Eastern Europe. This sense of the term draws upon the period usage and is an abbreviation of such commonly used descriptive phrases as *Ha-haredim li-dvar ha-Shem* (the wary of the word of God); *Ha-haredim al datam* (wary to safeguard their religion); *Haredim al dvar emunatam* (wary on the issues of their faith); *Ha-yere'im ve-ha-haredim ha-medakdekim be-mitzvot* (the wary and fearful who are exacting in ritual); *Ha-haredim ve-hayere'im mi-bnei ha-dor ha-yashan* (the wary and the fearful of the old generation), and simply *Ha-haredim ve-ha'yere'im* (the wary and the fearful). See, for instance, Mordecai Aharon Gintzburg, *Aviezer* (Vilna, 1864), 124; Shalom Ya'akov Abramovitch, *Sefer Toldot Hateva* 3 (Vilna, 1872), xxi; Peretz Smolenskin, *Kvurat Hamor* (A donkey's burden), *Ha-shahar* 4 (1873): 676, 724; Mordechai Ben Hillel HaCohen, *Kvar* (Once) (Warsaw: Shtibel, 1923), 208; "Cracow (Rebellious Runaway Girls)," *Ha-Maggid* 6, no. 48 (1897): 395. As a rule, the term *"Haredim"* did not carry a negative connotation, unlike other terms common in *maskalic* parlance such as *kana'im* (zealots or fundamentalists), *mordei or* (assailants of light), and the like. For a characterization of orthodoxy in Eastern Europe and its response to modernity, see Israel Bartal, "Reactions to Modernity in Eastern Europe: *Haskalah*, Orthodoxy, and Nationalism," in *Tzionut ve'Dat* (Zionism and religion), ed. Shmuel Almog, Yehuda Reinharz, and Anita Shapira (Jerusalem: Zalman Shazar Center and Tauber Institute, 1994), 21–32.

17. See Ginzburg, *Aviezer*, 17, 33, 66–67; Yehudah Leib Gordon, *Kitvei Yehudah Leib Gordon (Prozah)* (Writings of Yehudah Leib Gordon [prose]) (Tel Aviv: Dvir, 1960), 268–72; Lilienblum, *Ktavim Autobiography'im I* (Autobiographical notes), 84–86; Mendele Mocher Sfarim, "Reshimot le-Toldotai," in *Kol Kitvei Mendele Mocher Sfarim* (Collected writings of Mendele the bookseller) (Tel Aviv: Dvir, 1957).

18. Emden, *She'elat Yavetz*, 17, question 7.

19. I cite Rabbi Emden's statements in this context only because the very reference to studying grammar in the bathroom attests to the subordinate status in which grammar was held. Rabbi Emden himself dealt with grammar and encouraged instruction in it, and Rabbi Y. B. Levinsohn cites him as well as the Gaon, Rabbi Eliyahu of Vilna (HaGRA, 1720–97), to support his arguments in favor of grammar education. Yitzhak Baer Levinsohn, *Te'udah be-Yisrael* (Testimony in Israel) (Warsaw, 1879), 16, 21–23. See also note 21 below.

20. See note 10 above.

21. I don't claim that there were not important rabbis who knew grammar, applied it, and supported its instruction. Indeed there were such, including the Prague MaHaRaL (1512?–1609), Rabbi Ya'akov Emden, and the Gaon, Rabbi Eliyahu of Vilna, whose grammar text, *Dikduk Eliyahu's Grammar,* was published posthumously. See Assaf, *Mekorot* A, 468. Yet so far as the character of traditional education was concerned, the opponents of grammar had the upper hand, and the evidence suggests that their opposition increased as the *Haskalah* movement took root. See also note 86, below.

22. Amos Funkenstein and Adin Steinsaltz, *Ha-Soziologiah shel ha-Ba'arut* (Sociology of ignorance) (Tel Aviv: Misrad ha-Bitachon, 1987), 9–33.

23. The *Mishnah,* which according to Tractate *Avot* requires instruction for five years, wasn't taught in the *heder* either as a distinct subject. See Ya'akov Hocherman, "Tafkido shel ha-Heder be-Hayei ha-Yehudim ve-Hishtakfuto ba-Sifrut" (The Heder in Jewish life and its literary representations), *Hinuch va-Ma'as* 2 (1982): 31. Where *Mishnah* was taught, only a few select chapters were included. See Assaf, *Mekorot* A, 17.

24. For comparison, see Renee Balibar, "National Language, Education, Literature," in *Literature, Politics, and Theory,* ed. Francis Barker, Peter Hulme, Margaret Iverson and Diana Loxley (London: Methuen, 1986). Balibar argues that the French educational system undermined the goal officially declared in 1789 to form a language common to all citizens, by ranking educational establishments and eliminating instruction in Latin from elementary schools. Balibar maintains that proficiency in Latin gave students of secondary schools access to the nation's literary and cultural assets, while the exclusion of Latin from elementary schools denied their students access to such assets (135–36, 144).

25. William J. Bouwsma, *The Culture of Renaissance Humanism* (Washington, D.C.: American Historical Association, 1973), 6–12.

26. Eliezer Meir Lifschitz, "Ha-Heder" (The Heder), *Ha-Tkufah* 7 (1920): 323; Moshe Avital, *Ha-Yeshivah ve-ha-Hinuch ha-Mesorati be-Sifrut ha-Haskalah* (The Yeshiva and traditional education in Haskalah literature) (New York: Yeshivah University Press, 1977), 51, 70.

27. Lifschitz, "Ha-Heder," 345–46.

28. See, for example, Izik Hirsch Weiss, *Zichronotai* (My memoirs) (Warsaw: Ya'akov HaCohen Ginzburg, 1885), 61; Friedman, *Sefer ha-Zichronot,* 105.

29. Avital, *Ha-Yeshivah,* 48.

30. Ahad Ha'Am, *Pirkei Zichronot ve-Igrot* (Selected memoirs and correspondence) (Tel Aviv: Beit Ahad Ha'Am, 1931), 2.

31. Lifschitz, "Ha-Heder," 332; Zvi Sharfstein, *Ha-Heder be-Hayei Amenu* (The Heder in Jewish life) (Shilo, 1943), 100.

32. Rabbi Yehezkel Landau of Prague instructed that the Pentateuch be studied "only in commentary in Yiddish as is printed in the volumes issued in Berlin, Vienna and Prague." See Weiss, *Zichronotai,* 75. See also Sharfstein, *Ha-Heder,* 104; Yehiel Stern, "Heder un Beys Medresh" (Heder and Beit-midrash), *YIVO Bleter* 31–32 (1948): 37.

33. See Shaul Stampfer, "Heder Study, Knowledge of Torah, and the Maintenance of Social Stratification in Traditional East European Jewish Society," *Studies in Jewish Education* 3 (1988): 279; Hocherman, "Tafkido Shel ha-Heder," 34; Lifschitz, "Ha-Heder," 333. It should be noted that when scriptural texts of particular importance were about to be studied, instruction began not with the translated text but with a special tune for the legendary (*Agaadic*) materials called *oyseredenish.* Sharfstein, *Ha-Heder,* 100–108.

34. See Friedman, *Sefer ha-Zichronot,* 133; Zvi Kasdai, "Kit'ei Zichronot" (Fragments of memoirs), *Reshumot* 4 (1926): 219; Buki Ben Yogli, *Zichronot* (Memoirs) (Jerusalem: Mossad Bialik, 1947), 17; Lifschitz, "Ha-Heder," 325; Emanuel Gamoran, *Changing Conceptions in Jewish Education* (New York: Macmillan, 1925), 100.

35. See Ahad Ha'Am, *Pirkei Zichronot*, 79; Stampfer, "Heder Study," 280.

36. See Lifschitz, "Ha-Heder," 336; Friedman, *Sefer ha-Zichronot*, 134; Sharfstein, *Ha-Heder*, 114.

37. Gordon, *Kitvei Y. L. Gordon (Prozah)*, 475. To give a piquant illustration of "how widespread the ignorance of grammar is in much of this country, even among some of its prominent figures" RiBaL relates a humorous incident concerning "one especially famous divine" who could not distinguish among genders in the language. In the Sabbath after Purim, "after having abandoned the corporeal as was his wont, and becoming greatly agitated," he sought to convey words of wisdom for his disciples and "began by taking on an issue from the readings of the day, that is from the Book of Esther, and said: 'A great mystery have I found in this Book, although none of the interpreters or the received commentators has noticed it: Why is it that when the reference is to [King] Ahasuerus, it is written *"va-Yomer"* [and he said] with a *Yod* [a "y"], whereas in referring to [Queen] Esther it is written *"va-Tomer"* [and she said], with a *tav* [a "t"]?' (And great indeed is the wonder of it, for so it is throughout the Book!) And he said there were deep reasons for this which derived from secret knowledge yet he did not wish to disclose them to us as the present Age did not sufficiently merit it; however by way of hints he explained that the *Yod* of *va-Yomer* and the *tav* of *va-Tomer* indicate the building of the Holy Temple which had stood *tav* plus *Yod* years." Similarly, RiBaL adds: "And not long ago a fellow showed me the latest book of one divine who writes that whoever studies grammar is without a doubt a pimp, for reasons known to those who know, so he said, and surely that divine had considerable knowledge of grammar and ought to be believed for no one is so wise as he who speaks from experience." Levinsohn, *Te'udah be-Yisrael*, 22, comment 2. It may be noted that Mendele weaves this account into his *Be-Emek ha-Bacha* (In the valley of tears). His character Bentzi offers his resolution of the "mystery," and when Rafael informs him that *va-Yomer* is in the male gender, *va-Tomer* is the feminine gender, Bentzi furiously retorts: "feminine gender I know not of! Speech in the masculine and feminine is known only to Jewish criminals, a curse be upon them." Mendele, *Kol Kitvei*, 194.

38. For this opinion, see, for example, Sharfstein, *Ha-Heder*, 189; Avital, *Ha-Yeshivah*, 30.

39. Emden, *She'elat Yavetz*, 17, question 7.

40. See Assaf, *Mekorot A*, 18–26.

41. Boaz Shahevitch, "Arba Leshonot: Iyunim shel Sifrut bi-Leshon ha-Maskilim al-pi 'Ha-Measef'" (Four languages: Ha-Measef and the literary language of the Maskilim), *Molad*, new ser., 1 (1967): 236.

42. Yehudah Leib Ben-Ze'ev writes of these matters in his preface to the commentary on *Emunot ve-Deot* (The book of beliefs and opinions) by Rabbi Sa'adya Gaon: "And such was the manner of the First Wise Ones . . . they would abridge their expressions into compact statements. This for two reasons: for they valued wisdom and prized therefore concise adages; and furthermore they sought not to lighten the task for the discerning by making matters plain meanwhile for the boorish masses, who without toil and lacking appreciation of quality would strip away its veil of splendor by gropings crude." See Yehudah Leib Ben-Ze'ev, *Pirush ha-Emunot ve-ha-Deot* (Commentary to the book of beliefs and opinions) (Berlin, 1789), page A. For more on this point, see Brakha Fishler and Iris Parush, "Bein 'Mikra she-Katuv' le-'Mikra she-Ne'emar' bi-Yetzirato shel Mendele Mocher Sfarim" (Between "written Scripture" and "spoken Scripture" in the writings of Mendele Mocher Sfarim), *Mechkarim be-Lashon* 7 (1995): 110n14.

43. On this point, see Levinsohn, *Te'udah be-Yisrael*, 23–24; Fuenn, *Safah le-Ne'emanim*, 147; Weiss, *Zichronotai*, 76–77; Kasdai, "Kit'ei Zichronot," 223–24; Sharfstein, *Ha-Heder*, 85, 115, 119; Haramati, *Ivrit Hayah*, 230.

44. In 1886, in a conversation about the inferior status of Hebrew literature and the small size of its readership, M. Ben-Ami told Mendele Mocher Sfarim, "Try to estimate just how

many Jews understand Hebrew well enough to comprehend this literature." Mordechai Ben-Ami, *Ishei Dorenu* (Tel Aviv: Shtibel, 1933), 97. M. L. Lilienblum similarly writes in correspondence to Y. L. Gordon: "Here Hebrew literature is dead . . . the masses won't understand a thing in the Hebrew tongue and the so-called intellectuals hate it, its books and authors with the purest loathing." See Lilienblum, *Ktavim* B, 17.

45. Funkenstein and Steinsaltz, *Ha-Soziologia shel ha-Ba'arut*, 86–93.

46. On the view that those involved in Scripture are to be suspected of heresy, see Kasdai, *Kit'ei Zichronot*, 221; Buki Ben Yogli, *Zichronot*, 56–57. For the view that opposition to engagement with Scripture was an overreaction to the *Haskalah*, see Fuenn, *Safah le-Ne'e-manim*, 143; Lifschitz, "Ha-Heder," 321. Yet it must be noted that suspicions of heresy were raised mainly about those who were involved with grammar, as is attested by an amusing episode related by Friedman: "My grandfather prohibited us from studying Bible or the grammar of the Hebrew tongue. I recall one time after numerous entreaties my grandfather permitted me to study a '*kosher*' grammar book: *Tsohar ha-Teivah*. And it happened that as I began to peruse the book a piece of a cigarette rolled out and came into my hands. My grandfather saw this and said, sin follows sin in train, you take hold of a grammar book and already have a cigarette in hand! Thus ended my studies in grammar." Friedman, *Sefer ha-Zichronot*, 50–51. Friedman also says, "My grandfather did not permit me to study Bible and grammar, and told me, 'you will be a Rabbi of Israel, and a great rabbi has no need to know the Hebrew tongue'" (105).

47. Sharfstein, *Ha-Heder*, 111–17.

48. See, e.g., Lifschitz, "Ha-Heder," 320.

49. Stampfer "Heder Study," 271–83. In the context of his argument Stampfer attempts to justify the instructional methods of the *heder* as well. The fragmented instruction in the five books, for example, he explains by noting that a school need not be the only source of acquisition of knowledge and that a child may, if he so desires, hear from his parents the stories in the five books in their entirety. In his opinion, criticism of the fragmented instruction points not to any real problem in the methods used in the *heder* but rather exposes the ideological bias of its critics (ibid., 279). Yet, as I have shown above in discussing the methods used in Bible instruction, this response does not sufficiently address the fundamental questions such methods raise.

50. Literacy can cultivate free critical thought, but it may also serve conservative ends. Discrimination between populations on the basis of ethnicity, class, or gender need not be expressed by a complete withholding of basic literacy skills. Societies that do offer elementary reading capacities have often discriminated between populations by varying the educational inflections, so that skills are matched to the purposes they will serve in a given sociocultural context. Literacy is an instrument for freedom and progress when provided in ways that allow the student to apply literacy skills creatively, yet they remain an instrument for enforcing sociocultural conformism when they are distributed or applied selectively. See Kaestle, "History of Literacy," 33–36.

Writing was not taught in the traditional educational system. See Lifschitz, "Ha-Heder," 322, 329; Sharfstein, *Ha-Heder*, 119; Stampfer, "Heder Study," 277. This may serve as further evidence that Jewish society in nineteenth-century Eastern Europe acted to limit the creative use of literacy among most of those who learned to read. Interesting testimony to this effect is suggested by Nachum Meir Shaikevitch (Shomer), who notes in his memoirs that the *yeshivah* directors and the supervisors considered it a sin and a crime "if a student wrote some clever commentary." Shaikevitch, *Shirei Shomer ve-Zichronotavr* (Shomer's poems and memoirs) (Jerusalem: Ahiasaf, 1952), 60. The subject of the traditional educational system's attitude toward instruction in writing deserves separate treatment. Yet Shaul Stampfer's argument that such instruction was unnecessary, as contracts were written by special scribes while writing personal correspondence was precluded given the lack of an effective postal service, strains credulity. See Stampfer, "Heder Study," 278.

51. Rabbi Zvi Elimelech of Dinov, *Magid Ta'alumah* (Mystery teller) (1877), 425–27.

52. Compare Funkenstein and Steinsaltz, *Ha-Soziologia Shel ha-Ba'arut*, 53–54, and Rephael Mahler, *Ha-Hassidut ve-ha-Haskalah* A (Hassidism and Haskalah A) (Merhaviah: Sifriat ha-Poalim, 1954), 30–80. For an account of the complexity involved in direct access to biblical texts in the Reformation, see Euan Cameron, *The European Reformation* (Oxford: Clarendon Press, 1991), 136–44.

53. Shaul Levin, *Ktav Yosher* (An epistle of righteousness) (1894), 7a. For a satiric account of the attitude toward Scripture, see page 4a. Concerning Rabbi Shaul Levin, who was the senior justice of the religious court in Frankfurt, and the satire *Ktav Yosher,* published posthumously, see Moshe Samet, "Shaul Berlin u-Ktavav" (Shaul Berlin and his writings), *Kiryat Sefer* 43 (1968): 429, 432; and Perez Sandler, *Ha-Bi'ur la-Torah* (Mendelssohn's edition of the Pentateuch) (Jerusalem: Re'uven Mass, 1984), 97.

54. Lilienblum, *Ktavim Autobiography'im I,* 101.

55. Levinsohn, *Te'udah be-Yisrael,* 3–28, esp. 11; Immanuel Etkes, "Li-She'elat Mevasrei ha-Haskalah be-Mizrach Europa" (The question of the forerunners of the Haskalah in Eastern Europe), *Tarbitz* 57 (1988): 6–9.

56. David Baer Nathansohn, *Sefer ha-Zichronot* (Book of memoirs) (Warsaw, 1877), 116.

57. Mendele Mocher Sfarim, *Kol Kitvei,* 267.

58. Mordechai Breuer, "Mine'u Bneichem min ha-Higayon" (Keep your children from higgayon), in *Michtam le-David* (Ramat-Gan: Bar-Ilan University Press, 1978), 242–61; Dov Rappel, *Sheva Hochmot* (Seven wisdoms) (Jerusalem: Misrad ha-Hinuch ve-ha-Tarbut, 1990), 36–46.

59. Assaf, *Mekorot A,* 18–26.

60. Rappel's book deals with the dispute in Jewish history over the status of the "external wisdoms." It dwells principally on the efforts of those who took the word *Higayon* as denoting logic.

61. On this matter, see Meir Gilon, *Kohelet Musar le-Mendelssohn* (Mendelssohn's Kohelet Musar in its historical context) (Jerusalem: Ha-Academia ha-Le'umit le-Mada'im, 1979), 92.

62. Ibid., 160–61.

63. Shalom Ya'akov Abramovitch, *Ein Mishpat* (Eye of justice) (Zhitomir, 1867), 64–65.

64. Rabbi Yehezkel Halevi Landau approved Naphtali Hertz Wesseley's book, yet after Wesseley published *Divrei Shalom ve'Emet* (Words of peace and truth), Landau retracted his approval, became its leading detractor, and claimed that Wesseley "incited Israel to the study of natural and academic wisdoms." This episode is described in detail in the biography *Toldot Yehezkel Halevi Landau,* published in 1972 in Me'ah She'arim, accompanied by great praise for the rabbi's honesty and a warning against reading Wesseley's book: "And we are to consider the holy qualities of our Rabbi, who, though he himself had been among the supporters of this man's books, nonetheless did not hesitate to recant and ban him and say that he is a heretic and unfit to serve as a witness. (And one must take care to avoid reading this man's books and there are some who err in this as they do not know who he is and see in his book the approval of one of the Great Ones of Israel)." See *Toldot Yehezkel Halevi Landau* (The life of Yehezkel Halevi Landau) (Jerusalem, 1972), 13–16.

65. Yehezkel Landau, *ZaLaH [Tziun le-Nefesh Hayah]* (A tribute to the living soul) (Sdilikow, 1832), fol. 39b.

66. In his *Het'ot Neurim* (Sins of youth), Lilienblum relates how he had read the works of Yehezkel Landau and the Hatam Sofer so as to allay any doubts of the existence of a creator. Lilienblum, *Ktavim Autobiography'im I,* 116–18. About his influence, see also Weiss, *Zichronotai,* 61.

67. Hatam Sofer (Moshe Sofer), *Sefer Torat Moshe* (New York: Grossman, 1960), 21a–b.

68. On this issue, see Rephael Mahler, *Divrei Yemei Yisrael* B, 223.

69. Shlomo Kluger, *Ha-Elef Lecha Shlomo* (A thousand for you, Shlomo) (1911), 14, sec. 257.

70. Weiss, *Zichronotai*, 30. A similar conclusion—that the status of grammar was like that of the "external wisdoms"—follows from Rabbi Y. Emden's discussion regarding grammar study in the bathroom. See Emden, *She'elat Yavetz*, 17, question 10.

71. See, for example, Weiss, *Zichronotai*, 61, 71; Buki Ben Yogli, *Zichronot*, 56; Kasdai, "Kit'ei Zichronot," 219–22.

72. On this point, see, for example, Etkes, "Mevasrei ha-Haskalah," 97–98; Azriel Shochat, "Yachasam shel ha-Maskilim be-Russia el ha-Lashon ha-Ivrit" (The attitude of the Russian Maskilim toward the Hebrew language), in *Sefer Avraham Even-Shoshan* (Abraham Even-Shoshan book) (Jerusalem: Kiryat Sefer, 1985), 362, 368.

73. Moshe Pelli, "Tfisat ha-Melitzah be-Reshit Sifrut ha-Haskalah" (The concept of "Melitzah" at the beginning of the Haskalah), *Lashon ve-Ivrit* 8 (1991): 31–37.

74. On this issue, see Rappel, *Sheva Hochmot*, 12–45.

75. Naphtali Hertz Wesseley, "Rov Tov le'Veit Yisrael" (Great goodness for the house of Israel), *Divrei Shalom ve'Emet II* (Berlin, 1785), 5b.

76. Yitzhak Satanov, "Melechet ha-Shir" (The art of poetry), in *Sefer ha-Hizayon* (The book of vision) (Berlin, 1775), 4a. Satanov supported an expansion of Hebrew, drawing also on rabbinic language, yet sought to maintain the supremacy of biblical language. On this issue, see Iris Parush and Brakha Fishler, "Shikulei Lashon Sifrut ve-Hevrah ba-Vikuach al ha-Taharanut" (Religious, linguistic, literary, and social considerations in the transition from pure to synthetic language), *Mehkarei Yerushalayim be-Sifrut Ivrit* 15 (1995): 111–13.

77. Yehudah Leib Ben-Ze'ev, *Talmud Leshon Ivri* (Vilna, 1879), 342.

78. Shlomo Zalman HaCohen Hanau, "Teivat ha-Melitzah," *Tzohar ha-Teivah* (Vilna, 1733), A.

79. Etkes, "Mevasrei ha-Haskalah," 98.

80. Buki Ben Yogli, *Zichronot*, 153–54.

81. Also *zealotry;* the Hebrew is the same.—Trans.

82. Jonah Ibn Janah, *Sefer ha-Rikmah* (The book of embroidery) (Jerusalem: Mahadurat Wilensky, 1964), 14–15, 19.

83. HaCohen Hanau, author's preface to *Tzohar ha-Teivah.*

84. Rashi Fuenn makes a similar claim. In his opinion, during Mendelssohn's time the rise of Hebrew "came to a standstill and even retreated, as the *Hassidim* broke forth, . . . and in seeking an exalted inner truth to the Torah they scorned and ridiculed its literal meanings [*Pshat*] and took as it were a vow against study of the wisdom of the Holy Tongue, as well as against any other work of science or learning. And the masses of Talmud scholars . . . resisted and sought to multiply Talmud academies . . . so as to hold their ground against the *Hassidim.* And by putting all their efforts into the Talmud and its commentaries they too abandoned the literal understanding of Scripture, and gave no attention to knowledge of language, or the academic sciences." Fuenn, *Safah le-Ne'emanim*, 142–43.

85. See Yehudah Leib Ben-Ze'ev, *Otzar ha-Shorashim* (Treasure of roots) (Vienna, 1862). For the different justification provided for the engagement in Torah scholarship among the learned elite of Ashkenazi Jewry from the sixteenth century onward, see Etkes, "Mevasrei ha-Haskalah," 101–2.

86. Adam HaCohen, "Shir Shirah" (Sing a song), *Pirchei Tzafon II* (Vilna, 1844), 121.

87. Adam HaCohen, *Kinat Sofrim* (Author's lament) (Vilna, 1847), 42–43.

88. Ya'akov Lifschitz, *Zichron Ya'akov* B (Kovno, 1923–30), 2:18.

89. Reuven Fahn, *Sefer ha-Kara'im* (The book of Karaites) (Vienna: M. Hayk, 1929). In

extensive scholarship concerning relations between the *Maskilim* and the Karaites, Fahn argues that one of the causes of the *Maskilim's* fascination with Karaism was Karaism's linguistic and scientific research into Hebrew grammar and the Bible. He writes that "authors and Hebrew *Maskilim* in Russia who are active in promoting the *Haskalah* among Jews of the land are walking as intimate friends with the Karaite scholars, in close brotherly bonds" (107). In his opinion, Rabbi Fuenn "was enthralled by the idea of the *Haskalah* and the idea of criticism of Jewish life and its historical development, and thus was attracted to Karaism to a certain extent," and Y. B. Levinsohn resented him for this and attacked Fuenn in his *Nidachei Israel* (The outcasts of Israel) (108). Fahn writes also that "the *Maskilim* thought to find among the Karaites their intellectual predecessors—people with several hundred years' experience in criticism of the sayings of Our Rabbis, seekers who would not have Mount Talmud weighing upon them and would thus be free in their reasoning and their thoughts" (115).

90. Gide'on Katzenelson, *Ha-Milchamah ha-Sifrutit Bein ha-Haredim ve-ha-Maskilim* (The literary war between Haredim and Maskilim) (Tel Aviv: Dvir, 1954), 52–53.

91. Abramovitch, *Ein Mishpat,* 42.

92. Avraham Ya'akov Paperna, *Kankan Hadash Male Yashan* (New decanter, ancient contents) (Vilna, 1867), 49–51; Iris Parush, "Tarbut ha-Bikoret u-Vikoret ha-Tarbut" (The culture of criticism and the criticism of culture), *Mehkarei Yerushalayim be-Sifrut Ivrit* 14 (1993): 216–22.

93. On the theoretical basis of the distinction between "dominant language" and "subversive language," see Richard Terdiman, *Discourse/Counter-Discourse* (Ithaca: Cornell University Press, 1985), 25–81.

94. Sandler, *Ha-Bi'ur la-Torah,* 81–85; Fishler and Parush, "Bein 'Mikra she-Katuv.'"

95. It must be emphasized that the reference here is to the purist *ideal* of Haskalah literature. Klausner, *Sfat Ever Safah Hayah,* 68ff.; Haramati, *Ivrit Hayah,* 212–13. In practice the scriptural style was not the "unique Hebrew style that took control over modern Hebrew literature up to Y. L. Gordon (the later) and Mendele Mocher Sfarim," for the purism had mainly to do with *poetry.* Halkin, *Zramin ve-Tzurot,* 100–101. This also explains why the *Maskilic* threat was specifically identified with poetry and its *melitzah.*

96. Israel Hayim Taviov, "Sifrutenu ha-Hadashah va-Atidote'ha" (Our modern literature and its future), *Pardes* A (1891): 108.

97. Klausner, *Sfat Ever Safah Hayah,* 26, 98ff.

98. Parush, "Tarbut ha-Bikoret."

99. Brakha Fishler and Iris Parush, "Ha-Shibbutz ha-Mikra'i ki-Standard Beina'yim" (The inserted biblical text and the linguistic standard), in *Shay Le-Hadassah* (Hadassah Shy jubilee book), ed. Ya'akov Bentolila (Beer Sheva: Ben-Gurion University Press, 1997), 227–36.

100. Shmuel Versrs, "Ma'arechet ha-Zikot Bein ha-Sifrut ha-Yafah le-Vein Hochmat Yisrael" (Between Haskalah literature and Hochmant Israel), in *Megamot ve-Tzurot be-Sifrut ha-Haskalah* (Trends and forms in Haskalah literature) (Jerusalem: Magnes, 1990), 40–41.

101. Mahler, *Divrei Yemei Yisrael* A, 80–81.

102. See, e.g., Abramovitch, *Ein Mishpat,* 42.

103. Shalom Ya'akov Abramovitch, *Ha-Avot ve-ha-Banim* (Fathers and sons) (Odessa, 1868), 40–41.

104. Paperna, *Kankan Hadash Male Yashan,* 314.

105. Tzemach Tzimrion, *Ha-Me'asef—Ktav ha-Et ha-Moderni ha-Rishon be-Ivrit* (Ha-Me'asef—the first modern periodical in Hebrew) (Tel Aviv: Mif'alim Universitai'yim, 1988), 90–91; Shochat, "Yachasam shel ha-Maskilim," 353–430.

106. The promotion of the ideal of biblical purism was an attempt to reshape Hebrew as a monoglottic language and to impose such monoglossia on the emerging literature. Any follower of Bakhtin—who favors heteroglossia in all cases over a controlled, centralized, unitary

language—must view such an attempt as reactionary and negative, as it narrows the range of possible voices and restricts the expression of diverse worldviews. Yet in the particular historical situation being discussed, the path toward the democratization of language depended on just such a unification, that is to say, on replacing one monoglottic language with another. For a critique of Bakhtin based on Antonio Gramsci's concept of cultural hegemony, which is in line with the views expressed here, see Tony Crawley, "Bakhtin and the History of Language," in *Bakhtin and Cultural Theory,* ed. Ken Hirschkop (Manchester: Manchester University Press, 1989), 83–89.

Bringing Books to a "Book-Hungry Land"

Print Culture on the Dakota Prairie

Lisa Lindell

The dearth of reading material was a recurring lament in the writings and memoirs of Dakota settlers in the late nineteenth and early twentieth centuries. "I was born with a desire to read, . . . and I have never gotten over it," declared Henry Theodore Washburn, recalling his Minnesota boyhood and homesteading years in Dakota Territory, "but there was no way in those days to gratify that desire to any great extent."[1] This lack was indeed of consequence. In the pre-electronic era, print was a primary means of obtaining information, insight, and pleasure. High rates of literacy, sharp increases in book production, and falling costs all contributed to the pervasiveness of the printed word. Whether it promoted particular values or challenged them, reading played a vital role in shaping how individuals assigned meaning to their lives.[2]

Governing what and how much was read were geographical location, environment, economic conditions, educational levels, and amount of leisure time. For many early South Dakota settlers, reading was certainly not a prime activity or even a real option. Those who did actively involve themselves in the culture of print were variously motivated. From ordinary rural dwellers, to the educated elite, to book publishers and sellers, each had an agenda—whether to strive for cultural improvement, spread "right ideals," make a quick profit, or simply eke out a living. In any case, getting books to remote regions required initiative and perseverance. A historical examination of South Dakota's print culture, focusing on the experiences of those who supplied reading material and those who received it, can afford a valuable glimpse into the cultural aspirations and attitudes of a rural population in late nineteenth- and early twentieth-century America.

"There were but few books in any home in our community, in my early childhood," wrote Mabel Kingsley Richardson of her upbringing in southeastern Dakota in the 1880s. "I am proud to be country born, and in South Dakota. If I had my choice over, I'd choose to be born on the same hill, in the same house, by the same river, . . . but I would like more books." Among the family's small stock of printed materials were a Webster's dictionary, a brown leather Bible, almanacs, seed catalogues, and advertising material from which the children resourcefully clipped illustrations for homemade picture books. Richardson's keenest memories were of a lavishly illustrated gift book carefully stowed in her mother's trunk. Bound in "soft tan leather, with heavy gold tooling and gilt edges," the book was "filled with beautiful pictures in soft tints of dainty ladies in fluffy dresses and poke bonnets" accompanied by "grown up" poems and stories. When she learned that her father had presented this book to her mother the Christmas before they were married, Richardson decided that "it was reason enough for marrying any man."[3] The allure of the appearance and aura of books went beyond the enchanted reaction of a child. Indeed, for cultural aspirants in Victorian America, a reverence for books as objects and status symbols was a common response, something book publishers were quick to grasp and exploit.[4]

The Richardson family's few books were typical of the sparse holdings in many South Dakota homes. A survey of books owned by late nineteenth-century Hand County residents, for example, reveals that most of these households had a Bible, a schoolbook or two, and little else.[5] Specific references to the books of South Dakotans in this era are unfortunately scanty. Although many left written records of their pioneer experiences, Richardson's account is exceptional in that she provided a detailed description of her family's book holdings.

The voices chronicling life in South Dakota's territorial period and early years of statehood were mainly those of Euro-Americans whose settlement, at first confined to the southeast corner of the territory, spread progressively westward as the railroads advanced and millions of acres of Native American reservation lands were opened to homesteaders.[6] From 1878 to 1887, the years of the "Great Dakota Boom," the population of eastern Dakota Territory burgeoned, spurred by the railroads, aggressive advertising, and favorable weather patterns. The forcible opening of tribal lands in

1890, the year after South Dakota achieved statehood, and the period between 1904 and 1913 precipitated further land rushes, tripling the population in western South Dakota in the first decade of the twentieth century. Boom times, though, alternated with periods of drought, crop failure, and economic depression. As a result, the young state lost many settlers after only a short residency despite registering continuous population increases in its early years.[7]

Those who remained faced hard conditions in their attempt to wrest a living from the land. Thus it is hardly surprising that books and other reading matter were often not a priority. Determined readers who overcame the difficulties of access are indeed the more remarkable, as is illustrated by the example of Edna Jewett Allen and her husband, who, in 1881, transported their large personal library, reportedly consisting of a thousand "well chosen books," by train to their new home in Groton, Dakota Territory.[8] More modest was the collection of Stephen Street, a Grant County homesteader whose shanty accommodated "quite a row of books," including *The Adventures of Don Quixote* and *The Arabian Nights*. That Street was largely self-educated through reading could be discerned in his pronunciation of authors' names as they were spelled. In his system, Goethe became "Go-thee" and Bjornson "Be-jorn-son."[9]

While Street sought to boost his educational stature through books, filtering what he read through his English sensibilities, other settlers, especially the many recent immigrants populating South Dakota, approached books and other reading material as overt symbols of their traditions and culture. The 1900 census identified 22 percent of South Dakotans as having been born outside the United States and 39 percent of foreign parentage, thus significantly influencing what was read and how it was viewed and valued. Norwegian immigrant Walborg Holth was among those who maintained close ties to their homeland through reading, including, in her case, the Norwegian newspaper *Morgenblade*. Although the specific contents of the books and albums Holth proudly displayed in an alcove in the wall of her family's sod home remain unknown, they undoubtedly featured titles in her native tongue.[10] Religious faith shaped the reading habits of immigrants, as indeed of many settlers. Illustrative were the Trygstad family, early residents of Brookings County, who regularly read the devotional books, catechisms, and Bibles they had carefully transported from Norway, and Emma Westrum, also of Brookings County, who diligently studied her catechism and Bible while herding the family's cattle in Oslo Township.[11]

For settlers who desired fresh reading material and were fortunate enough to have the means to acquire it, books could be ordered through mail-order catalogues or directly from publishers.[12] Other Dakotans subscribed to newspapers, farm journals, or magazines, even to the point of financial hardship. Ethel Fish Riffle recollected that the only money her father ever borrowed ($5 from the local postmaster) was to pay his subscription to the *Orange Judd Farmer*, a Chicago-based farm weekly.[13] Newspapers served other practical purposes, as Jessie Andrews Sherard attested, describing her family's use of pages from the *Chicago Inter-Ocean* as window curtains in their sod shanty. And the Black family recalled stuffing newspaper into the cracks of their claim's walls to keep out the snow during a spring blizzard in 1881.[14]

That "hard winter" of 1880–81, long remembered for its frequent and heavy snowfalls, proved challenging for Dakota Territory's early newspaper publishers. A railroad blockade lasting into May and the consequent lack of supplies inspired many innovative newsprint substitutes, including wrapping paper, bleached flour sacking, and wall paper.[15] Despite the obstacles, newspapers became increasingly prevalent during the homesteading years, owing in part to the requirement that settlers publish, for a fee, five consecutive notices in the nearest newspaper stating their intention to gain title to their land. Contestants to these claims were obliged to pay the newspapers as well. The resulting proliferation of "final-proof" newspapers contributed to South Dakota's total of 275 publications in 1889.[16] Proof notices and ready-printed material, rather than substantive news or literary matter, formed the primary content of many of these early newspapers. These papers tended to be transitory as well, going out of business or moving on as regions became settled.[17]

Other ready sources of reading material remained in short supply throughout the late nineteenth century and well into the twentieth. In the 1880s a few bookstores emerged in Dakota Territory's developing towns. Among them were two businesses in the newly incorporated town of Brookings—in 1881, C. W. Higgins advertised books along with "Drugs, Chemicals, Paints and Oils, Glass, . . . Stationery and Cigars," and E. E. Gaylord marketed "Furniture, Books and Stationery." As a rule, storekeepers who sold books combined their trade in print wares with other merchandise.[18] A case in point was William Hyde's drugstore in Revillo, where "upon a certain shelf, noble in its solitude and as relieved of competition as the Washington monument, stood a gold-titled set of the novels of Charles Dickens."[19] Books were more plentiful in other stores, but selections were inevitably limited. And the location of these stores in scattered towns made them inaccessible to many rural households.

Libraries, too, were few and far between in South Dakota in the early years. Of those in existence at the time of statehood in 1889, nearly all began as subscription libraries or small reading rooms sponsored by individuals or organizations.[20] These rudimentary libraries, commonly located in parlors, churches, or above stores, were, despite determined fund-raising efforts and a few generous donors, susceptible to financial difficulties, lagging interest, and natural disasters. A fire in Howard, South Dakota, "swept away" the library in 1892, burning "400 volumes, the large bookcase, stove, table, lamps, chairs, etc., with no insurance."[21] An 1895 fire likewise decimated the Ipswich Library, founded in 1886, destroying all the books and records. Attempts to begin anew were temporarily defeated by another fire in 1898 that resulted in the loss of all but seventy-five books.[22]

Among the earliest towns to establish a reading room was Sioux Falls, advantageously located in the southeastern section of the state and destined to become South Dakota's largest municipality. Instigated by private citizen Louisa Gale, the reading room opened in 1875 above the Williams Brothers' store. The public-spirited enterprise proved transitory, closing after a short time; but the growing town was not long deprived of a library thanks to the successful efforts of two organizations, the Ladies' History Club and the Humboldt Club, in forming the Sioux Falls Library Association. By 1887 the library collection totaled 278 volumes, including works by Mark Twain, Ralph Waldo Emerson, William Thackeray, Bret Harte, and George Eliot. The struggling library was funded through membership fees, dues, fines, and fund-raising events until 1899, when the city voted a one-mill tax for library support.[23] Other South Dakota libraries would follow similar paths, but not until after the turn of the century did the pace of library development quicken.[24]

None of South Dakota's early libraries, in any case, was easily accessible to the inhabitants of villages and farms. The remote location, in addition to limited finances and education, served to curtail access to reading material. Nothing, though, could wholly stifle a basic yearning for books, and two methods in particular, subscription book selling and traveling libraries, attempted to fill the void.

Subscription book selling became a thriving industry in late nineteenth-century America. Drawn by the promise of riches and adventure, agents crisscrossed the country, gathering book orders and delivering door to door. South Dakota's isolated, undersupplied population presented a potentially fruitful field. Among those enticed to the book-selling enterprise was Eliza Jane Wilder, the future sister-in-law of author Laura Ingalls Wilder. A single woman homesteading in Kingsbury County, Dakota Territory, in the 1880s, Wilder struggled to make a living from her land. In a letter requesting the aid of the U.S. land commissioner in getting a patent for her claim after the requisite five-year residency, Wilder described the rigors of homestead life and vigorously defended her extended absences during the winter to earn money for necessary improvements to be made in the summer months, "the only time when work can be done in that climate on a farm."[25] A sometime schoolteacher who owned "50 or 60 books" of her own, Wilder spent a part of these long winter months selling books:

> In Nov. 1883 fall work being done, all bills paid[,] I found myself without fuel with but a scanty supply of food and $30.00 cash to face a long, cold winter. I made an engagement with Wm. Garrettson [Garretson] & Co. for canvassing for a book on the line of the C&N.W.R.R. [Chicago and Northwestern Railroad] (that I ought not be long from home at any time. There being much there requiring attention.) [I] bought a 1000 mile ticket and started with but $5.00 in my pocket to pay expenses until the books were delivered. In one month I had cleared $100.00.[26]

The conditions under which Wilder worked proved far from agreeable at times. She vividly recalled an intensely cold day in January 1884, spent outdoors in the young prairie town of Huron, with the thermometer registering forty degrees below zero. Despite this experience, Wilder renewed her engagement with William Garretson & Company in the fall of 1884.[27]

Wilder's status as a female book agent was not unusual. Indeed, many subscription publishers specifically catered to women, if sometimes condescendingly, as did the advertisement for an 1888 political campaign volume, which declared that "this is a book that ladies can sell just as well as men."[28] Other groups targeted as book agents included students, educators, and veterans. The American Publishing Company identified subscription book selling as "particularly adapted to disabled Soldiers, aged and other Clergymen having leisure hours, Teachers and Students during vacation, etc., Invalids unable to endure hard physical labor, Young Men who wish to travel, and gather knowledge and experience by contact with the world, and all who can bring industry, perseverance, and a determined will to work."[29]

Subscription selling was controversial. Although endorsed by partisans as a noble endeavor, the subscription industry was criticized with equal fervor. Detractors leveled accusations of "importunity and trickery" and denounced subscription publishers as self-serving profiteers who threatened the regular publishing industry.[30] Reflective of the widespread animosity toward subscription agents, and indeed toward all types of itinerant sellers, was the disparaging title of an 1879 publication: *How 'Tis Done: A Thorough Ventilation of the Numerous Schemes Conducted by Wandering Canvassers, Together with the Various Advertising Dodges for the Swindling of the Public.*[31]

Despite the criticism, subscription book publishing flourished. Supporters eagerly attributed this success to the industry's role in feeding what one

Figure 1. Dakota homesteader Eliza Jane Wilder was among the many "lady agents" canvassing books in late nineteenth-century America. Photograph courtesy of the Laura Ingalls Wilder Memorial Society, De Smet, South Dakota.

South Dakotan termed "a book-hungry land."[32] Among those lauding subscription agents for bringing books to the bookless was encyclopedia publisher and salesman F. E. Compton. "An army of book salesmen stormed
through the land, leaving behind them millions of books, good, bad, and
indifferent," he proclaimed. "Into communities remote from bookstores
and libraries they brought bibles, dictionaries, encyclopedias, textbooks,
histories, classics, children's books, and a flood of handy compendiums on
farming, law, medicine, and cookery."[33]

The staunchest champions were, not surprisingly, the subscription firms
themselves. William Garretson & Company, the firm for which Eliza Jane
Wilder worked, produced a thirty-page booklet for its agents, promoting
the book-selling business and offering tips and tricks for success. "An agent
with good books is a moral benefactor," the circular declared. "He goes
into the highways, byways and dark places of the land, and circulates
knowledge where it otherwise would not penetrate. His calling is a noble
one, and, when pursued with right motives, improving to his character."
The booklet gave canvassers advice in deflecting the negative reception they
might encounter. "People will tell you awful stories about having been
cheated by agents," it acknowledged. "Ask them if they have never bought
a hat or a pair of boots that failed to do them good service, and if so did
they determine to go bareheaded or barefooted for the rest of their days?"[34]

American Publishing's Elisha Bliss, a shrewd and calculating business-
man, fervently defended the subscription trade. "Instead of injuring the
regular book business," he loftily declared, "I think we create a thirst for
knowledge and thus increase the sale of all kinds of books. In the little
towns where there are no bookstores the book agent induces the people to
buy. One book thus sold is read with avidity by the whole household, and
when another agent comes it is ready to buy another book. In that way a
nucleus is formed for hundreds of thousands of little libraries throughout
the country, which never would have existed except for the book agent."[35]

Willard Dillman of Grant County, Dakota Territory, was eager to sign
on as a canvasser for the American Publishing Company. Dillman was
commissioned to sell Mark Twain's *Library of Humor,* published in 1888.
The works of Twain indeed dominated the publishing company's offerings.
Beginning with his *Innocents Abroad* in 1869, the prolific author had
elected to have most of his books sold through subscription, an immensely
profitable decision that eventually led to the formation of his own company.[36] Dillman, in his memoir, recounted his experience selling Twain's
book. "I had steeped myself in the sales literature that the publishers had
supplied," he reported. "I had set forth confidently. But after many weeks'
canvassing I came to doubt my talent as a book agent. No more than a
dozen sales had been consummated." Dillman did not lose his admiration

for the work he was selling, however. "I retained my personal copy of the book and it proved an education in its way," he declared. "It was really a noble example of the publisher's craft. . . . Purporting to be no more than a collection of humorous writings, it was scarcely less than an anthology of American literature. . . . This book became my winter and summer companion. If each of the dozen copies that had been locally distributed proved as potent, Mark Twain had his part in bringing culture to our town."[37]

Residents of the small town of Revillo, the Dillmans were, to be sure, exceptional in their enthusiasm for literary culture, reflected in Dillman's writing of his memoirs and the family's habit of sending for books and magazines by mail. Dillman recalled receiving "the old standard magazines," including the *Century, Harper's,* and *Scribner's,* as well as *McClure's,* "a new venture of fascinating quality," first issued in 1893. "We were not suffering intellectual starvation," he maintained, "though we dwelt beyond the border of culture."[38]

Dillman's book-selling career might well have prospered had he found more families like his own to target. The family's preoccupation with gaining "culture" made them ideal customers for book canvassers, and they were in fact frequent buyers of subscription books. Among their purchases was *Great Leaders and National Issues of 1896.* Dillman described the heavily illustrated and fancily bound publication as "a timely book if not great literature."[39] Prominently featured were the 1896 presidential campaign and the candidacies of William McKinley and famed orator William Jennings Bryan, then galvanizing audiences as Populism gained momentum in the Midwest.[40] Contemporary politics proved a popular topic of subscription books, its appeal to the Dillman family thus mirroring a widespread interest.

Despite the evidence that many subscription books did indeed sell well, booksellers' short-lived careers were by no means unusual. In his study of the American subscription publishing network in the nineteenth century, Michael Hackenberg characterizes local canvassers as "moonlighting individuals who briefly flirted with the hope of quick money and more often than not bowed rapidly out of the enterprise."[41] Although charges of dishonesty were in some cases deserved, many, if not most, agents set out with enthusiasm and good intentions, naïvely taking the glib hyperbole of the subscription publishers at face value.

That the job was by no means as rewarding as promised was a lesson painfully learned by aspiring book salesman John Merton Aldrich, an 1888 graduate of Dakota Agricultural College. Shortly before graduating, Aldrich sent for prospectuses for the three volumes he would be selling, a Bible history and campaign biographies of presidential and vice-presidential candidates Benjamin Harrison and Levi Morton, before accepting a commission for Day County, Dakota Territory. "Immediately after leaving Brookings, I plunged with much enthusiasm into the vocation of the book agent," he recalled. "Two days later, with less enthusiasm but more experience, I plunged out again."[42] Aldrich did not specify the reasons for his abrupt bailout, but his expectations were clearly too high. His observation that "everybody was poor, and it was very hard to accumulate even a few dollars" is telling.[43] Another likely factor was fear on the part of potential customers of being duped. Even those eager for books may have been deterred by the negative stories that had spread about traveling salesmen.

The book-selling experience of Ole Edvart Rølvaag, later to commemorate pioneer life in South Dakota through his acclaimed immigrant novels, was akin to Aldrich's. In the summer of 1899 the young Norwegian-American student signed on as a book agent, eagerly anticipating easy sales and ample earnings to support his education at Augustana Academy in Canton, South Dakota. He described his expectations in his autobiographical novel *The Third Life of Per Smevik*. "After I got out into the country, there would be nothing to do but rake the money in. Oh yes, I would succeed, no doubt about that."[44] Disillusionment quickly set in, however. Encountering indifference, mistrust, and long treks in miserable weather, Rølvaag's fictional alter ego, like Rølvaag himself, soon succumbed to discouragement, quitting after one month. "Since then I've been wandering around, sometimes working by the day, other times by the job. I've done almost anything you can name—dug wells, helped build windmills, butchered hogs, picked corn, and so forth. It hasn't always been fun and games either, that you must realize. Yet these things are nothing compared to being a book agent."[45] Rølvaag did not wholly reject the experience, however. The next summer he again sold books; and years later, as a college professor, he informed his students that "no one was truly educated who had not tried to sell books or aluminum-ware."[46]

Fellow subscription agent Albert Tallman Free took a less starry-eyed approach to selling books, adapting his education and experience to the exigencies of the trade. A graduate of the University of Iowa, Free arrived in western Dakota Territory in the early 1880s, serving as superintendent of Deadwood public schools and vice president of the Dakota Territory Board of Education. Free later relocated to the southeastern part of the territory, where he was a professor and ultimately president of Yankton College. As a sideline to these professional activities, he applied himself industriously to book selling.

Among the works Free was commissioned to sell was *Johnson's Universal Cyclopaedia*, published by A. J. Johnson & Co. of New York. After signing a contract in October 1886, he received a canvassing outfit, including order forms and weekly report forms, general advice on selling, testimonials

Figure 2. Norwegian immigrant Ole Edvart Rølvaag spent the summers of 1899 and 1900 selling books while attending Augustana Academy in Canton, South Dakota. Photograph courtesy of the Norwegian-American Historical Association, Northfield, Minnesota.

promoting the work, a sample of the book for sale, and a promotional pamphlet addressed to agents. "We have men at work on our Cyclopaedia who are making over $600 per month," the company claimed, "and in every instance they are men who, before they undertook the canvass, memorized the entire Description verbatim; and many of them have assured us their success has come from having followed our system." The company predictably warned against easy discouragement, asserting that "the subscription-book business is a trade, and is not to be learned in a day, a week, or a month. . . . It takes some talent and ambition, and a good deal of energy and perseverance. In fact, if you possess these qualities—perseverance and energy—follow our instructions, and labor hard, your success is only a question of time."[47]

Although Free surely did possess most, if not all, of these traits, he soon turned prudently to the more lucrative business of schoolbook subscription selling, representing North and South Dakota, first for D. Appleton & Co. and then for the American Book Company, formed in 1890.[48] Free received $100 a month for his service, which consisted of active fieldwork, visiting the counties where textbook adoptions were to be made, and promoting the company's list. Among the offerings were McGuffey's readers, Ray's arithmetics, and Appleton's geographies.

As Free quickly discovered, the competition between textbook publishers could be fierce. In its correspondence with the South Dakota agent, the company regularly complained of being "vigorously attacked in all directions" by rival agents. "Your most important business at this time is to correct the misinformation about us which is so sedulously scattered by our competitors," the company declared.[49] Ever diligent in protecting its interests, the company directed Free to travel regularly throughout his territory to ensure that its books were not "thrown out of the schools" in favor of competing texts.[50] In late 1890 Free's employment with the American Book Company ended, when the company rearranged its agents and their territories. A single agent was assigned to represent Minnesota and North Dakota, and another agent took charge of northwestern Iowa and South Dakota.[51] Obviously unswayed by the company's vilification of competing publishers, Free promptly offered his services to its key rival, Ginn & Co.[52]

The movement to establish textbook uniformity throughout South Dakota counties was followed closely by Free and other subscription schoolbook agents eager to have their products adopted in quantity. The lack of standardized, freely provided textbooks persisted for many decades, however, resulting in a jumble of readers, arithmetics, geographies, and spellers. In 1891 the passage of a school law amendment provided for uniform texts throughout South Dakota, but the implementation process was gradual.[53]

Also proceeding slowly, but continuing to gain momentum owing to the zealous efforts of state leaders and educators, was the development of school libraries. One who made a passionate case for good and varied reading material for students was library advocate William Henry Harrison Beadle, territorial superintendent of public instruction from 1879 to 1885. Protesting that "the same old text books for years, heard and repeated by successive classes, are not enough," Beadle contended that it was as much a duty to provide for libraries as it was to establish schools.[54] South Dakotan O. W. Coursey would no doubt have agreed. He and his classmates reused their schoolbooks year after year, he recalled, with the students beginning at the front and leaving off at about the same spot each school term. "At sixteen years of age," he wrote, "I was no farther ahead in any of my books than I had been when I came to Dakota, six years before." Despite their scarcity, schoolbooks were certainly influential, if only through sheer repetition and a lack of competing types of media, in shaping ways of thinking and in serving as an authoritative literary voice.[55]

A potentially promising step for school libraries in Dakota came in 1883 with the passage of legislation allowing school boards to spend up to $500 to purchase books to be rotated among the schools in townships or districts.[56] But because no financial provisions were made, the plan went for the most part unimplemented.[57] The concept of rotating libraries would live on, however, with the deployment of traveling libraries throughout the state.

Traveling libraries began tentatively but expanded steadily in the early decades of the twentieth century, with the ambitious goal of supplying the book needs of South Dakota's rural residents. Like subscription book selling, traveling libraries targeted remote populations, with the added attraction of free access. First promoted widely by New York State Librarian Melvil Dewey in 1893, the concept of traveling libraries for rural communities spread quickly throughout the nation. By 1900, around thirty states had established traveling library systems.[58]

In South Dakota, as in many states, women's clubs were the primary organizers of traveling libraries. Championing the causes of self-improvement and public education, South Dakota's Federation of Women's Clubs sent out several cases of books in the first decade of the twentieth century. Impeded, however, by the expense of the operation and the difficulties of management, the women strongly advocated a state-sponsored library network.[59] The recently organized South Dakota Library Association also promoted a traveling library system, estimating in 1912 that more than 80 percent of the state's population was still unserved by a public library.[60] Rejecting school libraries as a viable option for rural residents, given that most of these libraries did not circulate their collections (which in any case were meager), the association identified traveling libraries as "the only square deal for this state."[61]

Finally, in 1913, the efforts of these library enthusiasts were rewarded when provisions for a statewide traveling library system were codified into law with the establishment of the South Dakota Free Library Commission.[62] Ambitious field librarian Lilly Borresen at once set to work augmenting and publicizing the collection. The state's carpenter was employed in constructing wooden library cases "at a considerable saving to the book fund,"[63] and sample book collections were displayed at popular locales throughout the state, including the State Fair in Huron, the Alfalfa Palace in Rapid City, and the Corn Palace in Mitchell. The South Dakota Library Commission handed out hundreds of postcards at the state fair and other events; sent letters and advertisements to county superintendents, newspapers, and magazines; gave public addresses at conferences, teachers' institutes, and club meetings; and visited towns throughout the state.[64]

The publicity paid off. The number of libraries and books circulated continued to grow. Fifty traveling libraries were launched in September 1913, with fifty more following in March 1914. In its first year of operation, the commission estimated that, on average, each volume circulated nearly four times. Two years later, it boasted of a high of fourteen circulations per volume in the community of White, South Dakota. By 1920 the collection had grown to 251 traveling libraries, all constantly in use, with "thirty to fifty communities on the waiting list."[65] The books were typically lent for six months, with each community responsible for transportation costs.[66]

The lack of adequate funding and the consequent inability to accommodate all requests were persistent concerns. The *South Dakota Library Bulletin* complained that "the necessity of buying only the cheapest editions has caused recourse to clearance and bargain lists, with the unhappy result that where five or six copies of one book are needed only one could be procured. Then other titles had to be substituted, or the same ordered elsewhere."[67]

Judging from the many enthusiastic letters received by the South Dakota Free Library Commission (admittedly a partisan sampling), these concerns did not deter readers. Their testimonies reveal that the books the commission managed to acquire were eagerly welcomed and hungrily devoured. "We consider the traveling library as absolutely indispensible [*sic*]," declared one satisfied beneficiary.[68] "The winter months are very long and reading is about the only enjoyment people can get out here," observed another.[69] A third recipient, voicing her gratitude for the service, noted that she lived far from a railroad or post office and joined with many readers in characterizing traveling libraries as "a blessing to people in isolated sections of the state."[70]

Traveling book collections were frequently shared by groups of farm families, housed in their residences or in the local schoolhouse, where all in the neighborhood had easy access. "Perhaps only a pioneer in this vast portion of the west can so fully appreciate the value of even one book," asserted Nellie Vis, a Pennington County resident whose homestead served as an early traveling library station. Myrna Lyman of Potter County was likewise delighted to host a traveling library in her farmhouse. She proudly attested to the widening of mental horizons through the steady lending and re-lending of books to "every home in our community." [71]

The 1916 *South Dakota Library Bulletin* provided data on the state's traveling collections. In addition to homes, the books were located in general stores, schools, drug stores, public libraries, and post offices. Deemed the "most unique location for a traveling library" was a car belonging to A. W. Palm, the county extension agent for Codington County. Books as well as agricultural information and advice were thus regularly exchanged as Palm made calls throughout the county.[72]

Although they shared some of the same goals as book publishers and sellers, traveling library advocates were wary of the subscription business.

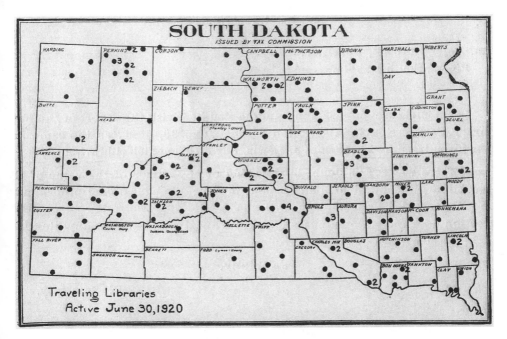

Figure 3. By 1920 traveling library stations were scattered throughout South Dakota, located in general stores, post offices, schools, and homes. From *Fourth Biennial Report of the South Dakota Free Library Commission* (Pierre, S.Dak.: The Commission, 1920), 4.

The remarks of T. A. Crisman, school superintendent of Spink County and ardent promoter of traveling libraries, are typical. While decrying the lack of reading matter in the average South Dakota farmhouse, Crisman was nonetheless dismissive of the efforts of itinerant booksellers. "What books will you find [in the country homes]?" he asked. "The Bible, nearly always. Usually an almanac advertising some patent medicine, with a few witty sayings thrown in as a bait. A book or two bought from an agent, just to get rid of her. . . . What a grand opportunity there is for the cultivation of the literary taste in most of our country homes!"[73]

The notion of the book agent as a nuisance to be "gotten rid of" clearly reflected the popular stereotype. The concern over literary taste, by contrast, was an issue primarily engaged by the educated and reform-minded, and it figured prominently in their criticisms of subscription book selling. Generally raised in a conservative literary tradition and roused by the reforming impulses of the Progressive Era, many educators and librarians saw books as a powerful and crucial force in effecting moral renewal and cultural uplift.[74] This stance was in part a response to the major social changes and unrest sweeping the nation in the late nineteenth and early twentieth centuries and the desire to retain, in the wake of rapid industrialization and modernization, a sense of stability and control. The proper, indeed only, role of literature, from this perspective, was to "enlighten, purify and elevate."[75] Representative of the era were the views of Charles Lugg, South Dakota's superintendent of public instruction, and George M. Smith, professor of pedagogy at the state's university. Focusing especially on children, Lugg criticized the reading habits of rural South Dakotans. "Too often the stuff they elect to read is not conducive to intellectual growth or the formation of moral fiber," he said, and he urged librarians to be diligent in providing better fare. George Smith, equating reading with character, argued that "unhealthful" reading instilled "wrong views of life" and made the startling declaration that "there can be no doubt that many of the strange and bizarre notions of the times are due to the literature of the day."[76]

The books sold by subscription agents, commonly perceived by the cultural elite as sensational, lowbrow, or even "trashy," thus failed to meet their definition of quality literature. An observation in the *Literary World,* maintaining that subscription books "cannot possibly circulate among the best classes of readers," was characteristic. Such elitist perceptions, however, neglected to take into account the wide variety of books sold by subscription agents as well as the mutable boundaries between "high" and popular culture.[77]

The book agents themselves would no doubt have defended the material they sold. Although none of the agents noted here left a record of how he or she might have responded to critics of the subscription trade, these booksellers seemed genuinely to believe in the value of what they sold and would have resented inferences of its being of lesser quality or class. Products of their time, the agents would have agreed on the importance of upholding moral standards but probably would have contended that the books they sold did just that. All were avid readers and viewed the works they sold as a means of promoting knowledge and culture. Rølvaag, especially, was convinced of the worthy task he was performing by selling books. Intellectually ambitious and a great believer in the power of reading, he was a little contemptuous of the farmers who refused to buy from him, complaining that "their highest interest" was "pigs, cattle, and horses" and proclaiming the desirability of shaping them into "thinking beings."[78] In effect, he saw himself as a cultural authority, just like those who would disparage him.

Through the early years of the twentieth century, elitist notions of what constituted quality literature continued to reign. The South Dakota Library Commission at first clung to its role in molding literary taste and closely monitored the content of the library collections.[79] As the twentieth century advanced, however, librarians' zeal for literary quality and moral guidance increasingly gave way to a commitment to meeting the desires and tastes of readers. The traveling libraries offered a mix of nonfiction, fiction, and children's books, with special agricultural collections available as well. By far the most popular was the fiction. Topping the circulation figures in South Dakota in 1916 were Eleanor Hallowell Abbott's *White Linen Nurse,* Alice Hegan Rice's *Romance of Billy-Goat Hill,* and Jean Webster's *Dear Enemy.* Among children's fiction, Julia A. Schwartz's *Beatrice Leigh at College,* Inez Haynes Gillmore's *Maida's Little Shop,* and Carroll Watson Rankin's *Adopting of Rosa Marie* were the most widely read. The Library Commission willingly supplied these novels, although they did hail the occasional request for nonfiction as a very "happy" and "refreshing" surprise.[80] By the mid-1920s, the commission had switched from a fixed book-collection system to an open-shelf system in which each community's needs and interests were taken into account when sending out the traveling libraries.[81]

Traveling libraries continued to fill a real need in South Dakota throughout the 1920s and into the 1930s, when approximately 80 percent of the population still lived on farms and in towns of fewer than a thousand inhabitants.[82] Getting books to these remote localities, given financial and transportation constraints, was an ongoing concern. A 1926 study of rural residents of Lake County revealed that only 38 percent had read any books in the previous year. The key reason given was a lack of access.[83] In 1931 Carroll P. Streeter of the *Farmer's Wife* magazine, speaking to an audience of South Dakota librarians and addressing the challenge of providing books to the thousands of farm families in South Dakota who wanted them, declared that it would require "showing missionaries' ingenuity, zeal and determination to surmount difficulties."[84]

Only with the establishment of county libraries and a growing number of public libraries, inspired in many cases by traveling book collections lent to the community, did the call for the traveling libraries gradually subside.[85] County libraries, designed to provide equal library service to both urban and rural residents within the county, fulfilled many of the same functions as the traveling libraries. Located in county seats, the libraries sent their books to strategic points around the county, including, according to a 1927 study, creameries, stores, post offices, telephone offices, churches, schools, and private residences. The same study found that while a mere 3.2 percent of South Dakota library borrowers were from rural households in counties lacking a county library, slightly more than half the borrowers were rural residents in the three counties with a county library.[86] The benefits of the traveling libraries were extended through these county-based services and, increasingly, through branch libraries, bookmobiles, and direct mail service.[87]

Despite insufficient funding and supplies, the traveling library system and subsequent forms of library outreach clearly were effective means of providing reading material to South Dakota's rural communities. The legacy of the subscription book industry is more ambiguous, but it, too, succeeded in delivering numerous books to isolated individuals eager to read. Debate over motives, methods, and questions of quality notwithstanding, subscription publications were, as scholar Keith Arbour recognizes, "all books that a significant number of Americans of the [nineteenth] century, and the first decade of the [twentieth] century—of all regions, ethnic affiliations, and walks of life—thirsted to consume."[88] The value and pleasure of reading clearly extended beyond narrow, often inconsistent definitions of "worthwhile" literature. Through the efforts of librarians, and book agents too, many of the state's rural residents discovered what fellow South Dakotan Mabel Kingsley Richardson called "the joy that lives in good books."[89]

Notes

1. Henry T. Washburn, *Genealogy and Other Writings of Henry T. Washburn* (Watertown, S.Dak.: Lambert Printing Co., 192?), 33.

2. For insight into the role of reading in late nineteenth-century America, see Christine Pawley, *Reading on the Middle Border: The Culture of Print in Late-Nineteenth-Century Osage, Iowa* (Amherst: University of Massachusetts Press, 2001), and Barbara Sicherman, "Reading and Middle-Class Identity in Victorian America" in *Reading Acts: U.S. Readers' Interactions with Literature, 1800–1950,* ed. Barbara Ryan and Amy M. Thomas (Knoxville: University of Tennessee Press, 2002), 137–60.

3. Mabel K. Richardson, "A Plea for County Libraries," *South Dakota Library Bulletin* 6 (Dec. 1920): 60, 61, 63, 64.

4. See Sicherman, "Reading and Middle-Class Identity," 142.

5. Information on the number of books, along with other articles of personal property, owned by early settlers of Hand County, South Dakota, is available from probated estate inventories. Of the few inventories that mentioned books (22 out of 210 households), around two-thirds (68 percent) had a Bible; nearly as many (64 percent) had one or more schoolbooks; and 50 percent owned other books, none exceeding a combined value of $10. Individual book titles were not listed, with the exception of a single mention of Webster's Dictionary, appraised at thirty cents. Hand County Inventory and Appraisement Records, 1891–1906, State Archives, South Dakota State Historical Society, Pierre.

6. Created in 1861, Dakota Territory became two states, North and South Dakota, in November 1889. For background on South Dakota's history, see Herbert S. Schell, *History of South Dakota,* 3rd rev. ed. (Lincoln: University of Nebraska Press, 1975); Howard R. Lamar, "Perspectives on Statehood: South Dakota's First Quarter Century, 1889–1914," *South Dakota History* 19 (spring 1989): 2–25.

7. Schell, *History of South Dakota,* 252–53, 256; Lamar, "Perspectives on Statehood," 14. The state's population grew from 98,268 in 1880 to 583,888 in 1910. *Thirteenth Census of the United States Taken in the Year 1910: Abstract of the Census; Statistics of Population, Agriculture, Manufacturers, and Mining for the United States, the States, and Principal Cities, with Supplement for South Dakota Containing Statistics for the State, Counties, Cities, and Other Divisions* (Washington, D.C.: Government Printing Office, 1913), 568.

8. Edna Jewett Allen, Brown County, Pioneer Daughters Collection, State Archives, South Dakota State Historical Society, Pierre (hereafter "Pioneer Daughters Collection").

9. Willard Dillman, *A Human Life: Memories of a Pioneer* (Excelsior, Minn.: Record Office, 1934), 114–15.

10. *Thirteenth Census of the United States, with Supplement for South Dakota,* 589; Lorna B. Hickok, ed., "A Pioneer's Letter," *South Dakota History* 6 (summer 1976): 310, 314.

11. Kristianna Trygstad, Brookings County, Pioneer Daughters Collection; Emma Westrum Sterud, Brookings County, Pioneer Daughters Collection.

12. The Montgomery Ward catalogue, for instance, devoted much space to book offerings, providing a thirty-nine-page list in their 1895 edition. For further analysis, see Pawley, *Reading on the Middle Border,* 33–34.

13. Ethel Fish Riffle, Charles Mix County, Pioneer Daughters Collection.

14. Jessie Andrews Sherard, Turner County, Pioneer Daughters Collection; Dorothy Louise Black, *History of Grant County, South Dakota, 1861–1937* (Milbank, S.Dak.: Milbank Herald Advance, 1939), 29.

15. Ruth Elizabeth Bergman, "Printing in South Dakota During the Territorial Period, with a Check List of Newspapers and Periodicals from the Beginning Through 1889" (master's thesis, University of Illinois, 1936), 152–53; Robert F. Karolevitz, *With a Shirt Tail Full of Type: The Story of Newspapering in South Dakota* (Freeman, S.Dak.: South Dakota Press Association, 1982), 29.

16. Bergman, "Printing in South Dakota," 160; Arthur C. Mellette, *Report of the Governor of Dakota: Made to the Secretary of the Interior for the Year 1889* (Washington, D.C.: Government Printing Office, 1889), 26.

17. For a firsthand account of operating a final-proof newspaper, see Edith Eudora Kohl, *Land of the Burnt Thigh* (St. Paul: Minnesota Historical Society Press, 1986); see also Schell, *History of South Dakota,* 186–87.

18. *History of Southeastern Dakota: Its Settlement and Growth* (Sioux City: Western Publishing Company, 1881), 257–305, 393–400, esp. 262. Advertisements of businesses

selling books along with other supplies also appeared in early South Dakota city directories and newspapers.

19. Dillman, *Human Life,* 96.

20. Towns with libraries or reading rooms at various stages of development prior to South Dakota's statehood in 1889 included Aberdeen, Howard, Huron, Ipswich, Milbank, Mitchell, Rapid City, Sioux Falls, and Yankton (*50th Anniversary of the South Dakota State Library Commission and Histories of South Dakota Libraries by Their Librarians: 1913–1963* [Pierre: The Commission, 1973], 12, 37, 39–40, 48–49, 52, 62, 65, 79).

21. Ibid., 37.

22. Ibid., 40.

23. Penny McLeod, "The History of the Sioux Falls, South Dakota, Public Library" (paper, University of Minnesota, 1971), 2–5; Dana R. Bailey, *History of Minnehaha County* (Sioux Falls: Brown & Saenger, 1899), 402–4; *50th Anniversary of the South Dakota State Library Commission,* 65–66; R. E. Bragstad, *Sioux Falls in Retrospect* (Sioux Falls: Bragstad, 1967), 61.

24. Despite an 1887 territorial law allowing for the establishment of free libraries, library growth was very limited. Revisions to that law and more favorable economic, social, and cultural conditions stimulated public library development after 1900. Dakota Territory Session Laws, 1887, chap. 56, sec. 1–9, pp. 160–62; Mary Lois Crouch, "The Library Movement in South Dakota with Special Reference to Some Outstanding Libraries" (master's thesis, University of Illinois, 1930), 22–23. Supplementing the few town libraries in South Dakota's early years were institutional libraries, primarily of the fledgling public and private colleges. Their service, though, was chiefly directed to their own constituencies. A list of institutional libraries and dates of establishment is provided in "Library Report," *Tenth Biennial Report of the Superintendent of Public Instruction, State of South Dakota,* 1909–10, 208.

25. Eliza Jane Wilder to Land Commissioner, Dept. of the Interior, n.d., Land Entry Files, Record Group 49, National Archives Building, Washington, D.C. In order to receive patents to their land, homesteaders were required to reside on and cultivate it for five years, never leaving for more than six months at a time. *U.S. Statutes at Large,* vol. 12, Act of 20 May 1862, p. 393.

26. Wilder to J. F. Chaffre, n.d., Land Entry Files, Record Group 49.

27. Ibid.

28. "Confidential Circular to Agents," (guide to selling the campaign book *National Contest*), Albert Tallman Free Family Papers, State Archives, South Dakota State Historical Society, Pierre.

29. Quoted in F. E. Compton, "Subscription Books," in *Bowker Lectures on Book Publishing* (New York: R. R. Bowker, 1957), 69.

30. S. R. Crocker, "Subscription Books," *Literary World* 5 (Aug. 1874): 40, quoted in Nancy Cook, "Reshaping Publishing and Authorship in the Gilded Age," in *Perspectives on American Book History: Artifacts and Commentary,* ed. Scott E. Casper, Joanne D. Chaison, Jeffrey D. Groves (Amherst: University of Massachusetts Press, 2002), 228. Cook's article provides a useful overview of the antagonism between the regular book trade and subscription publishers.

31. [Bates Harrington], *How 'Tis Done: A Thorough Ventilation of the Numerous Schemes Conducted by Wandering Canvassers, Together with the Various Advertising Dodges for the Swindling of the Public* (Chicago: Fidelity Publishing Co., 1879).

32. Edna Jewett Allen, Brown County, Pioneer Daughters Collection.

33. Compton, "Subscription Books," 69, 70.

34. William Garretson & Co., *Confidential Circular to Agents* (Nashville: Garretson, 1868), 12, 16. The William Garretson circular directed agents to woo prominent members of

the community, "men of influence, such as ministers, physicians, lawyers, editors, [Sunday School] superintendents, etc.," persuading them to head the subscription list, offering, if need be, lower rates or even a free copy. The circular further advised employees to carry only one book at a time to avoid dividing the potential buyer's attention, and to contrive to initially keep that book out of sight. Men were counseled to construct a false pocket, while "lady agents" could "carry their book under their shawl or in a little covered basket very neatly." The circular included several pages of text to commit to memory, which it urged agents to practice at length in order to avoid sounding "like a school-boy reciting a composition." Ibid., 13, 14, 24, 28–29.

35. Elisha Bliss, "Subscription Books," *New York Tribune*, 28 Oct. 1874, 8, quoted in Cook, "Reshaping Publishing and Authorship in the Gilded Age," 228. See also Hamlin Hill, *Mark Twain and Elisha Bliss* (Columbia: University of Missouri Press, 1964); Keith Arbour, "Book Canvassers, Mark Twain, and Hamlet's Ghost," *Papers of the Bibliographical Society of America* 93, no. 1 (1999): 5–37.

36. Cook, "Reshaping Publishing and Authorship in the Gilded Age," 247. At first highly successful, Twain's firm, Charles L. Webster & Co., eventually succumbed to mounting debt, exacerbated by the effects of the national financial crisis of 1893. John Tebbel, *A History of Book Publishing in the United States,* 4 vols. (New York: R. R. Bowker, 1972–81), 2:523–27.

37. Dillman, *Human Life,* 133.

38. Ibid., 149. For an analysis of the great national appeal of popular magazines in the 1890s, see Matthew Schneirov, *The Dream of a New Social Order: Popular Magazines in America, 1893–1914* (New York: Columbia University Press, 1994). For an examination of how culture was perceived and aspired to in nineteenth- and early twentieth-century America, see Joan Shelley Rubin, *The Making of Middlebrow Culture* (Chapel Hill: University of North Carolina Press, 1992), 1–33.

39. Dillman, *Human Life,* 145.

40. Populism, described by historian Howard Lamar as "a logical, almost inevitable response to economic problems brought on by drought, depression, railroad and grain elevator rates, deflation, and the world market," shaped the attitudes of many South Dakotans in the 1890s. Lamar, "Perspectives on Statehood," 11–12.

41. Michael Hackenberg, "The Subscription Publishing Network in Nineteenth-Century America," in *Getting the Books Out: Papers of the Chicago Conference on the Book in Nineteenth Century America,* ed. Michael Hackenberg (Washington, D.C.: Library of Congress, 1987), 52.

42. Aldrich Diary, 31 July 1888, Archives/Special Collections, Hilton M. Briggs Library, South Dakota State University, Brookings, S.Dak.; *Dakota Collegian,* Nov. 1888. John Merton Aldrich went on to become a professor of biology and ultimately an entomologist at the United States Department of Agriculture and United States National Museum (Smithsonian Institution).

43. Aldrich Diary, 8 Aug. 1888 (1932 insert).

44. Ole Edvart Rølvaag, *The Third Life of Per Smevik.* Translated from *Amerika-breve* (1912) by Ella Valborg Tweet and Solveig Zempel (Minneapolis: Dillon Press, 1971), 87.

45. Ibid., 93.

46. Ella Valborg Tweet, "Introduction," *Third Life of Per Smevik,* xvi. For more on Rølvaag's experience as a book agent, see Theodore Jorgenson and Nora O. Solum, *Ole Edvart Rölvaag: A Biography* (New York: Harper and Bros., 1939), 46–47, 51; Einar Haugen, "Rolvaag in South Dakota: Materials for Literary History," in *Siouxland Heritage,* ed. Arthur R. Huseboe (Sioux Falls: Nordland Heritage Foundation, 1982), 27.

47. A. J. Johnson & Co., "Confidential: To Be Read Carefully Before You Commence Canvassing" [1887], Free Family Papers.

48. The American Book Company was formed from the merger of Appleton and three other leading textbook publishers. Tebbel, *Book Publishing in the United States,* 2:565.

49. American Book Company to Albert Tallman Free, 20 June 1890, 1 Aug. 1890, Free Family Papers. Principal among these rivals was Ginn & Co. The American Book Company urged Free to "work against Ginn's books wherever you can find them" in order to keep the company too busy in defense to "apply all of their time in attacks upon us." Harper's and Porter & Coates were other companies eyed with suspicion. American Book Company to Albert Tallman Free, 1 May 1890, 7 July 1890, 16 July 1890, Free Family Papers.

50. Ibid., 4 Sept. 1890.

51. Ibid., 26 Nov. 1890.

52. Although unwilling to offer him a regular paying job, Ginn encouraged Free to introduce its books on commission, for which it would pay him half the net proceeds. Instead, Free turned to Silver Burdette & Co., who hired him to represent both Dakotas. Ginn & Co. to Free, 27 Dec. 1890; Silver Burdette & Co. to Free, 17 Dec. 1890, both in Free Family Papers.

53. *School Law of South Dakota with Session Laws Relating to Public Schools, 1891,* Appendix I, chap. 104, sec. 1–11, pp. 82–85.

54. William Henry Harrison Beadle, "Literature and School Libraries," in *A Teacher's Manual and Guide and Course of Study for the Common Schools of South Dakota* (Mitchell, S.Dak.: Mitchell Printing Co., 1892), 97. In 1890 fewer than 4 percent of South Dakota schools had a library. By 1900 the number had risen to nearly one in three, but holdings were sparse. School library statistics are from the *First Annual Report of the Superintendent of Public Instruction, State of South Dakota,* 1890, 75, 78; *Fifth Biennial Report of the Superintendent of Public Instruction, State of South Dakota,* 1899–1900, 342, 352.

55. O. W. Coursey, *Pioneering in Dakota* (Mitchell, S.Dak.: Educator Supply Company, 1937), 151. Likewise growing up in late nineteenth-century South Dakota, Willard Dillman acknowledged that some of his "primary notions" were obtained from schoolbooks (Dillman, *Human Life,* 115). For analysis of the role of schoolbooks, see Pawley, *Reading on the Middle Border,* 52–56; Ruth Miller Elson, *Guardians of Tradition: American Schoolbooks of the Nineteenth Century* (Lincoln: University of Nebraska Press, 1964).

56. Dakota Territory Session Laws, 1883, chap. 44, sec. 129–33, pp. 115–16.

57. "The Libraries of South Dakota," *Eleventh Biennial Report of the Superintendent of Public Instruction, State of South Dakota,* 1910–12, 381–82.

58. For further information on the history of traveling libraries, see Joanne E. Passet, "Reaching the Rural Reader: Traveling Libraries in America, 1892–1920," *Libraries and Culture* 26 (winter 1991): 100–118; William B. Shaw, "The Traveling Library: A Boon for American Country Readers," *American Monthly Review of Reviews* 17 (Jan.–June 1898): 165–70; Helen E. Haines, "The Growth of Traveling Libraries," *World's Work* 8 (Sept. 1904): 5231–34.

59. In 1904 the South Dakota's Federation of Women's Clubs, holding their annual convention in Watertown in conjunction with the inaugural meeting of the South Dakota Library Association, appropriated $50 to send traveling libraries to towns with populations of fewer than one thousand. The next year, meeting in Huron, the federated clubs reported that one case of books had been in circulation and that the clubs planned to send out three additional cases in the coming year. Letitia H. Stormo, "Sixty-Five Years with the South Dakota Library Association," *South Dakota Library Bulletin* 55 (July–Sept. 1969): 167–68; "Commission History," *South Dakota Library Bulletin* 11 (March–June 1925), 5–6. For more on the role of women's clubs in the growth of libraries, see Paula D. Watson, "Founding Mothers: The Contribution of Women's Organizations to Public Library Development in the United States," *Library Quarterly* 64 (July 1994): 233–69; Haines, "Growth of Traveling Libraries," 5233.

60. "Libraries of South Dakota," 380. By 1910 only twenty-four of South Dakota's fifty-three organized counties had a public library. Seventeen of these libraries were funded through

the Carnegie Library Building Program. Susan Richards, "Carnegie Library Architecture for South Dakota and Montana: A Comparative Study," *Journal of the West* 30 (July 1991): 70.

61. "Libraries of South Dakota," 379, 381.

62. South Dakota Session Laws, 1913, chap. 217, sec. 1–16, pp. 300–303. The commission was composed of the governor, superintendent of public instruction, state historian, and a member each of the Federation of Women's Clubs and South Dakota Library Association (*50th Anniversary of the South Dakota State Library Commission,* 5). After almost a decade of overseeing the nascent traveling library network, the Federation of Women's Clubs transferred their collection of nearly three hundred books to the newly formed commission. Stormo and Dorette Darling, "The South Dakota Library Association," in *Encyclopedia of Library and Information Science* (New York: Marcel Dekker, Inc., 1980), 28:280. In addition to these volumes, books for the traveling library system included 2,264 volumes from the state's Department of Education, 55 volumes from the Department of History, and 3,506 purchased volumes. *First Biennial Report of the South Dakota Free Library Commission* (Pierre: The Commission, 1914), 4.

63. *First Biennial Report of the South Dakota Free Library Commission,* 4.

64. "Traveling Library Notes," *South Dakota Library Bulletin* 4 (Sept. 1918): 98; "Some Results of Publicity," *South Dakota Library Bulletin* 2 (Dec. 1916): 42–43; *First Biennial Report of the South Dakota Free Library Commission,* 8.

65. *First Biennial Report of the South Dakota Free Library Commission,* 4, 8; "Traveling Library Notes," *South Dakota Library Bulletin* 2 (Sept. 1916): 38; *Fourth Biennial Report of the South Dakota Free Library Commission* (Pierre: The Commission, 1920), 4, 24.

66. "The Traveling Libraries," *South Dakota Library Bulletin* 2 (Jan. 1916): 14.

67. Ibid., 13.

68. *Fourth Biennial Report of the South Dakota Free Library Commission,* 18.

69. *Fifth Biennial Report of the South Dakota Free Library Commission* (Pierre: The Commission, 1922), 15.

70. *Seventh Biennial Report of the South Dakota Free Library Commission* (Pierre: The Commission, 1926), 16; *Eighth Biennial Report of the South Dakota Free Library Commission* (Pierre: The Commission, 1928), 17.

71. Nellie Vis, "Three Cheers for the Bookmobile," *South Dakota Library Bulletin* 24 (March 1938): 8; Myrna Lyman, "What the County Library Means to Me," *Dakota Farmer* 50 (1 March 1930): 264.

72. "Traveling Libraries," 14; *Eighth Biennial Report of the South Dakota Free Library Commission,* 4–5.

73. T. A. Crisman, "Libraries for Our Country Schools," *South Dakota Educator* 11 (March 1898): 61.

74. On this topic, see Esther Jane Carrier, *Fiction in Public Libraries, 1876–1900* (New York: Scarecrow Press, 1965), 12–31; Evelyn Geller, *Forbidden Books in American Public Libraries, 1876–1939: A Study in Cultural Change* (Westport, Conn.: Greenwood Press, 1984), 17–76; Dee Garrison, *Apostles of Culture: The Public Librarian and American Society, 1876–1920* (New York: Free Press, 1979), 67–87.

75. Carrier, *Fiction in Public Libraries,* 91.

76. Charles Lugg, "What the Teacher May Expect from the Library," *South Dakota Library Bulletin* 3 (Sept. 1917): 32; George M. Smith, "Some Psychological Aspects of the Library," *South Dakota Educator* 12 (Oct. 1898): 11. For a discussion of the importance of "character" in mid-nineteenth-century America, see Rubin, *Making of Middlebrow Culture,* 3–5.

77. S. R. Crocker, "Subscription Books," 40; David D. Hall, *Cultures of Print: Essays in the History of the Book* (Amherst: University of Massachusetts Press, 1996), 32. For insight

on the incentives of regular trade publishers to attack subscription books' lack of literary value as a means of "cloaking their own commercial motives," see Cook, "Reshaping Publishing and Authorship in the Gilded Age," 224–25.

78. Quoted in Einar Haugen, "Rolvaag in South Dakota," 27.

79. See, for example, "Book Censorship," *South Dakota Library Bulletin* 10 (Sept. 1924): 34–35.

80. "Traveling Library Notes," *South Dakota Library Bulletin* 2 (Dec. 1916): 57.

81. *Seventh Biennial Report of the South Dakota Free Library Commission*, 5; *Sixth Biennial Report of the South Dakota Free Library Commission* (Pierre: The Commission, 1924), 5.

82. *Eleventh Biennial Report of the South Dakota Free Library Commission* (Pierre: The Commission, 1934), 5.

83. W. F. Kumlien, *What Farmers Think of Farming*, Bulletin (South Dakota Agricultural Experiment Station), no. 223 (Brookings, S.Dak.: Agricultural Experiment Station, South Dakota State College of Agriculture and Mechanic Arts, 1927), 12–14.

84. Carroll P. Streeter, "Books and Farmers," *South Dakota Library Bulletin* 17 (Dec. 1931): 68.

85. The state's first county library was constructed in Hyde County in 1920; Tripp and Potter counties established county libraries in 1921 and 1925, respectively. Laws passed in 1917 and 1921 facilitated the establishment of county libraries in South Dakota. Crouch, "Library Movement in South Dakota," 62; South Dakota Session Laws, 1917, chap. 293, sec. 1–7, pp. 603–5; South Dakota Session Laws, 1921, chap. 163, sec. 1–8, pp. 260–62.

86. Kumlien, *Equalizing Library Opportunities in South Dakota*, Bulletin (South Dakota Agricultural Experiment Station), no. 233 (Brookings, S.Dak.: Agricultural Experiment Station, South Dakota State College of Agriculture and Mechanic Arts, 1928), 9, 20, 24.

87. South Dakota's bookmobile system, sponsored by the South Dakota Congress of Parents and Teachers and implemented through a Works Progress Administration project, began operating in South Dakota in 1938. In that same year the South Dakota Library Commission reported a total of eighty-two libraries, tax-supported and private, in South Dakota. *Thirteenth Biennial Report of the South Dakota Free Library Commission* (Pierre: The Commission, 1938), 6, 16.

88. Keith Arbour, *Canvassing Books, Sample Books, and Subscription Publishers' Ephemera, 1833–1951, in the Collection of Michael Zinman* (Ardsley, N.Y.: Haydn Foundation for the Cultural Arts, 1996), xii.

89. Richardson, "Plea for County Libraries," 63. Richardson pursued her love of books throughout her career, first as a country schoolteacher and then as a librarian. She headed the library at the University of South Dakota in Vermillion from 1907 to 1941.

Books Worthy of Our Era?

Octave Uzanne, Technology, and the Luxury Book in *Fin-de-Siècle* France

Willa Z. Silverman

Renovata resurgo [Renewed, I rise again].
—Motto appearing on Uzanne's first publications

"Octave Uzanne, the Bibliophile's dream!"[1] (Figure 1). So exclaimed the Belgian Symbolist painter Félicien Rops (1833–98) when describing his friend, a paragon of bibliophilia in *fin-de-siècle* France. During an era of intense bibliophilic activity spanning the last two decades of the nineteenth century and the first decade of the twentieth, Uzanne (1851–1931) was passionately and prodigiously engaged with the printed word as an author (more than fifty volumes of fiction and criticism), journalist (regular contributions to *L'Echo de Paris* and numerous other French and foreign periodicals),[2] bibliographer, and ad hoc publisher. He founded three influential reviews devoted to the book: *Le Livre: Bibliographie moderne* (1880–89), *Le Livre Moderne* (1890–91), and *L'Art et l'Idée: Revue contemporaine du dilettantisme littéraire et de la curiosité* (1892–93). A habitué of bibliophile societies, he ran two of his own, the Société des Bibliophiles Contemporains

I wish to acknowledge gratefully the National Endowment for the Humanities and the Research and Graduate Studies Office in The Pennsylvania State University's College of the Liberal Arts, whose generous support helped fund research for this manuscript. I wish to express gratitude as well to Antoine Coron for sharing his insights about bibliophilia in France, to Gabriel Weisberg for bibliographic leads, and to the anonymous readers of this manuscript, as well as to Jonathan Rose, for their many useful suggestions.

(1889–94) and the Société des Bibliophiles Indépendants (1896–1901).
Breaking with the tradition of antiquarian, retrospective bibliophilia solidly
established in France, Uzanne cast himself as a reformer, proclaiming that
"the future and success will belong to innovators."[3] He called for change
in all matters concerning the luxury book, especially in illustration, binding, and typography. This ally of the Symbolist poets and painters became
the foremost herald of a new type of bibliophilia, one that privileged close
collaboration between artists, authors, publishers, and collectors to create
illustrated editions of modern texts.

Among the many themes of Uzanne's work is a concern for the effects
of technology on book production. Superficially at least, he seemed optimistic about the many possibilities for creativity afforded by technological
advances. He relentlessly championed what he referred to as "the pretty
things of modern industry" (Cb 112) when applied to book production.
These "pretty things" were featured prominently at the 1894 Exposition
internationale du livre moderne et des industries du papier, held at the
Palais de l'Industrie in Paris. They included color illustrations, machine-
made bindings, and chemically tinted paper. Such novelties exemplified the
technological changes that had been radically transforming the book trade
throughout the nineteenth century to meet the demands of the burgeoning
market for print. Printing presses, for example, had become more complex
machines over the course of the century. Hippolyte Marinoni's rotary press
was introduced in France around 1866, coinciding with the replacement
of rag-based by wood pulp-based paper, to print twenty thousand copies
per hour of the popular daily newspaper, Le Petit Journal. Completed by
Ottmar Mergenthaler's linotype and Tolbert Lanston's monotype machines
(debuting in France at the 1889 and 1900 World's Fairs, respectively), these
inventions contributed to the phenomenal increase in the volume of printed
matter over the course of the century and assured the virtual disappearance
of the manual Gutenbergian atelier.

Uzanne valued the increasing sophistication of printing processes and
other such technological innovations. But he did so only insofar as they
helped advance an elitist aesthetic of the book based on originality, novelty, and fantasy. He disparaged technology's potential to replicate, leading
to overproduction and (worse, in his view) democratization of the type
of livre d'amateur he envisioned. He was, in fact, a peculiar herald, whose
desire for reform coexisted with conservative, even reactionary, leanings.
His elitism led him, in the end, to advocate two strategies for producers
of fine books in this age of mechanical reproduction. The first entailed
appropriating the most modern technologies but in ever more singular
ways, for the exclusive benefit of a select clientele of collectors. The second
also encouraged innovation, not by technological means but by a return to

Figure 1. Portrait-frontispiece of Octave Uzanne by A. Giraldon and Eugène Abot, *Le Livre Moderne,* vol. 1 (10 January 1890). The inscription in the open book reads: "The book, which is the clothing of thought, must express the artistic style and formal mode of an era."

traditional techniques associated with the woodcut. Uzanne's example suggests that during this period mechanical fabrication was not necessarily a dividing line between the sectors of large-scale and elite book production — between a sector, according to the sociologist of culture Pierre Bourdieu, "devoted to the market and to economic profit" and another "exclusively devoted to producing [books] for other producers."[4] Instead, each sector envisioned differing forms of appropriation of the new technologies in accordance with opposed conceptions of the book as either agent of democratization and progress or marker of social and cultural distinction. Rather than merely coexisting in opposition to one another, the sectors of commercial and fine book production were in fact closely interrelated, with technology serving as an essential link between them.

A Reactionary Modernist?

A glimpse at Uzanne's early career reveals a tension between modernism and anachronism that would characterize his attitude toward technology as well. Born into the commercial and office-holding bourgeoisie of Auxerre, Burgundy, Uzanne was soon sent to Paris after his father's death. As a boarder at the Collège Rollin, a training ground for the sons of the upper bourgeoisie and aristocracy, France's future elites, he received a rigorous classical education. A desultory attempt at a law career followed, soon abandoned when a well-timed inheritance in 1872 allowed him to pursue his literary inclinations. He became a habitué of the Bibliothèque de l'Arsenal in Paris, rendezvous for a coterie of erudite book lovers, all disciples of the author, and former Arsenal curator, Charles Nodier (1780–1844). These included the then-current Arsenal curator and lexicographer Lorédan Larchey (1831–1902), the journalist and critic Charles Monselet (1825–88), and the aptly nicknamed "Bibliophile Jacob" (Paul Lacroix, 1806–84), the Arsenal's curator of manuscripts.[5]

Uzanne's mentors conveyed to him a shared passion for the late seventeenth and eighteenth centuries and a dedication to reviving the reputation of their forgotten authors. Monselet's *Oubliés et dédaignés: figures de la fin du XVIIIe siècle* (1857) and Bibliophile Jacob's *XVIIIe siècle: institutions, usages, et costumes, France 1700–1789* (1875) may have provided models for Uzanne's four-volume series, *Poètes de ruelles au XVIIe siècle* (1875–88).[6] The series was published by Damase Jouaust (1834–93), whose "Librairie des Bibliophiles" collection, inaugurated in 1869, set the standard for refined limited editions until Jouaust's retirement in 1891. Uzanne completed his monumental task of resurrecting the works of forgotten eighteenth-century authors, especially those with a libertine bent, with three additional series published by the small firm of Albert Quantin. Uzanne devoted the more than twenty volumes in these series to the chroniclers, poets, and mores of the eighteenth century.[7]

The eighteenth-century revival thus led Uzanne backward, a journey in which he relied on his erudition and bibliographic talents to pay homage to the lesser-known authors of that century and the aristocratic culture that produced them. Indeed, his indefatigable editorial efforts, along with his reviews and bibliographic notices for the short-lived *Conseiller du Bibliophile* (1876–77), marked his emergence at age twenty-four as a critic, bibliographer, and bibliophile under the sway of the *ancien régime*. Yet Uzanne's devotion to the France of Louis XIV and Louis XV also led him forward, as a proponent of the neo-Rococo aesthetic and decorative arts that at the turn of the century inspired Art Nouveau. In this pursuit, his mentors were also bibliophiles — not the *érudits* of the Arsenal but aesthetes who, like Uzanne, were standard bearers for a curious blend of modernism and reaction: the Goncourt brothers.[8]

Uzanne's affinity for the eighteenth century, and for historical pastiche in general, were on display in one of his earliest works, *Le Bric-à-brac de l'amour* (1879) — one of several works for which he devised fanciful and decidedly nonscholarly titles. As suggested by its frontispiece, a neo-Rococo etching complete with cherubim and garlands, *Le Bric-à-brac* offered mildly licentious reflections on love written in a precious style (Figure 2). The traditional frontispiece of this work, however, was overshadowed by its technically groundbreaking two-tone blue cover, one of the earliest examples of a procedure developed in the mid-1870s by the second-generation printer-inventor, Charles Gillot (1853–1904). In 1850 Charles's father, Firmin, had developed the process known as *gillotage*, or zincography, whereby a line-drawn, etched, or lithographic image is transferred to a relief zinc plate. Gillot *fils* adapted his father's invention to the photographic image. Uzanne's experiment with photomechanical reproduction in *Le Bric-à-brac de l'amour* thus owed much to the pioneering work of Charles Gillot. Uzanne added rudiments of color reproduction to his book as well, using textured paper also invented by Charles Gillot to create subtle tone and shading effects.[9]

While *gillotage* would soon become the procedure most commonly used for book illustration by printers in France, in 1879 its use was still quite limited. Indeed, Uzanne's reliance on relief photoengraving placed him on the cusp of the photomechanical "revolution" brought about by new technologies and prepared by a half-century of experimentation. A great variety of printed products were working themselves into every feature of daily life during this "age of paper,"[10] signaled by the proliferation of

Figure 2. Frontispiece, Octave Uzanne, *Le Bric-à-brac de l'amour* (Paris: Rouveyre, 1879). Etching by Adolphe Lalauze.

newspapers, bank notes, travel guides, posters, and department store catalogues. Enlivening these printed products was a stunning diversity of images
that owed their appearance to new techniques, with lithographs and woodcuts giving way to the unparalleled verisimilitude afforded by processes
relying on photography.

Indeed, the development of photography in the late 1830s by Abel
Niepce de Saint-Victor and Jacques Daguerre in France and William Henry
Fox Talbot in England had by mid-century begun to generate numerous
techniques for applying photography to the not dissimilar technology of
printing. Known collectively as photogravure, these techniques exploited
diverse chemically treated surfaces (metal, wood, glass, stone) onto which
photographic images were transferred and often engraved to print the
equally varied types of illustrations now available to the public. The difficulty of adding shading and gradation to these illustrations was resolved
first with the use of textured paper and, most significantly in the 1880s,
with the introduction of halftone screens, anticipating the "color revolution" soon to come. The beginning of Uzanne's bibliophilic activities in
the early 1880s, then, coincided with the gradual displacement of manual
methods of illustrating print by photomechanical ones, as evidenced by the
flood of mass-produced, highly realistic images characteristic of the popular press and book publishing during this era.[11]

But while admittedly "looking for new procedures" (Q 159) with his
adoption of *gillotage,* Uzanne showed interest in photomechanical techniques not for their democratizing potential but rather for the esoteric
effects they could produce. He made this clear in the "iconographic prelude"[12] he wrote for a limited edition of the 1894 *Album Mariani.* Part
of a series that would eventually include eleven volumes, this first album featured photomechanically produced likenesses of seventy-five contemporary
"personalities" — politicians, journalists, actors, artists, novelists — accompanied by biographical sketches. The yearbook owed its publication to
the patronage of a wealthy Corsican scientist-entrepreneur, Angelo Mariani (1838–1914), creator of a wildly popular coca-laced wine tonic; indeed,
each celebrity in the album vaunted the virtues of the potent "vin Mariani."[13] Despite the blatantly commercial premise of these albums, their
material form, at least at the inception of their publication, was luxurious.
On behalf of the "distinguished and select public" for which this work
was destined, Uzanne praised Mariani, "a business *gentleman*" (and member of Uzanne's Bibliophiles Contemporains), for the superb Vosges paper
of the five hundred copies of the *édition de grand luxe.* Uzanne also noted
the yearbook's "remarkable" typography and skillful engravings on both
wood and copper, made from photographs of this "small Pantheon of our
contemporary glories," including Uzanne himself (Figure 3).

Figure 3. Portrait of Octave Uzanne from the 1894 "album Mariani." Wood engraving by Brauer from a photograph of Uzanne.

Shortly after the publication of the 1894 Mariani album, however, its status as a "unique Book," as Uzanne recalled in his preface, was jeopardized by a potentially enlarged, socially diverse readership—a "crowd of surging beggars, veritable throng incited by the excitement about the first volume." Faced with the disarming prospect of an elite product's becoming popular, Mariani (and Uzanne) devised a snob's response: "build a dam," in Uzanne's phrase, between the deluxe bibliophile edition of the album and its newly devised "popular edition." Any budget shortfall incurred by sales of the less expensive edition would be compensated by those of the pricey limited one. Thus, Uzanne concluded, "according to the sound principles of humanitarian bakers, the price of brioche will help lower the price of ordinary bread. It is good social policy to ask the richest and most delicate individuals to provide an opportunity to assist the masses."

The condescending pseudopopulism of Uzanne's preface revealed his feelings about the appropriateness for "the masses" of certain applications of technology. For this "veritable throng," he felt, such photorealistic images, in degraded form and unaccompanied by refined material support, were fitting. In fact, they typified what Uzanne perceived as an era in which "advertising is becoming brutally Americanized, when the millionaires of industry seek means of attracting attention through vulgar announcements, through clownish posters." For the elite, however, these same photomechanically produced portraits, enhanced by costly paper, elegant typography, and a small print run, only increased the allure of an album destined for the happy few.[14] It was not technology per se that Uzanne rejected, then. After all, as Mariani's example proved, even an industrialist could be an aesthete. Rather, Uzanne wished to distance himself from technology's association with "Americanization," a term that in his day equated the American republic with gigantism, mass production, industrial capitalism, ugliness, and conformity. In the introduction to the first issue of his review, *L'Art et l'Idée,* he bemoaned the "heart-rending, dismal and flat" appearance of photographic reproductions in school books, travel guides, and the press, blaming them for having "forbidden any fluttering of our imagination, so desirous of the great beyond."[15] Characteristically, in his bibliophilic pursuits Uzanne continued to turn to ever more esoteric, often hybrid photomechanical procedures that developed in the 1890s—phototypography, photolithography, photozincography—in search of the *livre unique.*

Exploiting new techniques to help create a vogue for fine illustrated books united Uzanne in a common effort with the publisher of *Le Bric-à-brac,* Edouard Rouveyre. An ambitious bookstore owner and publisher of collectors' editions three years Uzanne's senior, Rouveyre too was embarking on his career. He hoped to develop networks drawing together older, "retrospective" bibliophiles with those Uzanne considered "new strata of book lovers" (Q 155).[16] The activities of both Rouveyre's publishing house and bookstore and of a co-edited monthly review, *Les Miscellanées Bibliographiques* (1878–80), were part of a strategy elaborated by these "two daring men" (Q 156) (as Uzanne remembered the pair) in an effort to consolidate the field of fine book production. Within this field, Uzanne intended to exercise an extraordinary degree of editorial control over his publications, becoming their quasi-publisher while retaining the financial and technical support of an established firm. Writing about his work with Rouveyre, Uzanne described himself as "very intransigent about the decoration of his books" and noted that "already [in 1878] [he] intended to oversee the smallest details as well as the drawings, etchings, vignettes, page layout and the rest" (Q 156). An 1886 brochure put out by the firm of Albert Quantin went so far as to state that "M. Uzanne is the publisher as much as the author of his works,"[17] while Rops designated Uzanne the "inspirer and *moral director*"[18] of the Maison Quantin.

In Rops's view Uzanne was also the aesthetic heir of Paul-Auguste Poulet-Malassis (1825–78), publisher and friend of Baudelaire.[19] Poulet-Malassis had distinguished himself by his attention to the quality and originality of his books, attracting both like-minded authors and readers and earning a reputation as the "bibliophiles' publisher" until his 1862 bankruptcy. "[S]tudent of Malassis moreover, in all respects," wrote Rops, "[Uzanne] resembles Malassis greatly—morally." In the small-scale milieu of fine book production, publishers such as Rouveyre and Quantin, like Jouaust and Poulet-Malassis before them, were important cultural intermediaries, often the foremost shapers of a book's reception and symbolic value. Close collaborator of two of these publishers and symbolic descendent of two others, Uzanne exploited the multiple editorial functions he was accumulating to procure himself a decisive role in fostering a renaissance of the book arts in France.

The shock of the new combined again with a taste for reaction in Uzanne's audacious choice of a preface writer for *Le Bric-à-brac de l'amour*. Jules Barbey d'Aurevilly was seventy when he endowed the twenty-eight-year-old Uzanne's work with a sensational preface. As Uzanne recalled, this preface "exploded like a grenade in the world of letters in 1880 and was famous for a short while."[20] Five years earlier the man Uzanne remembered as an "impenitent and flamboyant romantic who exuded the extraordinary"[21] had written a notorious hallmark of decadent and Satanic fiction, *Les Diaboliques*. Barbey would provide Uzanne an entrée into the world of authors and artists within the realm of Symbolism, among them the occultist Joséphin "Sâr" Péladan and Rops, the illustrator of *Les Diaboliques,* both of whom were drawn, like Barbey, to what many *fin-de-siècle* Parisians deemed stylish "perversions." An "unfortunate and above all misunder-stood"[22] author (in his persecuted view of himself), Barbey felt he lacked the stature necessary to confer a "certificate of talent," even a "stupid . . . useless" one, on the fledgling author Uzanne. Nevertheless, Barbey praised Uzanne's broad knowledge, charm, and literary talent,[23] immediately invest-ing *Le Bric-à-brac* with a scandalous legitimacy derived from Barbey's fame as an *auteur maudit.*

For his part, Uzanne admired his *maître* (and fellow book lover) Barbey as an iconoclast and dandy. "Dandyism" for Barbey, and soon for his disciple Uzanne, manifested itself superficially as a distinctive personal style. In the lineage of Barbey, a legendary Latin Quarter personality known for his extravagant capes and scarlet vests (as well as his merciless verbal barbs), Uzanne emerges from contemporary accounts as an almost archetypal figure of the Belle Epoque—a "handsome monsieur with a beard" admired by Rops, an "elegant storyteller," according to Anatole France.[24] A rakish bachelor who frequented the tony Café Napolitain with Whistler and often sported a monocle, Uzanne was also, in his own words, "an impenitent *globe-trotter*"[25] whose travels took him to London, Venice, Cairo, and America. Yet dandyism expressed itself not only as a pose but also, more broadly, in a variety of aesthetic, social, and political positions. Common to them all was disdain for "mediocrity" and "vulgarity" in every domain—a snob's attitude that would clearly mark Uzanne's aesthetic of the book. Among the conservative, even reactionary positions embraced by the two men were intransigent Catholicism in the case of Barbey, anti-Semitic leanings in that of Uzanne,[26] and, on the part of both authors, a mixture of attraction to and disdain for women.

The "New Bibliopolis"

Conditioned by the elitist culture of dandyism, Uzanne seemed predisposed to scorn the effects of industrialization on book production. And his rants against "Americanization" convey to some extent a diffuse ambivalence shared by many of his contemporaries toward the "progress"—social, political, economic, and technological—associated with industrialization. Yet why and how he could maintain this position while at the same time exalting technology as crucial to the revival of book design at the *fin de siècle* is best understood with reference to the evolution of the book trade during this period. Changes in the quantity and quality of books produced, the social status of readers and collectors, and the availability of books deemed collectible all informed Uzanne's paradoxical stance.

Among the consequences of mechanization repellent to Uzanne, over-production seemed especially pernicious. Compounded by competition from the popular press, overproduction triggered the crash that destabilized the book market during a general economic downturn in France from the late 1880s through about 1900. The doubling of the number of works published in France between the middle and end of the nineteenth century had various causes, but industrialization of book production figured importantly among them. The increased output of print also corresponded to both the end of press and publishing restrictions in 1881 and growing demand from a reading public becoming more literate and socially diverse, a result of successive educational reforms. As Uzanne noted, a broad spectrum of social strata were now reading, "from the milkmaid selling her milk in the morning on the street corner to the duchess in her *chaise longue*" (*Cb* 89).

What this expanding public read was changing too. The massive output of print coincided with the consecration of a formerly maligned but now burgeoning genre, the "bourgeois" realist novel, and the decline in prestige of such classical genres as poetry and drama, soon to be reclaimed by bibliophiles. After initially praising the novel, Uzanne later railed against what the critic Charles Augustin Sainte-Beuve had termed "industrial literature"[27] — and its philistine readers — as "this intellectual nourishment of corrupt and decadent peoples, [which] reaches us from everywhere like a final plague from Egypt" (*Z* 4–5). Finally, in the proliferation of print spawned in part by mass production Uzanne observed numerous ancillary effects, all regrettable: critics could no longer identify new talent among the crush of review copies they received; writers became bitter over brutal competition and retreated to "the great legion of malcontents and misunderstood" (*Z* 17); publishers floundered. In short, the unfortunate marriage of technology and democracy, in Uzanne's view, had engendered a lamentable situation for the book, of which overproduction was the most notable symptom.[28]

Mass production and commercialism, Uzanne and others felt, had led not only to overproduction but also to a lowering of the material quality of books that accompanied the drop in manufacturing costs and sale prices. In the newspaper *Le Radical,* the author and book lover Albert Cim (1845–1924) denounced "these pitiful volumes printed at a discount, on cheap paper, dotted with typographical errors, inundated with inaccuracies, with no regular page justification."[29] The shabbiness of mass-produced novels, visible in their "modest yellow cover[s],"[30] made Uzanne despair. He bemoaned the state of bookshop windows, which confronted "the heart-broken eyes of the passerby with these sad exhibits of little yellow parallelepipeds, of such vulgarity that they evoke the edible memory of those packets of chocolate on sale in grocery stores."[31] Mass merchandise was again on Uzanne's mind when he dubbed the commercial publisher Flammarion "the Boucicaut of the book,"[32] an allusion to the founder, in 1852, of the immensely successful department store le Bon Marché. The inability to distinguish between books, foodstuffs, and other merchandise, for Uzanne, ominously foretold the advanced stages of commodification and desacralization of print brought about by industrial production.

Poor quality, Uzanne and others felt, marred not only the inexpensive best-seller but a certain type of luxury edition as well. This new variety of attractive illustrated book, as described by the publisher Edouard Pelletan (1854–1912), would be printed in runs of five hundred copies, not the one to two hundred copies more common for *livres de luxe*. They would cost fifty to sixty francs, thus positioning them in between, for example, paperbacks sold by the prominent literary publisher Calmann-Lévy for three and a half francs and the 525 francs paid at auction for Uzanne's copy of *Les Quatre Fils Aymon* (Q 82). The new fine books appealed to a readership that Pelletan identified as "educated, but middle class . . . whom circumstances have made buyers of what are considered luxury books."[33] Signs of the social and economic success of this class, such bourgeois *livres d'amateur,* however, soon found their detractors. In 1891 the publisher Damasc Jouaust retired in bitterness, bemoaning the "crisis" of "the luxury book as I have conceived of it, the real luxury book, solid and serious." This symbol of French artistic superiority had been displaced, continued Jouaust, by the "shoddy [luxury] book," leaving amateurs "beset, aggravated by the enormous quantity of so-called luxury books."[34] Uzanne concurred, complaining that as a result of the situation Jouaust described, "the inevitable, logical, predictable debacle took place, with production [of luxury books] far exceeding consumption" (*NB* 18). Faced with a glut of pseudo-*luxe* books, it became ever more crucial for "genuine" ones to distinguish themselves by all possible means. In the near future, Uzanne predicted, "works of veritable good taste" would surely be printed "*in a miniscule quantity,* according to very independent artistic formulae" (*LM* 355). Ironically, the solution Uzanne and others proposed to the inflated quantity and degraded quality of fine books that relied on technology for their production would entail increasingly distinctive uses of this same technology.

On one hand, then, Uzanne denigrated technology to distance himself from popular readers and their readings. These included, presumably, the status-seeking bourgeois book collectors described above, tainted by association with "industrial literature." On the other hand, he *championed* the products and techniques of modern industry to distinguish himself and like-minded bibliophiles from yet a different group, that of traditional, established bibliophiles. Typified by "a very old *monsieur*, scrawny, dry as a mummy, ill-dressed, wearing glasses and living peevishly in his *Bouquinerie* [old-book den] like a wolf in its lair" (*NB* 47), this prototypical bookworm may have belonged, in Uzanne's imaginings, to the venerable, largely aristocratic Société des Bibliophiles François. Founded in 1820 and directed for the half-century ending in 1894 by Baron Jérôme Pichon (1812–96), the society undertook, as its statutes indicated, to "publish or reprint rare or unpublished works, but especially those of interest for the study of French history, literature or language and perpetuating in its publications the traditions of old French printing."[35] Even the somewhat precious title of this society, with its Old French nuance, indicated its retrospective orientation, just as Uzanne's idiosyncratic (yet equally precious) lexicon, brimming with neologisms and Anglicisms, drew attention to the novelty of his endeavors.

In a milieu dominated by conservative, largely aristocratic fine book collectors, Uzanne's selective upholding of new technologies as they applied to fine book production may have served a strategic purpose. Such a position allowed him to legitimize the activities of his cohort of bibliophiles and establish what he termed "the new bibliopolis" (*NB*). Moreover, Uzanne's harangue against such stuffy, albeit erudite, bibliomanes, collectors of the Bible, of Virgil and Homer, was belied by an anxious question about the fate of rare book collecting in the second half of the century: what was left to collect? The torrent of rare books flooding France following the Revolution's confiscation of royal and clerical collections had been quickly bought, hoarded, or exported, inflating prices as their scarcity increased. At the same time, under the impetus of distinguished bibliophile-bibliographers like Nodier and Jean-Charles Brunet (1780–1867), the bibliophilic phenomenon had both expanded and been codified, as attested by the appearance of specialized publications such as Nodier's *Bulletin du Bibliophile et du Bibliothécaire* (founded in 1834) and Brunet's *Manuel du libraire et de l'amateur de livre*. A book's provenance and state of conservation, among other criteria, remained paramount for these antiquarian bibliophiles, idolaters of the past.[36]

Given the saturation of the bibliophilic sphere and its rigid codification, those eager to participate in the elite social practice of book collecting at the end of the century needed to elaborate a new bibliophilic subfield. By the 1890s this sphere was characterized by an allegiance, however discreet, to technological innovation. It had acquired its own institutions and spokesmen as well—collectors, societies, reviews, publishers, bookstores— all touted by their partisans as "new." In Uzanne's view, the new bibliophilia was a generational, and a collective, phenomenon. Born at the time of the disastrous 1870 French defeat by Prussia, members of the generation coming of age in the 1890s were eager, according to Uzanne, to help revive French pride through promoting a renewal of its decorative arts. However, the most prominent collectors of the *fin de siècle* appear to have been born a decade or two earlier than Uzanne suggests. Their social profile was changing, too. These were men from largely upper-bourgeois families whose social and economic success over the course of the nineteenth century was consecrated with the establishment in 1870 of the Third Republic, whose elites they would supply. These *haut bourgeois* bibliophiles included Uzanne himself; Henri Beraldi (1849–1931), a renowned collector who wrote prolifically on book collecting (in addition to his duties as a president of the Société des Amis des Livres); Eugène Rodrigues (1853–1928), a lawyer and president of the Société des Cent Bibliophiles who produced *catalogues raisonnés* of Rops's work; and the particularly colorful Paul Gallimard (1850–1929), whose son Gaston would dominate French publishing after World War I.[37]

Paul Gallimard was a vastly wealthy *rentier* who amassed an astonishing collection of Impressionist paintings, perhaps modeling his activities on his father Gustave's earlier patronage of painters of the Barbizon school. Gallimard *fils*—the "precious collector"[38] whose "natty youthfulness"[39] impressed the poet Stéphane Mallarmé—also cultivated a passion for books directed not toward *livres anciens* but toward an unconventional type of *livre de luxe:* the "rare" contemporary illustrated edition. In 1889 Paul Gallimard commissioned a three-copy edition, on Whatman paper and with etchings by Jean-François Raffaëlli, of Edmond de Goncourt's novel *Germinie Lacerteux*. The extravagant largesse bestowed by Gallimard on a book with no antiquarian value astounded Goncourt, the recipient of one of the copies, who described the unorthodox practice in his journal: "In this imbecilic world of bibliophiles, in this world of servants to old print, this Gallimard is really a revolutionary, who will spend 3000 francs to offer himself, like a tax-farmer, to give himself alone a luxury edition of a modern book."[40] Gallimard's gesture also impressed the painter Camille Pissarro, who in a letter to his son Lucien (a painter like his father, and a wood engraver) described the book collector: "Gallimard is the only man in Paris who will publish for himself three rare copies on fine paper of an illustrated novel by Goncourt."[41] To Goncourt, the iconoclastic Gallimard was the symbolic heir of the *ancien régime* tax collectors, many of whom amassed fabulous book collections with their substantial revenues. It is unsurprising that Uzanne proposed this "revolutionary" bibliophile and aesthete as a model the same year, when inviting Goncourt to join Uzanne's newly formed Bibliophiles Contemporains: "I'm dreaming," wrote Uzanne, "of a gathering of young and ingenious bibliophiles, more well-read in the *elegant* sense than scholarly (like Gallimard, to tell all)."

This cultivated assembly, Uzanne assured Goncourt, "will have nothing about it that is mummified, dried out, disagreeable."[42] While Goncourt declined Uzanne's invitation, the latter's attempt to entice a member of an older generation of bibliophiles by mentioning Gallimard indicates that this free-spending patron, no slave to old print or to antiquated methods, typified the "youth, reason, spirit of adventure and initiative" (NB 10)— not to mention the financial clout[43]—identified by Uzanne as characterizing the new bibliophiles.

Faced with a dearth of antiquarian editions, the traditional fare of bibliophiles, upper-bourgeois bohemians such as Uzanne and Gallimard legitimized as collectible the luxury edition designated in advance of its publication as rare and privileging the work of late nineteenth-century authors and illustrators. And faced with a commercial sector that valorized the largest possible market and the greatest profits, these rich patrons championed the smallest market possible—in Gallimard's case, a market of one—and economic indifference. The modern Maecenas, in turn, was connected to networks of institutions that further helped consecrate the new luxury books. Parisian bibliophile societies proliferated after 1870 for the first time since the founding of the Société des Bibliophiles François a half-century earlier.[44] Uzanne's Bibliophiles Contemporains and Bibliophiles Indépendents, two of about a dozen such societies, provided both supply and demand in regard to the new luxury books, offering a ready-made readership and also serving as publisher. These societies often worked in tandem with small firms that became the quasi-official publishing houses (and bookstores) of the bibliophile societies whose aesthetic visions they shared. The firm of Henry Floury thus joined forces with Uzanne in 1896 to publish Les Rassemblements for the Bibliophiles Indépendents, while the publisher and bookstore owner Léon Conquet (1848–97) was praised by the book collector Eugène Paillet for having "overturned the idol of the old book"[45] through the works he published for Paillet's Société des Amis des Livres. The gospel of newness was preached, finally, in specialized reviews and exhibits. Perhaps the most noteworthy of these, devoted to international modern fine book production, was mounted in 1896 in the gallery of the Art Nouveau impresario Siegfried Bing; its organizing committee included both Gallimard and Uzanne. An entire section of the exhibit displayed books illustrated by mechanical procedures, with examples showcasing both the popular press (Le Journal pour Rire) and luxury publications such as Bing's own review, Le Japon Artistique, for whose color printing Charles Gillot designed the plates.[46] Bing's exhibit provided a showcase for the judicious application of photomechanical procedures to fine book production.

By the 1890s, then, Uzanne's modern bibliopolis had acquired structures and a self-designation of newness, enabling it to challenge the hegemony of the durable Société des Bibliophiles François. To a certain extent, the rhetoric of newness may have served to mask divisions within the emerging pole of bibliophiles. Indeed, these amateurs were themselves quickly subdivided into cliques, separated, for example, by allegiances to particular techniques of illustration (woodcut, lithography, etching), divided over the question of whether image should be subordinate to text (Pelletan) or vice versa (Vollard).[47] Further, the older of the post-1870 societies, considered in the vanguard of fine book production at their inception, were quickly stigmatized by their successors as outdated; Uzanne founded his two groups in part in reaction against Paillet's Société des Amis des Livres, whose debut publication, Prosper Mérimée's *Chronique du règne de Charles IX*, reached far back into France's royal history. Uzanne considered the choice of texts and material quality of the works published by these "friends of books" too traditional and its members "lamentably closed to living art" (*NB* 187). In the end, though, this struggle to legitimize and interpret "newness," both at the expense of the old guard and within the emerging sphere of collectors, masked a competition for resources—commissions, readers, illustrators, publishers, and printers—within the relatively closed world of *fin-de-siècle* bibliophilia.

Yet, despite the real and symbolic divisions among those baptized by Uzanne as "neo-icono-bibliomanes" (*NB*), novelty, for many of them, encompassed openness to the use of technology in fine book production and set them apart from their predecessors. Such openness permitted a strategic rapprochement with related fields, such as graphic arts, which had proved receptive to photomechanical and other new techniques. Moreover, the rhetoric of newness was informed by struggles within not only the French bibliophilic sphere but the international one as well. During this climactic era of European nationalism and imperialism, international competition was enacted symbolically at the World's Fairs and other "universal" exhibits through displays of each country's technological prowess. Applications of photography to book illustration, for example, figured prominently in 1894 in Paris at the state-sponsored international exhibit of the book and papermaking industries.[48] Indicative of the competitive nature of this exhibit and those similar to it were the contrasts that journalists pointed out between France and other countries with respect to book production. One such visitor, for example, concluded that overall, "in first place, we must name Russia"—the country with which France had just concluded a crucial military alliance—while still contending that, "as concerns publishing, France holds first place here."[49] Similarly, the noted critic and collector of Japanese *objets d'art*, Philippe Burty, observed that the quality of French industrial bindings had improved since the 1878

World's Fair, at which "we were visibly outdistanced by English publishers."[50] Nearly two decades later, after visiting Bing's exhibit, the publisher Edouard Pelletan still found English luxury books superior to their French counterparts, deeming work by his compatriots "a veritable outrage to good taste."[51]

Such sizing up of France's diplomatic allies and enemies through the barometer of technological clout was typical of these pre–World War I exhibits. And the prickly tone of the French critics may convey to some extent the uneasiness with which they observed French industrial production lagging behind that of Germany, England, and the United States. It is surprising, however, to find echoes of such competition in the decidedly more *l'art pour l'art* milieu of the privately organized fine book exhibits. While Bing, for one, hoped that his exhibit would foster exchange between international artists of the book, the critics viewed this as improbable. If the show proved anything, asserted Edmond Cousturier in *La Revue Blanche,* it was the "decadence" of the French luxury book as compared to its English counterpart, a result, he felt, of the excessive influence of publishers and bibliophiles in France, to the detriment of illustrators.[52] After viewing this "frail display of the best we have produced," the critic concluded grimly that "for three centuries, the French have not produced a truly beautiful book." The exhibit's value for French luxury book producers, Cousturier felt, was essentially didactic, pointing out "imperiously, what we need to do."

The nationalist and often xenophobic ethos that pervaded the large-scale state exhibits during this prewar period, then, was not absent from smaller private shows frequented by elite collectors. Among the most vocal defenders of French traditions in the decorative arts, in fact, was Siegfried Bing, whose status as a German-born Jew naturalized in 1876 as a French citizen seemed to have made him particularly sensitive to the imperative of asserting his "Frenchness."[53] And if technology might promote French dominance, whether in book production or on the battlefield, Uzanne and his contemporaries proved eager to become its partisans. Their stance was consistent with the general receptiveness to the application of technology to luxury craftsmanship that distinguished France from both England and Belgium, whose craft reformers viewed mechanization as antithetical to artisanship.[54]

By the end of the century, then, fine books incorporating features of industrial production belonged to the personal libraries of many upper-bourgeois collectors. These were published by small firms such as that of Henry Piazza, whose 1898 edition of Etienne Dinet's *Antar* featured photo-mechanically reproduced watercolors. Uzanne's rallying cries of "let's be contemporary!" (*NB* 20) and "everything to the moderns" (Figure 4)—as a vignette from *Le Livre Moderne* urged—had thus succeeded in helping mobilize support for the new bibliophilia. Yet in Uzanne's lexicon "contemporaneity" and "modernity" had a peculiar twist. To be modern meant to create not a new democracy but a new aristocracy of taste, a snob's paradise from which would be barred both France's traditional aristocratic cultural elites and the expanding population of consumers of mass print culture. "Modernity" entailed lauding the marriage of industry and the book, but only to better renew a tradition of French preeminence in luxury craftsmanship. And it meant conceiving of the book not necessarily as agent of instruction and edification, but as object, artwork, fetish even.

Technology and the *Livre de Luxe*

"What we want," Uzanne proclaimed in 1890, "are books worthy of this era, which is witnessing a transformation of all received ideas . . . [and which] is beginning to . . . revolutionize logically and intelligently the simple-minded rules that habit alone made us respect until now" (*LM* 356). Technology, Uzanne felt, was essential to freeing books from "typographical and iconographic . . . traditions and prejudices" (*LM* 355) and helping create just such "books worthy of this era." He probably warmed to

Figure 4. "Everything to the moderns." Vignette featuring Octave Uzanne's initials from *Le Livre Moderne*.

Félicien Rops's suggestion that the pair visit the 1882 Exposition des Arts Industriels because, as Rops informed him, "they have machines there that are quite interesting for us!—We'll make two beautiful color books for next year."[55] What such machines would help the two rebels bring about, as Rops declared in an exalted letter that reads like a manifesto, was nothing less than the "*total reform of the illustrated book.*"[56] According to Rops, he and Uzanne would begin by experimenting with color printing techniques based on photography, although by Rops's admission the work "*won't be good*" at the beginning—no illusions!—we must create the engraver, the worker, the printer, *none of that exists.*" New techniques, new technicians, then, would endow books with what Rops deemed a "*modern allure,*" and experimentation would come to characterize a sector unconcerned with financial profit. He warned an older breed of bibliophiles: "Tough luck for the archaeologists of the book. We'll kick all that in the pants."[57]

Technical panache and flouting of tradition, then, were to be the hallmarks of the new *livres de luxe*. Unsurprisingly, given these criteria, the book Uzanne considered possibly "the most beautiful of the century" and "certainly the most original in terms of decoration of a new style and chromotypographic perfection" (Q 82) was the *Histoire des quatre fils Aymon, très nobles et très vaillans chevaliers,* published in 1883 by Henri Launette (Figure 5). Ironically, the subject of this book was hardly contemporary but was inspired by a twelfth-century epic poem recounting the struggle between the four sons of duc Aymes and Charlemagne. This updated *chanson de geste,* typifying the medieval revival of both the French and English *fin de siècle,* exemplified, for Uzanne, "popular literature" (Q 82), elevated here to the status of bibliophilic treasure. The publication signaled a remarkable collaboration between an artist, the Swiss-born lithographer Eugène Grasset (1845–1917), and the champion of photomechanical printing techniques who was also Grasset's patron, Charles Gillot. Each of the book's 240 pages boasted boldly integrated image and text (featuring a typeface designed by Grasset), dramatic asymmetrical compositions, elaborate ornamentation, and an emblematic style typical of both Celtic art and *japonisme.* Grasset's style revealed his aesthetic affiliation with English artists such as Walter Crane, and their common wish to revitalize book illustration by elevating it to the status of art.

The *Quatre Fils Aymon* broke new ground not only stylistically but also technically, as it marked the debut of four-color printing in France. Executed by Gillot "with fastidious care, in regard to the . . . placing of the blocks"[58] (as Uzanne pointed out for the English readership of the prominent decorative arts review, the *Studio*), four-color printing was used here to translate Grasset's original watercolors. This color-relief printing

Figure 5. Eugène Grasset, cover illustration for *Histoire des quatre fils Aymon, très nobles et très vaillans chevaliers* (Paris: Launette, 1883). Multicolor photo relief process. Reproduced with the permission of Rare Books and Manuscripts, The Pennsylvania State University Libraries.

technique—along with the special paper Gillot had developed to enhance effects of tone, grain, and shading—liberated color, much as it did in the posters by Grasset that Uzanne also appreciated.[59] The technique allowed color, in Uzanne's words, "to triumph in the modern decoration of books" (*NB* 28) and to stimulate the imagination, not merely to record reality, as photography would do.

Grasset's work in this large-format book revealed his simultaneous enthusiasm for both the medieval artisanal ideal and the most modern techniques of any era, from medieval weaponry and fortifications (visually depicted in great detail in the *Quatre Fils Aymon*) to nineteenth-century color printing.[60] As a fellow proponent of reconciling nostalgia and newness through a style, as Uzanne noted, both "very modern" and "strangely informed by archaism,"[61] Grasset undoubtedly pleased Uzanne, who became the artist's earliest and most zealous promoter in both France and England.[62] So new, in fact, did Grasset's images appear in this major work of his career as an illustrator that they failed to entice certain bibliophiles, even when printed on the imperial Japan or China paper of the limited edition of two hundred; until the late 1890s many amateurs preferred to collect books featuring illustrations executed with traditional methods.[63] And while much of Grasset's work was commercial—posters, calendars, invitations, stamps, sheet music—he also created the unique collectors' objects Uzanne valued. These included a set of elaborate Art Nouveau furniture for Charles Gillot's Parisian townhouse, a fitting setting for the printer's impressive collection of Japanese art. In Uzanne's view, then, Grasset had successfully navigated between "mass" and "class," producing works that Uzanne deemed appropriate for each.

Uzanne's "profound enthusiasm" (*Q* 83) over "the great perfection of the color printing"[64] of the *Histoire des quatre fils Aymon* revealed him to be a herald of the "color revolution" that would soon overtake Paris. Like the photomechanical revolution and in fact intertwined with it, the riot of color appearing in print by the *fin de siècle* had been prepared by nearly a century of experimentation in France, beginning with Godefroy Engelmann's 1837 patenting of color lithography. But it was only at the end of the century that several trends converged to foster the flowering of color in print. These included political developments (the 1881 French law on the freedom of the press, which legalized the placement of posters anywhere except on official buildings and required their printing on tinted paper); aesthetic currents (the captivating influence on many artists of Japanese color woodblock prints); and, again, technological advances (the invention, for example, of presses capable of holding very large lithographic stones). Soon color was enlivening the range of artistic techniques and print media. These included both the photomechanical technique of chromotypogravure, used to produce color images for the 1881 Christmas issue of the mass-circulation newspaper *L'Illustration,* and the traditional techniques of wood engraving, etching, and especially lithography, the privileged medium of printmakers and poster artists in the 1890s. Color also abounded on play-bills, sheet music, typefaces, religious iconography, and calendars. And it transformed the appearance of illustrated books, notably children's books, keepsakes, and nostalgic works such as Bibliophile Jacob's 1874 *Moeurs, usages, et costumes au Moyen Age et à l'époque de la Renaissance,* which evoked the rich color and gilding tradition of medieval manuscripts.

Unlike Uzanne, many in the artistic establishment disdained chromolith-ography, which they associated with reproductive industrial printing. For this reason, until 1899 color prints were banned from the official French artistic salon. At the same time, however, networks were emerging whose activities helped legitimize color printing as an artistic medium. A shared interest in the new technique brought together wealthy collectors; print and poster dealers such as Edmond Sagot; printers (notably Auguste Clot); specialized professional societies and journals such as André Marty's *L'Estampe Originale* (1893–95); and exhibits displaying the work of con-temporary printer-engravers, including the one held in 1896 in Ambroise Vollard's gallery.

While unified by a common allegiance to color printing, however, these new connoisseurs disagreed about the extent of the social benefits of the color revolution. Some of them, such as the art critic André Mellerio, direc-tor of *L'Estampe et l'Affiche* (1897–99), championed the educative advan-tages of democratizing color printing. He asserted that, in the interest of "further purify[ing] public taste," it "does not degrade the personality of the artist, thanks to means that science gives him, to be able to place, for very modest prices, true works of art within the reach of ever larger groups of people."[65] Such a pedagogical process, Mellerio continued, would have the salutary effect of eventually increasing the number of collectors, espe-cially among those "now numerous representatives of the middle class who dedicate their leisure time, a portion of their intelligence, and their money, to nosing about, to being interested in, and to buying" color prints and posters. Unlike Mellerio, however, other color printing enthusiasts— Uzanne among them—hoped that elevating high-quality applications of this technique from industrial product to art would render them inaccessi-ble to all but an elite. Therefore, when in 1897 Uzanne echoed many other critics in extolling the poster artist Jules Chéret as "the uncontested king of the contemporary polychrome mural" (*NB* 111), and praised posters as the "aesthetic banners of the new [artistic] schools" (*NB* 179), he was writ-ing from the perspective of a coterie of collectors who, in his words, were helping "augment the riches of [our] national art" (*NB* 92) by preserving

what some contemporaries considered ephemera. He lauded the color revolution, the avant-garde artists who embodied it, and its technological
underpinnings. But he did so, ironically, only to promote what this phenomenon might contribute to elite culture—the limited edition, not the wall
print; the collector's portfolio, not the cheap facsimile; form, not function.[66]

When Uzanne praised Grasset's and Gillot's work with color printing
and recalled the "joy of the bibliophile when I first saw this masterpiece,"[67]
he was writing as not merely a critic but also as a practitioner of this
new technique. In fact, he had been conducting his own experiments with
color printing and a range of other procedures at least a year before
Grasset's work appeared. His own "research in coloration, tints, inks . . .
the first experiments in heliography, printing on papers of varying weights"
(Q 161), materialized in a collection of loose pages he printed himself in
preparation for his 1882 and 1883 books, L'Eventail and L'Ombrelle, le
gant, le manchon, illustrated by Paul Avril, another of Uzanne's partners in
experimentation.[68] Uzanne considered these printed sheets "a document
for the future" (Q 161). Another edition of L'Eventail featured marine blue
paper, while a third, produced solely for Uzanne at his request, was printed
in monochrome, black ink on black paper—feats of technical bravura that
caused Uzanne to complain that "the material side of [L'Eventail] has
been gluttonously eating up all my time."[69] He found the overall effect of
this last volume "distinguished" but doubted that the public, "much taken
with color, oppositions of tones, gilding" (Q 161), would appreciate his
bold experiment. Further, he claimed, the subtle effects of etching and
typography would be lost on them. Refined and traditional in its subject,
L'Eventail betrays Uzanne's nostalgia for the elegance of bygone eras, as
evidenced by its wistful homage to the fan. At the same time, though, this
work, as well as its pendant, devoted to the parasol, the glove, and the
muff, figure among the first uses of the aquatint grain-color relief process.
In this procedure, minute crackle etched on the copperplate helps achieve,
after printing, an effect approximating the flat tints of wash or ink drawings. It was this and other modern techniques made available through the
development of industry, chemistry, and photography that would help
achieve rarefied effects, Uzanne believed, not for "the masses" but for an
elite group of connoisseurs.

Uzanne seemed somewhat less enthusiastic about the possible contributions of new technologies to binding than he did about their potential
for radically changing book illustration. Novelty and variety remained
his guiding principles: "I will never cease to preach," he wrote in one of
his two treatises on the subject, "the artistic renaissance of binding in all
its varieties of workmanship" (Rm 248). However, the real renaissance of
Uzanne's day was spawned not by artistic binding but by the spectacular

flourishing of industrial binding. Covers of cloth or percale, no longer bearing traditional motifs but eye-catching illustrations often lifted from within the text itself, were mass-produced with the help of hydraulic presses, circular shears, and other machines. These publishers' bindings were often accessorized with colorful satin and moiré endpapers, silk ties, and attractive boxes. They enclosed almanacs, keepsakes, prize books, and other genres appealing to the expanding categories of female and juvenile readers and offering them the novelty of modestly priced luxury. So unusual did these case-bindings (*cartonnages*) appear initially that they came to represent the avant-garde of binding, indeed furnishing a model for art binding until the last decade of the century, when the situation was reversed.[70] A relentless promoter of new techniques, Uzanne devoted a long chapter to industrial binding in his influential 1898 work, *L'Art dans la décoration extérieure des livres,* whose own eye-catching "poster binding" alluded to the ubiquity of the new medium of the color poster, at the juncture of art and industry (Figure 6).[71] Moreover, he praised Emile Carayon, who had built a reputation on attractive commercial bindings, as a "veritable artist of cloth binding" (*Rm* 256).

Yet, although Uzanne condemned an older generation of art binders as "stuck in tradition, mummified in the humdrum quality of their craft" (*Rm* 181), he was not prepared to anoint industrial or commercial binders, even "artistic" ones such as Carayon, as the next vanguard of talent in this domain. Rather, he considered much of their work mediocre, produced hastily for a growing clientele and always subject to the control not of the individual collector but of publishers. In the 1890s, under the sway of Art Nouveau (the aesthetic to which his review *L'Art et l'Idée* was unofficially dedicated), and convinced also that France was doomed to remain inferior in the realm of industrial binding (*Ad* 7–9), he emerged as a standard bearer for a younger generation of extraordinarily innovative binders of fine editions. In his view, these artists were spearheading a revolution comparable to the one reinvigorating all the decorative arts of the period (*NB* 38). His private library boasted volumes bound by about a dozen such "revolutionary" artists: the precursor Amand (d. 1900), whose allegorical bindings were among the first to incorporate scraps of Asian fabrics and paper;[72] the Lyonnais binder Lucien Magnin (d. 1953), whom Uzanne termed "a modern in every sense of the word" (*Rm* 187–88); and Pétrus Ruban (1851–1929), a master mosaicist versed in both traditional techniques and the stylistic and thematic novelties of Art Nouveau (Figure 7).

Uzanne reserved special praise for three binders from Lorraine's "Rococo" city, Nancy. Camille Martin (1861–98), René Wiener (1855–1939), and Victor Prouvé (1856–1943) were in the vanguard of reviving the decorative arts at the turn of the century. In the 1890s Martin perfected pyrography,

Figure 6. Louis Guingot, poster-binding (*reliure-affiche*) for Octave Uzanne's *L'Art dans la décoration extérieure des livres* (Paris: May, 1898).

Figure 7. Pétrus Ruban, binding for *L'Effort* by Edmond Haraucourt (Paris: Les Bibliophiles Contemporains, 1894).

a new binding technique reminiscent of the group's efforts in furniture making, in which designs were engraved directly on leather or wood with heated metal tools, thereby enhancing the sophistication and detail of the cover's graphics to create a painterly (and in certain cases sculptural) effect. Technically innovative, the bindings of the Ecole de Nancy also broke with tradition by featuring enameled panels, a brilliant range of colors, and spine designs integrated into the overall composition of the cover, thus transforming it into a unified surface.[73]

But the darling of individualistic amateurs such as Robert de Montesquiou, Edmond de Goncourt, and Uzanne himself was Charles Meunier (1866–1940), whose binding for the *Histoire des quatre fils Aymon* Uzanne deemed a "[m]asterpiece of binding; one of the most beautiful examples of incised leather of this time" (Q 82) (Figure 8). This "binder of the future, on hold for the beginning of the twentieth century," wrote Henri Beraldi in 1897,[74] had apprenticed with the renowned Marius-Michel (1846–1925), whose ornamental floral style and leather inlays he adopted. Yet, at twenty, the apprentice set up shop for himself in a stylish boutique near the Madeleine, signaling through his move to this newly fashionable upper-bourgeois neighborhood the increasing autonomy of fine books as a separate sector of the book market. Like Uzanne, he became both an influential intermediary

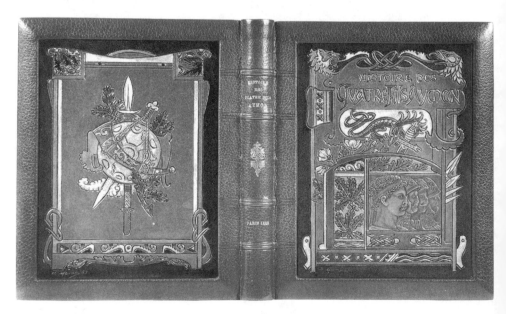

Figure 8. Charles Meunier, binding for *Histoire des quatre fils Aymon* (1883), with panels designed by J. Masson.

in this sector and a spokesman for the new bibliophilia. He invested profits from his bindery in both a review devoted to book arts, *L'Oeuvre et l'Image* (1900–1903), and a small press, La Maison du Livre. He established the latter largely to publish limited editions for the members of the bibliophile society he founded in 1908 and ran until 1924, Les Amis du Livre Moderne. His elite clientele valued his stunning, incised leather panels encasing the works of both nineteenth-century authors—Balzac, Baudelaire, Daudet, Maupassant, Verlaine, Zola—and illustrators such as the Symbolist Carlos Schwabe (Figure 9).[75]

Meunier's works featured a vast repertoire of symbols in harmony with the subject of each book, serving almost as a critical gloss on it. His expensive, esoteric materials, including "antique silks picked up . . . here and there"[76] by Edmond de Goncourt for work commissioned from Meunier, and the striking floral motifs adorning his covers, replaced the limited range of formal patterns distinguishing earlier fine bindings. Some *fin-de-siècle* bibliophiles, however, criticized the prolific Meunier for producing what they considered "gaudy and crudely executed commercial ventures pandering to the tastes of the . . . bourgeoisie."[77] While in fact Meunier did exploit the new technique of pyrography developed by Camille Martin and his collaborators in Nancy, in Uzanne's view this method was useful only insofar as it served an aesthetic of originality and uniqueness and did not promote the qualities of technical perfection and repetitiveness valued by many commercial publishers. Technical perfection concerned Uzanne little. He thus approved, for example, Meunier's unorthodox practice of refusing to polish down the coarse grain of the leather he used, resulting not in a smooth surface but in a handmade look. "Let's not tolerate only what is *well made*," Uzanne urged. "[T]rue talent is always a bit excessive, vivacious, innovative, uneven" (*LM* 356).

For Uzanne, "books worthy of this era" featured not only unique illustrations and bindings but also a third characteristic, which benefited at the end of the century from industrial developments and the proliferation of advertising: singular typography. The time had come, Uzanne proclaimed, to discard the tired Didot, Elzevir, and Gothic fonts (and their sometimes unseemly hybrids) standard in most nineteenth-century French publications. Instead, innovative foundries (such as that of Georges Peignot), publishers (Pelletan), and bibliophile societies collaborated in promoting the work of such rejuvenators of typography as George Auriol (1863–1938) and, again, Eugène Grasset. Auriol's work was featured on the cover of Uzanne's 1895 *Contes pour les bibliophiles,* co-written and illustrated by the futurist Albert Robida (Figure 10). To create the audacious mix of upper- and lowercase characters—an unorthodox break with the traditional typographical unity of the page typical of French publications at that time—Auriol relied

Figure 9. Charles Meunier, binding for Alphonse Daudet, *Sapho* (1897), leather with blind-tooling, incised, and polychromed panels designed by J. Masson.

Figure 10. George Auriol cover for Octave Uzanne and Albert Robida, *Contes pour les bibliophiles* (Paris: Quantin, 1895). Photomechanical color printing process.

on photographic enlargements and reductions of his original designs to permit greater accuracy in the engraving of the characters.[78]

A decade earlier, the same application of photography to typography had enabled, surprisingly, the experiments of the ferociously anti-industrial designer William Morris, who appeared to distinguish between machines that abased humanity and those that merely served as tools to simplify the work of book designers. From this perspective, the work of Morris's Kelmscott Press, "quintessential example of an arts-and-crafts longing for the pre-industrial age"[79] — but one that relied nevertheless on the sophisticated technological foundation of photography — seems informed by the same simultaneous acceptance and rejection of new technologies that is a leitmotif in Uzanne's writings and activities. Some French critics, however, saw only anachronism in Morris's versions of old Anglo-Saxon typefaces, and Grasset even dismissed them as "fetishistic . . . archaeological trifles."[80] Morris thus shared with Uzanne a longing for past eras of artisanal excellence combined with a desire to rely selectively on the most modern industrial technology to attain an aesthetic, noncommercial goal. The elitist Uzanne, however, shared none of Morris's socialist convictions. Indeed, it was only for an intimate circle of like-minded bibliophiles, not for "the masses," that Uzanne destined other of his works boasting equally striking Art Nouveau lettering and typographical ornamentation.

Technology, then, enabled Grasset's illustrations, Carayon's artistic case bindings, and Auriol's stylized typeface — all the markings of the *livre de luxe* of the turn of the century. At the same time, however, to Uzanne's displeasure, technology was progressively coming to serve the ideals of technical perfection and realism, which he denigrated, to the detriment of creativity and experimentation. In the early 1890s this frustration led him to reject the many industrial and commercial techniques he had touted so enthusiastically, in favor of traditional craftsmanship represented by the woodcut. Previously considered a rather "plebeian" genre and the most common one for book illustration until the 1880s, the woodcut was undergoing a revival in the last decade of the century. Motivating this movement in part was a desire to "rescue" the woodcut from the ravages wrought by the zinc printing block. According to Uzanne, prints made in this fashion, of a "dull exactitude,"[81] had replaced the work of xylographers in the popular press. Three avant-garde reviews — Alfred Jarry and Remy de Gourmont's *L'Ymagier* (1895–96), Paul Fort's *Le Livre d'Art* (1896), and Roger Marx's *L'Image* (1897) — led the crusade against photomechanical printing processes by featuring woodblock illustrations exclusively, prompting Edouard Pelletan to declare in 1896 that "the cause of the woodcut . . . has been definitively won."[82] Paradoxically, however, the traditional craft of wood engraving had itself been modified by new technologies, beginning

Figure 11. Félix Vallotton, woodcut portrait of Octave Uzanne, in *L'Art et l'Idée*, February 1892.

in the mid-nineteenth century with the introduction of electrotyping. This process involved the transfer of drawings on potentially fragile woodblocks to durable intaglio metal plates through the medium of molds created by electrolysis. Once again suspicious of the potential for mass production of woodcuts enabled by electrotyping, though, Uzanne advocated instead the artisanal, manual, and considerably more expensive methods of medieval wood engraving, familiar to him through the work of Morris's Kelmscott Press.

Uzanne's patronage of the Swiss wood engraver Félix Vallotton, closely associated with the avant-garde *Revue Blanche* and the Nabi group, exemplifies this turn toward traditional craftsmanship (Figure 11). In a laudatory article on Vallotton, Uzanne concurred that woodcutters had been "vanquished" by photomechanical techniques, and charged that they were misguided in attempting to "rival the precision of *gillotage*"[83] when they strove to produce ever more realistic effects. Because zincography and related techniques would soon afford "prodigious" levels of precision, Uzanne urged woodcutters to abandon their senseless turf war. Instead, they should embrace the "desired awkwardness" and "primitive workmanship" of sixteenth- and seventeenth-century xylographers, among them Holbein and Dürer, and such nineteenth-century successors as Gavarni.

Abandoning the etching needle for the penknife and the zinc plate for a block of pear wood, in the 1890s Vallotton was clearly Uzanne's man. The engraver supplied the cover and thirty woodcuts—if we are to believe the title page—for 220 copies of *Badauderies parisiennes. Les Rassemblements. Physiologies de la rue* (1896) (Figure 12). Fifteen of his fellow *Revue Blanche* collaborators contributed the texts, and Uzanne the preface, to this volume. The inaugural publication of Uzanne's Bibliophiles Indépendants, the *Badauderies* was produced by Henri Floury, a bookstore owner and publisher, notably, of the works of wood engravers. This satirical view of contemporary Parisian life and social types features the skewed perspectives, ingenious compositions, and large flat monochrome surfaces associated with both Japanese prints and the Nabi group with which Vallotton was affiliated. Moreover, as with all artists he admired, Uzanne appreciated Vallotton's originality, artistic vision, and willingness to break with "the grizzled methods of [his] elders" even while returning to a traditional technique. So while Uzanne conceded that "industrially treated images" were perfectly appropriate for "the mass public" (*le gros public*)—in fact he insisted that it would be "folly" to abandon them in this context—they had no place in "art books, works destined for an elite." Clearly, then, by the end of the century Uzanne had come to feel that not all readers were deserving of the "books worthy of this era"—perhaps "*his* era" is more fitting—that he envisioned.

Once again, however, in praising Vallotton Uzanne seemed to waver between dual allegiance to both past and future, craftsmanship and industry. Despite his description of Vallotton's style as "voluntarily reactionary and barbaric," he was also clearly interested in Vallotton as a modern in the artist's choice of subject matter. Vallotton did rely on traditional techniques; nevertheless, as a collaborator of both *La Revue Blanche* and the Nabis he was at the epicenter of the literary and artistic avant-garde, under the sway of Symbolism, *japonisme,* and anarchism. The "brutality" and "primitivism" of his technique was offset by the contemporary nature of his subject: Parisian scenes in which crowds of assorted gawkers (*badauds*) (schoolboys, workers, servants) assemble to view sidewalk performances, a presidential procession, and other new spectacles of modern urban life. These images were often almost identical to those Vallotton had produced for the popular illustrated press (*Le Courrier Français, Le Rire, Le Cri de Paris*). Vallotton and Uzanne's appropriation of these same mass-produced images in a *livre de luxe* destined for bibliophiles was in itself original. Much like the selective appropriation of new technologies, it exemplifies the fluidity of the boundaries between elite and popular book production at the *fin de siècle*.[84] In fact, the boundary nearly vanishes when considering the startling suggestion by Vallotton's biographer, the art critic Julius Meier-Graefe,

Figure 12. Félix Vallotton, cover illustration for *Badauderies parisiennes. Les Rassemblements. Physiologies de la rue* (Paris: Floury, 1896).

corroborated by two contemporary art historians, that Vallotton's illustrations for *Les Rassemblements* are not woodcuts at all but images produced photomechanically from the artist's drawings.[85] If this is indeed the case, it is possible that Uzanne may have passed off photomechanical images as woodcuts to better woo a clientele that by 1896 was enthralled by the work of artisans associated with the English Arts and Crafts movement and susceptible to the cachet of their techniques.

Uzanne the "Evolutionary"?

As suggested by the example of *Les Rassemblements,* the most modern technological procedure, photography, might be used to approximate a most traditional technique, the woodcut, itself updated by Vallotton and Uzanne to depict *fin-de-siècle* Parisian cityscapes. And this technique, once employed to illustrate popular chapbooks, might become the emblem of the dandified coterie of aesthetes that made up Uzanne's "independent bibliophiles." Yet the contradictions represented by *Les Rassemblements,* while quite notable, resonated widely in the field of print production during this period. Whereas prior to the nineteenth century, for example, printed illustrations had appeared at the two ends of a spectrum—in works for either an aristocratic elite or an often semiliterate peasantry—in the nineteenth century technology enabled images to permeate the variety of printed products and genres destined for a highly diverse readership. By the end of the century some of these illustrations, in the form of color lithographs, showed up both as inexpensive wall prints and in collectors' portfolios. Editions of newly "classic" authors such as Victor Hugo were available in both popular editions—the forty-three volume illustrated "monument" to this Republican hero published by Lemonnier—and in print runs of three hundred copies, as in the case of Quantin's 1885 edition of Hugo's *Le Pape.* And while small-scale publishers such as Launette and Morris's Kelmscott Press provided refined versions of popular legends for an elite audience, mass-circulation publications such as *Le Figaro Illustrée* featured the work of artists like Toulouse-Lautrec, soon associated with the *livre d'artiste.* Such blurring of commonly accepted dichotomies—tradition versus modernity, elite versus popular culture, art versus craft, the luxury edition versus the commercial book—did not result solely from technological change, of course. This breaking down of polarities also revealed the tensions exacerbated during this period by both the progressive social, political, and economic enfranchisement of ever more of the French, and by international competition soon to find one outlet in war.

While technology provided one means to dissolve these polarities, in the end it led to the creation of new ones. Under the banner of contemporaneity, Uzanne, for one, proved eager to appropriate technology to achieve the spectacular effects desired by an elite clientele and to enhance the prestige value of the book. In the end, then, the *livre unique* existed not only in spite of but because of technology. Yet, while both a spokesperson and practitioner of the new bibliophilia, Uzanne was at the same time a lover of the aristocratic eighteenth century and an inveterate dandy who despised all forms of "vulgarity" and "mediocrity." The progressive marriage of technology with commercialism and a dully realistic style led him at times to reject industrial techniques and promote ever more esoteric creations executed by master craftsmen, in line with the aesthetics of Symbolism. Uzanne eschewed the democratizing potential associated with technology by the French Third Republic and with craftsmanship by William Morris and his followers. Instead, Uzanne looked to both these means as marks of distinction and basis for a *haut bourgeois* elite culture, given physical form in the "new" luxury book and an archetype in Paul Gallimard, among other collectors.

That Uzanne proved successful in securing a new social grounding for aesthetic taste, which in turn served to reinforce the prestige of this social elite, is in part the measure of the influence he had accrued in his unique role as author, reader, publisher, critic, and collector of fine illustrated books. Such a multiplication of functions was typical of a milieu in which producers of fine books produced exclusively for their peers, unfettered by governmental censorship or expectation of profit. Such an accumulation of roles also allowed Uzanne to challenge the "old guard" represented by the aristocratic, "retrospective" Bibliophiles François. Yet, while Uzanne and others in his cohort were devotees of "newness," they nevertheless shared with their predecessors preoccupations common to all book collectors, for as Jean Viardot pertinently remarks, "each bibliophilic sphere always contains in it the germ of the following one."[86] What makes a book rare and collectible? What, and who, determines its value and beauty? The struggle between "old" and "new" bibliophiles at the *fin de siècle* thus often took the form of a symbolic contest over questions of taste, definition, and worth. And in this contest originality provided by the most unusual applications of technology became one of the distinguishing signs of a newly "rare" book.

It is tempting to consider Uzanne emblematic of a turn of the century that, Janus-like, pointed both backward and forward, toward past and future. Against a backdrop of rapidly accelerating change—near the outbreak of World War I Charles Péguy pronounced that the world had changed more in the previous thirty years than it had since Jesus Christ[87]—

Uzanne witnessed both the excitement and the anxiety generated by technology in an era when the electric light, telephone, phonograph, radio, cinema, bicycle, linotype, and myriad other inventions were transforming the shape and pace of daily life for many French. Uzanne characterized his self-contradictory vision as "evolutionary" and called for a compromise between "progressives" and "reactionaries," because "sudden revolutions," in his view, "have never fruitfully served the interests of sincere reformers" (*Ad* 2). And clearly Uzanne worried about where such "sudden revolutions" might lead and what radical innovations might mean for the future of the printed word. In 1895 he published a remarkably prescient short story entitled "The End of Books."[88] Prolonging this reflection, two years later he mused, "Who might tell us, in effect, what will be the state of Bibliophilia in the year 2000? Will the art of typographic impression still exist at that date, and will the phonograph . . . not definitively replace printed paper and illustration with some advantage?" (*NB* 41). Propagandist of the new bibliophilia, Uzanne skillfully articulated the challenges posed by technology to the book and its material means of support. And far from being removed from the debates generated by these challenges, the seemingly hermetic world of bibliophiles that he represented was in fact not far from their center, as privileged interlocutors of the printed word.

Abbreviations of Works by Octave Uzanne

Ad   *L'Art dans la décoration extérieure des livres en France et à l'étranger.* Paris: May, 1898.

Cb   *Caprices d'un bibliophile.* Paris: Rouveyre, 1878.

LM   *Le Livre Moderne* 5 (10 May 1890), 355–56 ("Block-notes d'un bibliographe").

NB   *La Nouvelle Bibliopolis: voyage d'un novateur au pays des néo-iconobibliomanes.* Paris: Floury, 1897.

Q   *Quelques-uns des livres contemporains en exemplaires choisis, curieux ou uniques, revêtus de reliures d'art et de fantaisie tirés de la bibliothèque d'un écrivain et bibliophile parisien dont le nom n'est pas un mystère.* Paris: A. Durel, 1894.

Rm   *La Reliure moderne artistique et fantaisiste.* Paris: Rouveyre, 1887.

Z   *Les Zigzags d'un curieux: causeries sur l'art des livres et la littérature d'art.* Paris: Quantin, 1888.

Notes

1. Félicien Rops to Léon Dommartin, n.d. (1972-A.847), Fondation Custodia, Paris. All translations are my own unless otherwise indicated.

2. Uzanne's collected articles in *L'Echo de Paris*, penned under the pseudonym "La Cagoule," were published as *Visions de notre heure: choses et gens qui passent; notations d'art, de littérature et de vie pittoresque* (Paris: Floury, 1899). Uzanne also contributed to *Art et Décoration, Connoisseur, La Dépêche de Toulouse, The Dial, Le Figaro, La Grande Dame, La Jeune France, Magazine of Art, La Plume, La Revue Bleue,* and *The Studio.*

3. Quoted in Antoine Coron, "Livres de luxe," in *Histoire de l'édition française*, vol. 4: *Le Livre concurrencé: 1900–1950*, ed. Roger Chartier and Henri-Jean Martin (Paris: Fayard/ Promodis, 1991), 433.

4. See Pierre Bourdieu, "Le champ littéraire," *Actes de la Recherche en Sciences Sociales* 89 (spring 1991): 7 and 6, for a discussion of what he perceives to be the opposition between the two sectors of the field of cultural production, one devoted to mass production (*grande production*), the other to "restrained" production (*production restreinte*). On the same relationship, see also Pierre Bourdieu, "The Market of Symbolic Goods," trans. R. Swyer, in Pierre Bourdieu, *The Field of Cultural Production,* ed. Randal Johnson (New York: Columbia University Press, 1993), 125–31.

5. Despite his prolific activity in a great variety of bibliophilic, literary, artistic, and journalistic circles at the *fin de siècle,* as evidenced by abundant references to him in correspondence, memoirs, and the press of the period, there is scant published biographical material on Uzanne. The most complete source of information on his life, though it covers only the first half of it, is Ahmed Fathi Glamallah, "Octave Uzanne, homme de lettres, bibliophile et revuiste (1851–1892)" (Ph.D. diss., Université Paul Valéry [Montpellier III], 1992). Also useful is an article by Uzanne's grandnephew: Yvan Christ, "Octave Uzanne, bibliophile 'évolutionnaire' de 1900," *Médecine de France* (Dec. 1973): 24–40. See also the entries on Uzanne in *Dictionnaire national des contemporains*, vol. 4, ed. C.-E. Curinier (Paris: Office Général d'Edition, 1899–1905), 66–67; *Dictionnaire des lettres françaises*, vol. 2, ed. Cardinal G. Grente (Paris: Fayard, 1972), 467–68; and the obituary by Pierre Dufay in *Mercure de France* (15 Nov. 1931): 247–50. Uzanne intersperses autobiographical material throughout many of his own writings, such as the 1894 auction catalogue of part of his own library (*Quelques-uns des livres contemporains*) or accounts of his travels such as *Instantanés d'Angleterre* (Paris: Payot, 1914).

6. *Poésies de Benserade* (1875), *La Guirlande de Julie* (1875), *Poésies de François Sarasin* (1877), *Poésies de M. de Montreuil* (1878). Each book in this series was accompanied by unpublished documents, a bio-bibliographical preface, and notes by Uzanne.

7. *Petits conteurs du XVIIIe siècle* (1878–83), *Petits poètes du XVIIIe siècle* (1879–85), *Les Moeurs secrètes du XVIIIe siècle* (1879–83).

8. On the Goncourts' role in the Rococo revival, see Debora L. Silverman, *Art Nouveau in Fin-de-Siècle France: Politics, Psychology, and Style* (Berkeley and Los Angeles: University of California Press, 1989), 17–39. On the Goncourts' bibliophilia, see Christian Galantaris, "Les Goncourt bibliophiles," *Le Livre & l'Estampe* 40 (1994): 7–63.

9. On the new printing processes developed by Firmin and Charles Gillot, see Daniel Renoult, "Les nouvelles possibilités techniques: Le triomphe de la mécanique," in *Histoire de l'édition française*, 4:36; and Phillip Dennis Cate, "Prints Abound: Paris in the 1890s," in *Prints Abound: Paris in the 1890s*, ed. Phillip Dennis Cate, Gale B. Murray, and Richard Thomson (Washington, D.C.: National Gallery of Art, 2000), 16–17.

10. The phrase refers to the title of a woodcut illustration by Félix Vallotton that appeared in *Le Cri de Paris* on 23 January 1898, shortly after the publication of Emile Zola's "J'Accuse . . . !" in the daily newspaper *L'Aurore.*

278 BOOK HISTORY

11. On the "photomechanical revolution" and the industrialization of illustration techniques during this period, see Catherine Bertho-Lavenir, ed., *Le Livre-Monde* (Paris: Flammarion, 1992), 120–29; Alain Mercier, ed., *Les Trois Révolutions du livre* (Paris: Imprimerie Nationale Editions, 2002), 381–404; Michael Twyman, *The British Library Guide to Printing: History and Techniques* (Toronto: University of Toronto Press, 1998), 46–75; and Geoffrey Wakeman, *Victorian Book Illustration: The Technical Revolution* (Detroit: Gale Research, 1973), 119–45.

12. Octave Uzanne, "Prélude iconographique," in *Figures contemporaines tirées de l'album Mariani* (Paris: Flammarion, 1894), iii–vii. The following quotations are all taken from these pages.

13. On both the "vin" and the "album" associated with Mariani, see George Andrews and David Solomon, eds., *The Coca Leaf and Cocaine Papers* (New York: Harcourt Brace Jovanovich, 1975), 243–46 and passim.

14. Writing in the *annuaire* of the Société des Amis des Livres, Motteroz concurred that illustration techniques based on photography needed to be appropriated differently by different groups of readers. While the mass public appreciated the savings of time and money such techniques provided in "works of vulgarization," "the man of taste," on the other hand, "who appreciates illustrations for their aesthetic value, must now study all the new methods of reproduction if he wishes to be able to recognize those worthy of belonging to artistic collections." The author concluded that, while reproductions were always "very inferior" to original illustrations, they might acquire artistic value at the hands of a skilled *retoucheur* (touch-up artist). Motteroz, "Les illustrations chimiques," Société des Amis des Livres, *Annuaire* (Paris: Imprimé pour les Amis des Livres, 1881), 114, 152.

15. Octave Uzanne, "Sensations d'art et expression d'idées: Notes successives sur le caractère de cette publication," *L'Art et l'Idée* 1 (Jan.–June 1892): 7.

16. Describing his first collaboration with Rouveyre, on *Caprices d'un bibliophile,* Uzanne wrote: "In 1878, it was the *belle époque* of the *livre d'amateur.* E. Rouveyre was starting out as a publisher in a narrow little shop on the rue des Saints-Pères and, very intelligent, very active, full of confidence in his strengths, he published some excellent works of bibliography and bibliophilia. . . . The Bibliophile [Uzanne] was scarcely known, Rouveyre hardly more than that. Nevertheless, he courageously made himself the publisher of this little book with the help of his new author and friend" (*Q* 155–56). Uzanne's dedication to Rouveyre of *Caprices d'un bibliophile* reads: "To the young *Bibliographe* the young publisher full of faith in his undertakings has come with an outstretched hand." Uzanne and Rouveyre would collaborate on three other of Uzanne's works, including *La Reliure moderne artistique et fantaisiste* (1887).

17. Quoted in Glamallah, "Octave Uzanne," 31. The substitution, on the cover of the works Uzanne published in Damase Jouaùst's Librairie des Bibliophiles series, of Uzanne's initials and motto ("Renovata resurgo") for the emblem of the printer-publisher Jouaust also alludes visually to Uzanne's preemption of certain of his publisher's functions. Ibid.

18. Félicien Rops to Léon Dommartin, n.d. (1972-A.847), Fondation Custodia, Paris.

19. Ibid.

20. Octave Uzanne, "Jules Barbey d'Aurevilly rue Rousselet," *Le Figaro* (13 Oct. 1923): 2.

21. Ibid.

22. Jules Barbey d'Aurevilly, "Préface," in Octave Uzanne, *Le Bric-à-brac de l'amour* (Paris: Rouveyre, 1879), vi.

23. "I am certain of only one thing, that You are charming! . . . You [are] . . . a scholar capable of making my ignorance tremble. . . . You are *above* all or *below* all . . . an Author . . . that is, what is most rare among those who write or believe they write!" (ibid., vii). On the relationship between Uzanne and Barbey, see Octave Uzanne, *Barbey d'Aurevilly* (Paris: La Cité des Livres, 1927) and his articles about the author: "Barbey d'Aurevilly, son

portrait," *Annales* 28 (Nov. 1909); "Un dandy stoïcien," *La Dépêche de Toulouse* (17 Feb. 1922): 1. See also Jean de Bonnefon, *Les Dédicaces à la main de M. J. Barbey d'Aurevilly* (Paris: Blaizot, 1908), for the revealing dedications to Uzanne of certain of Barbey's works, and Jacques Petit, *Barbey d'Aurevilly critique* (Paris: Les Belles Lettres, 1963), 598–600, 658–62. On bibliomania as a theme in Barbey's works and life, see Daniel Desormeaux, *La Figure du bibliomane: Histoire du livre et stratégie littéraire au XIXe siècle* (Saint-Genouph: Nizet, 2001), 171–89.

24. Félicien Rops, quoted in "Lettres de Félicien Rops à Octave Uzanne, écrivain et bibliophile (1832–1931)," ed. Maurice Kunel, *Bulletin du Bibliophile et du Bibliothécaire* 4 (1961): 298; Anatole France to Octave Uzanne, n.d., N.a.f. 15428, fol. 498, Bibliothèque nationale de France, Paris (hereafter BnF).

25. Octave Uzanne, *Jean Lorrain, l'artiste, l'ami: Souvenirs intimes, lettres inédites* (Abbeville: F. Paillart, 1913), 50. Traces of Uzanne's relationship with Whistler in the late 1890s can be found in letters (MS Whistler U37-40) held by the University of Glasgow Library.

26. While evidence of Uzanne's anti-Semitism is relatively circumstantial, his feelings of antipathy toward Jews appears to have been stronger than the diffuse anti-Semitism prevalent among certain sectors of French society at the *fin de siècle*. Whether out of ideological sympathy or opportunism, he helped find a printer for Edouard Drumont's *La France juive* (1886), the anti-Semitic blockbuster that was one of the greatest publishing successes in nineteenth-century France. He contributed to Drumont's anti-Semitic newspaper, *La Libre Parole*. On Uzanne's interactions with Drumont, see Edmond and Jules de Goncourt, *Journal: Mémoires de la vie littéraire*, ed. Robert Ricatte (Paris: Laffont, 1989), 3:572–73, and Elisabeth Parinet, *La Librairie Flammarion, 1875–1914* (Paris: IMEC Editions, 1992), 252–55.

27. Charles Augustin Sainte-Beuve, "De la littérature industrielle," *Revue des Deux Mondes* (1 Sept. 1839): 675.

28. On the so-called "krach de la librairie" and other changes in the literary field in *fin-de-siècle* France, see Christophe Charle, "Le champ de la production littéraire," in *Histoire de l'édition française*, vol. 3, ed. Roger Chartier and Henri-Jean Martin (Paris: Fayard/Promodis, 1990), 137–75, and Jean-Alexis Néret, *Histoire illustrée de la librairie et du livre français des origines à nos jours* (Paris: Lamarre, 1953), 267–71. On the growth of readership during this period, see James Smith Allen, *In the Public Eye: A History of Reading in Modern France, 1800–1940* (Princeton: Princeton University Press, 1991); Maurice Crubellier, "L'élargissement du public," and Jean Hébrard, "Les nouveaux lecteurs," both in *Histoire de l'édition française*, vol. 3, 315–41 and 526–67; and Martyn Lyons, *Readers and Society in Nineteenth-Century France: Workers, Women, Peasants* (New York: Palgrave, 2001), and "Les nouveaux lecteurs au XIXe siècle: Femmes, enfants, ouvriers," trans. Jean-Pierre Bordos, in *Histoire de la lecture dans le monde occidental*, ed. Guglielmo Cavallo and Roger Chartier (Paris: Seuil, 2001), 393–430.

29. Albert Cim, *Le Radical* (n.d.), in Damase Jouaust, *Aux bibliophiles: Utlima, notes et chroniques* (Paris: Jouaust, 1891), 17.

30. Octave Uzanne, "Couvertures illustrées de publications étrangères," *Art et Décoration* 5 (1899): 34.

31. Ibid.

32. Octave Uzanne, quoted in Parinet, *La Librairie Flammarion*, 359.

33. Edouard Pelletan, *Première Lettre aux bibliophiles* (Paris: Editions d'Art, 1896), 1–2.

34. Damase Jouaust, quoted in Francisque Sarcey, *Le XIXe Siècle* (n.d.), in Jouaust, *Aux bibliophiles*, 4, 7.

35. Quoted in Desormeaux, *La Figure du bibliomane*, 89.

36. For overviews of the evolution of fine-book production and of bibliophilia in France during the nineteenth and early twentieth centuries, see Coron, "Livres de luxe," *Histoire de*

l'édition française, 4:425–60; Jean Viardot, "Les nouvelles bibliophilies," ibid., 3:383–402; and Desormeaux, *La Figure du bibliomane,* 83–97 and passim.

37. Also sharing the same philosophy of collecting as his contemporaries Uzanne and Gallimard was Léon Schuck (1857–1930), about whom little biographical material is available. Despite belonging to the highly traditional milieu of provincial bibliophiles (in this case from Provence) and during an era when "most great bibliophiles idolized only the past," Schuck, as the sale catalogue of his collection notes, set himself apart as one of "the audacious ones who turned toward contemporary authors . . . rendering them confident homage by offering them the foremost place in their libraries." He owned an outstanding collection of works by Barbey d'Aurevilly. See *Catalogue de la bibliothèque de feu M. Léon Schuck* (Paris: Librairie L. Carteret, 1931), 1, and L. Carteret, *Le Trésor du bibliophile: Livres illustrés modernes 1875 à 1945 et souvenirs d'un demi-siècle de bibliophilie de 1887 à 1945* (Paris: Librairie L. Carteret, 1946), 2:105.

38. Stéphane Mallarmé to Robert de Montesquiou, 3 May 1896, in Stéphane Mallarmé, *Correspondance,* ed. Henri Mondor and Lloyd James Austin (Paris: Gallimard, 1959–85), 8:118.

39. Stéphane Mallarmé to [?], 11 May 1898, ibid., 10:183.

40. Edmond and Jules de Goncourt, *Journal,* 3:284. Nevertheless, in his 14 December 1890 journal entry Goncourt criticized Raffaëlli for having "delivered such rubbish, which will leave a stain on the beautiful typographical monument of [the fine-book printer Georges] Chamerot" (3:508). For more on Paul Gallimard, see *Les Archives biographiques contemporaines,* 1st ser. (Paris, 1906), 71–72; Pierre Assouline, *Gaston Gallimard: Un demi-siècle d'édition française* (Paris: Balland, 1984), 17–30; Frantz Jourdain, *Sans remords ni rancune: Souvenirs épars d'un vieil homme "né en 76"* (Paris: Corréa, 1953), 56–76; Sophie Monneret, *L'Impressionnisme et son époque,* vol. 1 (Paris: Denoël, 1978), entry on "Paul Gallimard."

41. Camille Pissarro to Lucien Pissarro, 14 May 1891, quoted in Anne Thorold, ed., *The Letters of Lucien to Camille Pissarro, 1883–1903* (Cambridge: Cambridge University Press, 1993), 222. Pissarro *père* had written his son to suggest he prepare an album of his finest wood engravings to show Gallimard.

42. Octave Uzanne to Edmond de Goncourt, [18?] Feb. 1899, N.a.f. 22477, fols. 186–87, BnF.

43. Of Paul Gallimard Camille Pissarro wrote to his son Lucien: "He showed me a volume by Verlaine illustrated by hand by Rodin, another volume whose cover is illustrated with drawings in pen mixed with writing on parchment by Raffaëlli. That must cost a pretty penny!" Camille Pissarro to Lucien Pissarro, 24 May 1891, in Camille Pissarro, *Lettres à son fils Lucien,* ed. John Rewald (Paris: Albin Michel, 1950), 250.

44. The following Parisian bibliophile societies were founded between 1870 and 1914: La Société des Amis des Livres (1873), La Société des Bibliophiles Contemporains (1889), La Société des Cent Bibliophiles (1895), La Société des Bibliophiles Indépendents (1896), Les XX (1897), Les Amis du Livre Contemporain (1903), La Société du Livre d'Art (1904), Les Amis du Livre Moderne (1908). While not necessarily bibliophile societies, the Société de Propagation des Livres d'Art (1888) and the Société Artistique du Livre Illustré (1890) also concerned themselves with the illustrated book. See Carteret, *Le Trésor du bibliophile,* 2:185–256; Jean-Paul Fontaine, "Les bonheurs historiques et existentiels des sociétés françaises de bibliophiles," *Le Livre & l'Estampe* 45 (1999): 107–112; Raymond Hesse, *Histoire des sociétés de bibliophiles en France de 1820 à 1950,* vol. 1: *Les Sociétés parisiennes d'avant-guerre* (Paris: Giraud-Badin, 1929).

45. Obituary from the *Bulletin du Bibliophile et du Bibliothécaire,* 15 Feb. 1898, in *Léon Conquet, Editeur, Libraire de la Société des Amis des Livres, 1848–1897* (March 1898), 9.

46. For more on the Exposition internationale du livre moderne at Bing's gallery, see

Edmond Cousturier, "Exposition internationale du livre moderne à l'art nouveau," *Revue Blanche* 11 (1896): 42–44; Colleen Denney, "English Book Designers and the Role of the Modern Book at L'Art Nouveau, Part II: Relations Between England and the Continent," *Arts Magazine* 61 (summer 1987): 49–57; "Notes d'art parisiennes (Le 'Livre moderne')," *L'Art Moderne* (28 June 1896): 203–4; P.-P. Plan, "L'Art du livre," *Le Figaro* (9 June 1896); Gabriel P. Weisberg, *Art Nouveau Bing: Paris Style 1900* (New York: Harry N. Abrams, 1986), 114, 119–25.

47. In discussing the first three volumes published by his firm, Les Editions d'Art, Pelletan stated: "It went without saying . . . that the nature of the written work brought about that of its visual interpretation." *Première Lettre aux bibliophiles*, 8. In the *Deuxième Lettre aux bibliophiles* (Paris: Editions d'Art, 1896), he reiterated this point, asserting that "a book cannot be beautiful if the text is not good" (4) or, simply, "[t]he book is a text" (8). By contrast, when the print dealer Ambroise Vollard began publishing illustrated books in 1900, his "interest first and foremost was in the artist and his chosen images. The author's work was . . . always secondary." Una E. Johnson, *Ambroise Vollard, Editeur: Prints, Books, Bronzes* (New York: Museum of Modern Art, 1977), 23.

48. Ironically, however, "scarcely any" machines were featured at the exhibit. "[I]n the section reserved for them, next to an electric machine that is a real buzzing spinning top, we find two machines for black and color printing, and that's it." G. Lequatre, "L'Exposition internationale du livre et des industries du papier," *Revue des Arts Décoratifs* 15 (1894–95): 36.

49. Lequatre, "L'Exposition internationale du livre," 35, 37.

50. Philippe Burty, "La reliure française," *La République Française* (25 Feb. 1881): no page numbers.

51. Pelletan, *Deuxième Lettre aux bibliophiles*, 1.

52. Cousturier, "Exposition internationale du livre moderne a l'art nouveau," 42–43.

53. This imperative may have seemed especially urgent to Bing in light of the sentiments revealed, for example, by Edmond de Goncourt in his 20 April 1896 journal entry: "Bing, this dirty and base Jew . . . clings to me, forces me to shake hands with him, solicits my help for an international exhibit of the modern book, overwhelms me with shows of affection and, at the door, again holds out his hand, which I don't take." (*Journal*, 3:1269).

54. According to Debora Silverman, it was "the luxury sector [in France] which successfully assimilated modern forms of technology to the craft process." *Art Nouveau in Fin-de-Siècle France*, 60.

55. Félicien Rops to Octave Uzanne, [1882], in Kunel, "Lettres de Félicien Rops à Octave Uzanne," 309.

56. Félicien Rops to Léon Dommartin, n.d. (1972-A.847), Fondation Custodia, Paris.

57. Ibid. Close friends and neighbors, Rops and Uzanne collaborated on Uzanne's *Son Altesse la femme* (Paris: Quantin, 1885), which featured three color rotogravures by Rops (*La Femme au pantin, L'Evocation* or *L'Incantation*, and *Le Bout de sillon*) displaying the artist's characteristic erotic and Satanic themes. Uzanne's *La Femme et la mode* (Paris: Quantin, 1892) and *La Nouvelle Bibliopolis* also featured frontispieces by Rops. Finally, Rops designed two ex-libris for Uzanne: *Daphné ou Le Livre Moderne* (a miniature woodcut version of which became an emblem for Uzanne's review of the same name) and *Le Terme,* bearing Uzanne's initials. For more on their relationship and collaboration, see Félicien Rops, *Mémoires pour nuire à l'histoire artistique de mon temps et autres feuilles volantes,* ed. Hélène Védrine (Brussels: Labor, 1998), 167–70; *Félicien Rops-Joséphin Péladan: Correspondance,* ed. Hélène Védrine (Paris: Séguier, 1997), passim; Kunel, "Lettres de Félicien Rops à Octave Uzanne," 297–332; Thierry Zeno, ed., *Les Muses sataniques: Félicien Rops* (Brussels: J. Antoine, 1985), passim.

58. Octave Uzanne, "Eugene Grasset and Decorative Art in France," *Studio* 4 (Nov. 1894): 39.

59. Uzanne considered one of Grasset's first commercial posters, for the "Librairie romantique" series launched in 1887 by the publisher E. Monnier, a "masterpiece," in part because of its nuanced chromatic palette. Uzanne, *La Nouvelle Bibliopolis,* 129.

60. Grasset's interest in modern technology was manifested allegorically in thirty vignettes commissioned by the bibliophile-publisher Edouard Pelletan for his 1901 *Almanach du bibliophile,* a work destined primarily for book lovers. The female figures embodying features of nineteenth-century French history, science, philosophy, and the arts in this work include "Electricity" and "Steam Power," the latter an incarnation of progress depicted by Grasset as a muscular woman surrounded by a railroad engine and factories. See Anne Murray-Robertson-Bovard, *Eugène Grasset: Une certaine image de la femme* (Milan: Skira, 1998), 36–40.

61. Octave Uzanne, "A mes collègues de l'Académie des Beaux Livres: Salut présidentiel," *Annales littéraires des Bibliophiles contemporains* (Paris, 1890), xi.

62. See the article on Grasset by Uzanne in his own review, "Les artistes originaux: Eugène Grasset, illustrateur, architecte et décorateur," *L'Art et l'Idée* 2 (July–Dec. 1892): 193–220; his piece in the *Studio;* and the article he published to coincide with the first major Grasset retrospective: "L'Exposition récapitulative d'Eugène Grasset aux Artistes Décorateurs," *Art et Décoration* 20 (1906): 173–86. For more on *Les Quatre Fils Aymon* see the 15 May 1894 issue of *La Plume* devoted to Grasset's work; L. Carteret, *Le Trésor du Bibliophile* (Paris: Librairie L. Carteret, 1947), 3:34; Phillip Dennis Cate and Sinclair Hamilton Hitchings, *The Color Revolution: Color Lithography in France, 1890–1900* (N.p.: Peregrine Smith, Inc., and Rutgers University, 1978), 5; Anne Murray-Robertson, *Grasset pionnier de l'Art Nouveau* (Lausanne: Editions 24 Heures, 1981), passim; Eleanor M. Garvey, Anne B. Smith, and Peter A. Wick, eds., *The Turn of a Century, 1885–1910: Art Nouveau-Jugendstil Books* (Cambridge: Department of Printing and Graphic Arts, Houghton Library, Harvard University, 1970), 46.

63. See Murray-Robertson, *Grasset pionnier de l'Art Nouveau,* 147.

64. Uzanne, "Les artistes originaux," 195.

65. André Mellerio, *La Lithographie originale en couleurs* (Paris: L'Estampe et l'Affiche, 1898), trans. Margaret Needham as "Original Color Lithography," in Cate and Hitchings, *Color Revolution,* 95 (and 96 for the following quotation).

66. On the proliferation and reception of color printing in *fin-de-siècle* France, see especially Cate and Hitchings, *Color Revolution,* and Michel Melot, *The Impressionist Print,* trans. Caroline Beamish (New Haven: Yale University Press, 1996), 231–35.

67. Uzanne, "Eugene Grasset and Decorative Art," 39.

68. Uzanne deemed a later collaboration with Avril (who was also an engraver) on *Le Miroir du monde: notes et sensations de la vie pittoresque* (Paris: Quantin, 1888) "incontestably the most successful from the standpoint of what the drawings yield based on the use of diverse procedures (heliogravure, Gillot facsimiles, chromogravure . . .). An essentially new type of book . . . that provides evidence, for those in this craft, of a thousand difficulties vanquished and of decorative daring happily crowned with success. The Bibliophile, as artistic editor, feels some vanity in having failed nothing in the very complex production of this book" (*Q* 170). On the pair's collaboration on *L'Eventail* and *L'Ombrelle,* see Phillip Dennis Cate, "The 1880s: The Prelude," in Cate and Hitchings, *Color Revolution,* 5.

69. Octave Uzanne to Germain Bapst, 18 [Sept.?] 1881, N.a.f. 24540, fol. 209, BnF.

70. On the development of industrial binding in nineteenth-century France, see Sophie Malavieille, *Reliures et cartonnages d'éditeur en France au XIXe siècle (1815–1865)* (Paris: Promodis, 1985).

71. On poster bindings, see Roger Devauchelle, *La Reliure en France de ses origines à nos jours,* vol. 3: *Depuis 1850* (Paris: J. Rousseau-Girard, 1961), 105–6 (and, on Carayon's *cartonnages,* 108–12).

72. Of the binder-gilder Amand, Uzanne wrote, "for the past twenty years [he] has fought for the triumph of his ideas," despite being "followed by only a small number of faithful and curiosity-seekers, interested in innovative fantasy." He attributed Amand's lack of success in the form of prizes to "bourgeois narrowness" and the traditionalism of juries (*Rm* 182–87).

73. On the binders of the Ecole de Nancy, see *René Wiener, relieur et animateur de la vie artistique au temps de l'Ecole de Nancy,* ed. Martine Mathias (Nancy: Musée Lorrain, 1999), and Christian Debize, *Emile Gallé et l'école de Nancy* (Metz: Editions Serpenoise, 1998), 86–87. For more on Uzanne's assessment of contemporary artistic binders, including Martin, Prouvé, and Wiener, see his chapter on "La reliure d'art et les maîtres relieurs contemporains" (*Ad* 157–260).

74. Henri Beraldi, "Préface," in Hesse, *Histoire des sociétés de bibliophiles en France,* 1:106.

75. On Meunier, see Henri Beraldi, *La Reliure du XIXe siècle* (Paris: Conquet, 1897), 4:103–6; "Bindings by Charles Meunier," *Bookman* (Jan. 1907): 532; Carteret, *Le Trésor du Bibliophile,* 2:16; E. de Crauzat, *La Reliure française de 1900 à 1925* (Paris: R. Kieffer, 1932), 1:35–44; Devauchelle, *La Reliure en France,* 3:98–104; Hesse, *Histoire des sociétés de bibliophiles en France,* 1:93–102; Eiluned Rees, "Bookbindings in the National Library of Wales: Charles Meunier," *National Library of Wales Journal* 26, no. 2 (1989): 223–23; Léon Thévenin, "Opinion sur la reliure moderne: Étude sur Charles Meunier," *Mercure de France* (1 April 1914): 514–24; Nancy Zinn, "Charles Meunier and the French Bookbinders," *Fine Print* 2 (Jan. 1976): 5–6. A portion of Meunier's bindings from his own collection were sold at auction in 1908. See *Catalogue de livres modernes ornés de reliures artistiques exécutées par Charles Meunier et provenant de sa bibliothèque particulière* (Paris: Henri Leclerc, 1908).

76. Edmond and Jules de Goncourt, *Journal,* 3:1015.

77. Alistair Duncan and Georges De Bartha, *Art Nouveau and Art Deco Bookbinding: French Masterpieces, 1880–1940* (New York: Abrams, 1989), 137. While considering Meunier a "virtuoso of incised leather," Raymond Hesse felt that an overabundance of floral and other ornamentation sometimes flawed his work (*Histoire des sociétés de bibliophiles en France,* 1:93). E. de Crauzat contended that Meunier's obsession with symbols "often verged on the grotesque; on occasion he was even guilty of bad taste" (*La Reliure française de 1900 à 1925,* 1:36).

78. On the application, by Auriol, Grasset, and others, of new technologies to typography at the *fin de siècle,* see Philippe Thiébaut, *La Lettre art nouveau en France* (*Les Dossiers du Musée d'Orsay* 55) (Paris: Editions de la Réunion de Musées Nationaux, 1995), 41–51. On the development of typography in France in the late nineteenth century, see Gérard Blanchard, "La typographie française de 1830 à 1885," in *Histoire de l'édition française,* 3:365–68, and René Ponot, "La création typographique des Français," in *Histoire de l'édition française,* 4:367–83.

79. William S. Peterson, *The Kelmscott Press: A History of William Morris's Typographical Adventure* (Berkeley and Los Angeles: University of California Press, 1991), 82. On Morris's use of photography in typeface design, see ibid., 81–95.

80. Eugène Grasset in André Marty, *L'Imprimerie et les procédés de gravure au vingtième siècle* (Paris: Marty, 1906), quoted in Thiébaut, *La Lettre art nouveau,* 42–43.

81. Octave Uzanne, "La Renaissance de la gravure sur bois: Un néo-xylographe, M. Félix Vallotton," *L'Art et l'Idée* 1 (Jan.–June 1892): 117. On the revival of the woodcut at the *fin de siècle,* see Coron, "Livres de luxe," in *Histoire de l'édition française,* 4:445–47; Rolf Söderberg, *French Book Illustration, 1880–1905 (Acta Universitatis Stockholmiensis/Stockholm Studies in History of Art)* 28 (Stockholm: Almqvist and Wiksell International, 1977), 85–95, and Wakeman, *Victorian Book Illustration,* 69–81.

82. Pelletan, *Deuxième lettre aux bibliophiles,* 4.

83. Uzanne, "La Renaissance de la gravure sur bois," 115–17, and for the following quotations, 117–19.

84. Luce Abélès, "Tradition et modernité: *Les Rassemblements,* un livre de transition," in *L'Illustration: essais d'iconographie,* ed. Maria Teresa Caracciolo and Ségolène Le Men (Paris: Klincksieck, 1999), 317. To balance the stylistic crudeness of Vallotton's images, unorthodox in books for bibliophiles, Uzanne chose François Courboin, an artist with a more traditional technique and illustrator of Uzanne's *Les Modes de Paris* (1898), to produce the vignettes for *Les Rassemblements* (318). For Vallotton's own brief comments on his work for *Les Rassemblements,* see Félix Vallotton, *Documents pour une biographie et pour l'histoire d'une oeuvre,* ed. Gilbert Guisan and Doris Jakubec (Lausanne-Paris: La Bibliothèque des Arts), 1:133–34.

85. Meier-Graefe's assertion is corroborated by the fact that Vallotton's images do not appear in the *catalogue raisonné* of his engravings and lithographs. See Abélès, "Tradition et modernité," 317, 323. Both Richard S. Field and Phillip Dennis Cate support Meier-Graefe's contention that Vallotton's work for Uzanne's *Rassemblements* consisted of photomechanically reproduced images. See Cate, "Prints Abound," 46n44.

86. Jean Viardot, "Les nouvelles bibliophilies," in *Histoire de l'édition française,* 3:386.

87. See Eugen Weber, *France fin de siècle* (Cambridge: Harvard University Press, 1986), 235.

88. Octave Uzanne, "La Fin des livres," *Contes pour les bibliophiles* (Paris: Quantin, 1895), 125–45. Translated, this story appeared as "The End of Books" in *Scribner's Magazine* 16 (July–Dec. 1894): 221–31.

THE WRITER, THE CRITIC, AND THE CENSOR

J. M. Coetzee and the Question of Literature

Peter D. McDonald

Seen against the background of the vast scholarly and polemical literature on censorship, J. M. Coetzee's *Giving Offense* (1996) stands out as an avowedly singular intervention. As Coetzee himself points out in the preface, the twelve essays that make up the volume, most of which originally appeared between 1988 and 1993, constitute neither a "history" nor a "strong theory" of censorship. Rather they represent an attempt, first, "to understand a passion with which I have no intuitive sympathy, the passion that plays itself out in acts of silencing and censoring," and second, "to understand, historically and sociologically, why it is that I have no sympathy with that passion."[1] These prefatory remarks prepare the way for a wide-ranging interdisciplinary study that is at once psychoanalytic, literary, historical, sociological, and autobiographical. They also make plain the antirationalist spirit of Coetzee's enquiry, which centers not so much on legislative history or the practice of censorship as on the passions revealed and concealed in writings for or against it. One of the most important essays, "Emerging from Censorship" (1993), seeks, for instance, to understand the curiously "contagious power" of the censor's "paranoia" (37). Why is it, Coetzee asks, that writers—and here he includes himself—so often "record the feeling of being touched and contaminated by the sickness of the state" (35)?

The antirationalist spirit of this question is as evident in the essays on specific censors and dissident writers as it is in some of Coetzee's own general arguments against censorship. "Censorship is not an occupation that attracts intelligent, subtle minds," he notes at one point, adding that it "puts power in the hands of persons with a judgmental, bureaucratic cast of mind that is bad for the cultural and even the spiritual life of the community" (viii, 10). Characteristically, given the focus of his enquiry, he bases his objection not on matters of principle but on judgments about the censors' quality of mind and the pernicious public effects of their authority. A similar logic underlies his analysis of the censors' more immediate impact on writers. What concerns him most in this case is the psychological damage censorship inflicts irrespective of whether or not a writer's works are banned, an effect he feels he can represent only in an arrestingly precarious series of gendered and highly sexualized figures. In ideal conditions, the "inner drama" of writing could, he suggests, be construed as a transaction between the writer and the "figure of the beloved," the internalized reader whom the writer "tries to please" but, as important, "surreptitiously to revise and re-create" as "the-one-who-will-be-pleased." "Imagine what will happen," he then asks, "if into this transaction is introduced in a massive and undeniable way the dark-suited, bald-headed censor, with his pursed lips and his red pen and his irritability and his censoriousness—the censor, in fact, as a parodic version of the figure-of-the-father." The logical consequence of this consciously Freudian chain of figures is inevitable. "Working under censorship is like being intimate with someone who does not love you, with whom you want no intimacy, but who presses himself in upon you. The censor is an intrusive reader, a reader who forces his way into the intimacy of the writing transaction, forces out the figure of the loved or courted reader, reads your words in a disapproving and *censorious* fashion" (38).

Once again Coetzee conducts the argument not in terms of principle—he makes no appeal, say, to the language of rights—but through a "speculative" analysis of the censor's passion and the effects of his "contagious power" (37). He also argues from personal testimony. Though never banned, he did have the misfortune to begin his publishing career in the 1970s, one of the worst decades in the history of South African censorship under apartheid, and so his striking image of the censor as an unwelcome, "intrusive reader" is all the more disconcerting because it comes, as he notes, partly from introspection.

Yet he did not intend this to be merely an autobiographical exercise. His purpose was to analyze the discourse he shared with other writers working under censorship, whether in South Africa or elsewhere, and to situate it historically. His image of the censor as a patriarchal monster or censorious bureaucrat was, he recognized, not particularly unique or new, nor was it untouched by the paranoia he detected in the censors themselves. It was part of his European cultural inheritance, reflecting his continuity with a tradition of increasingly "settled and institutional" hostility between artists and "governmental authority," which he dated from the late eighteenth century. Artists, he notes, have over the past two centuries assumed it as "their social role, and sometimes indeed as their vocation and destiny, to test the limits (that is to say, the weak points) of thought and feeling, of representation, of the law, and of opposition itself, in ways that those in power were bound to find uncomfortable and even offensive" (9). Though Coetzee himself is acutely sensitive to the potential pitfalls of this heroic authorial self-construction—he analyzes this powerfully in essays on Solzhenitsyn and André Brink—he is equally aware of the extent to which the countervailing idea of the censor as adversary has shaped the institution of literature in modernity. The censor, as hateful guardian of the Law, is an opponent the transgressive modern writer has somehow needed.

Just how these nightmarish censor figures, who have for so long haunted Western literary culture, relate to the all-too-human censors of history, particularly in the case of apartheid South Africa, is not always easy to predict. Indeed, what makes the once secret history of Coetzee's own fate at the hands of the apartheid censors so challenging and significant is the unexpected gulf the archives reveal between the reality of his felt experience under censorship—which was, of course, not just his—and the official response to his work. Though there were many censors in the system with a "judgmental, bureaucratic cast of mind," and no doubt many who could be cast as *dramatis personae* in Coetzee's version of the writer's "inner drama," those who read and reported on his own novels seem disturbingly miscast for their role. *In the Heart of the Country* (1977) and *Life and Times of Michael K* (1983) were, as I reported in an article in the *TLS* in May 2000, read and passed by an unusually sophisticated group, appointed in part for their literary expertise: Anna Louw, a respected Afrikaans writer; H. van der Merwe Scholtz, a minor poet and professor of Afrikaans literature; F. C. Fensham, a professor of Semitic languages; and Rita Scholtz, an educated "ordinary" reader with special literary interests. Their reports echo the praise Coetzee received from many of his earliest critical champions, and at times even read like fairly interesting literary criticism. Anna Louw, in fact, very quickly reworked her Afrikaans censorship report on *In the Heart of the Country* into two local newspaper reviews, praising it as her book of the year for 1977, and a decade later she published a more elaborate English version in the British scholarly journal *PN Review,* where she responded enthusiastically to the novel as an allegory of a Calvinist consciousness.[2]

A report on a third novel, *Waiting for the Barbarians* (1980), which has only recently come to light, confirms this unexpected pattern. In this instance, the censor and chair of the relevant reading committee was Reginald Lighton, an elderly (he was born in 1903) retired professor of education at the University of Cape Town.[3] A former teacher and inspector of schools, Lighton was, like Merwe Scholtz, firmly part of the censorship establishment by 1980. He had served on the early Publications Control Board as a member and then as vice chairman from 1970. After the new censorship system was set up in 1975, he was an assistant and then deputy director of the new Directorate of Publications. He was also something of a literary man. A minor novelist, a children's writer, and a literary anthologist, his modest success was not harmed by the fact that he was also a school inspector. His one novel, *Out of the Strong: A Bushveld Story* (1957), an uplifting moral tale for teenage boys, went through two editions and four reprintings, no doubt partly because it was, like his anthology *Stories South African,* prescribed for white secondary schools. Lighton did, it seems, have a bureaucratic cast of mind—he served on endless councils and committees, and clearly enjoyed being an administrator—but, if his report on *Waiting for the Barbarians* is anything to go by, he was not especially judgmental or censorious. Like the others who read Coetzee's work, he was also not disapproving.

Waiting for the Barbarians, like the other two novels, reached the censors, via customs in Cape Town, who intercepted the first consignment of the Secker and Warburg hardback edition and submitted a copy to the Directorate on 25 November 1980. Following the usual practice, the copy was then passed on to the principal reader, in this case Lighton. Dated 7 December and written in English, his report began with the required brief synopsis of the story, which he introduced with a series of quotations from the confrontational blurb that Coetzee had either written or authorized. "For decades (an) old Magistrate had [*sic*] run the affairs of a tiny frontier settlement, . . . occupying himself in philandering & antiquarianism, ignoring the confluence of forces . . . leading to war between the barbarians (frontier nomads) & the Empire he serves [*sic*]." The Magistrate's situation "is that of all men living in unbearable complicity with regimes which elevate their own survival above justice & decency."[4] Having set this out, Lighton immediately noted: "The locality is obscure; some oasis in an arid region north of the equator, where winters are icy." What he wanted to stress was that "it is nowhere near Southern Africa, nor is there any white populace" and that "there are no apparent parallels," though he added, "some symbols may be found." The rest of his summary comprised a sketchy account of the plot and a short character analysis of the magistrate, whom he described as "a compassionate, sincere man, a loner who has gone 'semi-native,' to the extent that he antagonises the police & military authorities—for he reveals some sympathy with the barbarians." It was, in his view, a "sombre, tragic book," which ended "with the bloody but always unbowed Magistrate heading the dispirited remnants of the populace 'waiting for the barbarians.'" No doubt the ironies of his use of the much-cited phrase from "Invictus," W. E. Henley's bombastic late-Victorian poem about manly heroism in the face of death, were not intended—his experience as a writer of stories for boys seems to have colored his interpretation of the ending.

The passages Lighton thought "may possibly be regarded as *undesirable*" almost all fell under Section 47(2)(a) of the 1974 Publications Act, which dealt with what might be "indecent or obscene or offensive or harmful to public morals." Most centered on the magistrate's various real or imagined sexualized encounters with the young barbarian girl (30, 40, 44, 55, 63, 66, 149), a town girl (42), and an older woman (151), but he also highlighted the scene in which the magistrate voyeuristically witnesses sex between the town girl and a young boy (97).[5] Though he underlined those pages containing scenes of full intercourse (63 and 97), he remarked that all these "sex incidents" were "generally vague, implicit." Under clause (a), he also noted scenes of "brutality," especially Colonel Joll's public flogging of the captured barbarians (103–8) and Warrant Officer Mandel's torturing and mock hanging of the magistrate (115–16, 119–21). For the rest, he simply counted up the words "fuck" ("8 times") and "shit" ("6 times")— he found the soldier's abusive language on page 138 especially noteworthy. The only passage he felt might be undesirable in other ways was the scene in which Mandel first reads the charges, ranging from incompetence to treason, against the magistrate (84). From the page number, it is most likely that he was concerned about the magistrate's comments on the bureau's cynical abuse of due process. "They will use the law against me as far as it serves them, then they will turn to other methods. That is the Bureau's way. To people who do not operate under statute, legal process is simply one instrument among many." Lighton may also have been worried about his subsequent analysis of Mandel's character, however. The magistrate goes on to describe Mandel as one of those "men who might as easily go into lives of crime as into the service of the Empire (but what better branch of service could they choose than the Bureau!)." In Lighton's view, these comments might be deemed "prejudicial to the safety of the State, the general welfare or the peace and good order" (47[2][e]).

Yet, despite these potential difficulties, he was in no doubt that the novel was "not undesirable." His reasoning, which in effect became the committee's recommendation, is worth citing in full.

This is a somewhat Kafkaesque type of narrative, with the narrator an elderly somewhat Quixotic Magistrate, for long posted at a little frontier outpost, who has sought a modus vivendi if not operandi with the nomadic tribes (the barbarians). But the officiously overbearing Imperial police & military find in him an impediment to their plan to extend Imperial sway to subduing the barbarians. So there is tension between the ambitious authoritarians and the indulgent magistrate. He loses position & authority, & suffers severe battering. Doom, brutality and suffering suffuse this sombre book unrelieved by any lighter touches. The few across the line sex incidents are almost entirely inexplicit & in no case lust-provoking. The locale is as obscure as Erewhon, and any symbolism more so—apart from the arrogant tyranny of State [*sic*] senior ideologists—their blinkered ideological outlook & ruthlessness. [*Added as an afterthought:* Further symbolism could with diligence be extracted. All is of world-wide significance, not particularized.] Though the book has considerable literary merit, it quite lacks popular appeal. The likely readership will be limited largely to the intelligentsia, the discriminating minority. There are less than a dozen "offensive" words, and all are commonplace & functionally in context. We ["I" *crossed out*] submit there is no convincing reason for declaring the book undesirable.

The other committee members, including Rita Scholtz (who would go on to chair the committee on *Michael K*) and F. C. Gonin (who had passed *In the Heart of the Country*), simply endorsed this conclusion, which the Directorate subsequently agreed not to appeal.

Now that reports justifying the release of all three novels have been unearthed—*Dusklands* (1974) and *Foe* (1986) were not scrutinized—it is possible to make some general remarks about the official response to Coetzee's work. To begin with, it is clear that all the censors recognized that his novels tested the limits of the 1974 act, especially on matters of public morals and state security. They included sexually frank episodes and scenes of torture and brutality, and they were directly or indirectly critical of the apartheid state or its agents. Their political subversion was especially evident in *Michael K,* but, as Fensham noted, *In the Heart of the Country* also displayed "traces of protest literature," and Lighton recognized that the agents of the bureau and the empire, for all their lack of specificity as "symbols," had some local resonance.[6] His comments on torture, Joll, and Mandel are particularly noteworthy, given Coetzee's subsequent reflection on *Barbarians,* the torture chamber, and the ethics of writing. *Barbarians* was, Coetzee noted in "Into the Dark Chamber" (1986), "about the impact of the torture chamber on the life of a man of conscience," a subject that made it potentially complicit with the apartheid regime, since there was "something tawdry about *following* the state . . . making its vile mysteries the occasion of fantasy."[7] He would later develop this line of argument more fully, not least in his challenging critique of Brink.[8] Yet complicity was only one side of the "dilemma proposed by the state." Ignoring, as opposed to exposing, its "obscenities" was equally unacceptable. *Either* self-censorship *or* complicity—such were the grim alternatives the censor's intrusive gaze seemed to impose. For all his candor about the "contagious power" of this gaze, Coetzee nonetheless felt that the writer's "true challenge" was "how not to play the game by the rules of the state, how to establish one's own authority, how to imagine torture and death on one's own terms."[9] In the absence of the detailed information contained in the censors' reports, it was not possible—though it was of course for some always tempting—to judge to what extent Coetzee managed to rise to his own challenge. It is worth recalling that while the censors' decision not to ban any of the three novels they scrutinized was a matter of public knowledge at the time—the fact that the books were embargoed and then released was noted in the press—it was not known which censors acted in his case or how they justified their recommendations. On the basis of this new evidence, we can now make a more informed retrospective assessment of the censors' response to Coetzee's own struggle to avoid the state's dilemma. Unexpectedly, this turns on their openness to, and idea of, the literary, since, for all the readers, the committees, and ultimately for the Directorate itself, his novels' *potential* undesirability was mitigated by their manifest literariness.[10] They were not banned because they were *sufficiently* literary.

This of course begs a number of large questions, not least because it meant various things. The novels were literary first in the sense that they had, as Lighton put it, no "popular appeal." Their readership was restricted to the "intelligentsia, the discriminating minority." This quasi-sociological conception of the literary did not simply mean that the novels were passable because their impact in South Africa was expected to be slight. It also assumed that undesirability was relative. No content was inherently or absolutely undesirable, since its power to offend or threaten depended on the number and kind of readers it was likely to reach and/or on the way in which those putative readers were likely to respond to it. To this extent, the censors' conception of the literary depended in part on their construction of the "literary reader." As Rita Scholtz claimed in her report on *Michael K,* its "sophisticated & discriminating" readership would "experience the novel as a work of art."[11] This conviction was inseparable from the censors' second, more aesthetic understanding of literariness. The novels were also literary, and likely to be read as literature, they argued, because of their formal and rhetorical complexity, subtlety, or obscurity. This was particularly important in relation to public morals. The novels' aesthetic qualities functioned as a kind of protective covering that rendered any potentially undesirable sexual or violent content innocuous. Anna Louw, for instance, felt that the disturbed first-person narrative mode of *In the Heart of the Country* made tolerable the rape scenes "that might, *in a different context,* be questioned as undesirable" (emphasis added).[12]

This idea of literature as a privileged aesthetic space, set apart from more ordinary forms of discourse, including less literary novels, was not based just on assumptions about form, however. Aspects of the novels' content and themes, in particular their temporal and spatial settings, were also important, not least in relation to their potential subversiveness. They did not pose a threat to the apartheid state, the censors argued, since, as literature, their settings were either universal or did not simply, essentially, or directly reflect the *contemporary* South African situation. On this issue their judgments were not always predictable. In the case of *Waiting for the Barbarians,* Coetzee's most antirealist novel, with its largely invented geography and nonspecific setting in a colonial past, it is hardly surprising that Lighton emphasized its redeeming universality, not only through his comments on its setting but through his various allusions to the canon of Western literature ("Kafkaesque," "quixotic," "Erewhon"). Though it could be argued that the novel resists this kind of reading—for one thing, South Africa is covered by Lighton's term "world-wide"—it is of all Coetzee's fictions the one most amenable to those committed to the belief in canonical art's universality. (Elsewhere I have argued that his novels resist nation-centered readings and the equally reductive pieties of the particular.)[13] It is also, for the same reasons, the novel that leaves Coetzee most vulnerable to the charge of self-censorship, not, as he thought, complicity. Yet on this issue he clearly could not win. The dogma of universality—canonical literature is about everywhere and all times—was simply too entrenched in the censor's thinking. For Rita Scholtz, *Michael K's* universality—she privileged a reading of it as an allegory of the alienated human condition in the late twentieth century—enabled it to rise above the concretely realized setting and the explicitly "derogatory" comments on the state; she did not mention that the novel is set in the future. Like Lighton, she used the appeal to universality to downplay, if not erase, what she took to be its relatively direct relevance to contemporary South Africa. Though Anna Louw echoed this wishful universalizing tendency in her individual comments on *In the Heart of the Country,* the committee, in their general report on that novel, took a different approach to its narrative displacements. They argued that its portrayal of interracial sex was "perfectly acceptable" because the story was set sometime in South Africa's colonial past.[14] In each case, then, the novels were passed not only because they were not popular, or because their aesthetic qualities rendered them harmless, but because their real or imagined spatiotemporal displacements—into South Africa's past or future, into a universal contemporary situation, or into the realm of pure imagination—and their manifest canonical status deemphasized or overwhelmed their relevance to contemporary South Africa. All these factors ensured that despite their potential undesirability they could be officially approved because they were not going to cause offense or threaten the state. They were *too literary* to warrant banning, or, to be more precise, they were too readily amenable to the censors' idea of the literary and ways of reading to be proscribed.

That the apartheid state put a group of censors so committed to defending the literary in such a powerful position is startling enough. Things become more disconcerting, however, if we set these censors' relatively uncensorious judgments in the context of the critical reception of Coetzee's work in the late 1970s and 1980s. This is partly because some critics did not fit the censors' construction of the "literary reader." Indeed, while the censors secretly judged Coetzee's novels acceptable because they were too literary, some leading critics, particularly in South Africa but also elsewhere, openly considered them objectionable on the same grounds. If we take Coetzee's own much-cited essay "The Novel Today," which he originally delivered as a talk in Cape Town in November 1987, as a testament to the way in which he felt critics were responding to his work at that time, then the challenges posed by the censors' approval become all the more acute. On that occasion, and to that local audience, which he assumed was hostile, Coetzee portrayed himself as a "member of a tribe threatened with colonisation," his provocative figure for the novelist whose own specifically literary discourse was in danger of being appropriated by the discourses of politics, ethics, and, most notably, history.[15] The main point of his talk was, as he put it, to oppose the "powerful tendency, perhaps even dominant tendency, to subsume the novel under history," where history was taken to be a fixed, self-evident reality to which the novel was supposed to bear witness. He also wanted to correct the misperception that novels, like his own, that were not "investigations of real historical forces" were somehow "lacking in seriousness."[16] This negative assessment, according to which his novels were at best irrelevant or at worst inimical to the struggle against apartheid, was of course only strengthened by the fact that they were never banned.

According to the dominant view, only those novels that in a realist mode put their literariness in the service of ethics, politics, and history deserved to be valued and taken seriously in the pressing circumstances of South Africa in the 1980s. This concerned Coetzee not just because it devalued his own work but because it assumed that literary discourse has no public value or authority per se. This assumption could be articulated in two ways. Where proponents of the "dominant tendency" recognized literariness, they did so because it made possible especially effective ways of judging or bearing witness to history (e.g., "from the inside," as Stephen Clingman's Lukacsian study of Gordimer had it). This weaker formulation, which was the focus of Coetzee's critique, granted the literary some, albeit only instrumental, value. According to the stronger formulation, which Coetzee acknowledged only implicitly, the value of the literary was at best negligible, at worst nugatory. In this view, the literariness of a novel is irrelevant, or relevant only negatively as obfuscation, since its value is wholly dependent on its status as a social document dealing with issues of race, class, and gender. This view is implied in Coetzee's sardonic comment that "There is a game going on between the covers of the book, but it is not always the game you think it is. No matter what it may appear to be doing, the story is not really playing the game you call Class Conflict or the game called Male Domination or any of the other games in the games handbook."[17]

His answer to both the stronger and the weaker forms of instrumentalized reading was emphatic. Not content simply to defend his own novelistic practice, he insisted on literature as a specific kind of discourse, distinct from the discourses of history, politics, and ethics, or, as he put it, "storytelling as another, an other mode of thinking."[18] This appeal to distinctiveness did not simply mean that, contrary to the weaker version of the "dominant tendency," literature was an autonomous rather than a supplementary discourse, since for Coetzee distinctiveness also entailed rivalry. Against the stronger version of the dominant view, the version that sought to efface literariness altogether, he insisted that the literary existed in a rivalrous relationship to the discourses of politics, ethics, and history. Read as literature, in other words, his novels could be seen not simply to disturb but to displace the authority of the historical categories—including race, class, and gender—pervading, and often deforming, the wider public discourses in and about apartheid South Africa. This further move was not without risk, a point I shall develop later.

Coetzee's formalist appeal to the literary as a discourse with its own distinct or, more strongly, rivalrous mode of existence looks like a version of the censors' privileged aesthetic space, an affinity that would of course invite further suspicions of self-censorship and compound the historical ironies. Far from being patriarchal monsters determined to usurp the position of the beloved reader, it seems that the unexpectedly literary censors, not the politicized critics, were Coetzee's closest allies in the 1980s. For Anna Louw this was not surprising. Coetzee, she felt, was on her side. In her *PN Review* article, she eagerly noted some reservations he had expressed about "politically committed literature" in an interview of 1978, before adding that such writing had, in her view, "reached a fever pitch in both English and Afrikaans literary circles" in South Africa.[19] Yet the bogus drama of this next unexpected turn—it is not difficult to imagine the head-lines: "Great Writer Loved by Censors, Hated by Critics"—obscures a more testing set of reversals, which reflect more profound theoretical and ulti-mately cultural anxieties about the literary. In the febrile political context of South Africa in the 1980s, Coetzee's novels did not just fall victim to the censorious critics or, perhaps more damningly, to the censors' approval. This was partly because the censors were not simply state functionaries who applied the law mechanically. It was also partly because the critics did not see themselves only as evaluators and interpreters of Coetzee's novels. The situation was made more challenging, and worse still for Coetzee, because both the censors and the critics took on the additional task of policing the category of the literary, of deciding what constituted literature or, more narrowly, what could count as serious literature, which they of course defined in opposite ways.

Their opposing definitions can be summed up briefly if we follow the cogent formula Stanley Fish proposed in a major theoretical essay of 1973 (revised in 1980). To summarize two dominant attitudes to the literary in Western thinking, both of which relied on a purely linguistic analysis of the difference between literary language and a supposedly normative ordinary language, Fish outlined what he termed "message-plus" and "message-minus" approaches to the question. "A message-minus definition," as he put it, "is one in which the separation of literature from the normative cen-ter of ordinary language is celebrated; while in a message-plus definition, literature is reunited with the center by declaring it to be a more effective conveyor of the messages ordinary language transmits."[20] One of the chief difficulties with these traditional formulations, Fish then pointed out, is that, while purporting to be universal in scope, and to define literature once and for all in purely linguistic terms, each entailed a set of specific, and wholly opposed, aesthetic valuations. "Message-minus theorists are forced to deny literary status to works whose function is in part to convey infor-mation or offer propositions about the real world. . . . Message-plus theo-rists, on the other hand, are committed to downgrading works in which elements of style do not either reflect or support a propositional core."[21]

The relevance of this seemingly abstruse theoretical problem to the murky circumstances of Coetzee's reception in the 1980s is not difficult to see. The censors, who were adherents of the "message-minus" definition, passed Coetzee's novels because they were sufficiently literary on their terms. As literature they were far enough removed from more ordinary dis-courses, including less literary novels, that would, with the same content, be offensive or subversive. By contrast, the critics, who at best followed the "message-plus" view, downgraded Coetzee's novels because they were too literary according to their definition. They lacked seriousness because they did not engage effectively (i.e., realistically) enough with the struggle against apartheid.

Fish's essay is worth invoking in this context not only because it clarifies the stakes involved in this strange, previously invisible contest between the censors and the critics in a usefully concise way. It is also especially pertinent because it influenced Coetzee's own thinking about the category of the literary, as evidenced in his 1987 talk. At one point, for instance, he updated Fish's arithmetic—all the plusses and minuses—bringing it into the age of the desktop computer. "There is no addition in stories. They are not made up of one thing plus another thing, message plus vehicle, substructure plus superstructure. On the keyboard on which they are written, the plus key does not work. There is always a difference; and the difference is not a part, the part left behind after the subtraction. The minus key does not work either: the difference is everything."[22]

This explicitly allusive passage, one of many in the talk as a whole, casts a different light on Coetzee's defense of the distinctiveness of the literary, and on his relationship to the censors. Though his talk was quite clearly a defense of literature's autonomy, it was not in any way an endorsement of the censors' morally compromised faith in subtraction, where the literary becomes an aesthetic covering that sets canonical novels apart and renders them innocuous. Nor did it offer any backing for his critics' morally laudable faith in addition, where the literary becomes an effective supplement to more ordinary discursive modes. In his view, literary discourse was neither more nor less than the discourses of politics, ethics, and history. It was just different—though, as I have intimated, his further insistence on its status as a *rival* discourse goes beyond mere difference, problematically reinscribing the literary in a broader cultural struggle for power and privilege. To the extent that he insisted on difference, however, Coetzee was as far from the censors as he was from his more adversarial critics, who were, at least at the level of theory, rather more like each other than they would have liked to acknowledge. For one thing, both assumed that "form" and "content" are in principle separable; and, for another, both presupposed that the literary could be defined only relative to a putatively fixed norm of a message-bearing ordinary discourse. These were two assumptions that Coetzee's appeal to distinctiveness—"the difference is everything"—was intended to repudiate. As he argued in "The Novel Today," with reference to the critics (and a year earlier in "Into the Dark Chamber") with the censors in mind, literature's authority, and his claim to seriousness as a novelist, lay in its irreducible power to intervene in the public sphere on its own terms, since its effectiveness, including its political effectiveness, and its literariness were inseparable. The trouble was, despite Coetzee's efforts, surreptitious or otherwise, to court a beloved ideal reader, few actual readers appeared willing or able to recognize, let alone endorse, this idea of the literary in the 1970s and 1980s.

To Coetzee it looked at that time as if his particular literary project was imperiled by two very different and especially intrusive kinds of reader: the judgmental, wholly unliterary censor on the one hand; and the appropriative, politicized literary critic on the other. Yet, as I have tried to show, the situation was made all the more trying because the actual censors who read his novels behind the scenes were not quite the opponents they seemed. Now that their detailed reports have emerged from the shadows it is possible to offer a new retrospective reading of the situation, which links the censors and the critics in unexpected ways and puts the question of literature at the center of things. On the basis of this new evidence, Coetzee could still be figured as the embattled member of a marginal tribe threatened with colonization by two opposing but equally intrusive forces: censorship and literary criticism. But we would now have to acknowledge that both were directed toward a common goal: misrecognizing the distinctiveness of his novels by assimilating them into their contradictory conceptions of the literary. In this analysis, it could be argued that Coetzee emerges as a hero of the margins, as, say, a Kafkaesque hunger artist working in the tradition of a minor literature, always against the odds.

This is still a popular image of Coetzee-as-novelist, one that he, of course, partly authorized in his polemical 1987 talk, particularly when he shifted the locus of his argument from difference to rivalry. Yet championing him in this way only complicates matters further, in my view. For one thing, the move from difference to rivalry had the unhappy effect of implicating Coetzee in a troubled European high-cultural tradition of "metacultural discourse," as Francis Mulhern has usefully termed it, according to which the literary represents not only a distinct mode of discourse but also a genuine alternative, particularly when set alongside the political. "What speaks in metacultural discourse is the cultural principle itself," Mulhern notes, "as it strives to dissolve the political as locus of general arbitration in social relations."[23] Coetzee's claims about rivalry echo this tradition insofar as they present the literary as a real choice, in the logic of an either/or, set *against* some abstractly conceived "political discourse." In so doing, I would argue, he threatened to undermine his powerful claims about difference by overstating his case and by mirroring the equally exaggerated distortions of his most outspoken opponents: where he tended toward a hyperinflation of the literary at the expense of the political, they did the opposite.[24] None of this rests easily with an idea of Coetzee as an embattled hero of the margins.

Championing him in this way can be limiting in other, more general respects as well, especially if it entails stabilizing his particular definition of the literary or turning it into yet another universal. Doing so would simply repeat the mistakes of the censors and critics and so risk ignoring the most significant lesson of Fish's essay: "All aesthetics . . . are local and conventional rather than universal, reflecting a collective decision as to what will count as literature, a decision that will be in force only so long as a community of readers or believers (it is very much an act of faith) continues to abide by it."[25] In this respect it is important to remember that, for all his indebtedness to Fish in "The Novel Today," Coetzee spoke in 1987 as a novelist, not as a literary theorist. His object was not, following Fish, to expose the logical impossibility of ever establishing a stable, "objective" definition of the literary on purely linguistic grounds. It was to intervene in a collective debate about what counts as literature and to persuade a community of readers to change their ideas. As his own often hyperbolic language reveals—all that rhetoric of rivalry and colonization—he was defiantly defending his own heterodox literary faith against orthodoxies that were more powerful (because more widely shared) but no more solidly founded. Though aimed at his more adversarial critics, this challenge could, as I have argued, equally have been directed at the approving censors.

If this less enchanted analysis does not exactly rally to Coetzee's cause, neither does it undermine the value or persuasiveness of his case. On the contrary, it makes it all the more compelling because it insists on the literary, not as a universally fixed or "natural" category, or as a privileged discourse above the fray, but as the site of constant cultural, legal, political, and ethical struggle in which Coetzee, as novelist, is just one relatively powerless figure among many. Nor does this perspective prevent anyone from endorsing his particular literary faith. Though his conception of the literary as a *rival* to the discourses of history and politics, in my view, risks pushing the important argument about *difference* too far and closes down too many possibilities, especially considering the long tradition of satirical fiction, I, for one, would rather be a "Coetzeean" than anything else when it comes to literary matters. Difficulties would arise only if this commitment was seen as anything other than a corroborating act of faith in our time.

This admittedly rather dispassionate stance would not only have important consequences for literary criticism, however. It would also oblige us to open up more effective lines of communication between literary theory and cultural history, including book history. If the first stage in the argument is to move against the censors and the critics by shifting the locus of literariness from the text to the reader, the second is to historicize the resulting "interpretive communities" more radically, as Fish always insisted, and so make possible a "truly new literary history."[26] Relocating the question of literature in larger and more richly realized sociopolitical contexts, encompassing numerous intersecting communities, including censors, critics, writers, publishers, teachers, and so-called "ordinary" readers, requires a parallactic style of cultural history, which privileges no single point of view. Written from neither the critic's nor the writer's perspective—the vantage points for most traditional literary histories—this kind of narrative would involve a particularly comprehensive, if never impossibly totalizing, account of how the overdetermined, often conflicting, and always volatile desires of various interest groups ("communities" perhaps presupposes too much) have shaped literary history—or, more accurately, have shaped the category of the literary in history. Such an approach would necessarily pay particular attention to the fractious and now also wholly globalized public arena ("public sphere" implies an unwarranted degree of coherence) in which the sometimes costly effects of specific definitions of the literary are worked out and felt. It is here that books are banned or approved, writers praised or blamed, and seemingly innocent matters of taste linked to larger questions of social and political power—all in the name of what "we" (who exactly?) call literature. Moreover, it is in this arena that the apparently abstract question of literature confronts an unpredictable world in which censors are not just state functionaries serving oppressive regimes but also morally compromised devotees of the literary, where progressive critics can be self-appointed literature police, where writers constantly risk making it new, and where everyone dreams up his or her own version of the ideal "literary reader." Above all it is in this arena that the paradoxical authority of the literary—not as a privileged discourse above or outside the law, history, or politics, but as the most fragile of categories—is revealed most acutely and poignantly.

Notes

1. J. M. Coetzee, *Giving Offense: Essays on Censorship* (Chicago: University of Chicago Press, 1996), vii. Hereafter cited parenthetically in the text.

2. Anna M. Louw, "*In the Heart of the Country:* A Calvinist Allegory?" *PN Review* 14, no. 2 (1987): 50–52. See also: "'n Onvergeetlike indruk" (An unforgettable impression), review of *In the Heart of the Country, Die Burger* (2 Dec. 1977): 2; and "'n Fyn geslypte metafoor" (A fine, polished metaphor), review of *In the Heart of the Country, Beeld* (23 Jan. 1978): 10.

3. The biographical details are all contained in the forms each censor was required to fill in when applying to be a reader. Publications Control Board Archive, reference IDP 1/5/3, vol. 1, National Archives of South Africa, Cape Town.

4. Reginald Lighton, censors' report on *Waiting for the Barbarians,* Publications Control Board Archive, reference P80/11/205, National Archives of South Africa, Cape Town.

5. All page references keyed to J. M. Coetzee, *Waiting for the Barbarians* (London: Secker & Warburg, 1980).

6. Peter D. McDonald, "'Not Undesirable': How J. M. Coetzee Escaped the Censor," *TLS* (19 May 2000): 14–15.

7. J. M. Coetzee, *Doubling the Point,* ed. David Attwell (Cambridge: Harvard University Press, 1992), 363–64.

8. Coetzee, *Giving Offense,* 204–14.

9. Coetzee, *Doubling the Point,* 364.

10. For a more detailed account of the bureaucratic process of the censorship system, see McDonald, "'Not Undesirable,'" 14–15. It is worth briefly mentioning that the relationship between the (government-appointed) Directorate and the (government-appointed) readers/committees was complex. On the one hand, the Directorate could (and sometimes did) manipulate recommendations by choosing to send books like Coetzee's to sympathetic "literary" readers; on the other hand, the Directorate could appeal any recommendation and request that it be reviewed by the Publication's Appeal Board, the final arbiter in the post-1974 censorship regime.

11. McDonald, "'Not Undesirable,'" 15.

12. Ibid.

13. Derek Attridge's essay "Oppressive Silence: J. M. Coetzee's *Foe* and the Politics of the Canon," in *De-colonizing Tradition: New Views of Twentieth-Century "British" Literary Canons,* ed. Karen R. Lawrence (Urbana: University of Illinois Press, 1992), 212–38, to which I am especially indebted, is an indispensable guide through the questions of particularity, universality, and canonicity in relation to Coetzee's work. See also Peter D. McDonald, *"Disgrace* Effects," *Interventions* 4, no. 3 (2002): 321–30.

14. McDonald, "'Not Undesirable,'" 15.

15. J. M. Coetzee, "The Novel Today," *Upstream* 6, no. 1 (1988): 3. See also Gaye Davis, "Coetzee and the Cockroach Which Can't Be Killed," *Weekly Mail* (13–19 Nov. 1987): 19. It is worth noting that, despite a number of opportunities, Coetzee has not permitted this talk to be published outside South Africa in a more accessible form. It appeared in its entirety only in *Upstream,* a small local scholarly journal. The *Weekly Mail,* a courageously critical anti-apartheid newspaper launched in 1985, which organized the Book Week at which Coetzee spoke, also included an abridged version of it in the issue for 13–19 November 1987. Despite the fact that he reasserted his commitment to some of its terms in an interview with Joanna Scott ten years later (see below), the essay has remained a highly occasional piece, charged with the heat of a very particular moment, a point I hope my own reading of it respects. Coetzee's target was both general and specific. As his own formulation of the "colonising process" suggests, he had in mind a dominant Lukacsian style of reading (antimodernist, broadly realist) popular among critics in South Africa at the time, to which, in Coetzee's view, the *Weekly Mail* was especially committed. In the talk he noted that the occasion was "arranged by an active and unashamed proponent of this colonising process" (3). Though Coetzee, who was already an internationally acclaimed Booker Prize winner, clearly felt the local pressures most acutely, it should be noted that South African critics were not the only ones skeptical about his work at the time. There is not enough space here to give an extended analysis of the history of his critical reception in the 1970s and 1980s, but the following pre-1987 pieces give a preliminary idea of some of the more notable critical responses: for *Barbarians,* see Abdul R. JanMohamed, "The Economy of Manichean Allegory: The Function of Racial Difference in Colonialist Literature," *Critical Inquiry* 12, no. 1 (1985): 72–73; and for *Michael K* see Nadine Gordimer, "The Idea of Gardening," *New York Review of Books* (2 Feb. 1984): 3, 6, and Z. N., "Much Ado About Nobody," *African Communist* 97 (1984): 101–3. Also worth mentioning in this regard are Stephen Clingman's *The Novels of Nadine Gordimer: History from the Inside* (1986), which praises Gordimer for engaging directly and critically with the historical realities of apartheid South Africa, and David Attwell's *J. M. Coetzee: South Africa*

and the Politics of Writing (1993), which makes a powerful positive case for the reflexive historicity of Coetzee's fiction. I am extremely grateful to David Attwell for clarifying Coetzee's reference to the *Weekly Mail* in the talk.

16. Coetzee, "The Novel Today," 2.

17. Ibid., 3–4.

18. Ibid., 4.

19. Louw, "*In the Heart of the Country*," 50. Louw was interpreting circumspect comments Coetzee had made in an interview with Stephen Watson in *Speak*. She probably had in mind his remark that he doubted "that the political thinking of writers is of any more interest or value than anyone else's," and perhaps his subsequent comments about some black South African writers "working with models which I regard as very dubious." In the same interview, he also observed that the description of the "political situation" as an "inhibiting factor" (Watson's words) "could be belied at any moment by the emergence of one or two Black writers who can achieve—I know this is a dirty word nowadays, but let me use it—that necessary distance from their immediate situation." See "Speaking: J. M. Coetzee," interview with Stephen Watson, *Speak* 1 (May–June 1978): 22–24. Louw's rather loaded article is in many ways a rare example of apartheid thinking in a reasonably sophisticated literary-critical context. She took it as axiomatic, for instance, that "indigenous black writing" was in its "infancy" (this in 1987), and focused her attention on white writing and Coetzee's "mixed English and Afrikaans" background, praising him as an "authentic South African voice." In her view, this background set him above other English writers, like the "competent Nadine Gordimer with her obsession with the urban African political scene," and others, like Alan Paton, Jack Cope, and Guy Butler, who "often sound like the first generation Colonial writing letters home, sometimes over-romanticizing, at other times complaining rather impotently about the other white racial group, the Afrikaners" (50).

20. Stanley Fish, *Is There a Text in This Class? The Authority of Interpretative Communities* (Cambridge: Harvard University Press, 1980), 103. The essay "How Ordinary Is Ordinary Language?" originally appeared in *New Literary History* 5, no. 1 (1973): 41–54. Though Fish made some slight changes to the essay when he republished it in *Is There a Text in This Class?* he did not alter the passages I cite. For ease of reference I have keyed all the quotations to the more widely accessible 1980 version.

21. Fish, *Is There a Text*, 104.

22. Coetzee, "The Novel Today," 4.

23. Francis Mulhern, "Beyond Metaculture," *New Left Review* 16 (July–Aug. 2002): 86. In *Culture/Metaculture*, Mulhern identifies "metacultural" tendencies both in the well-established European tradition of "Kulturkritik," which he traces from Matthew Arnold to Adorno through Benda and Leavis, among others, and in the younger, apparently antagonistic tradition of British "cultural studies" from Williams to Hall. In my view, Coetzee's arguments about rivalry can be linked to the former tradition. For an extended discussion of this see Francis Mulhern, *Culture/Metaculture* (London: Routledge, 2000) and, as important, the lengthy exchange with Stefan Collini: Collini, "Culture Talk," *New Left Review* 7 (Jan–Feb. 2001): 43–53; Collini, "Defending Cultural Criticism," *New Left Review* 18 (Nov.–Dec. 2002): 73–97; Mulhern, "What Is Cultural Criticism?" *New Left Review* 23 (Sept.–Oct. 2003): 35–49.

24. Coetzee's subsequent reflections on Erasmus's *In Praise of Folly*—first published in 1992—in particular his account of Erasmus's desire to define a non-position outside the contests of ideological rivals, might suggest that he too came to have doubts about his earlier emphasis on the literary as a rival discourse. Yet it is worth recording that he restated his commitment to the term rivalry in a 1997 interview. This was in response to a question referring to Attwell's conception of the relationship between fiction and history as complementary. See

Coetzee, *Giving Offense,* 83–103, and Joanna Scott, "Voice and Trajectory: An Interview with J. M. Coetzee," *Salmagundi* (spring–summer 1997): 100–101.

25. Fish, *Is There a Text,* 108.

26. Ibid., 97–98. Derek Attridge made a similarly compelling case for a new approach to literary history in his introduction to *Peculiar Language* (London: Metheun, 1988), esp. 14–16.

READING

The State of the Discipline

Leah Price

When William James wanted to explain "the stupidity and injustice of our opinions, so far as they deal with the significance of alien lives," the example that he chose was reading:

> Take our dogs and ourselves, connected as we are by a tie more intimate than most ties in this world; and yet . . . how insensible, each of us, to all that makes life significant for the other!—we to the rapture of bones under hedges, or smells of trees and lamp-posts, they to the delights of literature and art. As you sit reading the most moving romance you ever fell upon, what sort of a judge is your fox-terrier of your behaviour? With all his good will toward you, the nature of your conduct is absolutely excluded from his comprehension. To sit there like a senseless statue when you might be taking him to walk and throwing sticks for him to catch! What queer disease is this that comes over you every day, of holding things and staring at them for hours together, paralyzed of motion and vacant of all conscious life?[1]

James's example points to one of the central difficulties of a history of reading: how to analyze an activity that's too close for critical distance, and perhaps for comfort. What's "alien" here is not simply the relation of readers to illiterates (human or canine), but also one reader's relation to another. Writers on reading have lamented its unknowability or savored its ineffability as far back as Wilkie Collins's 1858 essay "The Unknown Public." This is the assumption that book historians have come to combat, either in practice (by uncovering the physical gestures and material artifacts that can make one reader knowable to another), or in theory (by tracing the origins of a Cartesian dualism that severs reading from the hand and the voice).[2] For all the polemics that have shaped the field—about extensive reading, about technological determinism, about whether to determine the texts read by a particular demographic group or to define the audience reached by an individual text—historians seem united in the urge to contest James's characterization of reading as a literally "senseless" act.

This doesn't, however, imply any agreement about what the history of reading is. As David Hall has pointed out, different scholars have understood the term to encompass enterprises as various as the social history of education, the quantitative study of the distribution of printed matter, and the reception of texts or diffusion of ideas.[3] Reading means something different to literary critics (for whom it tends to feed either into case studies focused on the reception of particular texts or into theories of hermeneutics) than to historians (for whom it can become a subset of social or intellectual history). Among the former, reader response is now a field established enough to have its classics (Janice Radway, *Reading the Romance: Women, Patriarchy and Popular Literature* [Chapel Hill: University of North Carolina Press, 1984]), its historians (Elizabeth Freund, *The Return of the Reader: Reader-Response Criticism* [London: Methuen, 1987]), its anthologies (*The Reader in the Text,* edited by Susan Suleiman and Inge Crosman [Princeton University Press, 1980], and *Reader-Response Criticism: From Formalism to Post-Structuralism,* edited by Jane Tompkins [Baltimore: Johns Hopkins University Press, 1980]), even its anthology-pieces (Stanley Fish's "Is There a Text in this Class?" or Robert Darnton's "First Steps Toward a History of Reading," in *The Kiss of Lamourette: Reflections in Cultural History* [New York: W. W. Norton, 1990]). Yet reader response still looks less like a field than a battleground: its manifestations range from structuralist neologism to folksy case studies to mad scientism. (This last culminates in Victor Nell's *Lost in a Book* [New Haven: Yale University Press, 1988], which marries pieties about readerly pleasure with a report on readers' salivation rates, cardiovascular responses, and distinctly unpleasant-sounding electrogastrograms). Nor is an interest in reading confined to historicist literary critics. Their formalist colleagues have long saddled the reader with a series of alliterative adjectives: implied, inscribed, intended, ideal.[4] The relation among these models remains to be theorized. Even the basic distinction between a work's reader and a text's addressee is less commonly accepted than that between author and narrator. A critic as eminent as Tzvetan Todorov, for example, still cavalierly substitutes inscribed readers for empirical audiences, complaining (one hopes tongue in cheek) that "One of the difficulties in studying reading is due to the fact that reading is so hard to observe: introspection is uncertain, psycho-sociological investigation is tedious. It is therefore with a kind of relief that we find the work of construction represented in fiction itself, a much more convenient place for study."[5]

Convenient but reductive: in fact, some of the most interesting cases are those in which the implied reader differs sharply from what we know about the empirical audience. Thus Roger Chartier demonstrates the diffusion of aristocratic letter-writing manuals among peasants in chapbook reprints, while Jonathan Rose reconstructs a working-class audience for the Edwardian public-school yarn; Kate Flint shows that middle-class girls in the same period preferred the *Boy's Own Paper* to its putatively gender-appropriate spin-off, the *Girl's Own,* and so on.[6] The question here is not simply the gulf separating inscribed from implied audience, or even audience from market, but also the relation among the disciplines that study those different phenomena. Only the rare argument that combines historical sensitivity with interpretive ambition, like Garrett Stewart's *Dear Reader: The Conscripted Audience in Nineteenth-Century British Fiction* (Baltimore: Johns Hopkins University Press, 1996), manages to carve out a space (in Stewart's words) "between sociohistorical studies of the popular audience, on the one hand, and so-called reader-response criticism, on the other—between . . . purchasing or processing ends": such a middle course, he shows, is the only way to avoid either redefining the text as "an affective structure of effected meaning" or displacing it "from linguistic effect to social artifact" (8).

Part of the problem is that literary critics tend to act as if reading were the only legitimate use of books. They forget that the book can take on a ritual function (even, or especially, for nonliterates); it can serve as a gift (Natalie Davis, *The Gift in Sixteenth-Century France* [Madison: University of Wisconsin Press, 2000], and Jason Scott-Warren, *Sir John Harrington and the Book as Gift* [Oxford: Oxford University Press, 2001]), an investment (Philip Connell, "Bibliomania: Book Collecting, Cultural Politics, and the Rise of Literary Heritage in Romantic Britain," *Representations* 71 [2000]: 24–47), even an engineering challenge.[7] As long ago as 1968, Jack Goody's edited volume *Literacy in Traditional Societies* highlighted the role that literacy plays even in those cultures that earlier scholars had assumed to be insulated from the written word. The place of reading within anthropology today can be gauged from a very different collection, Jonathan

Boyarin's *The Ethnography of Reading* (Berkeley and Los Angeles: University of California Press, 1992), which brings together case studies from ancient and modern Israel, Anglo-Saxon England, premodern Japan, contemporary Indonesia and Colombia, upper-middle-class neighborhoods in Texas, and an Indian reservation in California, as well as a theoretical overview by Johannes Fabian with excurses on the role that transcription and writing more generally play in fieldwork. Elizabeth Long's unabashedly populist chapter, "Textual Interpretation as Collective Action," uses an analysis of contemporary reading groups to counterbalance the traditional trope of solitary reading. Empirical studies of mid-twentieth-century American adults have shown that reading correlates with social involvement: readers need others to set an example, to provide a sounding board for reactions to texts, to recommend and criticize and exchange books. Long's emphasis on the influence of oral and communal interactions on what's been imagined for several centuries as a silent and solitary activity thus inverts Natalie Davis's exhortation for critics to "consider a printed book not merely a source for ideas and images, but a carrier of relationships."[8]

This is as true of book historians as of anyone else: here, then, are some thoughts on recent developments in the field, inevitably skewed by the occupational blind spots of a card-carrying Victorianist literary critic. (Any history of reading is also a meditation on the reading of a particular writer.) If one took readership seriously, one could organize a review essay like this not by topic but by audience: scholarly monographs, edited collections, trade books, mass-market anthologies, digital databases. Even within the first of those categories, studies of reading take a variety of forms: some are organized around a particular reading public (Kate Flint's *The Woman Reader,* Jonathan Rose's *The Intellectual Life of the British Working Classes,* and Jacqueline Pearson's *Women's Reading in Britain, 1750–1835*), others around a category of book (Radway's *Reading the Romance*), still others around a particular form of evidence (H. J. Jackson's *Marginalia: Readers Writing in Books*). A historiography of reading could also categorize books according to the disciplinary affiliations of their readers. A study addressed to literary critics (like *Problèmes actuels de la lecture,* edited by Lucien Dällenbach and Jean Ricardou [Paris: Clancier-Guenaud, 1982], which makes up in neostructuralist diagrams what it lacks in quantitative tables) differs recognizably from one addressed to historians (for example, David Vincent's *Literacy and Popular Culture: England 1750–1914*) or to social scientists (Brian V. Street's *Literacy in Theory and Practice* and Harvey Graff's *The Literacy Myth*) or to psychologists such as Victor Nell. Yet as far as their inscribed reader goes, all of these have more in common with each other than with a popular study such as Alberto Manguel's *A*

History of Reading (London: HarperCollins, 1996), a series of bravura meditations that wear their learning lightly. In turn, Steven Roger Fischer's *A History of Reading* (London: Reaktion, 2003) shares little more than its title with its predecessor. The wider geographical scope of this second *History of Reading* may explain its breathless pace, but not its portentous tone or one-sentence paragraphs: where Manguel marries the essayistic with the encyclopedic, Fischer yokes platitudes with typos. Teachers looking for a classroom text on the history of reading may prefer to supplement Manguel with the relevant essays in *The Book History Reader,* edited by David Finkelstein and Alistair McCleery (London: Routledge, 2002).[9]

To act on Meredith McGill's argument that "unauthorized reprinting makes publication distinctly legible as an independent signifying act,"[10] we might add another category: recent reprints of older books in the field, especially Richard Altick's *The English Common Reader: A Social History of the Mass Reading Public, 1800–1900* (Chicago: University of Chicago Press, 1957; reprinted, with a preface by Jonathan Rose, by Ohio State University Press, 1998) and Q. D. Leavis, *Fiction and the Reading Public* (1932), reprinted, with an introduction by John Sutherland, by Pimlico (2000), as well as the collected work of the now curiously dated Holbrook Jackson (*The Anatomy of Bibliomania, The Reading of Books,* and *The Fear of Books,* all by University of Illinois Press, 2001). As a third taxonomy, however, we could distinguish monographs from anthologies, essay collections, and of course the eponymous "readers." Some of these are organized by author: thanks to the University of Massachusetts Press series in book history, scattered essays have been assembled in volumes such as David Hall's *Cultures of Print: Essays on the History of the Book* (1996) and D. F. McKenzie's *Making Meaning: 'Printers of the Mind' and Other Essays* (2002). But the field has been defined most decisively by multiauthor collections. *Reading in America,* edited by Cathy Davidson (Baltimore: Johns Hopkins University Press, 1989), juxtaposes essays whose methodological reflections have much to teach non-Americanists (especially Davidson's introduction and Robert Darnton's "What Is the History of Books?") with readers' digests of several important monographs in the field (Davidson's own *Revolution and the Word,* for example, and Janice Radway's study of the Book-of-the-Month Club).

Based on conference proceedings rather than on previously published sources, *The Practice and Representation of Reading in England* (Cambridge University Press, 1996), edited by James Raven, Helen Small, and Naomi Tadmor, assembles trailers for (and outtakes from) several equally important recent monographs, including William Sherman's *John Dee: The Politics of Reading and Writing in the English Renaissance* (Amherst: University of Massachusetts Press, 1995) and a characteristically dense chapter on the physiology of reading drawn from Adrian Johns's *The Nature of the Book* (Chicago: University of Chicago Press, 1998). The volume also includes provocative studies of particular readers (John Brewer on an eighteenth-century culture vulture), oeuvres (Kate Flint on the inscribed reader in Thackeray), and audiences (Helen Small's tour de force on Dickens's public readings). *Histoires de la lecture* (Paris: Maison des Sciences de l'homme, 1993) and *Pratiques de la lecture* (Marseille: Rivages, 1985) bear the editorial stamp of Roger Chartier, also a force behind two more general multivolume collections that have much to say about reading, the *Histoire de la vie privée* and *Histoire de l'édition francaise*. Its origins in a conference may explain the asymmetrical organization of *Histoires de la lecture*: its first half consists of variably ambitious surveys of national traditions (Spanish, Dutch, Italian, German, English, American, Russian), while the second contains more focused discussions of methodological problems such as the relation of the history of reading to the history of the book (Jean-Yves Mollier) and to the history of literature (Jean-Marie Goulemot).

Despite Darnton's insistence that "books do not respect limits, either linguistic or national"—a maxim substantiated by case studies like Elizabeth Eisenstein's *Grub Street Abroad* (Oxford University Press, 1992)—most of those collections are national in scope. The case is different for single-author works, which have focused increasingly on movements across national or colonial borders. Where "circulation" was once a metaphor for the transmission of ideas, recent books by James Raven, Priya Joshi, and Franco Moretti have conspired to remind us just how literally books circulate in space.[11] (The history of the book is also a geography of the book.) But reference works and encyclopedic essay collections still tend to take a single nation as their topic, even when—as in *Readers in History: Nineteenth-Century American Literature and the Contexts of Response,* edited by James L. Machor (Johns Hopkins University Press, 1993)—they have implications for other case studies. Others limit their focus chronologically, as in *Books and Their Readers in Early Modern England,* edited by Jennifer Andersen and Elizabeth Sauer (University of Pennsylvania Press, 2002); *Reading, Society and Politics in Early Modern England,* edited by Kevin Sharpe and Steven Zwicker (Cambridge University Press, 2003); Isabel Rivers's *Books and Their Readers in Eighteenth-Century England: New Essays* (Continuum, 2002), a sequel to her earlier *Books and Their Readers in Eighteenth-Century England* (St. Martin's Press, 1982); and John O. Jordan and Robert L. Patten's *Literature in the Marketplace: Nineteenth-Century British Reading and Publishing Practices* (Cambridge University Press, 1995), a collection that manages to place Simon Eliot's charts and graphs in dialogue with J. Hillis Miller's deconstructive reading of a fictional valentine.

In contrast, neither space nor time limits *A History of Reading in the West*, edited by Guglielmo Cavallo and Roger Chartier and translated by Lydia G. Cochrane (1999). International not only in its coverage but in its authorial makeup and publication history (translated from a Franco-Italian co-production and co-published in Britain by Polity and in the United States by the University of Massachusetts Press), this volume collects newly commissioned essays that speak to students and specialists. Taken together, the chapters trace a rough chronological progression, from silent reading in classical Greece to the emergence of the codex in the Roman world to medieval reading techniques (there are chapters on scholasticism and Jewish reading communities, as well as M. B. Parkes on graphic conventions and Paul Saenger on silent reading). The one constant across this encyclopedic range is the progressive disappearance of the reader's body. Thus Guglielmo Cavallo's "Between *Volumen* and Codex: Reading in the Roman World" describes classical medical works that include reading among healthful forms of physical exercise (75). The volumen had to be held with both hands (only the codex would liberate one hand so that writing could accompany reading); the body participated as much as the voice.[12] In Paul Saenger's account, however, word separation, word order, and syntactic punctuation enabled silent reading, which engendered heterodoxy in turn. Armando Petrucci's concluding chapter brings this narrative up to the present, showing that the emergence of the public library has trained readers to efface their own bodies: the proper thing to put on tables is books, not feet; pages must not be touched with dirty hands or gummy fingers. But Petrucci's survey also steps back far enough to question triumphalist celebrations of the spread of literacy. Although book production has been boosted rather than deterred by the growth of new media, UNESCO figures show that only half of that production occurs outside Europe; and while literacy rates are gradually rising, in absolute terms the number of illiterates is continually growing. As we learn in Martyn Lyons's chapter "New Readers in the Nineteenth Century: Women, Children, Workers," the first generation to accede to mass literacy (at the end of the nineteenth century) was also the last to see the book unchallenged as a communications medium. This volume contains other stories as well: Anthony Grafton's witty analysis of the material conditions of humanists' reading; Dominique Julia on literacy and illiteracy in the Counter Reformation; Reinhard Wittmann reopening the debate about whether intensive reading really gave way to extensive at the end of the eighteenth century. Throughout we can see the places of reading change, from the open spaces of antiquity (gardens, porticoes, squares, streets) to the closed sites of the Middle Ages (churches, monks' cells, refectories, courts). But reading practices reshape those spaces in turn: silent reading carved out privacy within communal institutions such as the coffee shop, the public library, and the railway carriage. (Which of us has not used a newspaper, or a copy of *Book History,* as a shield?)

All that unites the case studies that make up *A History of Reading* is a fascination with ways of reading that now appear marginal or even unthinkable—most prominently, various forms of vocalization. Book historians' interest in reading aloud bears two allegorical charges.[13] One is that the scene of one person reading to others restores a social dimension to an activity now more often parsed as individual or even individualistic. The Roman reader standing up and using hand gestures (an emblem in Cavallo's chapter in *A History of Reading*) or a lector declaiming pages of *The Count of Monte Cristo* in a Cuban cigar factory (Manguels's most engaging character) stand opposite the solitary, silent reading that contemporary academics idealize and intermittently practice. In reconstructing sociable forms of reading, book historians make one reader knowable to another.

Even the genre that most powerfully allies writing with individual freedom—the American slave narrative—reminds us that literacy is inherently a social skill. When Douglass's mistress teaches him to spell words of three or four letters, her husband "forbade her to give [him] any further instruction." That prohibition confirms our culture's triple association of literacy with upward mobility, with spiritual liberation, and with political progress (a myth that even Levi-Strauss hardly dented). What comes next is less often quoted: "the determination which he expressed to keep me in ignorance only rendered me the more resolute to seek intelligence. In learning to read, therefore, I am not sure that I do not owe quite as much to the opposition of my master as to the kindly assistance of my amicable mistress." Michael Warner's *The Letters of the Republic: Publication and the Public Sphere in Eighteenth-Century America* (Harvard University Press, 1990) insists that reading was not just a neutral medium that whites happened to monopolize, but rather a defining feature of white identity—and one that depended crucially on the illiteracy of blacks. Like literacy, illiteracy fulfills a social function.

Social, but also sociable. David Henkin's *City Reading: Written Words and Public Spaces in Antebellum New York* (Columbia University Press, 1998) deploys "unobtrusive street signs, imposing commercial advertisements, incendiary political broadsides" (x) as emblems of how little of the world's reading actually takes place in private. As Henkin points out, our own association of reading with privacy feeds into "a cluster of myths, some of which romanticize the written word, others of which romanticize a preliterate world of oral communication" (6). Yet reading in nineteenth-century New York was just as likely to take place outdoors as indoors—in the same way that our reading today can take place in airports or doctors' waiting rooms.

Scholars working on reading have sometimes imagined their field as more pluralistic, more democratic, or somehow more transgressive than the study of authorship. (Robert Gross has cautioned against imagining the history of reading as "a Whiggish contest between liberty and power"; as James Secord puts it in his massively researched *Victorian Sensation,* "a critical emphasis on fragmentation and interpretative freedom has sometimes slipped into a celebration of the Victorian values of liberal pluralism . . . accounts of audience response illustrate diversity, but little else.")[14] Others see themselves as puncturing a traditional consensus that showed more interest in writing than in reading: one active, the other reactive; one originary, the other belated. It's true that any simple opposition between productive writers and passive readers has given way to a new consensus that readers make meaning. Jean Marie Goulemot summarized the new orthodoxy when he declared that "to read is to constitute a meaning, not to reconstitute one" ("Lire un tableau: Une lettre de Poussin en 1639" in *Pratiques de la lecture,* 91, my translation).

Such a narrative would not be entirely unfounded: certainly it's possible to see ours as an age of readers. Within literary criticism proper, the reception theory that flourished in the German-speaking world in the 1970s shifted the making of meaning from authors to readers; so did Stanley Fish's interest in "communities" that determine (or at least allow us to predict) readers' responses—but also, just as important, in the unfolding of a single reader's response through time. Fish's innovation was not simply to replace the author with the reader as a maker of meaning, but also, more subtly, to substitute a temporal act (reading) for a spatial object (the text). Arguing against those New Critics who dismissed the reader's activities as "the disposable machinery of extraction," Fish redirected attention to "the developing responses of the reader to the words as they succeed one another on the page: the making and revising of assumptions, the rendering and regretting of judgments, the coming to and abandoning of conclusions, the giving and withdrawing of approval, the specifying of causes, the supplying of answers, the solving of puzzles." Fish gives the "making" in "making sense" its most literal force: the consumer also produces meaning.

Even outside reader-response theory itself, literary critics' basic unit of measure has become consumption, not production. Where earlier feminists discussed texts about women or texts by women, scholars now are as likely to discuss what Edwardian girls made of the self-proclaimed boys' books that they borrowed from their brothers. And that shift from authorship to readership extends outward to popular culture. Even in the turn-of-the-millennium paperback industry, the shift from reprint series based on authors' identity (such as Virago) to others based on readers' identity (such as Oxford Popular Classics, made up largely of turn-of-the-century best-sellers) reflects a new emphasis on consumers as agents.

Yet such a Whig history also risks overstating the novelty of reader-response criticism, for wherever you look in history, the reader, like the novel and the middle class, always seems to be rising. The wealth of research on readership in eighteenth-century Britain (including the work by Rivers, Brewer, and Pearson already mentioned) reflects that century's pivotal role in the shift from a criticism based on production to one focusing on consumption. Trevor Ross's *The Making of the English Literary Canon: From the Middle Ages to the Late Eighteenth Century* (McGill-Queen's University Press, 1998) has reexamined a whole range of issues, from copyright to canonization, in light of this new interest in the circulation of cultural commodities. In contrast, Regenia Gagnier's *The Insatiability of Human Wants* (University of Chicago Press, 2000) situates that shift a century later, juxtaposing the rise of the reader with the development of microeconomics as twin manifestations of a new interest in consumption.

Rather than seeing some cultures as author-centered and others as reader-focused, then, it may be safer to say simply that the relation of reading to writing varies with time and place. (The theory of imitatio once bound them together more tightly than today's creative writing courses do.) David Hall has shown that in eighteenth-century New England reading was taught before writing, and the situation is similar elsewhere in the early modern West.[15] We tend to think of reading as connoting passivity, but Kevin Sharpe reminds us that patronage—and its paratextual corollaries such as the dedication—place the reader in a position of greater power than the writer.[16]

Book historians have a vested interest in the interplay of reading with writing, for writing about reading and writing while reading are among the best sources we have. One produces external evidence (in genres ranging from autobiographies to inquisitorial records); the other generates internal evidence (marginalia, commonplace-books). Traces of reading practices can also take nonverbal and even nonbibliographical forms, however: we have as much to learn from the layout of libraries and bookshops as from furniture like the reading wheel, which allowed humanists to compare and collate passages from different books.

Familiarity makes reading appear deceptively knowable: it's part of the daily experience of any historian or literary critic. But scholars are also well positioned to know how easily reading can become a self-consuming act. The most impassioned reading destroys its own traces. The greater a reader's engagement with the text, the less likely he or she is to pause long enough to leave a record: if an uncut page signals withdrawal, a blank margin just as often betrays an absorption too rapt for note taking. Can a book mark us if we mark it?

As a result, studies drawing on autobiography or marginalia alike are biased toward certain kinds of readers and styles of reading. Conversely, projects such as the *Reading Experience Database* (http://www.open.ac.uk/Arts/RED/), which combats this problem by assembling "evidence from lives in which reading appears to have been peripheral," are inevitably opportunistic in their cherry-picking of decontextualized "reading experiences" from sources whose own structure and content differ widely. Michel de Certeau compared readers to poachers, but historians of reading may be more like magpies.[17]

Yet that miscellaneity can also be an advantage. Scholars in the field have culled sources as various (in Jonathan Rose's words) as "memoirs and diaries, school records, social surveys, oral interviews, library registers, letters to newspaper editors, fan mail, and even the proceedings of the Inquisition" (Rose, *Intellectual Life of the British Working Classes* [Yale University Press, 2001], 1). *The Reader Revealed,* edited by Sabrina Baron (Folger Shakespeare Library, 2001) draws inferences about reading from marginalia but also "from the kinds of reading readers received; from the dominant texts of the culture and the ways they were presented, distributed, and used; and from the paratexts of early modern books—frontispieces, tables, commendatory verses, indices, plates, and, most intriguingly, those dedications and addresses in which writers, publishers, and printers at once imagined and conjured the early modern patron, reader, and marketplace for books" (13).

Part of the question is what exactly such texts and artifacts form evidence for. The title of an important recent collection, *The Practice and Representation of Reading in England,* suggests the fundamental gap that differentiates sociohistorical studies of literacy from art-historical or literary-critical studies of the motif of the reader. (Or novelistic ones: *Don Quixote* can stand as the first in this line.) Yet those works that attempt to reconstruct the former are inevitably products—even manifestations—of the latter. Some of the most persuasive recent studies are those that face up to the constructed nature of their evidence. Exemplary in this respect is Kate Flint's *The Woman Reader,* which marshals a dizzying range of representations of women's reading—visual and verbal, descriptive and prescriptive. (Flint points out how many of the latter focus on what *not* to read: the energies of Victorian social criticism are characteristically negative.) Avoiding the temptation to flatten out her sources, Flint takes the time to think about why women's reading should be celebrated in particular genres (autobiography, for example) and attacked in others (medical and psychological manuals). If men's reading was associated with the mind, she shows, women's reading was tarnished by association with the body.

While Annaliste social historians like François Furet and Jacques Ozouf concentrated on large-scale quantitative studies, to shift our attention from authors to readers does not necessarily mean moving from the individual to the mass.[18] Case studies of particular individuals have been central to the field from the very beginning (witness Ginzburg's *The Cheese and the Worms* [Johns Hopkins University Press, 1980] and Darnton's "Readers Respond to Rousseau"). In "Studied for Action: How Gabriel Harvey Read His Livy," *Past and Present* 129 (Nov. 1990): 30–78, Lisa Jardine and Anthony Grafton tease an extraordinary number of inferences out of the marginalia to Harvey's *History of Rome*. Harvey returned to this text over and over between 1568 and 1590, reading the same text in different ways at different moments in order to perform services for present or potential patrons. Harvey's habits pose a challenge to later conceptions of reading as self-directed and disinterested—even if twenty-first-century academics should be well placed to understand reading as a mode of career advancement. (Today, an in-flight advertisement for audio summaries of business books claims that "just as there are personal trainers for your body . . . think of us as your 'personal reader' to advance your career.") Kevin Sharpe's *Reading Revolutions* (Yale University Press, 2000), too, works outward from the diary, commonplace-books, and library of a seventeenth-century English landowner. And the reading of individual writers forms the starting point of Robert DeMaria's *Samuel Johnson and the Life of Reading* (Johns Hopkins University Press, 1997), Brian Stock's *After Augustine: The Meditative Reader and the Text* (University of Pennsylvania Press, 2001), and William Sherman's *John Dee: The Politics of Reading and Writing in the English Renaissance.*

But this model has also extended to studies of groups of readers. Janice Radway's *Reading the Romance* launched a movement whose influence can still be seen in recent studies such as Elizabeth McHenry's *Forgotten Readers: Recovering the Lost History of African American Literary Societies* (Duke University Press, 2002). Indeed, some of the most interesting recent work on nineteenth-century American women's reading—that of Barbara Hochman and Mary Kelley, for example—has stressed precisely the impossibility of separating individual reading practices from literary communities. From a slightly different angle, Jon Klancher's *The Making of English Reading Audiences, 1790–1832* (University of Wisconsin Press, 1987) argues that "the intense cultural politics of the Romantic period obliged writers not only to distinguish among conflicting audiences, but to do so by elaborating new relations *between* the individual reader and the collective audience" (11). And Patrick Brantlinger's *The Reading Lesson: The Threat of Mass Literacy in Nineteenth-Century Britain* (University of Indiana Press, 1998) argues that the heuristic distinction between a singular addressee and a multifarious public in itself responds to anxieties about the mass public.

It's appropriate, in this context, that several studies use library records as a clue to the reading habits of their patrons: scholars of British history, for example, can consult Simon Eliot's *A Measure of Popularity: Public Library Holdings of Twenty-Four Popular Authors, 1883–1912* (London: History of the Book On-Demand Series 2, 1992) or Jan Fergus's "Eighteenth-Century Readers in Provincial England: The Customers of Samuel Clay's Circulating Library and Bookshop in Warwick, 1770–1772," *Papers of the Bibliographical Society of America* 78:2 (1984). But such instrumental mining of library records needs to be distinguished from studies of the library itself as a social institution, either theoretical—in R. Howard Bloch and Carla Hesse's *Future Libraries* (University of California Press, 1995)—or synoptic (e.g., *Histoire des bibliothèques françaises,* edited by André Vernet [Paris: Promodis-Editions du Cercle du librairie, 1988–], or Alastair Black's *A New History of the English Public Library . . . 1850–1914* [London: Leicester University Press, 1996]).

As an early generation of polemicists acknowledged—Q. D. Leavis comes to mind, but so does Richard Hoggart's *The Uses of Literacy,* first published in 1957 and still in print—the question of what people at some distant historical moment read rarely lies very far from the question of what people here and now should read. The success of Jonathan Rose's *Intellectual Life of the British Working Classes*—the only recent book other than Manguel's to reach the kind of serious general audience for which it forms an elegy—suggests how lively those debates remain. Not the least of the achievements of this loose, baggy monster is Rose's attack on recent culture warriors' unexamined assumption that the task of widening access to culture is coextensive with the enterprise of broadening the canon. Pointing out that multiculturalist critics more often project their own concerns onto a hypothetical mass audience than excavate the desires of that audience itself, *The Intellectual Life* asks what books influenced working-class readers—but also, just as interestingly, what books did not. (Marx is prominent in the latter category.) Drawing on questionnaires, oral histories, library records, and above all memoirs, Rose's richly researched project exemplifies both the power and the limits of autobiographical evidence. "Memoirists are not entirely representative of their class," Rose acknowledges, "if only because they were unusually articulate." His introduction discounts "bowdlerization" on the grounds that most of these autobiographies were unpublished or self-published, but this is to ignore that authors can alter evidence themselves as easily as their publishers can. Not only are autobiographers by definition highly literate, but the dominance of rags-to-riches stories (not just in autobiographies or surveys of Labor MPs) makes it hard for the adult narrator not to read his middle-class milieu backward into the experiences of the working-class youth described. Can a person—or a culture—be trusted to self-diagnose its reading habits?

In short, as Robert Darnton wrote in his often-reprinted "What Is the History of Books?" "reading remains the most difficult stage to study in the circuit that books follow." Depressingly, much of what we know about standards for evidence is negative. Bowman and Woolf point out that studies of literacy are more notable for the generalizations they debunk than for those they develop. The received wisdom has been replaced by received skepticism: literacy is not a single phenomenon that can be studied across different cultures; it does not in itself cause social progress or economic growth, or (at an individual level) social mobility or rationality; "literates do not necessarily think differently from illiterates, and no Great Divide separates societies with writing from those without it."[19] In *Reading and the Social Order: Reading and Writing in Tudor and Stuart England* (Cambridge University Press, 1980), David Cressy cautions scholars against taking Tudor writing masters and preachers as reliable narrators: by definition, such occupations have a vested interest in exaggerating the centrality of literacy within their culture. The strength of the academic study of literacy (self-reflexivity) is inseparable from its weakness (narcissism).[20]

It's telling, in this context, that the two most striking essays in David Resnick's *Literacy in Historical Perspective* (Washington, D.C.: Library of Congress, 1983) debunk received wisdom: Thomas Laqueur's, on reading in eighteenth- and nineteenth-century England, questions triumphalist theories of literacy as an index to social progress, while M. T. Clanchy's cautions against technological determinism by showing how many of our assumptions about literacy and the book predate the invention of print. Of the same vintage is Gerd Baumann's *The Written Word* (Oxford University Press, 1986), which reprints classic essays on literacy by Walter Ong and Keith Thomas, among others.

Literary critics have long taken their own immersion in print culture too much for granted to discuss literacy as such. Some of the most sophisticated recent work on literacy is self-reflexive, taking its subject to encompass not just literacy itself but successive endeavors to chart and promote it. David Vincent's *Literacy and Popular Culture: England 1750–1914* reads literacy as part of a larger history of nationalism, of centralization, and of statistical method itself.[21] Provocatively, Vincent declares that the self-educated reader is as much a myth as the self-made millionaire: the longstanding association of reading with autonomy or personal liberation should not blind us to the extent to which reading is communally learned and used. (This may be true in part because the value of literacy commanded such a wide cross-class consensus in Britain by mid-century, at least in theory; in the slave-holding American South, matters were rather different.)

If literacy risks being taken for granted by literary critics, for historians the problem may be the reverse: as David Cressy argues, "scholars . . . in a modern mass-literate society . . . risk being misled by our own high valuation of literacy into misunderstanding its place, or its absence, in the world we have lost." Cressy nuances such work by insisting that the differential distribution of literacy is more interesting than the effects of literacy itself: like so much else, literacy is a system of differences. In "Labourers and Voyagers," Chartier insists that the distinction between literacy and illiteracy does not exhaust the range of different relationships to writing. On the contrary, as literacy spreads across societies, how and what people read replaces whether they read as a mark of social status. For the historian, then, the issue becomes what Chartier elsewhere calls "contrasting uses of shared objects or competences."[22]

The paradigmatic case of those contrasting uses may be the shift from intensive to extensive reading first hypothesized by Rolf Engelsing. Engelsing's description of a late eighteenth-century shift from the rereading of a few prized texts to the consumption of many ephemeral ones will be familiar to most readers of this journal.[23] Before that time, Engelsing argues, people of all social classes owned a few books that they read "intensively": slowly, repeatedly, reverently. The classic example of such reading would be the Bible, a book read year after year, never outdated, but paradoxically linked via inscriptions on the flyleaf with the passage of time in readers' own lives. Toward the end of the eighteenth century, in Engelsing's account, the proliferation of new books gave rise to a model of "extensive" reading—skimming and skipping, devouring and discarding—from which we have yet to emerge.

Like the shift from vocalization to silent reading, Engelsing's historical model has been extensively discussed and intensively criticized.[24] (It has also been substantiated in other national contexts, such as New England in William Gilmore-Lehne's *Reading Becomes a Necessity of Life* [University of Tennessee Press, 1989] as well as, more skeptically, in David Hall's "The Uses of Literacy in New England: 1600–1850," in *Printing and Society in Early America*, 1–47.) Few historians dispute the changes in the production and circulation of books on which Engelsing's thesis rests—the contrast between a backlist of books passed from generation to generation and a cycle of fashionable ephemera as soon outdated as a newspaper—but their consequences for reading are less clear. Some genres—particularly the novel—appear to have elicited a newly intensive reading at precisely the historical moment to which Engelsing traces its decline: witness Darnton's use of fan mail to reconstruct readers' self-consciously intense engagement with *La Nouvelle Héloïse*. In fact, the very distribution mechanisms that Engelsing blames for the spread of extensive reading appear to have been perfectly compatible with reverent rereading: the connection readers felt with Rousseau is precisely what allowed booksellers to turn a profit by renting out his novel by the hour.[25] From a different angle, Cathy Davidson has called attention to the moral overtones of Engelsing's narrative, revealing the hypothesis of a "reading revolution" as the story of a fall. Such a contrast between reverent readers and passive consumers, she argues, fuels a conservative distaste for modern mass culture and mass markets.

This is not to say that anyone questions the distinction between "intensive" and "extensive" reading practices; rather, what's at issue is the extent to which that contrast can be plotted onto a chronological axis. Where Engelsing distinguished mutually exclusive practices, his critics see a repertoire of styles that readers could switch on and off at will. Elizabeth Eisenstein uses the example of early eighteenth-century journals to argue that rather than one mode of reading replacing the other, both coexisted in any given historical moment. Eisenstein quotes Francis Bacon—"some books are to be tasted, others to be swallowed and some few to be chewed and digested"—but takes his aphorism one step further, showing that a single book could be read extensively by one reader and intensively by another.[26] Or, indeed, by the same reader in a different context, a point that resonates with the lived experience of most book historians, who (like Samuel Johnson in Robert DeMaria's account) shuttle daily and even hourly between both styles of reading.

Contra William James, what makes reading hard to study is not (or not only) that it's alien: the complementary challenge is to establish any critical distance from a field whose message is also its medium. Peter Stallybrass's recent work on how early modern readers navigated the codex—a history of reading encapsulated by the bookmark—brings exotic gestures close to home. Redefining the book from a container of meaning to an occasion for operations both mental and manual, his analysis shows the intellectual implications of physical forms; our own culture relegates "study skills" to the remedial classroom, but an essay like Ann Blair's "Annotating and Indexing Natural Philosophy" makes clear that the Post-it note has a long history.[27] For all its interest in marginalia and marginalized persons, the history of books is centrally about ourselves. It asks how past readers have made meaning (and therefore, by extension, how others have read differently from us), but it also asks where the conditions of possibility for our own reading come from.

Notes

1. William James, "On a Certain Blindness in Human Beings" (1899), in *Selected Papers on Philosophy* (London: Dent, 1917), 1–21. Thanks to Melisssa Shields for help with the research for this essay.

2. For a critique of this model, see David Henkin, "Solitary, Intimate, and Exclusive: The Myth of Private Reading" (unpublished paper, 2002).

3. David Hall, "Readers and Reading in America: Critical Perspectives," in *Cultures of Print: Essays on the History of the Book* (Amherst: University of Massachusetts Press, 1996), 169–88.

4. Wolfgang Iser, *The Implied Reader* (Baltimore: Johns Hopkins University Press, 1974); Wayne Booth, *The Rhetoric of Fiction* (Chicago: University of Chicago Press, 1961); Gérard Genette, *Figures III* (Paris: Seuil, 1972).

5. Tzvetan Todorov, "Reading as Construction," in *The Reader in the Text,* ed. Susan Suleiman and Inge Crosman (Princeton: Princeton University Press, 1980), 78–79.

6. Kate Flint, *The Woman Reader, 1837–1914* (Oxford: Clarendon Press, 1993); Jonathan Rose, *The Intellectual Life of the British Working Classes* (New Haven: Yale University Press, 2001); Roger Chartier, "Des 'secrétaires' pour le peuple? Les modèles épistolaires de l'ancien régime entre littérature de cour et livre de colportage," in *La correspondance: Les usages de la lettre au XIXe siècle,* ed. Roger Chartier, Alain Boureau, et al. (Paris: Fayard, 1991), 159–278.

7. Henry Petrowski, *The Book on the Bookshelf* (New York: Knopf, 1999).

8. Natalie Davis, *Society and Culture in Early Modern France* (Stanford: Stanford University Press, 1975), 192.

9. For a fuller discussion of this anthology, see my "Tangible Pages," *London Review of Books* 24 (31 Oct. 2002): 36–39.

10. Meredith McGill, *American Literature and the Culture of Reprinting, 1834–1853* (Philadelphia: University of Pennsylvania Press, 2003), 5.

11. James Raven, *London Booksellers and American Customers: Transatlantic Literary Community and the Charleston Library Society, 1748–1811* (Columbia: University of South Carolina Press, 2002); Priya Joshi, *In Another Country: Colonialism, Culture, and the English Novel in India* (New York: Columbia University Press, 2002); Franco Moretti, *Atlas of the European Novel 1800–1900* (London: Verso, 1998).

12. On the role of embodiment in reading, see also Georges Perec, "Lire: esquisse socio-physiologique," *Esprit* 44 (Jan. 1976): 9–20.

13. On this interest, see, e.g., Roger Chartier and Pierre Bourdieu, "Comprendre les pratiques culturelles," in *Pratiques de la lecture,* ed. Roger Chartier (Marseille: Rivages, 1985), 218–39, esp. 219–20.

14. Robert Gross, "Seeing the World in Print," unpublished lecture; James A. Secord, *Victorian Sensation: The Extraordinary Publication, Reception, and Secret Authorship of Vestiges of the Natural History of Creation* (Chicago: University of Chicago Press, 2000), 521.

15. David Hall, "Introduction: The Uses of Literacy in New England, 1600–1850," in *Printing and Society in Early America,* ed. William Joyce et al. (Worcester: American Antiquarian Society, 1983), 24.

16. Kevin Sharpe, *Reading Revolutions* (New Haven: Yale University Press, 2000), 40.

17. Michel de Certeau, *The Practice of Everyday Life,* trans. Stephen F. Rendall (Berkeley and Los Angeles: University of California Press, 1984), 174.

18. François Furet, *Reading and Writing: Literacy in France from Calvin to Jules Ferry* (Cambridge: Cambridge University Press, 1982).

19. Alan K. Bowman and Greg Woolf, "Literacy and Power in the Ancient World," in

Literacy and Power in the Ancient World, ed. Alan K. Bowman and Greg Woolf (Cambridge: Cambridge University Press, 1994), 2–3.

20. Ibid., 1.

21. For a narrower account of the growth of literacy in nineteenth-century Britain, see David Mitch, *The Rise of Popular Literacy in Victorian England* (Philadelphia: University of Pennsylvania Press, 1992).

22. Roger Chartier, "Labourers and Voyagers," *The Book History Reader,* ed. David Finkelstein and Alistair McCleery (London: Routledge, 2002), 47–59; Roger Chartier, *Correspondance,* 9, my translation.

23. See, e.g, Rolf Engelsing, "Die Perioden der Lesergeschichte in der Neuzeit," *Archiv für geschichte des Buchwesens* 10 (1970): 945–1002.

24. See, e.g., Reinhard Wittmann, "Was There a Reading Revolution at the End of the Eighteenth Century?" in *A History of Reading in the West,* ed. Guglielmo Cavallo and Roger Chartier (Amherst: University of Massachusetts Press, 1999): 284–312.

25. Robert Darnton, "Readers Respond to Rousseau," in *The Great Cat Massacre and Other Episodes in French Cultural History* (London: Allen Lane, 1984), 215–56.

26. See Cathy Davidson, *Revolution and the Word: The Rise of the Novel in America* (New York: Oxford University Press, 1986), 69–79; Darnton, "Readers Respond to Rousseau," 249–52; and Wittmann, "Was there a Reading Revolution?" 284–312.

27. See Peter Stallybrass, "Books and Scrolls: Navigating the Bible," in *Books and Readers in Early Modern England,* ed. Jennifer Andersen and Elizabeth Sauer (Philadelphia: University of Pennsylvania Press, 2002), 42–79; and Ann Blair, "Annotating and Indexing Natural Philosophy," in *Books and the Sciences in History,* ed. Marina Frasca-Spada and Nick Jardine (Cambridge: Cambridge University Press, 2000), 70–89.

CONTRIBUTORS

Shlomo Berger (Ph.D. 1987, Hebrew University of Jerusalem) teaches in the department of Hebrew and Jewish Studies at the University of Amsterdam, The Netherlands. He has published extensively on early modern Yiddish, and his publications include *Travels Among Jews and Gentiles: Abraham Levie's Travelogue (Amsterdam 1764)* (Brill-Styx, 2002). He is now preparing a new study of Amsterdam Yiddish book culture in the seventeenth and eighteenth centuries.

John A. Buchtel was recently appointed Curator of Rare Books in the Sheridan Libraries of Johns Hopkins University. He previously served as Curator of Collections at Rare Book School at the University of Virginia, where he will continue to co-teach his RBS introductory survey course, "The History of the Book, 200–2000." He recently completed his doctoral dissertation, *Book Dedications in Early Modern England: Francis Bacon, George Chapman, and the Literary Patronage of Henry, Prince of Wales,* in the University of Virginia's Department of English.

Barbara Hochman is Chair of the Department of Foreign Literatures and Linguistics, Ben-Gurion University of the Negev. She has published widely on nineteenth-century American fiction. Her most recent book is *Getting at the Author: Reimagining Books and Reading in the Age of American Realism* (University of Massachusetts Press, 2001). In 2003 she received an NEH Fellowship for her project, *Uncle Tom's Cabin and the Reading Revolution*. The present essay grows out of research for that project.

Thomas S. Kidd is Assistant Professor of History at Baylor University. He is the author of the forthcoming *From Puritanism to the Protestant Interest: Changing Identities in Provincial New England* (Yale University Press, 2004). His next book project, also to be published by Yale University Press, is *Awakenings: The First Generation of American Evangelical Christianity.*

Cree LeFavour is in the final stage of completing her dissertation, "'Who Reads an American Book?': British Reprints and Popular Reading in America, 1848–1858," in the American Studies Program at New York University. Her other work on transatlantic print culture includes a study of W. M. Thackeray's *Vanity Fair* in the American market, an analysis of Susan Warner's *The Wide, Wide World* as an example of Anglo-American reading and writing practices, and research on the trope of the "edible book" as an expression of anxiety over female reading in 1850s America.

Lisa Lindell is a Catalogue Librarian at South Dakota State University in Brookings. Her research interests and publications focus on the history and literature of the Great Plains.

Peter D. McDonald is a Fellow of St. Hugh's College and a Lecturer in English at the University of Oxford. He is the author of *British Literary Culture and Publishing Practice, 1880–1914* (1997), and co-editor, with Michael Suarez, of *Making Meaning: "Printers of the Mind" and Other Essays,* by D. F. McKenzie (2002). He has also co-edited, with Derek Attridge, a special issue of the journal *Interventions* (autumn 2002) on J. M. Coetzee's *Disgrace*. He has published widely on the linkage between book and literary history, and he is currently writing a study of the category of the literary, focusing on South African writing of the apartheid era.

Iris Parush is a Professor of Hebrew Literature at Ben-Gurion University of the Negev. Her book *National Ideology and Literary Canon* (in Hebrew, Mossad Bialik, 1992), explores the impact of national ideology on the formation of the modern Hebrew literary canon. She is also the author of *Reading Women: The Benefit of Marginality* (in Hebrew, Am-Oved, 2001). An English edition of the book, entitled *Jewish Women's Reading: Marginality and Modernization in Nineteenth-Century Eastern Europe*, will be published in 2004 by the University Press of New England. She is currently writing a book on the "reading-biography" of young nineteenth-century yeshiva students as they underwent a process of enlightenment.

Leah Price is Professor of English at Harvard University. She is the author of *The Anthology and the Rise of the Novel* (2000, paperback 2003) and co-editor of *Literary Secretaries/Secretarial Film* (2004). She also contributes regularly to the *London Review of Books*. With Seth Lerer, she is co-editing a special issue of *PMLA* on "The History of the Book and the Idea of Literature." Her current projects include two monographs, *The Secretarial Imagination* and *Novel Media,* as well as an anthology, *Victorian Readers: A Reader.*

Neil Safier is Assistant Professor of History at the University of Michigan and a postdoctoral fellow in the Michigan Society of Fellows. His research focuses on the history of travel and exploration in colonial Latin America and the circulation of scientific knowledge in the early modern Atlantic world. His current project examines the sociocultural and bibliographical practices of Spanish and Portuguese naturalists in colonial Brazil and the borderlands of the Amazon River basin.

Willa Z. Silverman is Associate Professor of French and Jewish Studies at The Pennsylvania State University. Her research on author-publisher relations, authorial strategies, and the ideological dimensions of publishing in late nineteenth-century France has been published in *Contemporary French Civilization,* the *French Review, Historical Reflections/Réflexions Historiques,* and *Nineteenth-Century French Studies.* She is currently working on a book, tentatively titled *The New Bibliopolis: French Book-Collectors and the Culture of Print, 1880–1914.*

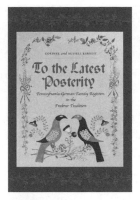
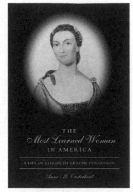

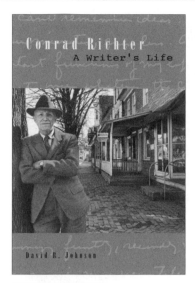

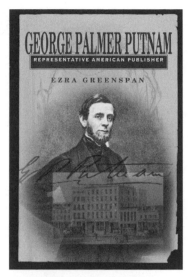

CONRAD RICHTER
A WRITER'S LIFE
David R. Johnson

"Biographer Johnson portrays Richter through letters and diaries as a serious, self-castigating artist, one as worried about his income as his storytelling. . . . Richter's self-doubt and his prickly relationship with his publisher, Alfred Knopf, continued throughout his career, even when his autobiographical novel, *The Waters of Kronos*, won the National Book Award in 1961. In the brief acceptance speech that the pathologically shy author had Knopf read for him, Richter described 'hardship into gain' as the theme of his pioneer novels, but it could apply equally to his life, well and thoroughly depicted here by Johnson."

—*Publishers Weekly*

432 pages | 20 b&w photos | $42.95 cloth
Penn State Series in the History of the Book

GEORGE PALMER PUTNAM
REPRESENTATIVE AMERICAN PUBLISHER
Ezra Greenspan

"I would like to say that Greenspan's work is a model for modern scholarship in publishing history, but it presents an example that may be difficult to follow. . . . We can only hope that undiscovered manuscript troves will find their way to libraries, and, in the meantime, we can enjoy the product of Greenspan's labors and make more well-informed surmises about other publishers based on his exemplary scholarship."

—Melissa J. Homestead,
Resources for American Literary Study

584 pages | $48.95 cloth
Penn State Series in the History of the Book

penn state press

820 N. University Drive, USB 1, Suite C I University Park, PA 16802 I fax 1-877-778-2665 I www.psupress.org
AVAILABLE IN BOOKSTORES, OR ORDER TOLL FREE 1-800-326-9180

AS EVER YOURS
THE LETTERS OF MAX PERKINS
AND ELIZABETH LEMMON
Edited by Rodger L. Tarr

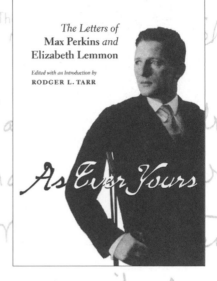

The Letters of
Max Perkins *and*
Elizabeth Lemmon

Edited with an Introduction by
RODGER L. TARR

As Ever Yours

"When I found these cigarettes you had left I thought at first to keep them as a rememberance. But I am far from needing a rememberance."
—From Max Perkins's first letter to Elizabeth Lemmon, dated 14 April 1922

Maxwell E. Perkins, famed editor of such literary luminaries as F. Scott Fitzgerald, Ernest Hemingway, Zora Neale Hurston, Marjorie Kinnan Rawlings, and Thomas Wolfe, was a man whose personal and professional lives often intersected. Nowhere is this more evident than in his correspondence with Elizabeth Lemmon, the Virginia socialite who became his long-distance confidante. Despite the platonic nature of their relationship, others realized the intensity of their connection. The letters contained in *As Ever Yours,* published here for the first time, reveal an epistolary love story—and they provide fresh insights into Perkins the man and Perkins the editor.

304 pages | 19 illustrations | $29.95 cloth
Penn State Series in the History of the Book